Liberal Arts through the AGES

Interdisciplinary Art Historical Inquiry

Published in the United States of America in 2011 by
Augustana College, 639-38th Street,
Rock Island, Illinois 61201-2296.

First Edition 2006, Revised Edition 2007, 2008, 2011

ISBN 0-9714345-5-7

Liberal Arts through the AGES

Augustana General Education Studies

Catherine Carter Goebel
Paul A. Anderson Chair in the Arts
Editor

Katherine Elizabeth Goebel
Assistant Editor

Steven C. Bahls
President of the College
Introduction

Pareena G. Lawrence
Dean of the College
Introduction to Liberal Studies

Elizabeth Parker Ducey
Graphic Design

Megan MacCall
Electronic Web Gallery

Sherry Case Maurer
Catalogue Checklist

Catalogue 90, detail

"Modernity...to extract from fashion the poetry that resides in its historical envelope, to distill the eternal from the transitory...."

Charles Baudelaire, *The Painter of Modern Life (1863)*

To my husband

Dr. Gary James Goebel

in celebration of our 31st anniversary

and in appreciation for his

profound encouragement and support

through many wonderful years

of collaboration.

And to our children

Thomas James and Katherine Elizabeth

who continually amaze and

inspire.

Catalogue 59, 26 and 63, details

"Study the science of art. Study the art of science. Develop your senses—especially learn how to see. Realize that everything connects to everything else."

Leonardo da Vinci (1452-1519)

Acknowledgments

Liberal Arts through the AGES: Interdisciplinary Art Historical Inquiry represents an important multidisciplinary collaboration at Augustana College. And with this edition, the project returns to its roots in the *Origins of Modernity* (2004-5) as a comprehensive interdisciplinary faculty/student collaborative project. Since then, for the past five years, three editions of *Liberal Arts through the AGES* (2006, 2007, 2008-11) have been constructed, each built from the foundation of the modernity project in order to be relevant to the evolving goals for Liberal Studies. All artwork represented here complements the liberal arts curriculum and art historical goals of establishing contexts for the past through critical analysis and research of art, in order to deepen our understanding of both the past and present. These works have been carefully selected, researched and documented by current and former Augustana students as well as a number of members of the faculty and administration.

This undertaking continues to be primarily supported through the Paul A. Anderson Chair in the Arts. The profound insight of alumnus Paul A. Anderson, whose successful life was cut tragically short in 1992, established this endowed chair so that the beauty and intellectual stimulation of the visual arts would have a strong and lasting presence at Augustana. Paul wanted students to see original works of art in person and become knowledgeable about the aesthetics, meaning and history of that art within a supportive academic environment. These resources serve to enhance the teaching mission of Augustana College in general and of the Department of Art History in particular. The majority of works included here were purchased, gifted or facilitated through the Anderson Chair in order to develop a pedagogically-based art history collection that represents a broad historical and cultural range from ancient Greek black and red-figure pieces through contemporary art. By building an art history teaching collection, and supporting its related programming, Paul's endowment has enriched multiple areas within Augustana College, resulting in an impressive collaboration of many committed people—professors, students, alumni, administrators, staff, donors and art dealers—reflecting the ideals of the liberal arts college.

In my role as the Paul A. Anderson Chair, I have enjoyed overseeing the many aspects of this project, from building the art history teaching collection, in coordination with our museum director and the Office of Advancement, to orchestrating and editing five AGES publications, now in their seventh year as a common text for Liberal Studies. *Liberal Arts through the AGES* is an unprecedented interdisciplinary art history education model that resonates on an international level. It has been well-received at the Oxford Round Table, the College Art Association, the Association for General and Liberal Studies, and the Association of American Colleges and Universities as well as at the Art Institute of Chicago and through exhibition at the Figge Art Museum. In the spring of 2011, I was honored to chair an interdisciplinary Augustana faculty panel on this project for the Association for Core Texts and Courses conference at Yale University. The panel included Thomas Bengtson, Earl H. Beling Professor in Mathematics; Ellen Hay, Professor of Communication Studies; Dell Jensen, Associate Professor of Chemistry; Taddy Kalas, Professor of French; and Emil Kramer, Associate Professor of Classics. The conference was sponsored by Yale University and co-sponsored by Boston and Augustana Colleges.

My initial thesis for this undertaking, of providing students with fundamental primary documents—including artwork—enables them to engage in critical research and writing, guided by their professors, specialists in a number of disciplines. We have clearly broken new ground in the interdisciplinary use of the liberal arts museum as a classroom, and perhaps more importantly, with the classroom used as a relevant forum for original works of art. I would like to thank my former BA and MA art history professor and advisor, Thomas B. Brumbaugh, Professor Emeritus of Fine Arts, Vanderbilt University, whose many gifts and loans of works of art collected through his forty years of teaching have greatly impacted and enormously enhanced the intrinsic relevance of our art history teaching collection to all liberal arts disciplines. The Dr. Thomas B. Brumbaugh Art History Collection is indeed integral to this publication and our mission. Dr. Brumbaugh inspired my own goal to establish a rich art history teaching collection at Augustana. I also wish to acknowledge my former professor, Ljubica Popovich, Professor Emerita of Fine Arts, Vanderbilt University, for her further scholarly influence and direct contribution to Augustana's art history and museum programs through a public lecture and scholarly consultation on the Anderson purchase and booklet publication of our Russian icon. Finally, I want to note the profound influence of my doctoral advisor, Susan Hollis Clayson, Professor of Art History and History and Bergen Evans Professor in the Humanities, Northwestern University, for instilling in me a deep understanding of the importance of seeking rich and creative interdisciplinary contexts in art history. She nurtured such methodology through my dissertation on the critical reception of American expatriate artist, James McNeill Whistler (1834-1903), and it remains central to my art historical viewpoint and scholarship. She has lectured twice at Augustana and shared her scholarship here. This foundation also provided the philosophical basis, combined with Professor Brumbaugh's appreciation and critical understanding of original art, for this interdisciplinary project which effectively engages faculty and students across the curriculum. In this manner, I aim to acknowledge my teachers who have been instrumental in defining my own world view, as well as students and colleagues, both past and present, who continually enrich and expand that viewpoint through genuine and generous faculty/student collaboration.

In addition to art contributions from Paul A. Anderson and Professor Thomas B. Brumbaugh, many additional patrons have lent and gifted artwork or made possible specific art acquisitions included in this exhibition and volume. These include my parents, Dr. Thomas William and Barbara Lee Carter, Dr. Jeff Abernathy, Mr. Alex M. Adelman and Mr. Luis Robert Ubillus, Professor Irma Adelman, Josef and Anni Albers Foundation, Andy Warhol Foundation, Drs. Richard and Paula Arnell, Paul A. Arnell, Art History Alumni in Honor of Dr. Mary Em Kirn, Audubon Elementary School, Augustana College Art and Art History Department, Augustana College Art Association, Augustana College Art Collection, Augustana College Class of 1951, Augustana College Department of Art History, Augustana College Department of Geology, Augustana College Department of Physics and Astronomy, Augustana College Thomas Tredway Library Special Collections, Mr. James Beebe, Mr. and Mrs. Michael Barooshian, Mr. and Mrs. Victor H. and Isabel Bartolome, Mr. Barry Bauman, Mr. James A. Bergquist, Dr. James K. Billman, Mr. and Mrs. LeRoy and Margaret Carlson and Family, Dr. Kurt Christoffel, Dr. Daniel Culver, Mr. Dan Churchill, Adam J. DeSimone, Al and Lynne DeSimone, David A. DeSimone, Elizabeth and John Ducey, Emily Ducey, Robert Ducey, Mr. Daryl Empen and Dr. Cynthia Empen, Polly Fehlman, Betty L. Beer Franklin and Dr. Woody Franklin, Drs. Gary James and Catherine Carter Goebel, Katherine Elizabeth Goebel, Thomas James Goebel, Mr. and Mrs. Edward Hoban, Dr. Reynold Emanuel and Johnnie Gause Leak Holmén Endowment Fund for the Visual Arts, Mrs. C. L. Horberg, Lynn Jackson, Kathy Bulucos Memorial Collection, Drs. Mary Em and Michael Kirn, Sonja Knudsen, Mr. James Konrad, Dr. Dan and Ruth Lee, Lohrey Family Limited Partnership, David and Cyndy Losasso, Mr. and Mrs. Frank Lufrano, Mr. and Mrs. Michael Moss, Mr. Carlton Neville and Stephanie Strass, George and Pat Olson, Olson-Brandelle North American Indian Collection, Dr. Richard E. Parker, Paul A. Anderson Estate, Paul and Marty Pearson, Dr. Paul Plante, Thomas E. Rassieur, Mr. George J. Schlenker, Dr. Erick O. Schonstedt, Mr. Harris Schrank, Mr. Allen Schuh, Dr. Alex and Mrs. Martha Stone, Adrian R. Tió, Mrs. Jean F. P. W. Walgren, Rebecca Wee, Dr. Eugene C. and Mrs. Barbara B. Wittenstrom and Mr. Clarence F. and Mrs. Barbara B. Wittenstrom, Jr., and Dr. Karin Youngberg. Additional funding support was provided through a summer 2011 Presidential Fellowship, by the Department of Art History, Augustana College Art Exhibits program, and friends of Augustana College. We are particularly fortunate to include a large number of important works graciously and anonymously lent from private collections. I would also like to acknowledge the considerable research and collection assistance of Alex M. Adelman, Marylene Charmont, Bruce Duncan, Geoffrey Heeney, Hollie Powers Holt, Zeljko Lah, Bruce Loch, Ron Povlich, Harris Schrank, Luis Robert Ubillus and Matt Wrubican.

Our College administration has been tremendously supportive of this vast undertaking. I thank President Steven C. Bahls for his genuine enthusiasm and fine introductory essay as well as his contribution on Pieter Bruegel; Pareena G. Lawrence, Dean of the College and Professor of Economics, for her further introduction and contribution on the Mughal India pieces; Margaret Farrar, Associate Dean, for her encouragement; Lynn Jackson, Vice President for Advancement, for her guidance and gifted work by Mary Cassatt; and Paul Pearson, Vice President of Business and Finance, for his gifts related to Andy Warhol as well as his support for our projects. I am grateful to have been awarded a 2011 Presidential Reasearch Fellowship.

Many contributors to the catalogue must also be acknowledged. I especially thank my colleague, Mary Em Kirn, Professor Emerita of Art History, who has always been the ideal senior colleague and continues as such during retirement. Her significant contributions are too numerous to list. Thomas Banks, Professor Emeritus of Classics and Dorothy J. Parkander Professor Emeritus in Literature, has been fundamental to the project as were Thomas Bengtson; David Ellis, Associate Professor of History; Naoko Gunji, Assistant Professor of Art History; Ellen Hay; Dell Jensen; Emil A. Kramer; Taddy Kalas; and Margaret Morse, Assistant Professor of Art History.

Many members of the administration and faculty contributed essays on works of art related to their interests, including Umme Al-Wazedi, Assistant Professor of English; David Arbesu, Assistant Professor of Spanish; Steven C. Bahls; Thomas Banks; Thomas Bengtson; Erin Bertram, Fellowship Instructor in English; Allen Bertsche, Director of International and Off-Campus Programs and Professor of Spanish; Noelle Birondo, Visiting Assistant Professor of

Philosophy; Ann Boaden, Adjunct Associate Professor of English; Deborah Bracke, Assistant Professor of Education; Lendol Calder, Professor of History; Lee Carkner, Associate Professor of Physics and Astronomy and Director of the John Deere Planetarium; Kurt Christoffel, Professor of Chemistry; Roger Crossley, Professor Emeritus of French; Daniel Culver, Henry Veld Professor of Music; Kelly Daniels, Assistant Professor of English; Kirsten Day, Assistant Professor of Classics; David Dehnel, Professor of Political Science; Kristin Douglas, Associate Professor of Biology; Elizabeth P. Ducey, Art History Graphic Designer and Secretary; Leslie Dupree, Director of Web Services and New Media; Bohdan Dziadyck, Professor of Biology and Director of Field Stations; Robert Elfline, Assistant Professor of Music; Don Erickson, Professor Emeritus of English and Dorothy J. Parkander Professor Emeritus in Literature; C. Kevin Geedey, Professor of Biology; Meg Gilette, Assistant Professor of English; Naoko Gunji; Virginia Johnson, Director of the Reading and Writing Center; Robert Haak, Professor of Religion and Associate Dean and Director of the Center for Community Engagement; Stephen Hager, Associate Professor of Biology; Ellen Hay, Professor of Communication Studies; David Hill, Professor of Philosophy; Sarah M. Horowitz, Special Collections Librarian; Jennifer Horrell, Assistant Professor of Scandinavian Studies; Nancy Huse, Professor Emerita of English; Scott Irelan, Assistant Professor of Theatre; Dell Jensen, Associate Professor of Chemistry; Ruth Ann Johnson, Professor of Psychology; Virginia Johnson, Director of the Reading and Writing Center; Taddy Kalas; Adam Kaul, Associate Professor of Anthropology; Mary Em Kirn, Professor Emerita of Art History; Peter Kivisto, Professor of Sociology and Richard A. Swanson Professor of Social Thought; Stephen A. Klien, Associate Professor of Communication Studies; James Konrad, Adjunct Professor of Art; James M. Lambrecht, Professor of Music and Director of Bands; Emil A. Kramer; Daniel Lee, Professor of Religion and Director of the Center for the Study of Ethics; Megan MacCall, Art History Director of Digital and Visual Resources; Sherry Maurer, Art Museum Director; Joseph D. McDowell, Professor of English; Barbara Melaas-Swanson, Assistant Professor of Religion; Margaret Morse; Kristy Nabhan-Warren, Associate Professor of American Religions; Mari Nagase, Assistant Professor of Asian Studies; Jamie L. Nelson, Special Collections Librarian; Michael Nolan, Adjunct Instructor of English; Dorothy Parkander, Professor Emerita of English and Conrad Bergendoff Professor Emerita in the Humanities; Melbert E. Peterson, Professor Emeritus of Chemistry and Director Emeritus of the John Deere Planetarium; Jennifer Popple, Adjunct Instructor in English and Liberal Studies; Richard Priggie, College Chaplain; Margaret Rogal, Reference Librarian; Nirmala Salgado, Professor of Religion; Larry E. Scott, Professor of Scandinavian Studies; Lisa Seidlitz, Assistant Professor of German; Patricia Shea, Assistant Professor of Education; Jane Simonsen, Associate Professor of History and Women's and Gender Studies and WGS Coordinator; Marsha Y. Smith, Professor of Sociology; David Snowball, Professor of Communication Studies; Heidi Storl, Professor of Philosophy; Molly Todd, Assistant Professor of History; Roald Tweet, Professor Emeritus of English and Conrad Bergendoff Professor Emeritus in the Humanities; Sharon Varallo, Professor of Communication Studies and Violet M. Jaeke Professor of Family Life; Dara Wegman-Geedey, Professor of Biology; Christopher Whitt, Assistant Professor of Political Science; Michael B. Wolf, Professor of Geology; Leslie F. Wolf, Fellowship Instructor in Philosophy; Karin Youngberg, Professor of English and Conrad Bergendoff Professor in the Humanities; and Cyrus Zargar, Assistant Professor of Religion and Islamic Studies.

Many students and alumni from a variety of majors and minors ranging from first-year through seniors contributed essays on individual works for this textbook. Alumni contributors include: Jennifer Jaskowiak; Elizabeth D. Olton and Beth Repay Swanson, Class of 1987; James Beebe and Anthony Merino, Class of 1988; Paul Bacon and Deann Thoms, Class of 1990; Cynthia Wiedemann Empen, Class of 1992; Kathryn Hannen Walker, Class of 1993; Michelle Richmond, Class of 1995; Emily Vokt Ziemba, Class of 1998; and Amy DeLamoreaux, Erin Granet, Lauren Habenicht, Robert Lopez, Angela Granet Lynch, Class of 2001. Alumni from the class of 2005 include: Brian Allured, Matthew Brownley, Errin Copple, Megan Crandall, Dana Kau, Nikki Kromphardt, Beth Luebke; Joe Marusarz, Jason Myers, Megan O'Brien and Michael Skelton. Contributors from the class of 2006 include: Paul Arnell, Kate Felde, David Freeman, Regina Gorham, Colleen Jaycox; Jennifer Johnson, Carol Marquardsen, Kim Weidner and Ewa Wojewoda. Class of 2007 authors include: Mikeda Cannon, Beth Cloud, Mary Feeney, Katie Gedrimas, Chris Johnson, Sneha Konda, Laura Kurczodyna, Gayln Landem, Courtney Olson, Dan Pearson, Kelly Volkert, Jessica Whetzal, Jennifer Windmiller and Dana Zingato. Contributors from the Class of 2008 include: Katie Arnold, Jennifer Bock, Kaitlin Bradley, Jessica Feinman, Beth Gilmartin, Thomas J. Goebel, Julius Gylys, Randi Higel, Lisa Johnson, Aron Lees, Cristy Martinez, Kristin McLinden, Anne Motto, Amanda Nordstrom, Katie Otter, John Regan, Andrea Ritchie, Erin Reeverts, J. D. Rotzoll, Joe Scurto, Johanna Voorhees and Jeffrey Weiland. Class of 2009 contributors include: Julianne Medel, Megan O'Connor and Joshua Schipp. Class of 2010 writers include: April Bernath, Margaret Maksimovich and Mark Leveling. Class of 2011 contributors include: Brooke Bryant; Emily Cox, Stephanie Loria, Victoria Richmond and Helen Reinold. Class of 2012 authors include: Melanie Battistoni, Matthew Bowman, Emma Burns, Rebecca Hodgson, Griselda Mata,

Amanda Miller, Eric Safranski and Veronica Smith. Class of 2013 contributors include: Alyssa Anderson, Kate McCormick and Emily Timmons. And Class of 2014 writers include: Amanda Greenlee, Elizabeth Jakaitis, Jessica Lemek, Alexis Long and Chase Matzinger.

Special thanks and gratitude are extended to our graphic designer and secretary, Elizabeth Parker Ducey. Beth has spent seven years now, tirelessly working with me through summers as well as many evenings and weekends toward the *Origins of Modernity* and all four editions of *Liberal Arts through the AGES*. Her good-humored dedication to these projects is laudable and her fine eye for design is reflected in every beautiful page of these publications. Beyond the design work, she has served as project manager for this book and was instrumental in coordinating the drafts and final manuscript, especially complicated through my teaching on fall 2011 London term. She was assisted by work-study students, Logan Douglass, who standardized all citations and constructed a collated bibliography, and Veronica Smith, who oversaw permissions for reproducing works of art. Sherry Case Maurer, Director of the Augustana College Art Museum, must also be thanked for her contributions, particularly her assistance with the compilation of the exhibition checklist, used as captions for the artwork in the catalogue, and conducting Liberal Studies class tours in the art museum. Megan MacCall, Director of Digital and Visual Resources, has also been integral to this venture and particularly toward constructing the electronic web gallery for these works of art to facilitate their usage by faculty and students. I would also like to acknowledge the assistance of the Thomas Tredway Library staff, particularly Carla Tracy, Director, as well as Margi Rogal and Connie Ghinazzi, Reference Librarians, and Jamie Nelson and Sarah Horowitz, Special Collections Librarians. In addition, Information Technology Services Director Chris Vaughan as well as Fernando Rios furthered this undertaking. Darlene Link, College Controller has continually and graciously reinforced our endeavors over the years for all aspects of this project.

In addition, I wish to acknowledge the late art professor, James Konrad, for his skillful conservation and consultation regarding many paintings on exhibit. Barry Bauman, Conservator of Paintings and Fine Works of Art for Non-Profit Organizations, also kindly conserved key pieces for exhibition. Dick Oberg photographed all artwork for this publication and Fidlar Printing Company courteously provided professional resources toward the planning and production stages for all five books. Finally, I want to generally thank all, too numerous to mention, who have in any way contributed to the successful completion of this 2011 edition of *Liberal Arts through the AGES: Interdisciplinary Art Historical Inquiry*. The faculty, students and administration who have embraced this project and its potential for our students are truly remarkable. I am profoundly grateful, in particular, to members of the Augustana faculty who graciously lent their time and impressive expertise toward this significant collegial collaboration. Each has provided a distinct lens on the liberal arts that richly contributes toward the greater illumination of our first-year students as they prepare to focus on the large picture of their education.

I am most indebted to my husband, Dr. Gary James Goebel, who has been continuously patient, supportive and encouraging toward my many diverse professional projects and especially for this particular one, originally planned as a one-year enrichment, which clearly became much larger and longer than anticipated. I am grateful to my mother, Barbara Lee Carter, who introduced me to the beauty and importance of visual and written language and my late father, Dr. Thomas William Carter, whose example of excellence and service remain a beacon in my life. My sister, Patricia Carter Deveau, first suggested I take an art history class in college, a decision which led to a most satisfying career. I especially want to thank my children, Thomas James Goebel and Katherine Elizabeth Goebel, who reinforce their mother's preoccupation with such professional projects for the college. Tom was an enormously valuable resource, offering perspectives and insights, for the first three books in general and in particular as volunteer assistant editor for the further sesquicentennial edition. Katie proved integral and indeed essential to the current edition as volunteer assistant editor, adeptly editing longer essays from past contributors to transition effectively to the new format for this book. Both Tom and Katie also wrote their own multi-source research essays included in this edition. Their inspiration, guidance and contributions have thoroughly enhanced the quality of this project and its relevance for their contemporaries. Without my family's enthusiasm and encouragement this project would never have been undertaken or completed.

Catherine Carter Goebel, *Editor*

An Introduction to the Liberal Arts and AGES

Thomas R. Banks, *Professor Emeritus of Classics*
Dorothy J. Parkander Professor Emeritus in Literature

Diana of Gabii, After Praxiteles—(Greek, ca. 375-340 BCE) ca. 1850
Catalogue 6

The concept of the liberal arts has been an evolving human achievement, not a motionless given. From the classical period to our own time, civilizations have examined the experience of their forebears and their own circumstances, then created studies that seemed most likely to develop the happy—the truly happy—person. As the name suggests (Latin *liberalis*, free) this happiness was known to require freedom of mind, body and spirit. The *artes liberales* were to enable that freedom. The tradition of the concept eventually counted seven liberal arts and called them the Trivium (the written word, the spoken word, and logic) and the Quadrivium (arithmetic, geometry, astronomy, and music). We would know them by other names and expanded concerns: the humanities, mathematics, natural science, social science, the fine arts, and the critical thinking that accompanies them all.

The origin of this concept, and its evolution since, was practical in so deep a way that it has to be considered idealistic as well. The ideal practicality lay in the goal of preparing a person to be in the deepest sense happy: fulfilled in mind, body, and spirit. This happiness would require the ability to fulfill a calling in many senses: in economic capability, in civic duty and leadership, and in the life of the mind as it confronts all the other richness and challenge of life. Further—and this deeper practicality especially distinguished the liberal arts—this learning must prepare one to meet opportunities and agonies never seen before. If learned well, then, the liberal arts are an ever-new resource for an unknown future.

At Augustana today, our enactment of the liberal arts is the curriculum called Augustana General Education Studies (AGES). Crucially, this begins with the courses we call Liberal Studies. These are introductions to the fundamental questions of the liberal arts. As such, they are the basis for deeper happiness, whether sought in citizenship, private life, or vocation. They are in effect—let us be emphatic here—the roots of any major field of study: not preliminary to the major, not in addition to the major, but where a major itself begins.

AGES continues with the Learning Perspectives and Learning Communities. The Learning Perspectives are the modern enactment of the Trivium and Quadrivium. They are the ways of inquiring into answers to serious questions. But the power of these ways, these perspectives, is weakened if isolated. The liberal arts are parts of a whole. Therefore the third component of AGES, the Learning Community, shows how to integrate learning from more than one perspective. Knowing the questions, knowing how to research and formulate answers, and knowing how to do this in a collaboration both of methods and of colleagues will be the means to achieve that deepest happiness—within self, society, and cosmos. Thus the mission statement of Augustana:

> *Augustana College, rooted in the liberal arts and sciences and a Lutheran expression of the Christian faith, is committed to offering a challenging education that develops qualities of mind, spirit and body necessary for a rewarding life of leadership and service in a diverse and changing world.*

Catalogue 17, detail

"Both to those alive now and to those of later time we will be a source of amazement."

Thucydides (Athenian, ca. 460-400 BCE)
reporting Pericles's Funerary Oration
History of the Peloponnesian War 2.41.

Introduction to *Liberal Arts through the AGES: Interdisciplinary Art Historical Inquiry*

Steven C. Bahls, *President of the College*

Throughout its history, Augustana College has transformed lives. For some students, the wide range of opportunities—intellectual, creative, physical and spiritual—challenges their thinking, while providing balance to their personal growth. For others, the inspiration of meeting a professor head-on with new ideas, spontaneously and even at odd times or places, stretches their perceived boundaries. They find themselves becoming thoughtful leaders, capable of influencing, advancing, understanding and questioning the world in which we live.

Whatever their individual experiences, it is their liberal arts education that makes such transformation possible. And at Augustana, it is our steadfast commitment to the way we interpret and engage liberal arts that makes such transformation happen. We focus and build on a primary strength long held by the college: close, intentional relationships between professors and students within a strong academic program based in the liberal arts. We recognize liberal arts education to be not simply an exposure to a wide array of ideas to tantalize the intellect, but an integration and application of learning gathered from the great thinkers across the spectrum of human achievement. When Augustana students find themselves making essential connections among ideas—purposely promoted in this effort by their faculty mentors—they are transformed.

Transformation itself is something we address within our liberal arts curriculum, beginning with the first-year liberal studies program. Through this first-year sequence, our students learn that a liberal arts education at Augustana is generous and human, imaginative and intuitive. We agree with John Henry (Cardinal) Newman when he observed that those educated in the liberal arts "apprehend the great outlines of knowledge, the principles on which it rests, the scale of its parts, its lights and its shades, its great points and its little" (Newman 93).

Art, we believe, is a particularly effective vehicle for students to think about the "lights and…shades" of the human experience. That is why, during the winter term, the first-year liberal studies curriculum incorporates this interdisciplinary textbook, *Liberal Arts through the AGES* (Augustana General Education Studies) and complementary exhibition. As evident in the catalogue, which includes over two hundred works of art, the college's pedagogical art history collection is designed first and foremost to educate our students. Thus, the museum includes collections from Europe, Asia, Africa, Australia, as well as various regions in the Americas.

The works of art found in *Liberal Arts through the AGES* embody Augustana's commitment to the liberal arts and each work of art is reproduced with an analysis written by faculty, students, alumni and administrators at the college. According to the creator and editor of this project, Dr. Catherine Carter Goebel, the Paul A. Anderson Chair in the Arts and Professor and Chair of the Department of Art History, this book is designed to help our students "realize that our contemporary worldview has actually evolved over time." She believes that understanding the past "enables us to better discern our present….Works of art—original texts—offer an ideal historical and multidisciplinary lens through which we might examine the past as it relates to the various eras and themes under investigation" (xix).

This book permits our students to look at the world through the eyes of others, both those of the artists in their historical contexts and those of the Augustana faculty, students and administrators who researched and wrote about these works through their own perspectives. *Liberal Arts through the AGES* recognizes that different viewers may see different messages in the art, and that sharing these different messages with each other enriches our understanding of the past, provides integrative opportunities for learning in the present, and models how we should strive to build a better world for the future.

Under Dr. Goebel's leadership, the college decided that during the winter term of our first-year liberal studies course, historic works of art should be viewed as primary texts to research and study. Dr. Goebel's book, *Origins of Modernity*, and its progeny as exemplified in four different editions (including this one) of *Liberal Arts through the AGES*, constitute a common text for first-year students. Approximately half the essays were contributed by Augustana students and alumni from the classes of 1987-2014, with a number of different majors and minors, who critically analyzed and researched original works of art. And nearly half the essays published here were written by Augustana faculty and administrators, from various disciplines across the curriculum, who lent their expertise toward the interdisciplinary interpretation of original artwork—a profound accomplishment of multidisciplinary collaboration. This book thus serves to celebrate our community, engaged in the beauty and truth exemplified in this art historical textbook, representing the generosity of spirit and intellectual goals of Augustana College coming to full fruition through faculty/student research.

To have a full "life of the mind," the mind at times needs soothing. We aim to help our students understand not only the historical dimensions and complexities of visual images, but also to view the arts as spiritual sustenance and solace. But a liberal arts college and its art should do more than soothe our souls. For students, in particular, studying art allows us

to delve into ideas that will challenge our minds, in a way perhaps less threatening than a lecture or debate as it invites a one-to-one engagement with the artwork. Art often makes an understated point, and we can study it with greater deliberation. Art allows us time and space to linger and reflect. If we are challenged by the art, we can grapple with the artist's ideas and contexts at our own pace.

Art and literature have challenged my own thinking about my vocation. As an attorney, educator and college president, I find that the most difficult decisions to make are those in which one combines justice (what people deserve) with mercy (forbearance from giving people what they deserve). My views of justice have been deeply influenced by Pieter Bruegel's *Justicia* (image **#1**), which I analyzed for this publication. This 450-year old work of art is as relevant today as during Pieter Bruegel's time.

Art provides a way to connect with other cultures and other times, without an airplane ticket (or a time machine). The Paul A. Anderson Chair has overseen building a pedagogical art history collection, in coordination with the museum director as well as generous donors and dealers, that spans recorded history from ancient Greece (image **#2**) through the twentieth century (image **#3**), encompassing all major western historic periods between (images **#4-14**). In addition, incorporating many diverse cultures (images **#15-16**), as well as art historical expertise in these areas, similarly enrich the multicultural perspectives of the liberal arts at Augustana College.

I believe Martin Luther was right that art helps us deepen our understanding of faith. I believe that God can speak through the hands of great artists. In the same way, I believe the study of art history helps us to deepen our understanding of ourselves and our world.

Luther wrote that "singing, poetizing, and painting" serve to "praise God's words." This "blessing," he writes, "does not leave us or part from us; it goes through death with us, tears us out of it, and brings us to eternal life, where there is neither death nor fear of dying" (Luther 131). Just as our faith can sustain us throughout this life and the hereafter, the gift of art does not leave us or part from us. Art enhances the life of the mind in a way that neither hardship nor illness can tear away. That is why Augustana has committed itself to giving generations of students the gift of understanding and appreciating original art created throughout the world and throughout time.

Catalogue 56, detail

"...the business of art lies just in this—to make that understood and felt which, in the form of an argument, might be incomprehensible and inaccessible."

Leo Tolstoy, *What is Art?* (*1896*)

Liberal Arts through the AGES: An Introduction

Pareena G. Lawrence, *Dean of the College and Professor of Economics*

Welcome to Augustana College! We are excited that you are undertaking your college journey with us and I can think of no better way to begin your academic career at Augustana than with the carefully crafted curriculum that we proudly call *Liberal Arts through the AGES*. We at Augustana are committed to educating students in the long established traditions of the liberal arts.

Liberal education is a program of personal development. The focus is on who you can become and not just what you can do with your degree, though that is important. This tradition is even more important today as the world is rapidly changing and becoming increasingly interconnected. Knowledge of another language, human culture, the physical and natural world, critical inquiry, and communication skills are vital in today's global and interconnected society. A genuine liberal arts education is not only about the curriculum, but is also about the methods of discourse and the environment in which it is offered. A residential campus, small class sizes, pedagogical methods that focus on engaging students in learning and discovery, all important elements of an authentic liberal arts college experience that creates a community of scholars who challenge and support one another.

The writings that are part of the collection for the winter term Liberal Studies course allow you to access original texts from across disciplines and cultures and time periods. As you read and reflect on these works, we hope that you will better understand the diverse perspectives on human thought and its evolution over time. The rich and unique collection of art that has been specifically selected for this curriculum is also exhibited in the College's art museum. Art has served many purposes in human history. It uplifts, inspires, pleases, but it can also horrify and make us uncomfortable. It is a visual record of history. Art communicates the human experience and the human condition. Leo Tolstoy in his 1896 work, *What is Art?* wrote, "the business of art lies just in this—to make that understood and felt which, in the form of an argument, might be incomprehensible and inaccessible" (102). It is our hope that you will engage with this collection and that this opportunity will help you grow in your understanding and appreciation of the world around us and our shared past.

The next four years that lie ahead will be a very special experience for you. It will provide you with multiple opportunities and the potential to grow and change in profound ways. However, learning is a process, and process takes time. Don't be in a rush to grow and change—that will happen organically as you absorb everything that is happening around you. As you begin this educational journey, challenge yourself, be passionate, explore, lead, disagree, learn to reason and not rationalize, remember to listen, question your assumption and biases, and above all be civil. That is the quintessential liberal arts way of learning.

Catalogue 86, detail

"Observe carefully and extract from nature everything that can be extracted. Above all, light! Seek its radiance, its flash, render it down, hunt out its warmth."

Eugène Boudin *(1824–98)*

Discerning Texts from Past to Present: Art History as Liberal Arts Bridge

Catherine Carter Goebel, *Professor and Chair of Art History*
Paul A. Anderson Chair in the Arts

Liberal Arts through the AGES is an important part of your unique first-year learning experience. While many colleges have first-year readers, *Liberal Arts through the AGES* not only includes written texts but also utilizes the rich resources of the Augustana College Art Collection. These texts provide a foundation for first-year courses. They have been selected by faculty teaching the courses as cornerstones for your studies.

Liberal Arts through the AGES offers first-year students immediate access to primary documents—original texts—dating from various periods, cultures and disciplines through the history of civilization. The texts that are included present a wide perspective on human thought and come from many different disciplines. While we often think our view of the world is one that has always been common, the texts in this publication help us realize that our contemporary worldview has actually evolved over time. Reading words, some dating back to oral traditions, written by great thinkers of the past, enables us to better discern our present. It is also an integral step toward becoming fully educated in the liberal arts—and "in the deepest sense happy: fulfilled in mind, body, and spirit" (Banks xi). The fundamental questions of the Liberal Arts are touched upon in these readings. As described by two former Augustana first-year students, this book "looks at history through firsthand accounts. And some of these accounts happen to be works of art," since "predating the written word, art transcends all language barriers" (O'Connor and Petry).

1

2

Works of art—original texts—offer an ideal historical and multidisciplinary lens through which we might examine the past as it relates to the various eras and themes under investigation. Diverse scholarly approaches are used to explicate artwork, including stylistic analysis, iconographic (symbolic) language, sociological and psychological interpretation, as well as scientific and technical consideration. Art historians increasingly account for the context in which works of art were created and the manner in which such accomplishments mirror their time periods. By studying artwork from a given epoch, we can learn more about that time. Furthermore, as we

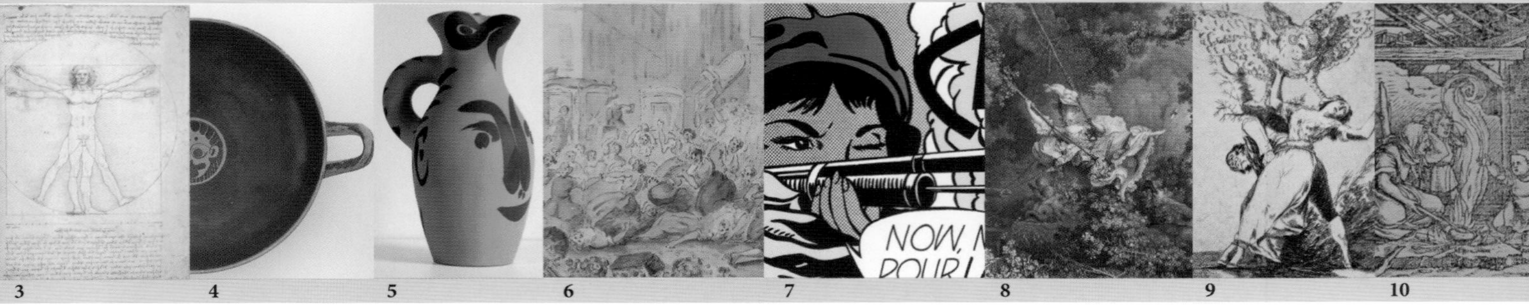

trace the development of art along a timeline, we may note places where traditions and past styles (#**1**: catalogue 2—ca. 340-320 BCE) have impacted the present (#**2**: catalogue 143—1898) as well as innovations that occur that are particular to a specific period.

Liberal Arts through the AGES is thus a major pedagogical resource for teaching critical thinking, comparative analysis and chronological developments. Studying original works of art, rather than merely consulting photographs or electronic images, is crucial because reproductions cannot adequately present perceptual subtleties of scale, surface, color and line quality or conceptual details found within the work's content. Augustana's art collection has been carefully developed in order to effectively complement the liberal arts curriculum of the college; it therefore establishes an important visual education resource for students and faculty. As evidenced by this publication, professors and administrators, as well as alumni and undergraduates ranging from the first through senior year with a multitude of majors and minors, have benefited from the opportunity of directly studying these works of art in person. And the benefit increases, as their writing further informs as you utilize this book for your own research. This dynamic creates an ongoing dialogue with the work of art and with others who interpret it, designed to facilitate both contemplation and action.

You are likely, historically, one of the most visually adept generations, capable of quickly assessing a variety of images, as you input and access data. But don't settle for the immediate satisfaction of the *quick read*. Instead, learn to carefully examine primary texts, consult secondary sources, discuss your ideas and interpretations with other students and with your professors (specialists in a number of fields, many referenced in this book) and look for larger patterns. Countless new ideas trace their origins in creative interpretations of the past. Renaissance master Leonardo da Vinci, for example, carefully sketched the famous *Vitruvian Man* (#**3**: figure 1—ca. 1492). Yet the concept was not his own, but stemmed instead from Leonardo's reading of a theory on *ideal* mathematical proportions for the human figure by first-century BCE Roman architect Vitruvius: "For if a man be placed flat on his back, with his hands and feet extended, and a pair of compasses centered at his navel, the fingers and toes of his hands and feet will touch the circumference of a circle described therefrom. And just as the human body yields a circular outline, so too a square figure may be found from it" (Vitruvius 690). Leonardo's drawing after Vitruvius, in turn, stimulated contemporary novelist Dan Brown, centuries later, to reproduce the *Vitruvian Man* in a very different medium, as a complex symbol to launch the plot for his fictional bestseller, *The Da Vinci Code*.

In similar manner, LS students can make connections through art historical comparisons (note examples of first-year student comparative essays—pages 20-29). For example, they might discover origins in ancient Greek pottery (#**4**: catalogue 1—ca. 520-500 BCE) for artist Pablo Picasso's modern ceramic designs (#**5**: catalogue 194—1963). They can examine the emerging empowerment of women as defined during the French Revolution (#**6**: catalogue 56—late 18th century) and reinvestigated through pop imagery from the 1960s (#**7**: catalogue 200). Capricious (#**8**: catalogue 38—

late 18th century) as well as tragic female roles (#**9**: catalogue 62—18th century) are apparent. Themes on mortality might be traced centuries back to a Renaissance woodcut of a skeletal figure of *Death* seizing a child within a domestic interior (#**10**: catalogue 20—1538) and re-investigated in a Romantic image of Shakespeare's tragic hero, Hamlet (#**11**: catalogue 68—1801), holding the skull of his former court jester and ruminating over the fragility of life. Yet in sharp contrast, Impressionist Mary Cassatt depicted blissful maternal *bonding* (#**12**: catalogue 95—1908), unchallenged by such heartbreaking realities of life. Renaissance master Raphael Sanzio centered his composition on great men as philosophers (#**13**: catalogue 17—1509), yet Rembrandt van Rijn focused on Christ as illumination (#**14**: catalogue 26—1652). Realist Honoré Daumier saw the future in science and technology (#**15**: catalogue 77A—1862) while Andy Warhol illustrated the dehumanization that modern technology increasingly facilitates (#**16**: catalogue 199 A & B—1982-84). Symbols of peaceful meditation (#**17**: catalogue 35—n.d.) may be contrasted with sobering realities of war (#**18**: catalogue 80—19th century). Exploring the past through such juxtapositions enables students to recognize significant links that deepen our understanding of the human condition.

The origins for our present may thus be traced through a number of cultural and historical movements. In fact, the very nature of being *modern* may pertain to such a wide range of artistic periods that one must repeatedly attempt to frame modernity within its appropriate context. Many art historians, for example, feel nineteenth-century American expatriate artist James McNeill Whistler (#**19**: catalogue 116—1897) effectively defined the position of the modern artist. Whistler was a highly original individual who transformed Romantic alienation into a virtue and indeed made it a necessity for success. One cannot imagine a better role model for the modern pose than Whistler, an artist who flaunted patrons, sued a critic, enjoyed being incomprehensible and wrote a book to celebrate it all. In fact, his publication, *The Gentle Art of Making Enemies*, has long been hailed as a virtual sourcebook for modern artists.

In applying this term through the liberal arts model, itself a concept representing, according to Thomas Banks, Professor Emeritus of Classics and Dorothy J. Parkander Professor Emeritus in Literature, an "evolving human achievement, not a motionless given" and across various disciplines within the liberal arts program, varied diverse definitions and interpretations result. Such complexity furnishes "introductions to the fundamental questions of the liberal arts...an ever-new resource for an unknown future" (Banks xi). And as with the classical basis for such examination, this book begins with Greek civilization. Perhaps the very nature of being *modern*, implies constant flux as the *new* is evaluated, and often replaced, by the next generation.

In defining the historical *modern age*, productive interpretative disagreements ensue. As David Ellis, Associate Professor of History, states: "Many historians in the west consider the modern era to have begun sometime around either 1500 or 1789. Those in the first camp point to a number of crucial developments that occurred within fifty years or so of 1500. These include the introduction of the movable printing press, European voyages of discovery and subsequent transcontinental exchanges, significant expansion and solidification of the Ottoman Empire...[and]

the beginning of the Protestant Reformation(s)...Those who favor the time around 1789 (give or take fifty years) as the beginning of the modern era point to another cluster of comparably important events and processes that start around that time. These include important developments in imperialism..., the American Revolution..., the various phases of the French Revolution [and]...the beginnings of the Industrial Revolution...Historians of Europe often resort to a *modus vivendi* [an accommodation] that partly reconciles the two positions...[into a] distinction between the *early modern* and the *modern* eras."

The so-called early modern period might be traced in such Renaissance works as Giorgio Ghisi's engraving after Michelangelo's *The Erythraean Sibyl* (#**20**: catalogue 16—1508-12) at the Sistine Chapel in Rome. As he did in the famous scene of the *Creation of Adam*, from the same location, Michelangelo sought to reconcile classical idealism and anatomical investigation with Roman Catholicism. Such renderings reflect a careful balance of art and science with theology, reinforced by the artist's own deep faith and belief that if indeed man was made in God's image, then by studying cadavers the artist could both learn how to accurately portray the human figure and spiritually gain greater insight into the nature of God. In the same manner, Northern Renaissance master, Albrecht Dürer (#**21**: catalogue 19—1510), utilized architect Filippo Brunelleschi's mathematical invention of linear perspective, which improved upon ancient illusionism by effectively creating the look of a third dimension through a logical system of parallel and perpendicular lines on an otherwise two-dimensional surface.

Following on the heels of such innovations, the Reformation brought about profound changes in seventeenth-century Baroque subject matter. For example, Dutch etcher, Rembrandt van Rijn, although illustrating a religious event in *Christ Preaching* (#**22**: catalogue 26—1652), adopted an approach which reflects less interest in the visionary side of religion and instead presents an approachable holy figure who, although emphasized through *chiaroscuro* (the contrast of light and shadow), seems to compete with the assemblage of interesting personalities surrounding him. Rembrandt was a master of atmosphere and characterization and his works responded to a growing interest in searching beyond classical idealism toward individuality. In similar manner, artist and diplomat, Peter Paul Rubens in *The Hunt of the Hippopotamus and the Crocodile* (#**23**: catalogue 28—1615-16) illustrated the quest for exoticism based in further voyages of discovery. The privileged humanistic position of man over nature is fragile, lending itself to a more emotional and precarious depiction, with a similar sort of modern appeal as today's action movies. Even the medium of printmaking reflects an increasing democratic approach to art by making it more accessible to a larger number of people, both by virtue of its multiple images as well as its resulting lower price.

In most recent art historical studies, however, the modern period seems to be most broadly defined by the eighteenth-century Enlightenment and the various important events that followed in its wake. In an era marked by a return to classicism and order, further fueled by the rediscovery of the lost Roman cities of Pompeii and Herculaneum and the consequent Neoclassical movement, Rococo images of decadent, pampered female Parisian aristocrats engaged in

recreation (#**24**: catalogue 38—ca. 1767) or depicted as goddesses such as *Hebe* (#**25**: catalogue 40—mid-18th century) would soon be replaced by desperate women in revolt (#**26**: catalogue 56—late 18th century), demanding a means by which to feed their children. Artists pursued the *Grand Tour*, considered an essential finishing element to gentlemen's formal education, and sculptors found a ready market for marble copies of ancient Greek and Roman works such as *Minerva* (#**27**: catalogue 58—n.d.). British entrepreneur Josiah Wedgwood effectively marketed the classical for popular consumption through his invention of jasper ware (#**28**: catalogue 59—1791) which imitated ancient Roman glass. At the time, the so-called *father of art history*, Johann Winckelmann, encouraged young enthusiasts: "There is but one way for the moderns to become great, and perhaps unequaled; I mean by imitating the ancients" (Winckelmann 6). Yet through such historical example, the French Revolution was fueled (#**29**: catalogue 54—ca. 1784).

Furthermore, Denis Diderot and Jean d'Alembert co-authored their *Encyclopédie*, which aimed at presenting a rational compendium of past and present knowledge ranging from astronomy to zoology (#**30**: catalogue 48 A & B—1751-72). Such publications attempted to portray a rational new world devoid of superstition. At the same time, they made information more precise and available to a larger number of people. Artists such as Sebastiano visited Athens and Rome on the Grand Tour in order to examine and record such antiquities in person (#**31**: catalogue 49—late 18th century), while academies in France and Britain, patronized by royalty, developed to reinforce appropriate artistic training and exhibition (#**32**: catalogue 44—1787) of didactic artwork. These art academies also determined the types and hierarchy for works of art. History was deemed the highest level and consisted of stories from ancient or recent history, including religious or mythological subjects. It was the most prestigious since it was generally considered morally edifying. Also in descending order, the hierarchy included portraits, genre (scenes of everyday life), landscape and still life.

It seemed that the American Revolution would provide the perfect Enlightenment subject for artists of the day. Yet in a young country which prided itself on freedom from oppression, dramatically illustrated by Paul Revere (#**33**: catalogue 50—ca. 1770), there were inherent challenges as to how to appropriately portray grand history painting related to the revolutionary cause. John Trumbull's image of the *Declaration of Independence* (#**34**: catalogue 51—1786-94), representing perhaps the triumph of Enlightenment philosophy, suffers from the very nature of the newly created country where straightforward Yankee realism and accuracy outweighed bombastic historicizing. Another problem arose in this new republic, without princes and popes, as to who would patronize such large, expensive works? The same quality might be seen in the consummate if unfinished portrait of *George Washington* (#**35**: catalogue 53—1796), which retains its credibility by portraying a simple, straightforward interpretation of the first president of the United States.

Romanticism furnished many seeds for modernity. The image of the suffering artist found its source in such works as Francisco Goya's *The Sleep of Reason Produces Monsters* (#**36**: catalogue 63—1793-98), a self-portrait of the painter

himself who, although a child of the Enlightenment, was disillusioned by intolerant rulers, peasant sorcery and ignorance as well as the Spanish Inquisition. An illness left him deaf, further isolating him from the aristocratic society of his patrons. This image breaks the barrier from the rational world to the imagination, which according to Goya, when accompanied by reason, was the "mother of the arts," yet when abandoned, produced "impossible monsters" (Johnson 32). Goya's fascination with the subject of dreams opened a realm of mystery that would be the focus of twentieth-century Surrealists. At the same time, painters like Thomas Lawrence explored mortality through literary sources such as William Shakespeare. *Hamlet* (#**37**: catalogue 68—1801), for example, holds the skull of his former court jester, Yorick, a *memento mori* (reminder of death) in order to examine the frailty of the human condition. Both images and sources also touched upon the subject of depression and insanity, which would be further explored by twentieth-century psychology.

Multiculturalism—or perhaps orientalism—was increasingly probed through images such as the *Burial of Atala* (#**38**: catalogue 69—1808), which illustrates the tug-of-war experienced in the New World by François-René de Chateaubriand's literary figure of Atala. She could only reconcile the pull between her religious conviction, illustrated by the priest on the right, and her love for the young Native American boy on the left, by tragically committing suicide. The piece, having elements of both Neoclassicism and Romanticism, might also be seen as illustrating the competing schools of the time. In the same manner, exotic subjects reflecting colonization were also explored through Sir David Wilkie's study (#**39**: catalogue 65—1835) for *Sir David Baird Discovering the Body of the Sultaun Tippoo Sahib*, Eugène Delacroix's sketches of lions (#**40**: catalogue 66—1832-61) and the anonymous image of *Our Lady of Guadalupe* (#**41**: catalogue 25—early-mid 19th century).

Romanticism also accompanied the age of modern nineteenth-century science. Dell Jensen, Associate Professor of Chemistry, has suggested: "Modernity cannot be defined without looking at the development of science, because it provided the basis for advancement and betterment of society through the understanding of the natural world. From this perspective, it can be said that modernity started with the great thinkers of the Renaissance (Leonardo da Vinci and Galileo Galilei [#**42**: catalogue 29—ca. 1832 image of Galileo in 1632]). They were followed by many other individuals (Isaac Newton, Francis Bacon, Antoine Lavoisier and Benjamin Franklin) who made significant contributions to our understanding of the modern world...[Furthermore] John Dalton and Charles Darwin...laid the foundation for modern science. Dalton's Atomic Theory (1807) provided the basis for much of our understanding of chemistry and Darwin's book, *Origin of Species* (1859), solidified the concept of natural selection and evolution. During this four hundred year period, the world underwent profound changes and many of those changes involved the understanding of the natural world and its role in society." Yet, such a narrative of progress often sat uneasily with Romantics, whose appreciation for the power, beauty and uniqueness of nature was coupled with a bitter sense of the loss of mystery, which many expressed with poignant irony.

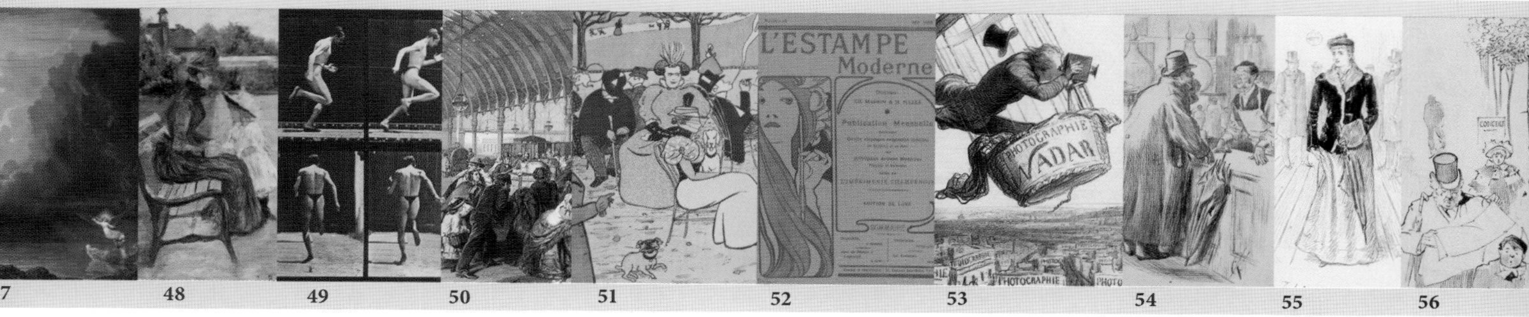

Artistic parallels in science might be traced to John James Audubon's series, including *Whippoorwill* (#**43**: catalogue 71—1830), which aimed at recording all the native birds of North America depicted in their natural habitats. The illustrator attempted to capture the immediacy of the specimens, either drawn from life or freshly shot and wired into position, exhibited against a blank background allowing them to be read in a careful analytical manner, with some aesthetic interpretation for effect. Such scientific analysis is further illustrated in the images of *Metamorphoses* by Maria Merian (#**44**: catalogue 133 A & B—1717). In similar manner, English Romantic painter John Constable beautifully combined the meteorological interests of his age with art through dozens of cloud studies, captured on sight through the invention of portable oil paints which allowed artists for the first time to paint outdoors directly from nature (#**45**: catalogue 67—1813). Although Constable lovingly depicted the subtle nuances of cloud banks and individual trees; his scientific interest, like Michelangelo's before him, was reinforced by a profound belief that such natural phenomena were aspects of God's divine order. Yet never before had an artist so effectively captured the moods of nature, which would have immediate influence on the development of Realism and Impressionism in France.

American artist Thomas Cole would similarly straddle Romanticism and Realism. His *Voyage of Life* series raised landscape to the level of history through its predictable moral metaphor for the river of life, the meaning accessible to a large audience. In scene two of the four-part series, *Youth* (#**46**: catalogue 73—1849), the baby from scene one is now a young man in the summer of his youth (as well as that of landscape) who optimistically steers his boat with the hourglass masthead toward a castle in the sky. By scene four, *Old Age* (#**47**: catalogue 74—1849) is inevitable. Although the elements are carefully and scientifically rendered after nature, Cole's greater purpose was to deliver the message of time's passing and the consequent *ages of man* inherent in history painting.

By the second half of the nineteenth century, artists had largely abandoned such themes and focused, with Impressionism's interests in capturing everyday life, on utilizing new theories such as the physics of light. Michel-Eugène Chevreul published his law of simultaneous contrasts in 1839, which likely influenced Impressionist and Post-Impressionist approaches to color. Impressionist paintings including Berthe Morisot's *Young Woman and Child in a Garden* (#**48**: catalogue 93—ca. 1888-94) reflected these new ideas, as well as the utilization of atmospheric perspective based on the scientific observation that colors appear cooler and details less distinct in the distance. Such imagery also offered no apology for simply representing modern life, with no pretense of greater purpose.

By the mid nineteenth century, following the Industrial Revolution, city populations were growing at rapid speed, as people moved from the countryside. This new middle class was accommodated by urban adjustments. Thomas Bengtson, Professor of Mathematics and Earl H. Beling Chair in Mathematics, has noted: "The fine arts were greatly affected by advances in technology and gains in wealth. Art came to be produced not only for the aristocracy, but rather for those with the means to pay for it. Subjects depicted in art changed to include themes of interest to a

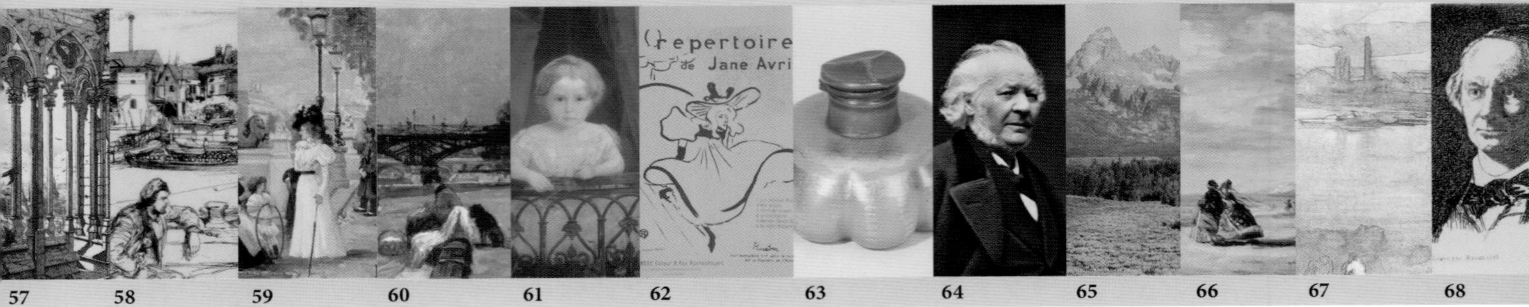

growing middle class. Entirely new subjects became available, too, such as railroads and buildings of inexpensive iron and steel. Technology provided new means, such as photography [#**49**: catalogue 117 A & B—1887] and steel engravings, with which to produce art…Consider *The Railway Station* [#**50**: catalogue 114—1866], an engraving after an original painting by William Powell Frith. The subject includes a train and a train station. Fifty years earlier, trains did not exist and neither did the architecture of an open iron lattice for the station. Steel engraving techniques had only recently become available, making the print affordable to a growing middle class."

In response to the growing *bourgeoisie* (middle class), newspapers and journals multiplied to educate and entertain the masses (#**51**: catalogue 137—1896 and #**52**: catalogue 131—1898). Artists such as Honoré Daumier (#**53**: catalogue 77A—1862), Charles Keene (#**54**: catalogue 111—1884), George du Maurier (#**55**: catalogue 113—1891) and Phil May (#**56**: catalogue 112—1896) delighted their audiences with narratives, astutely drawn and engraved, that illustrated the many facets of modern urban life. Yet their field, based on quick and brilliant sketches, would soon be eclipsed by photography.

Many artists and writers regretted the sweeping changes that accompanied urban modernity. As the new Paris was being designed by Baron Haussmann for Emperor Napoleon III, clearing away much of the historic medievalism of the city, artists such as Charles Meryon in *La Galerie Notre Dame* (#**57**: catalogue 75—1853) recorded national treasures that were now in jeopardy. In like manner, James McNeill Whistler depicted the colorful dockside views along the Thames River in London, such as *Black Lion Wharf* (#**58**: catalogue 76—1859), destined to be irrevocably erased through the building of an embankment. Although such changes brought large boulevards (#**59**: catalogue 90—n.d.), well-engineered bridges (#**60**: catalogue 88—ca. 1860-70) and better living conditions (#**61**: catalogue 94—1872), there was a wistful sentimentality as to the price of *progress*. Decorative arts even reflected rejection of the mass production of post-Industrial Revolution society by designing functional art that retained careful craftsmanship, part of the *Arts and Crafts* movement, with results such as Henri de Toulouse-Lautrec's elegant and reductive music book cover (#**62**: catalogue 129—1893) and the elegant *Tiffany Favrile Glass Inkwell* (#**63**: catalogue 139—1899).

With such renditions of modernity initially aided by technology, many artists further questioned the advances that they enabled. Whistler suggested: "The imitator is a poor kind of creature. If the man who paints only the tree, or flower, or other surface he sees before him were an artist, the king of artists would be the photographer" (Whistler 128). Portraits (#**64**: catalogue 77B—1877) and landscapes (#**65**: catalogue 168—1882) could now be captured on film, so what was left for an artist to do? Such modernist dilemmas might be illustrated by comparing Eugène Boudin's *Beach at Trouville* (#**66**: catalogue 86—1864) with James McNeill Whistler's *Early Morning* (#**67**: catalogue 85—1878). On the surface, though similar in composition and atmospheric effect, they both emerge from very distinct philosophies which ultimately defined the course of modern twentieth-century art.

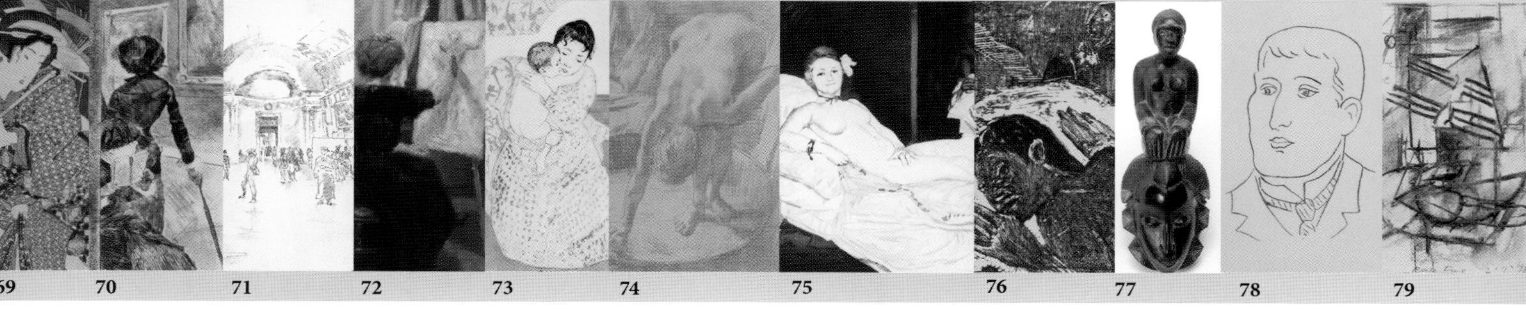

69 70 71 72 73 74 75 76 77 78 79

Both artists were initially influenced by writer and theorist Charles Baudelaire (#**68**: catalogue 84—1865), who postulated in his 1845 essay on the *heroism of modern life*: "We do not lack for subjects or colors with which to make epics. The painter, the true painter for whom we are searching, will be the one who can seize the epic quality of contemporary life and make us see and understand, with brush or with pencil, how great and poetic we are in our cravats and patent-leather boots....the true seekers may grant us the extraordinary joy of celebrating the advent of the *new*!" (Baudelaire 37).

66

67

Boudin's works directly relate to such ideas as he was one of the first French artists to paint *en plein air*, before an outdoor subject, at fashionable bourgeois resorts. He aimed to capture the climatic effects of the landscape, as well as the fashionable participants who inhabited it. Like Constable, Boudin focused on the transient qualities of the atmosphere, yet in a more secularized Impressionist manner. His works would inspire his most direct follower, Claude Monet, the leader of the French Impressionist movement, who described the influence of Boudin: "Suddenly a veil was torn away. I had understood—I had realized what painting could be. By the single example of this painter devoted to his art with such independence, my destiny as a painter opened out to me" (Seitz 13). By capturing instantaneous views, further informed through photography, portable tube oil paints and new scientific theories on light and color, such works epitomized the epic quality of modern life. Sketches and finished paintings now expressed the same sort of *unfinished* quality that invited the viewer's eye to complete the impression, ultimately leading to Paul Cézanne's description of Monet: "He is only an eye, but *my* God what an eye!" (Parsons and Gale 45). Monet himself admitted the difficulty of achieving his goals: "It is enough to drive one raving mad, to render the weather, the atmosphere, the ambience...the sun sets so fast that I can't follow it" (Monet 138). Boudin and Monet thus shared the naturalist passion of Constable, devoid of his spiritual associations.

Whistler, on the other hand, by 1878 had evolved away from such Realist concerns and increasingly withdrew from competing with technology. Instead, he advocated the theory of *Art for Art's Sake*, a more elitist philosophy that placed aesthetics above replication. Analogies were made between the parallel connections of music, poetry and art, as he stated: "As music is the poetry of sound; so is painting the poetry of sight, and the subject-matter has nothing to do with harmony of sound or of colour" (Whistler 127). In this manner, he reasserted his traditional position as an artistic genius who would *improve* the scenery: "Nature contains the elements, in colour and form, of all pictures,

as the keyboard contains the notes of all music. But the artist is born to pick, and choose, and group with science, these elements, that the result may be beautiful—as the musician gathers his notes; and forms his chords, until he brings forth from chaos glorious harmony. To say to the painter, that Nature is to be taken as she is, is to say to the player, that he may sit on the piano" (Whistler 142-43).

Given his *modern* sense of aesthetics, we can see Whistler's landscape, along the Thames River in London, softened and made more elegant through an atmospheric envelope. A critic at the time, in response to such effects, humorously suggested that perhaps there was no fog in London until Whistler created it. Whistler thus transformed the murky urban industrial landscape, as he described in his publication *The Gentle Art of Making Enemies*: "And when the evening mist clothes the riverside with poetry, as with a veil, and the poor buildings lose themselves in the dim sky, and the tall chimneys become campanile, and the warehouses are palaces in the night, and the whole city hangs in the heavens, and fairy-land is before us...Nature, who, for once, has sung in tune, sings her exquisite song to the artist alone, her son and her master—her son in that he loves her, her master in that he knows her....In all that is dainty and lovable he finds hints for his own combinations, and *thus* is Nature ever his resource and always at his service, and to him is naught refused" (Whistler 144-45).

Whistler and Boudin were thus two leaders of the nineteenth century who developed works of art that were highly original, yet at the same time reflected the theories of artists and writers of their age. As in the case of these works, at times their images bore striking similarities to one another, yet in theory, they were at opposite ends of the spectrum. Boudin represented the scientific and technological advancements of the day that enabled artists to better portray perceptual realities of nature on their canvases. Whistler, on the other hand, offered a more conceptual response which encouraged the development of twentieth-century abstraction. Both clearly were beacons for the modern era.

Along with reactions to technology and science, new viewpoints were inspired from interactions with other cultures. In particular, the reopening of trade with Japan, virtually isolated from the West for one hundred fifty years, introduced Oriental porcelains, and perhaps more importantly, Japanese woodblock prints to an appreciative western market. The influence that such bold, cropped and flattened images had on nineteenth-century approaches might be demonstrated by comparing a Japanese pillar print (#**69**: catalogue 97—ca. 1822) with Impressionist Edgar Degas' etching of *Mary Cassatt at the Louvre* (#**70**: catalogue 98—1879-80). Degas' work acknowledged not only the subject of women in museums, and the Louvre (#**71**: catalogue 115—1894) as Parisian art center, but their training and acceptance as artists (#**72**: catalogue 163—1890-1900). Such *Japonisme* (European adaptation of Japanese aesthetics) revolutionized modern art. Renaissance perspective was abandoned in favor of more abstracted artforms. Japanese *ukiyo-e* (images from the floating world) subjects also encouraged artists to pursue more common everyday scenes in a bolder manner, exemplified by Cassatt's straightforward approach to bonding in *Maternal Caress* (#**73**: catalogue 101—1891) and Degas' suggestion that the modern Venus, as a female nude, might be found in bourgeois households and houses of prostitution, as in *Le Bain* (#**74**: catalogue 106—1889). Édouard Manet furthered this implication in his infamous *Olympia* (#**75**: catalogue 83—1865).

92 93 94 95 96 97 98 99 100 101 102

Further multiculturalism—or orientalism—can be found in Post-Impressionist Paul Gauguin's intentionally primitive woodcut, *Spirit of the Dead Watching* (#**76**: catalogue 132—1894-95), inspired by his life in Tahiti and his response to native mythology. In like manner, African art (#**77**: catalogue 203 A & B—n.d.) and its *magical* brutality would stimulate twentieth-century leaders such as Pablo Picasso and Henri Matisse to pursue more conceptualized and abstract directions. Matisse explored the emotive, expressionist qualities of such images, and Picasso, the more formal and geometric patterns. Lyric poet Guillaume Apollinaire (#**78**: catalogue 156—1952), one of the great critics of the early twentieth century, encouraged interpretation of such sources: "Consequently the artistic 'handwriting' of all kinds of styles—those of the hieratic Egyptians, the refined Greeks and the voluptuous Cambodians, the works of the ancient Peruvians, the African statuettes proportioned according to the passions which have inspired them—can interest an artist and help him to develop his personality" (Apollinaire, *La Phalange*, 483-84).

Artists Picasso and Georges Braque advanced the style of Cubism, as beautifully depicted in Perle Fine's *Sketch for a Cubist Still Life* (#**79**: catalogue 158—1938). Apollinaire recognized that these innovators built upon Whistler's aesthetic model and were "moving toward an entirely new art which will stand, with respect to painting as envisaged heretofore, as music stands to literature. It will be pure painting, just as music is pure literature" (Apollinaire, *Art History*, 1036). Although still based in natural observation, the pieces of the still life are seemingly broken into parts and built along a mathematical grid. Color is secondary to form, the whole rejecting linear perspective, in favor of a sort of composite view consisting of the intersection of multiple viewpoints—presumably adding time, as a suggested fourth dimension, to the ensemble.

Although nearing abstraction, it was the German Expressionists who accomplished the momentous break with reality. Apocalyptic imagery often appeared in the works of *Blue Rider* painters, German Franz Marc (#**80**: catalogue 154—1914) and the *improvisations* of Russian Vasily Kandinsky (#**81**: catalogue 153—ca. 1909-1914) during the years preceding World War I. They responded to world events, not with the careful, mathematic precision of the Cubists, but instead with the expression of full emotive color and imagery, continuing the course of Whistler's philosophy. Kandinsky wrote in *Concerning the Spiritual in Art* (1911): "Color directly influences the soul. Color is the keyboard, the eyes are the hammers, the soul is the piano with many strings. The artist is the hand that plays, touching one key or another purposely, to cause vibrations in the soul" (Kandinsky 1028). Such interpretation led Kandinsky to ultimate abstraction based on pure color and line as perhaps taken to its ultimate conclusion in the work of Josef Albers (#**82**: catalogue 196—1962) and Sonia Delaunay (#**83**: catalogue 197—ca. 1970).

In contrast, events leading to America's involvement in World War II encouraged artists to reject such European modernism in favor of familiar scenes of American genre, as illustrated in Grant Wood's *Seed Time and Harvest* (#**84**: catalogue 182—1937), John Bloom's *Seining on the Mississippi* (#**85**: catalogue 184—1938) and Thomas Hart Benton's *Sunday Morning* (#**86**: catalogue 181—1939). These works continued the comfortable realism of nineteenth-

century depictions by artists such as Boudin. Wedged as they were between the Great Depression and the Second World War, they presented a sort of predictable pattern and perhaps even escapism during an age of profound uncertainty. These traditional images could just as well have been based on nineteenth-century imagery as twentieth and reflect a national preference for the observed fact, traceable back to such benchmarks as the *Declaration of Independence* (#**87**: catalogue 51—1786-94) and portrait of *George Washington* (#**88**: catalogue 53—1796). Benton, in contrast to African American artists such as Charles Alston (#**89**: catalogue 179—1934) and Romare Bearden (#**90**: catalogue 202—1972), illustrated a more traditional approach that ignored the inequalities illustrated by Alston as well as the roots of African heritage (#**91**: catalogue 203A & B—n.d.) embraced by Bearden.

Such interactions between conceptual and perceptual viewpoints, historical revivals and rejections as well as innovations and cultural influences might be noted throughout this book. One might discern renewed sources from the past, such as the beautiful patina of the ancient Roman glass bowl (#**92**: catalogue 5B—4th-ea. 5th century), an accident of nature's chemical process over time, scientifically replicated as an inkwell by decorative artist, Louis Comfort Tiffany (#**93**: catalogue 139—1899). Also intriguing is the balance of the written word with visual imagery, as in the medieval illuminated manuscript (#**94**: catalogue 12—1425-50) contrasted against Henri de Toulouse-Lautrec's modernist advertising poster for the Moulin Rouge (#**95**: catalogue 130—1896). At the same time, the bold, clean elements of the Renaissance woodcut from Hans Holbein's *Dance of Death* (#**96**: catalogue 20—1538) might be traced in the disillusioned 1940s German workers of Erich Heckel (#**97**: catalogue 152—1946). Or equestrians can morph from auspicious Chinese tomb effigies (#**98**: catalogue 8A & B—7th century) toward aggressive vehicles in the court of Qajar Iran (#**99**: catalogue 34A—ca. 1585) to American instruments for scientific discovery (#**100**: catalogue 117A—1887). And the elegant figurative patterns originally carved in ancient Roman cameo glass (25 BCE), lovingly reproduced in jasper ware in the Neoclassical period (#**101**: catalogue 59—1791), were masterfully simplified and reversed in tonality through Henri Matisse's deceptively simple *Blue Nude I-IV* (#**102**: catalogue 191A-D—1952).

Within modernity, twentieth-century landscapes can vacillate between the brilliant evocations of Sven Birgen Sandzén (#**103**: catalogue 169—1928), the ethereal visions of William Wendt (#**104**: catalogue 170—n.d.), the classical metaphysical discomfort of Georgio de Chirico (#**105**: catalogue 159 & 160—1921) and the abstracted signage of Robert Indiana (#**106**: catalogue 201—1969). We might even note the manner in which Edward S. Curtis in his quest to establish photographic records for what, at the time, many thought was a *vanishing breed*, depicted Native American Fannie Nampeyo with an anachronistic lens (#**107**: catalogue 171—1906) that belies the modernist originality of her traditionally based, yet abstracted, ceramics (#**108**: catalogue 172—1920-25). At the same time, Frederick Remington effectively immortalized the image of the American cowboy (#**109**: catalogue 176—n.d.). René Magritte additionally noted surreal anonymity in the *Son of Man* (#**110**: catalogue 162—1964), further abstracted by

a Russian artist (#**111**: catalogue 161—1922), and seemingly consumed by his *hat* in Henry Moore's unsettling *Helmet Head* (#**112**: catalogue 195—ca. 1963). Finally, one can only marvel at the visual concordance between Gavin Hamilton's elevated allegory of classical perfection in the *Allegorical Figure of Painting* (#**113**: catalogue 55—1768-85) as it translates into a mechanistic Art Deco-inspired woman, machine-like yet whimsical (#**114**: catalogue 157—1928) within a modern twentieth-century urban structure. What other comparisons, contrasts, distinctions and definitions might be observed? I invite you to examine the pieces in this book, digest the information written in the catalogue, investigate even further and draw your own conclusions.

As we confront our own diverse and changing world, we might observe twentieth-century newspaper and magazine illustrations, such as Norman Rockwell's idealized American family from the *Saturday Evening Post* (#**115**: catalogue 187C—1943), visually colliding with Abstract Expressionist canvases, constructed with dripping and flung paint (#**116**: catalogue 188—1980). In the wake of the explosion of the first atomic bomb, it appears that artists found reality too difficult to confront, thereby producing descriptions that were either too good or narrow to be true, or simply avoided recognizable imagery altogether. Henri Matisse took a magic carpet ride to the "Arabian Nights" (#**117**: catalogue 190—1950) as a form of escape from the times and his own physical agony while Marc Chagall created ethereal atmospheres, colored by memories of his Russian-Jewish heritage, further enhanced through hopeful imagination (#**118**: catalogue 193—1963). The traditional privileged position of humanity, so powerfully immortalized in the *Vitruvian Man*, was clearly challenged by the twentieth century.

In our own more recent times, we are perpetually bombarded with photographic, computer-generated and video/film media, which have become primary texts as well. At the same time, such multiplicity allows us easier access to artifacts from diverse cultures including Aborigine (#**119**: catalogue 207—1995), Inuit (#**120**: catalogue 206—1986), Haitian (#**121**: catalogue 204—1986) and Peruvian (#**122**: catalogue 205—2009). Yet in an age dominated by ***I's—I-Pads, I-Phones, I-Pods, I-Tunes*** and ***I-Ms***—with communications swiftly disseminated and just as quickly eliminated, what archaeological records will *I* or *you* truly leave for future generations to examine? Many, I hope. Your liberal arts education at Augustana aims to provide you with the tools you need to critically read the texts of others, as well as to thoughtfully construct your own. Enjoy this year—your historic first at Augustana!

Pottery through the AGES: Picasso and the Greek Kylix

Sample Comparative Essay

Yan Face Catalogue 194
Pablo Picasso (ca. 1963)

Attic Black-figure *Kylix* Catalogue 1
Artist unknown (ca. 520-500 BCE)

The field of art is constantly changing. New styles, ideas and techniques are always being conceptualized and utilized to give birth to innovations in the art world. Artists often look to the past to fuel their creativity and produce new creations based on old concepts. This idea is easily seen in the work of Pablo Picasso. His ceramic pitcher, *Yan Face*, looks as if he borrowed techniques from pottery artists of the early Greek period. By examining the Greek *Kylix* and Picasso's *Yan Face*, it is possible to draw parallels between the modern work of Picasso and the ancient works of the Greeks.

The design of the *Kylix* had the consumer of wine in mind. The outside of this particular *Kylix* has what appears to be a pair of eyes and a lion in the middle of them. As the user finished his drink, he would find a Gorgon's head at the bottom of his chalice. The Gorgons were said to be a group of sinister sisters who had snakes in place of hair and had the power to turn men to stone with their gaze.

Picasso used red clay full of earth tones and a black overtone very similar in composition to the ancient Greek *Kylix*. The red earthy body is complemented with a black face and bird's head that appear to be painted over the clay. Picasso adapted the design of the clay pitcher to advantage when he pinched the top for the bird's head. *Yan Face* is a classic example of borrowing from old art traditions and applying them to modern concepts. This work is simple, yet it shows the diversity and innovation of Picasso.

It may be said that both the artist of the *Kylix* and Picasso used the same medium to construct their creations. Both works have the similar composition of terracotta clay with black accents. Each has the potential to hold liquid. Another similarity between the works is the presence of faces and eyes on the body of both vessels, each of which appears to be looking at the patron as if he were engaging in some kind of contact. The media and composition resemble each other closely, but their uses are different. The *Kylix* had a known function but although the ancient Greek *Kylix* may have given birth to the idea and medium for Picasso's *Yan Face*, Picasso clearly did not intend for the valuable pitcher to be used in a practical manner, not to mention a wild drinking symposium.

[Mark Leveling, *Class of 2010*]

Motherhood through the AGES: Cassatt and Kollwitz

Sample Comparative Essay

The Manicure Catalogue 95
Mary Cassatt (ca. 1908)

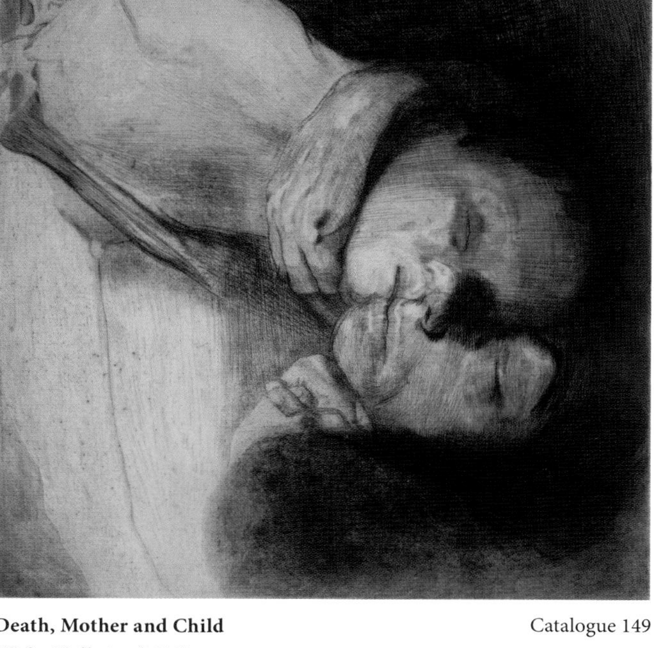

Death, Mother and Child Catalogue 149
Käthe Kollwitz (1910)

The Manicure by Mary Cassatt and *Death, Mother and Child* by Käthe Kollwitz share the common theme of the relationship between mother and child. However, they each provoke different emotions for their audience. Cassatt represented the maternal bond through an everyday domestic scene while Kollwitz portrayed it through the tragedy of death.

The Manicure is a touching Impressionist genre scene. The mother gently grooms the child as she softly touches her mother's hand. Such tenderness is suggested in the artwork that one can feel the true joy of what it is to be a mother. The soft delicate outlines capture an impression of an everyday moment in time, common in Impressionist subject matter.

Death, Mother and Child is an Expressionist portrait of a mother with her dead child. Kollwitz's use of iconography evokes an emotionally charged scene. A skeleton bone symbolizes death separating the mother and child. Light and dark effects suggest gloom while sketchy lines indicate "frantic emotion" (Goebel 216). The mother and child appear to clench hands together while another hand is held around the child's neck as if death is attempting to ultimately separate them.

Despite their feminine theme, most women artists at the beginning of the 20th century faced chauvinistic attitudes. Cassatt was determined to gain acceptance as a professional artist despite inherent challenges in a male-dominated art market. Kollwitz encountered chauvinism as well as Nazi propaganda that labeled her artwork as *degenerate*. Yet both women successfully persevered.

They clearly worked in distinct styles and found inspiration in different places. Japanese woodblock prints and middle class subjects influenced Cassatt as evidenced in her choice to depict a common genre scene. Kollwitz experienced harsh conditions among the poor who were treated by her husband, a physician. Cassatt depicted a perceptual view of blissful motherhood while Kollwitz envisioned a conceptual, macabre scene.

Models are another source of contrast. Kollwitz posed her own son here and the mother may thus be a self-portrait. The fact that he died young in World War I renders this a disturbing *premonition* (Prelinger 175). Having no children of her own, Cassatt often employed models, preferring those of lower-class since they were accustomed to handling their children.

Although both works share common themes, these women artists chose to express the maternal relationship in very different ways. Furthermore even though both pieces were constructed in the same medium, they are depicted in completely different manners. Overall, both artists represented their respective art movements effectively through their personal expressions of style in depicting the relationship between a mother and child.

[April Bernath, *Class of 2010*]

Enlightenment in Art: Raphael and Rembrandt

Sample Comparative Essay

School of Athens, Catalogue 17
After Raphael Sanzio (ca. 1509)

Christ Preaching Catalogue 26
Rembrandt van Rijn (ca. 1652)

Enlightenment is knowledge for which humans have always strived. Because this is a consistent theme in life, it has been depicted in many works of art. According to Plato, knowledge should be shared because"...the law does not exist for the exclusive benefit of one class in the city" (Plato 24). In the *School of Athens* and *Christ Preaching*, the spread of enlightenment is depicted in two different ways that are indicative of their respective periods in the history of art.

In the *School of Athens*, engraved by Joannes Volpato after the famous High Renaissance fresco by Raphael, Plato (left) and Aristotle (right) are deep in thoughtful conversation. These central figures are surrounded by other Classical greats, including Pythagoras, Euclid and Ptolemy. Not all figures can be identified, so perhaps these include future intellectuals who might be worthy to stand in their presence (Bell 638).

The second piece, *Christ Preaching*, was etched by Rembrandt Van Rijn during the Dutch Baroque era. Christ is depicted as enlightening those around him. His divinity is symbolized by his halo and *orant* position (hands raised in prayer). His followers vary in socioeconomic status, but he seems to concentrate on teaching the neediest. The composition is relatively simple with a humanistic perspective indicative of Christ's focus.

The medium of printmaking allowed these prints to reach a large audience through multiple copies. Despite this similarity, they differ in subject matter. *School of Athens* represents Renaissance idealism and Classical revival which stressed the intelligence of men and what we can learn from them. *Christ Preaching* differs from this perspective in that it focuses on a dramatic Baroque composition that reinforces that faith in God can teach those who listen.

A similarity between these works is discernible in the idea of enlightenment. In both, the artists wanted viewers to visualize people learning within each work while their example in turn teaches us how knowledge spreads through discourse. Art in itself is a form of dialogue between artist and audience. Rembrandt communicated the importance of religion while Raphael focused on intellect. The *iconography*, symbolism, in both is indicative of their respective stylistic periods. *Christ Preaching* is framed around Christ who represents the whole realm of Christianity. Created after the Reformation, Rembrandt downplayed Christ's divinity and instead stressed his humanity. In contrast, gifted philosophers encompass Raphael's iconography. They represent passion for attaining and sharing wisdom. The spread of enlightenment thus as a theme, although consistent throughout time, is clearly subjective to each artist's individual perspective framed within its historic context.

[Stephanie Loria, *Class of 2011*]

Transition in Art: From Impressionism to Post-Impressionism
Sample Comparative Essay

The Beach at Trouville Catalogue 86
Louis-Eugène Boudin (ca. 1864)

The Luxembourg Gardens Catalogue 90
Emma Ruff (n.d.)

The Impressionist Era was a period of beautiful artistry. French artists successfully portrayed reality and rejected traditional academic approaches. They created art from the life that surrounded them. One of the most beloved artists of this time was Louis-Eugène Boudin. His *Beach at Trouville* epitomizes Impressionism. His influence lived on into the Post-Impressionist era through Emma Ruff. Her work, *The Luxembourg Gardens* emphasizes Impressionist color but forged its own sense of Post-Impressionist style. She began an artistic renaissance where such naturalism was modified in favor of vibrant and exaggerated Post-Impressionism.

These late nineteenth-century French oil paintings share many similarities. The *bourgeoisie* (middle class) is vividly depicted in both with color and beauty radiating from the canvases. A sense of wealth pervades both works as they depict *le joie de vivre* (the good life). Both artists painted *en plein air* which aided in capturing the immediacy of the subject. One cannot ignore the two artists' connection to the famous Impressionist, Claude Monet, who links them together. While Boudin greatly impacted the work of Monet, Monet in turn influenced Ruff. Boudin instructed Monet on the proper method of creating seascapes. And like Monet, Ruff emphasized landscape instead of figures in her paintings.

The paintings also differ in many respects. On a technical and stylistic level, Ruff used tighter brushstrokes as in the rich details of the painstakingly detailed flowers. Boudin, by contrast, employed loose, short Impressionist brushstrokes for the people on the beach. Upon closer examination, these are actually simply blobs of paint that appear as people from far way. Ruff's use of tight brushstrokes reflects her academic roots. Boudin depicted Parisians at a beach resort as Ruff illustrated a day in a Parisian park while also incorporating symbolism. She included the *Fontaine de l'Observatoire* with its four bronze women bearing the weight of the world. Ruff probably centered this image to mirror the strength of women. Boudin, on the other hand, was simply creating a work of art at Trouville by the sea.

The movements of Impressionism and Post-Impressionism both contrasted and complemented each other. Post-Impressionism arose from the ashes of Impressionism. Ruff forged her own path through academic approach and the use of her imagination to portray the ideal Parisian atmosphere. Today we appreciate the mold that was broken by this Post-Impressionist mastermind. Ruff was not afraid to move art in a different direction and take what she learned from her Impressionist forefathers, such as Boudin, and climb her way to the top of the ambitious Post-Impressionist movement.

[Matthew Bowman, *Class of 2011*]

Tracing Feminine Roles through the AGES: Cassatt and the Rococo

Sample Comparative Essay

Maternal Caress Catalogue 101
Mary Cassatt (1890-91)

Hebe Catalogue 40
Artist unknown (mid 18th century)

Artwork through the ages varies significantly due to the struggles and occurrences during each artist's lifetime. These result in individual characteristics during various eras. A comparison of *Maternal Caress* and *Hebe* illustrates how works from different historic periods are impacted by a combination of artistic viewpoints framed within historic contexts. With their focus on women, they are similar but also differ due to the eras in which they were created.

The Rococo period focused on soft, feminine imagery in keeping with aristocratic taste of the time. Women were in positions of influence and held salons to reinforce artistic patronage. Portraits were common, but women were flattered as patrons to the point of becoming mythical goddesses. *Hebe* elevates this unknown sitter, depicted as the goddess of eternal youth, in a dreamy atmosphere.

A century later, Impressionists created perceptual images focused on middle class subjects. Photography informed their quest for instantaneous views of the world around them. Mary Cassatt aimed to move beyond the traditional role of women as subjects to also include women as artists, on an even professional footing with their male counterparts. Impressionists pushed academic standards toward new modern perspectives. *Japonisme*, Japanese influence inspired by the reopening Japan to the West, informed her innovations.

In comparing these works, several differences emerge. *Maternal Caress* is a perceptual, everyday scene stylistically impacted by Japanese *ukiyo-e* prints. In response to such works, Cassatt's colors are bold and her perspective edges away from traditional Renaissance linear perspective to a flatter, more abstract approach. *Hebe*, in contrast, is more conceptual. Although based in a portrait of a real woman, she is dressed in expensive clothing and portrayed as a mythical goddess, pouring the *waters of life*. Cassatt's mother and child, in contrast, appear to live ordinary lives. These works also differ in detail and color. The Rococo piece exhibits soft tonal subtleties toward capturing three-dimensional illusionism while the Impressionist work utilizes simple bold patterns and colors bordering on abstraction.

Although vastly different, these works do have similarities. Both portray soft, graceful women in roles with years of artistic tradition behind them: females as goddesses and mothers. *Hebe* seems to make direct eye contact with the viewer while Cassatt's honest depiction of maternal *bonding* appears as a candid, timeless image. Since Cassatt never had children of her own, perhaps she longed for this traditional role while breaking the boundaries professionally for her gender. Both images beautifully combine the goals of their respective eras as well as those of each individual artist.

[Eric Safranski, *Class of 2012*]

Women in Art throughout Time

Sample Comparative Essay

Minerva Catalogue 58
Ernesto Gazzeri (n.d.)

Femme à la cruche Catalogue 157
Fernand Léger (1928)

Art history provides a means toward understanding the past since before written language, visual art recorded history and described daily life, affording a glimpse into earlier times. One of the most recurrent artistic subjects is the female figure. From earliest times, women have symbolized such ideals as beauty, fertility, compassion and power. During the Classical era, artists sought perfection by sculpting goddesses and the female figure still persists as a viable subject in contemporary art.

Classical nudes were typically goddesses in contemplation, causing viewers to respond intellectually, as with the Neoclassical figure of *Minerva*, the Roman goddess of war. Her idealized nudity demonstrates the artist's renewed pursuit of Classical beauty. Her *contrapposto* (weight-shift stance), *wet* drapery and thoughtful pose reinforce such Classicism. The helmet symbolizes her power in war while the tiara acknowledges her divinity.

Modern art encouraged further exploration of form. Following the invention of photography, artists no longer felt compelled to be representational. Cubism added the concept of time, a fourth dimension, to artistic perspectives. The viewer could now simultaneously perceive multiple viewpoints, shattering tradition while allowing for a more composite whole.

Femme à la cruche represents a somewhat cubistic simplification of a woman, depicted through various combined viewpoints. Parts of the figure are flat while others appear round. Her eyes do not connect with the viewer, making her appear dehumanized. Her geometry and primary colors render her appearance more in synch with the industrial age. She offers a window to the future while reflecting current changes surrounding her.

The marble versus colored print media for these works contrast dramatically. *Minerva* is a goddess and Leger's woman seems average, demonstrating a difference between artistic concepts of idealism and the mundane. Gazzeri pays homage to the Classical past while Leger comments on contemporary society. His figure appears expressionless, seemingly gazing into a time to come. She is not about repeating the past but instead offers a glimpse into the future.

It is important to notice similarities in these works. Both focus on a woman who portrays a sense of female empowerment. Minerva reveals idealized beauty while *Femme à la cruche* depicts an entirely different but no less powerful position. Dressed perhaps in a contemporary business suit, she holds a pitcher that seems like a complex piece of machinery. This view of a woman embracing the mechanized and ordered future demonstrates a certain control over her world akin to the helmet beneath *Minerva's* foot following victory. Both represent their respective periods while acknowledging the inherent vital role of women throughout time.

[Melanie Battistoni, *Class of 2012*]

Degas and Lichtenstein: Comparing Modern Women

Sample Comparative Essay

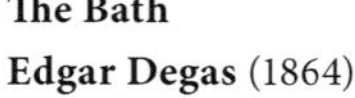

The Bath Catalogue 106
Edgar Degas (1864)

Crak!, Catalogue 200
Roy Lichtenstein (1964)

Across oceans and decades, views of women have changed significantly. In nineteenth-century France, women who bore all for art were considered scandalous, whereas in the United States in the 1960s, French women were portrayed as strong and revolutionary. In order to achieve a better understanding of the evolving portrayal of women through art, a comparison of *The Bath* and *CRAK!* is instructive.

These lithographs, separated by nearly a century, both focus on women. Degas used brown ink, likely inspired by Japanese woodblock prints and photographic sequencing popular in his time. Lichtenstein employed the red, yellow, black and white of his comic book sources. Degas sketched in geometric patterns echoing the circular tub and the round contours of the woman's body. Lichtenstein, on the other hand, used *benday* dots mimicking commercial printing. In his style, "voluptuously contoured anatomy" is "quickly and brutally ironed out by the two-dimensional conventions" (Rosenblum 193). This is not true in Degas's work. His style softens and actually enhances the female form, as "the foreshortened forearm, the flattened curve of the upper back, the rhythmic line of breast and stomach" make the woman appear more realistic (Rich 105).

Stark differences continue in the emotion and purpose behind each piece. *CRAK!* portrays immediate passion—a woman aggressively firing a gun. *The Bath*, on the other hand, conveys a woman bathing, through a soft technique that reinforces a calm, candid mood. While each artist aimed to portray a new modern woman, her definition clearly changed over time. Degas' new woman was middle class and perhaps even read by some contemporaries as a prostitute, since this was the type of woman who willingly disrobed and bathed often in an attempt to ward off disease. Degas' nudes were often negatively reviewed because they were controversial—people were uneasy viewing a naked women, rather than Classical goddesses. Yet he successfully defined an appropriate modern woman. Lichtenstein, on the other hand, illustrated an independent zealot standing up for her country as "the dominant female stereotype of the postwar era, the complement to the macho war heroes he was portraying in his paintings" (Waldman 117). Lichtenstein's French figure conveys dramatic beauty while wielding a dangerous weapon—a revolutionary new image for women. This approach was generally well-received because a woman taking action in the 1960s was a newly acceptable feat. Pop art, however, was perhaps a bit more difficult to accept. Both pieces were worlds apart, yet they achieved a shared goal of portraying women in a new and challenging light appropriate for their times.

[Emily Timmons, *Class of 2013*]

Imaging Women: A Comparison in Bronze

Sample Comparative Essay

Crouching Girl Catalogue 147A
Aristide Joseph Bonaventure Maillol (ca. 1900)

Playdays Catalogue 148
Harriet W. Frishmuth (ca. 1938)

The image of a nude woman may be portrayed in several ways, even within the same time period. By comparing the bronze sculptures *Crouching Girl* by Aristide Maillol and *Playdays* by Harriet W. Frishmuth, the different portrayals are clearly seen. The sculptures are of the same medium and purpose and yet their meanings are opposite; Maillol's symbolizing vulnerability and melancholy versus Frishmuth's symbolizing innocence and free-spirit.

Frishmuth's sculpture, *Playdays*, is lively and displays what could be considered a pivotal moment in a young girl's life. She is becoming a woman and taking a step into the unknown. As she tickles the frog with her toe, the gradual transition from childhood to womanhood is metaphorically represented. She is nude, yet not meant to portray sensuality, but instead the idealism of a young girl. She is beautiful with a graceful body of pure innocence. The viewer feels the burst of life and joy from this energetic sculpture. The verde patina adds character and motion to her slender body. Harriet W. Frishmuth became a sculptor during a critical time period for women's equality in America. Women were fighting for their right to vote along with the right to produce respectable art (Rubinstein 209). Frishmuth tried to make her statues more conservative and innocent, but one could still see signs of this new sense of the woman's body. Like other women artists, she sculpted slender figures, several of them dancing and overall signifying that the times had changed (Rubinstein 146).

On the other side of the art spectrum, is Maillol's *Crouching Girl.* She is nude as well, but is shown in a provocative manner with sensuality and eroticism in mind. This French sculpture is of a woman, possibly middle aged, yet still possessing beauty. She, unlike *Playdays*, however, is not playful or innocent. The sculpture appears more serious, voluptuous, and revealing. She seems as if she may be reflecting on her past and yet thinking ahead to the future. This leaves the viewer wanting a glimpse into her thoughts and dreams.

Maillol's sculptures cannot be considered to be a part of a specific era or style like Frishmuth's sculptures (George 47). "Maillol is well-versed in the science of structural form, sacrificed anatomy to rhythm" (Chevalier 12). The art of sculpting became his primary focus for medium and as he developed his own style of art, his goal became to produce art that would stand for "European morality, its system of values and its idea of mankind" (George 113). "He endows his wise virgins with medieval masks, but links them with torso and pelvis modeled with delicate idealism which unveils the throbbing life and reveals his own sense of perfection" (George 47).

In taking a quick glance at these two sculptures, they appear to be quite similar because of their bronze facade and since they were created around the same time period in the early twentieth century. They were also both meant to be outdoor décor in a garden or plaza. Despite the many similarities, if analyzed by an artistic eye, they are discovered to be considerably different and are appreciated for their own unique presence.

[Alyssa Anderson, *Class of 2013*]

Glass through the AGES: From Ancient Rome to Tiffany

Sample Comparative Essay

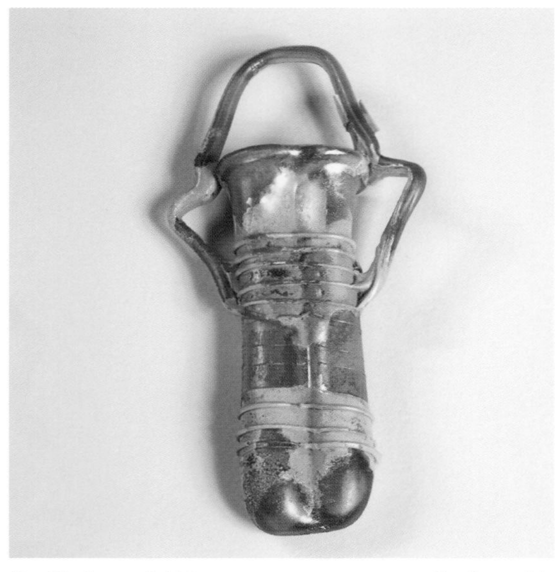

Double Cosmetic Tube  Catalogue 5A
Roman workshop (4th century CE)

Favrile Inkwell Catalogue 139
Louis Comfort Tiffany (1901)

The importance of glass can be taken for granted, especially when it comes to art. There are two beautiful examples of glass in the Augustana College Art Collection: a double cosmetic tube of free-blown glass made in a fourth-century Roman workshop and an inkstand made by Louis Comfort Tiffany in 1899. By comparing and contrasting these works, glass-making techniques and uses over time can be understood.

The glass for the double cosmetic tube was originally greenish yellow. It changed color due to climatic conditions that caused its chemical composition to break down. This transformation adds to the rich history related to glass surviving from ancient Rome. The process was not much different than today's. The glass blowing technique involved a globule of molten glass attached to a tube, inflated and shaped with the help of gravity and other techniques. The handles were likely drawn out thin and folded back and forth at the point of attachment (Stern).

Roman glass had many uses and was not highly valued in comparison to precious metals such as gold and silver. Yet the industry was important because it provided glass, much as it does today, to everyday Romans who could not afford precious metal. This object is part of a kit that would have held components for eyeliner similar to modern cosmetics. The applicator is missing for this piece.

The inkwell reflects Tiffany's goal to combine the vibrant colors of ancient and medieval glass with texture that suggests draperies in glass. This new glass, known as *favrile*, meaning handmade, was composed of various colors fused together during the molten state. Tiffany achieved the technology to create iridescence through careful study of the natural decay of glass (Feld 105).

The techniques Tiffany used will probably never be fully understood as he did not openly share them. The basic process included adding small quantities of glass in different colors and textures to an incandescent ball of glass as it came out of the furnace. The ball was then returned to the fire to be heated. This process could have been repeated up to twenty times in order to get the desired color and texture for the glass (Feld 105).

Favrile glass ultimately became a status symbol. Tiffany aimed to produce luxurious everyday objects that have escalated in value. The gold iridescent color of the inkwell links Tiffany's glass back to the common glass, transformed through time, of ancient Rome. Tiffany's color and opalescent quality reflect sophisticated craftsmanship that is difficult to replicate.

Glass is an important part of art history that can easily be overlooked. Roman glass, however, demonstrates how the technology of glassmaking began and transformed over time. The inkstand evidences how Tiffany strove to replicate such historic effects. Glass thus represents a key aspect of history and is a fascinating medium toward historical analysis.

[Jessica Lemek, *Class of 2014*]

Appreciating Nature Across Time and Culture: the Peacock and the Whippoorwill

Sample Comparative Essay

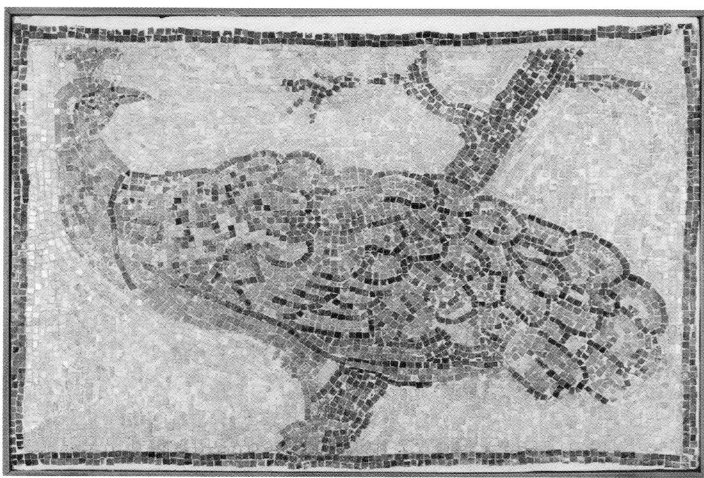

Pavo (peacock) Catalogue 3
Artist unknown (300–400 CE)

Whippoorwill Catalogue 71
John James Audubon (1830)

Presented here are two contrasting pieces from the Augustana Art Collection: a hand-colored engraving of John James Audubon's *Whippoorwill* and a mosaic entitled *Pavo* from Ancient Rome. *Whippoorwill* is from a collection of prints entitled *Birds of America*, which was completed in 1838 and contains life-size renderings of 489 American birds (Vedder 5). Alhough the identity of the artist who created *Pavo* has been lost to time, it is estimated that the mosaic was made around 300-400 CE in Ancient Rome (Banks 32). These works have contrasting media and purposes, but both relate a common love for birds.

The two artists used varying methods in the creation of their works. Like many mosaics from ancient Rome, *Pavo* was constructed with small cubes of stone, called *tesserae*, set in mortar and decorated at times with other materials such as glass, gold, precious stones, pumice and shells. Audubon, on the other hand, created *Birds of America* by first making watercolors of each bird, which were then reproduced in large quantities as prints (Vedder 22). These prints were made by first constructing an engraving plate and printing the image onto paper, and then applying hand-coloring to each copy (Vedder 32). While both works of art have similar subject matter, their methods for depicting the birds are very different.

Pavo and *Whippoorwill* were also created for different purposes. The original use for *Pavo* is not certain, but it was most likely made as a decoration for either a wealthy home or religious temple (Banks 32). In ancient Rome, the peacock was seen as a sign of extravagance and served as a symbol in both pagan and Christian religions. Peacocks were a pagan symbol for the goddess Juno, while also an early Christian symbol for eternal life (Banks 32). John James Audubon's intentions in creating *Birds of America* and *Whippoorwill* were much more scientific. In each watercolor, Audubon depicted birds in their natural habitat eating their common prey, and even included a scientific description for each bird (Vedder 22, 35). The two works of art were therefore not created for the same reason.

Nevertheless, the varying media and intentions of the works do not hide the fact that both artists' creations were fueled by their appreciation of nature. John James Audubon, while an artist, was also both a woodsman and a hunter (Vedder 5). He once expressed his love for birds, stating "I have lost nothing in exchanging the pleasure of studying men for that of admiring the feathered race" (Vedder 5). The inhabitants of ancient Rome had a deep appreciation for birds as well (Rome, Ancient). The pagan belief system taught that gods resided in all living things and that inexplicable events in nature, such as the flight of birds, were direct actions of the gods (Rome, Ancient). These two works—*Whippoorwill* and *Pavo*—both share a clear love for birds that crosses the boundaries of time, culture and geography.

[Chase Matzinger, *Class of 2014*]

Catalogue 67, detail

"In such an age as this, painting should be understood, not looked on with blind wonder, nor considered only as a poetic aspiration, but as a pursuit, legitimate, scientific, and mechanical."

John Constable *(1776–1863)*

Catalogue

1

Attic Black-figure *Kylix*, ca. 520–500 BCE
Class of the Top-Band Stemlesses (Greek) [D. Caccioli]
Ceramic, 7.8 x 23.8 x 17.3 cm., 3-1/8 x 9-3/8 x 6-7/8"
Paul A. Anderson Chair in the Arts Collection Purchase, Augustana College Art Collection, 2000.54

The *kylix* was a popular drinking cup in ancient Greece. Such vessels were often used at all-male drinking parties called *symposia*. These recreational activities were restricted to wealthy aristocrats who indulged in the pleasures life could offer (and their class could afford)—particularly related to wine, sex and music.

This particular kylix was created in the black-figure style, which entailed painting figures in black slip over the natural terracotta-colored clay. Details were added either by incising lines into the black slip to reveal the body color beneath or by painting red or white decorations over the black pattern (Boardman 9). The exterior of this kylix is separated into black and red bands. The top one depicts a centered lion framed by two eyes between the handles on both sides, further enclosed by two *palmettes* (stylized leaf patterns) placed next to the handles. The interior is painted entirely black except for the circular mask of a *gorgon* (called a *gorgoneion*), which stands out in red relief. The gorgons were three hideously ugly mythological sisters who were said to have had snakes for hair. According to the legends, they turned men who looked at them to stone. The humor of this piece is seen both in the *gorgoneion* inside the cup and the face that is formed by flipping the cup upside down. Though originally serving a protective function, the purpose of gorgons over time became diluted to one of general amusement. After draining one's cup, the patron would be confronted with the comical face of a staring gorgon. Such imagination combined with skillful technique reflects the extraordinary creativity of the ancient Greeks.

[Errin Copple, *Class of 2005*]

Red-figure Dish with Running Female Figure with Wreath and Ivy-garnished *Phiale*, ca. 340–330 BCE
Middle Apulian "Milan Orpheus Group" (South Italian) [D. Caccioli]
Ceramic, 5.8 x 24.9 x 24.9 cm., 2-3/8 x 9-7/8 x 9-7/8"
Paul A. Anderson Chair in the Arts Collection Purchase, Augustana College Art Collection, 2000.55

In its revelation, this pot seems to anticipate a poetic form soon to be created by Theocritus (about 300–260 BCE), the *eidyllon*: an idyll or snapshot-like image of a unique personality caught unawares while engaged in an archetypal event of life. Theocritus' verbal portraits deliberately evoke and riddle more than they explain, suggesting the unique within the archetypal. The artifact as a whole is of red-figured pottery. That ceramic technique, whereby major shapes were left undecorated to acquire the distinctive red color of the unpainted, fired clay against a painted black background, flourished in Greece and Greek colonies from around 530 to 300 BCE (Caccioli 18). The date of this particular pot is placed more precisely to 340–330 BCE (Caccioli 18).

The shape of this pot is that of a *phiale*, a shallow, dish-like, handleless cup. Its function par excellence was for libation: that is, the pouring of liquid offerings to divinities and the spirits of the dead. On the rim of the interior is painted a wreath of laurel. As laurels were conventionally an award for victory, that plant would be suggestive of use at a festivity involving contests of some sort, though not definitively so. In the tondo—the inner circle, double-banded—is centered the figure of a young woman in haste. The figure grasps in the left hand, extended ahead for balance, a decorated garland. Jane Borelli identifies this as a myrtle garland (Borelli 18), a plant associated with Aphrodite. This would put in place a second suggestion (after her phiale itself) of a festive or ritual occasion. One could assume this is a bride, hastening in preparation for the wedding that would not take place in life, hastening poignantly to a premature death and a symbolic wedding to the god of the underworld (Caccioli 18).

[Thomas R. Banks, *Professor Emeritus of Classics*
Dorothy J. Parkander Professor Emeritus in Literature]

3

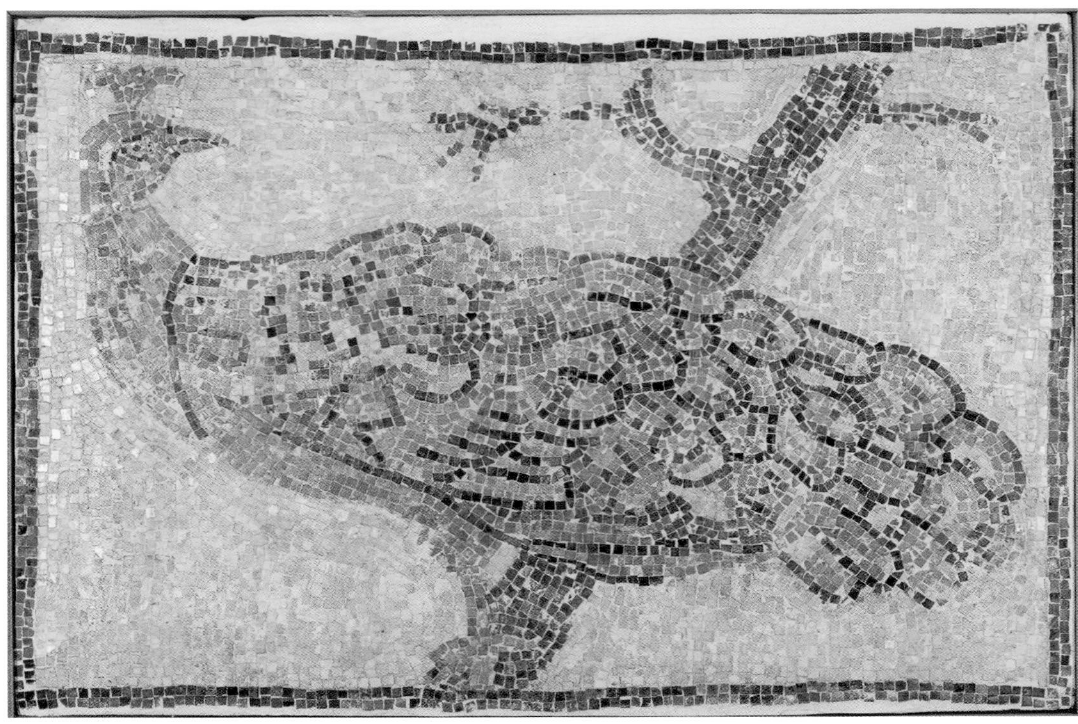

***Pavo* (peacock),** 300–400 CE
Artist unknown (Roman)
Mosaic of lifted ancient tesserae fragments, restored with ancient tesserae, mounted in plaster, 47.5 x 69.7 cm., 18-1/2 x 27-1/2"
Paul A. Anderson Chair in the Arts Collection Purchase, Augustana College Art Collection, SDC 2003.12

This peacock, shown in mosaic, looks over his shoulder and proclaims the importance of provenance in looking at ancient art: Where did I come from? When exactly was I made? Alas, like so much of the portable ancient art we value, he surfaced in unknown ways. The Paraskevaides Museum believes the mosaic can be traced back only as far as an old English collection—i.e., it was not stolen, by current understandings—while it began life in the Roman world between 300 and 400 CE. Thus, in our ignorance, we can see three contexts for it, three possible meanings for *Pavo*.

One context to fit into such a broad span in time and area would be religious—the pagan beliefs and rites associated with the goddess *Juno*. The peacock was Juno's bird. For pagans the peacock was associated with reverance for the immortal goddess. Thus the emperor Hadrian dedicated a golden, bejeweled peacock at the temple of Juno near Mycenae (Pausanias 17.6).

A later religious context, the Christian, took up the peacock as a symbol of immortality itself, one to be known in the resurrection of the flesh. St. Augustine (ca. 350-430 CE —perhaps, that is, a contemporary of *Pavo*) asks us, "Who but God, the creator of all things, granted to the flesh of the dead peacock not to putrify?" (Augustine xxi.iv). Hence we may note the appearance in later Christian art of the peacock presaging the Resurrection of Christ (Ferguson 95).

A third possibility would be secular, perhaps from the decor of an opulent private home. For this bird could also be a symbol of luxury, as we read in the *Satyricon* of Petronius. There, the *nouveau riche* Trimalchio tries to impress his guests with an *hors d'oeuvres* tray shaped like a bird warming a clutch of eggs—peacock's eggs for them to eat (Petronius xxxiii). Pliny the Elder credits the orator Hortensius with first serving the peacock as food, in the first century BCE. That occasion was a banquet celebrating Hortensius' inauguration into the college of the priesthood (Pliny the Elder 10.23).

Not knowing which if any of these provenances to choose, we are constrained to a bare museum description for facts alone. Nevertheless, those bare facts, and the fact of the artistry, still permit us to enjoy *Pavo's* handsome reappearance into the light in our century, immortal indeed.

[Thomas R. Banks, *Professor Emeritus of Classics*
Dorothy J. Parkander Professor Emeritus in Literature]

4

Four Doves on a Bowl, 300–400 CE
Artist unknown, after Sosus of Pergamum (Greek second century BCE)
Mosaic of lifted ancient tesserae fragments, restored with ancient tesserae, mounted in plaster, 46.8 x 45.4 cm., 18-1/2 x 17-7/8"
Paul A. Anderson Chair in the Arts Collection Purchase, Augustana College Art Collection, SDC 2003.13

Not every proud household in the Roman world could afford original masterpieces. So-called "imitations" or "copies" or—less prejudicially—echoes of famous classics reverberated across time and territory into the provinces. There, despite remoteness and limited finances, locally prominent hosts still wanted to display their taste. The echoes did that for them.

The dove mosaic before us is such an echo. The provenance of these doves on the large bowl is, like that of the peacock *Pavo* on the adjoining page, a mystery. The date would be around the fourth century CE, the place unknown (Paraskevaides Museum). But the classical model being emulated is clear enough. In this case, the classic (which caused more than one echo) was created in the second century BCE—some 500 years before ours. The original is famously recorded by Pliny the Elder in his *Natural History* (36.62). The artist was one Sosus of Pergamum, Pliny says, and Sosus, renowned for the verisimilitude of his images, created a mosaic where one dove drank from a party goblet (*cantharus*), its shadow darkening the water, while other doves sunned themselves and preened on the lip of the bowl. The mosaic was still famous in Pliny's time (died 79 CE), some two hundred years later.

The best-known echo of Sosus' work was stunningly loud. A masterpiece itself, it emanated from the palatial villa of the emperor Hadrian (emperor 117-138 CE). In the eighteenth century, treasure hunters exploring the villa found a Roman "copy" of Sosus' original. (See the Capitoline Museums in Rome.) One might note that this bowl is not exactly Pliny's *cantharus*. *Canthari* had upright, fixed, handle loops. Instead this shows a small basin with hinged handle loops. Nor are its attached tripod stubs the typical *cantharus* stem (Cf. illustrations in Thayer).

Our echo has drooping handle loops similar to that of Hadrian's. Its foot, however, is more like that of Pliny's *cantharus*, having a goblet-like stem. The shape of the whole is also different. The doves from Hadrian's villa are set in a rectangle. Ours are in a circle. That would make it plausible that the original placement of ours was a typical *emblema* or centerpiece to a mosaic floor.

That's the classical model and two variations. But what of the meaning? Were doves just doves? Probably not. Doves in antiquity often had associations with goddesses in their romantic aspect: Aphrodite in the Greek world; in Asia Minor (as around the Pergamum of mosaicist Sosus, where the procession began) doves came with Astarte, Semiramis, and the Magna Mater. As for the *cantharus*, the god Dionysus is often depicted waving one in a spirit of amiable intoxication—though one filled with wine, not water as with the doves (Mikalson). Despite the fourth century dating, the connotations of the image seem more loyal to its pagan origin than evocative of the later, single dove of the Holy Spirit of Christians (Matt. 3:16-17).

In sum, we may well see in this mosaic a focus for a hospitable dining room. The focus suggests an ambiance of educated taste and an appreciation of nature, of tender human emotions, and of the gentler blessings of Dionysus.

[Thomas R. Banks, *Professor Emeritus of Classics*
Dorothy J. Parkander Professor Emeritus in Literature]

5A&B

5A

Double Cosmetic Tube, 4th century CE
Roman workshop (Eastern Mediterranean) [D. Caccioli]
Free-blown glass, 13.6 x 6.7 x 3.3 cm., 5-3/8 x 2-11/16 x 1-5/16"
Gift of Estate of Paul A. Anderson, Augustana College Art Collection, 2001.9

5B

Bowl, 4th–early 5th century CE
Roman workshop (West Roman) [D. Caccioli]
Free-blown glass, 6.5 x 7.2 x 7.2 cm., 2-1/2 x 2-7/8 x 2-7/8"
Gift of Estate of Paul A. Anderson, Augustana College Art Collection, 2001.8

The two pieces of Roman glass in our collection wonderfully reflect the story of glass itself, and also reveal some of the many links between antiquity and our present day. Indeed, the first of these (item A), stunningly links ancient Egypt with the cosmetics counter at your local department store. What you are viewing is an ancient eyeliner kit. The basic design of the kit, double tubes to hold the components of the eyeliner and an applicator (missing in our piece), seems to have developed in Egypt during the period of the New Kingdom (ca. 1587–1085 BCE) (Dayagi-Mendels 40-44). Remarkably, the design remained essentially the same into the later Roman Empire (200–400 CE), the period in which blown glass versions of the kit appear to have become popular—a span of almost 2000 years (Caccioli 20). Kits of this sort would have been used to make the highly exaggerated eyes typical of Egyptian portraiture. Surviving applicators are similar to those in modern eyeliner kits: one end was broad and flat, the other pointed (Dayagi-Mendels 36).

The other example of Roman glass in the Paul A. Anderson Collection (item B) carries us across the Mediterranean and into the northernmost reaches of the western Roman Empire where important centers of glass production had grown up around the Roman legionary bases along the Rhine river (Isings 4-13). This diminutive blown glass bowl (Caccioli, notes 4 and 5) would be at home in any kitchen or on any table, ancient or modern. Bowls of this sort were manufactured primarily in cities along the Rhine during the later Roman Empire (from the late 3rd through the 5th century CE), a time when Rome was frequently challenged by incursions of Germanic tribes (Isings 113-114).

Ironically, the remarkable colors that make these pieces so distinctive are accidents of time; both of our pieces were originally a uniform yellowish-green color. The present appearance of the pieces is the result of weathering over the last 1500 years. When glass is exposed alternately to wet and dry conditions over such a span of time, the surface of the glass begins to break down chemically. This process ultimately produced the varied hues of bright green, gold, and blue evident on the eyeliner kit, and the shimmering iridescent patina of the bowl. These transformations serve as a reminder that artifacts of antiquity—material and also literary—sometime acquire meaning and significance never envisioned by their creators.

[Emil A. Kramer, *Associate Professor of Classics*]

Diana of Gabii, after 4th century BCE original, ca. 1850
After Praxiteles (Greek)
Carved marble, 149.8 x 45.8 x 48.3 cm., 59-1/8 x 17-15/16 x 19-1/16"
Gift of Dr. Thomas William and Mrs. Barbara Lee Carter, Augustana College Art Collection, 1998.16

The piece shown here is a reproduction of a Roman copy of a marble statue of *Diana* (Artemis) by the Greek sculptor Praxiteles. Praxiteles was active between 375-340 BCE. Thus, he worked during the Late Classical period, about one hundred years after the great classical sculptors Pheidias and Polykleitos. The Late Classical period witnessed a number of innovations in sculpture, including the following: an increased use of marble (as opposed to bronze); "emotional expressiveness" and "dramatic poses;" a greater range of types and textures of clothing; and, the appearance of the female nude (Grossman 64; Boardman 289; Dillon 48). Praxiteles himself contributed to many of these developments. For example, Praxiteles often worked in marble, though he also produced some bronze sculptures; and, his *Aphrodite of Cnidus*, which Pliny the Elder claimed to be the best sculpture ever produced, was apparently the first large-scale female nude (Grossman 84). It is possible that Praxiteles' original sculpture of *Diana* (Artemis) was painted—many Egyptian, Greek, and Roman sculptures were painted, and Pliny reports that Praxiteles said that his favorite sculptures were those that had been painted by Nicias, which indicates that at least some of Praxiteles' own sculptures were painted (Pliny *Natural History* 35.133).

Many scholars believe that none of Praxiteles' original sculptures have survived, and his work is primarily known to us through Roman copies and literary descriptions. It is important to note that ancient copies were often imperfect, even when created in the same medium as the originals on which they were modeled (Boardman 282-83; Grossman 36). Even so, the Roman copy of Praxiteles' *Diana* (Artemis) is an extraordinary piece, and it is clearly the work of a master sculptor.

Some words about the piece are in order. The subject of the statue is Artemis, whom the Romans identified with Diana. Many scholars believe that at least some of the most important gods and goddesses worshipped by the ancient Greeks were borrowed from the ancient Near East; and, some scholars believe that reference to Artemis in Greece can be found in Linear B writing dating to 1400-1200 BCE (Parker 250-52). Artemis was certainly an ancient deity, and she was also a very important one. In fact, the ancient Greeks regarded her as one of the twelve most important divinities, a group that also included Zeus, Athena, and Apollo, who was Artemis' twin brother (Parker 248; Price 11-12). Artemis was variously associated with the wilderness, hunting, childbirth, etc. Her cult was extremely important in ancient Greece, and references to her can be found in works ranging from Homer's *Iliad* to the New Testament (Acts of the Apostles 19:28). Many scholars believe that the ancient Romans worshipped the goddess Diana since at least the sixth century BCE (Green xvii). Eventually, the Romans identified Artemis with Diana. Like Artemis, Diana was variously worshipped as a goddess of the wilderness, hunting, and childbirth (Green 112ff; Rives 84).

Many Greek and Roman statues of Artemis/Diana show her reaching over one shoulder to retrieve an arrow from a quiver. Here, the goddess is shown reaching toward one shoulder in order to fasten her *diplax* (a kind of cloak) (Grossman 40). This is unusual; ancient statues of gods and goddesses do not typically show them in the act of dressing. Has Artemis given up the hunt, or is something else afoot?

[Leslie F. Wolf, *Fellow of Philosophy*]

7

Maya Polychrome Tetrapod High-shouldered Plate with Agouti Feet, Late Classic period, 600-900 CE
Artist unknown (Maya) [Elizabeth D. Olton]
Ceramic, 10.2 x 28.3 x 28.4 cm., 4 x 11-1/8 x 11-3/16"
Gift of Dr. E. Richard Parker, Augustana College Art Collection, 2005.30.1

The subject of this brief essay, a Maya polychrome tetrapod plate, is an object that comes to Augustana, like many ancient works, lacking some basic information. By looking at this plate's formal qualities and comparing it to similar painted vessels, it can be dated to the Late Classic period of the Maya civilization 600-900 CE. Its visual features suggest the piece was likely made in an area that today is defined by eastern Guatemala and Belize.

Although the plate does not have hieroglyphic writing, imagery from the interior of the plate depicts symbols that we understand today. Two circular bands and a large round frame organize the interior space. Within the outermost band are four red "water stacks" and four groups of five red vertical lines. Most likely these lines represent the number five, while the stacked motifs can be read as signs for "surface of the water." Groups of circles decorate the second interior band, the most significant being the four *quincunx* designs. Each sign is arranged like a square and is composed of four circles at the corners, with one in the middle. A quincunx with its four cardinal directions and center symbolized the universe. A seated figure in profile view occupies the central frame. His skull-like face and discolored left arm might refer to death; his unnaturally thin body and padded costume, in turn, might allude to a mummy bundle. Supporting the plate are four legs modeled to look like the head and snout of an *agouti*, which is a large rodent that still lives in Central America in burrows under the earth's surface.

The plate's iconography and context tell us it was used in funerary ritual. The water stacks and agouti heads might refer to breaking through the surface of water and earth, actions which were central to Maya burials. The number five is at the core of the Maya numerical system and the quincunx describes their worldview.

Among the ancient Maya, polychromed ceramic pieces were usually reserved for use by the elite class. The pedestal legs provided the dish with height, while its colors and graphic designs added visual drama. Most of these painted ceramics were found in elite burial contexts, where they were used once and then ritually interred. Augustana's vessel is part of this tradition. It is in excellent condition, with rich colors and a smooth shiny surface.

[Elizabeth D. Olton, *Class of 1987*]

8A&B

Straw-glazed pottery equestrian figures: younger woman (A) and older woman (B), 7th century
Artist unknown (Chinese), early Tang Dynasty
Cast ceramic, A: 32.0 x 9.9 x 25.9 cm., 12-5/8 x 3-7/8 x 10-3/16;" B: 31.4 x 10.2 x 26.1 cm., 12-1/4 x 4 x 10-1/4"
Paul A. Anderson Chair in the Arts Collection Purchase in Honor of Cyrus and Mildred Churchill,
Augustana College Art Collection, 2007.24 a,b

The two yellow-glazed pottery equestrian figurines, datable to the early Tang period (618-907), represent a change in women's roles and behaviors that were influenced by cultural exchanges, primarily from a surge of foreigners via the Silk Road into the cosmopolitan capital of Chang'an. According to Katheryn Linduff, the two equestrians were probably non-Han in origin from western China due to the fact that non-Han Chinese rode horses astride, while Han women in earlier times rode with both legs on one side of the horse side-saddle. Contrary to the Confucian gender hierarchy, many historical and visual sources attest that Tang women were not sheltered in their household but they went outside riding horses and playing polo (both of which are foreign in origin) with men. The costume of the equestrians also suggests female independent status affected by non-Han influence. Although the Augustana pieces epitomize female high social status and their high fashion costumes differ from those prior to the Tang dynasty, their function is deeply rooted in the long tradition of mortuary art. They are *taoyong*, the Chinese term, which refers to a pottery piece in a human form buried with the dead in the grave. These were buried with luxurious objects (i.e. bronze vessels and jade ornaments) that were either used by the deceased during his lifetime or were dedicated to him at his funeral. The provenance of the two mounted figurines in the Augustana College permanent art collection is undocumented, but several similar works were unearthed from the elite burials in Shaanxi province.

[Naoko Gunji, *Assistant Professor of Art History*]

9

Icon with Scenes of the Four Feasts: Annunciation, Transfiguration, Entry into Jerusalem, Washing of the Feet, late 17th century
Russian Workshop [L. Popovich]
Oil on panel, 27.4 x 23.4 cm., 10-3/4 x 9-1/4"
Paul A. Anderson Chair in the Arts Collection Purchase in Honor of Ljubica Popovich, Professor Emerita of Fine Arts, Vanderbilt University, Augustana College Art Collection, 2000.63

Created by an unknown artist, Augustana's Russian icon dates from the late seventeenth century. Possibly a part of a larger series of scenes depicting the life of Jesus, the four panels were attached to canvas, reset on a wooden backing and reframed. Note how the restorer painted cracks on the frame to approximate the original. The bright red border is typical of icons from Russia (Popovich 1).

In terms of content, the first panel depicts the Annunciation in which Angel Gabriel conveys to Mary that she will become the Mother of God. Note that Mary holds a red thread as she spins yarn for the Temple curtain which is torn upon Jesus' death (Popovich 2). The second panel tells the story of the Transfiguration. Jesus ascends a mountain to pray, accompanied by three disciples. The little party is visited by Moses and Elijah, and Jesus is transfigured into his heavenly splendor, thus revealing both his divine and human natures. In the third panel, Jesus enters Jerusalem though one must look hard for the "hosanna-shouting" crowds, so prominent in the Biblical accounts, possibly symbolized by the group of boys situated by the tree at the top of the picture (Popovich 4). To the right, the men of Jerusalem meet Jesus and his entourage. Jesus' washing of the feet of the disciples forms the subject of the fourth panel. Though the expected basin of water is missing, Jesus holds a towel and appears to be drying Peter's feet. Through this act, Jesus models the ideal of *servanthood* which forms the basis of the disciples' continued ministry in the world.

Icons play an integral part in the practice of faith amongst Eastern Orthodox Christians. Whether painted by a monk or a secular artist, the creation of Augustana's icon would have been approached as a devotional act resulting in a holy object believed to be imbued with divine purpose. The artist would have prepared for his task through prayer, fasting and acts of penance. Strict rules govern the creation of icons including use of materials, symbols, colors and the employment of models for drawing Biblical figures, along with their attributes, so that characters and scenes are easily recognized by those familiar with the stories. The flatness of the composition suggests an *otherworldly* dimension as do the golden haloes (*nimbi*) surrounding the heads of the figures. Icons are never signed, suggesting that credit is due not to the artist's merit but to divine inspiration and gift.

Given its sacred nature, it is perhaps good to acknowledge the intended home for the icon is not an art museum but the setting for worship. The size of Augustana's icon suggests its probable original placement in the "beautiful corner" of the patron's home, a monastic cell or a chapel (Popovich 6). In these places, the icon best fulfills its purposes to tell the stories of the faith, to instruct in its teachings, to inspire to prayer and to be a "window to heaven" through which the faithful on earth are cheered on and encouraged by the "cloud of witnesses" (Hebrews 12:1) who inhabit God's heavenly realm.

[Barbara J. Melaas-Swanson, *Assistant Professor of Religion*]

10

A Crowned Female Saint, ca. 15th century
Westphalian Workshop (German)
Carved oak with vestigial traces of polychrome,
66.3 x 22.3 x 14.1 cm., 26-1/8 x 8-3/4 x 5-1/2"
Paul A. Anderson Chair in the Arts Collection
Purchase in Tribute to Dr. Mary Em Kirn,
Augustana College Art Collection, 2000.65

This gracefully curved statue of a standing female saint is an outstanding example of late Gothic woodcarving in northern Europe. Oak was one of the approved woods based on guild by-laws and until the 1480s, it was common practice to cover the surface with paint (Steyaert 31-34). In fact, surface color was so important that the painters were paid more than the woodcarvers. Thus, this figure originally would have looked quite different than it does today. We can only imagine the brilliant colors, including the probable use of gold leaf, which would have covered the entire surface. Today, small traces of the original red paint are still evident on the back.

Beginning in the early Middle Ages, individual saints began to be identified with attributes or symbols that specifically relate to some aspect of their lives or deaths. The narrow pointed crown circling this figure's head suggests royalty and it was common for female saints from aristocratic backgrounds, such as St. Catherine of Alexandria and St. Barbara, to wear crowns (Hall 40 & 58). However, St. Barbara would also have been identified by the tower she carried and St. Catherine of Alexandria by her wheel and a sword. Unfortunately, this image cannot be identified with a specific saint because her lower arms and attribute are missing.

The original location of this image also remains a mystery. We know that carved statues of both male and female saints were often part of elaborate winged altarpieces created in northern Europe from the mid-14th through 16th centuries (Kuhn 14). Carved saints were also found on contemporary choir stalls and tabernacle shrines.

Experts in late medieval sculpture have difficulty identifying a particular image with a specific geographic area because carvers often moved from place to place, however it has been suggested that this figure is stylistically similar to sculpture from the area of Westphalia. At the beginning of the 19th century, the military occupation of Westphalia by Napoleon resulted in the dissolution of monasteries, the closure of churches and the widespread destruction of religious images. It is possible that this image was removed from its original location at that time.

[Mary Em Kirn, *Professor Emerita of Art History*]

11

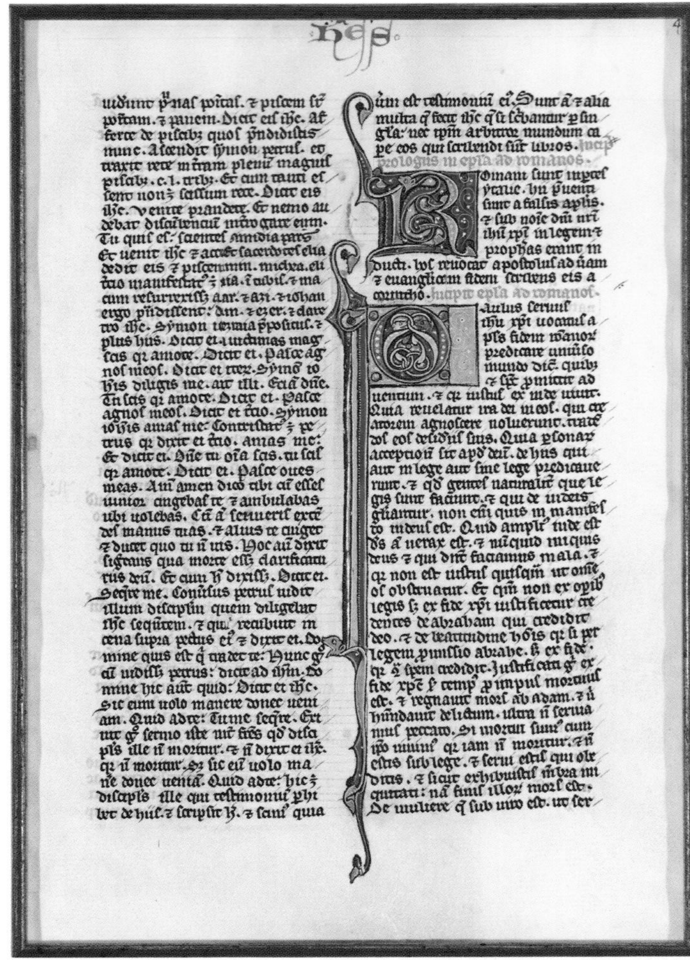

Vulgate Bible Page: Gospel of John and Prologues to the Epistle of St. Paul the Apostle to the Romans, ca. 1247
Attributed to Johannes Grusch Workshop (French)
Ink, gouache and gold leaf on vellum, 29.1 x 19.2 cm., 11-1/2 x 7-5/8" sheet
Paul A. Anderson Chair in the Arts Collection Purchase in Memory of James Breckenridge, Professor of Art History, Northwestern University, Augustana College Art Collection, 2006.40. a and b

The illuminated manuscript of the *Vulgate Bible*, written on vellum, is in gothic script. The stunning illuminations of the initials R and P have been attributed to the workshop of Johannes Grusch (France, ca. 1247). The presence of gold and the color blue—which was very expensive, as it could only be obtained from the mineral lapis lazuli, found in Asia—indicate that vast quantities of money were put into making this manuscript. The folio on display (*recto*, f. 4) is written in two columns, each with forty-eight lines of text. The first column contains the end of the *Gospel of John*—chapter 21—which ends in the first line of the second column. The text that follows is Saint Paul's *Epistle to the Romans*, as indicated by the rubric *Incipit epistola ad romanos* (here begins the letter to the Romans). What is interesting is that in the standard *Vulgate Bible*, the *Acts of the Apostles* is included between these two books, while in this version it has been omitted, or moved somewhere else. More interesting, however, is the *Prologue* to the epistle, also indicated by a rubric—*Incipit prologus in epistola ad romanus.* In addition to the Biblical text, the *Vulgate Bible* contains seventeen prologues, sixteen of which were written by Saint Jerome, and one of them is, indeed, a general prologue to the Pauline epistles. However, the short prologue included here is one of the so-called "Marcionite prologues," which were composed by Marcion of Sinope, one of the most prominent heretics in early Christianity. The original Greek text of these prologues has been lost, but as this folio attests, Latin translations survive in most *Vulgate* manuscripts (their heretical source having been forgotten):

> Romani sunt in p*ar*tes ytalie. hii preuenti sunt a falsis ap*ostol*is. et sub no*mine* do*mi*ni no*stri* ih*es*u xp*ist*i in legem et proph*et*as erant inducti. hos reuocat apostolus ad ueram et euange*li*cam fidem scriuens eis a corintho. [The Romans are in the regions of Italy. They were reached by false apostles, and under the name of our Lord Jesus Christ they were led away into the law and the prophets. The apostle calls them back to the true and evangelical faith, writing to them from Corinth.]

[David Arbesu, *Assistant Professor of Spanish*]

12

Book of Hours: Crucifixion Scene Opening the Hours of the Cross, ca. 1425–50
Parisian Workshop (French)
Hand painted with gold leaf on vellum, 15.5 x 11.6 cm., 6-1/8 x 4-1/16"
Paul A. Anderson Chair in the Arts Collection Purchase, Augustana College Art Collection, 2000.13

Over sixteen hundred years ago, during the Roman Empire, a major shift occurred in how information was stored, moving from the system of a roll or tablet to the format of a *codex* (book) (Brown 42 and 119). Thus, from the 4th century to the 1450s, all codices were written and illustrated by hand (Calkins 201-231). Using parchment or vellum (paper made from animal skins), these hand-written manuscripts were laboriously created by scribes in imperial workshops and later in monasteries and secular workshops.

By the fourteenth and fifteenth centuries, among wealthy aristocrats, the most popular format for a personal prayer book was a "book of hours" (Wieck 9-10). Usually small-scale, these highly portable hand-written books were divided into the eight canonical hours of the day and images of the Crucifixion are usually found in one of two places (Wieck 79-81). Based on the text, we are looking at the opening section of the Hours of the Holy Cross.

The narrative of Christ's passion begins in the lower right. Wearing a crown of thorns, Christ is being pulled toward Calvary by a man whose tongue lolls from his mouth, an indication that physical ugliness is connected to spiritual disbelief. To the lower left an angel kneels in prayer and gazes at the prominent image of the Crucifixion (Hall 81-86). The narrative of Christ's passion begins in the lower right. To Christ's right are his mother Mary, dressed in her traditional colors of blue, red and white and his "most beloved" disciple, John the Evangelist, who is always shown as a young man. To Christ's left, are two men, probably representing the disbelievers who scoffed at His suffering. Thus, this 15th-century French book of hours is an exquisite example of the period when hand-written and illustrated books were the major method of storing and disseminating information.

[Mary Em Kirn, *Professor Emerita of Art History*]

13A

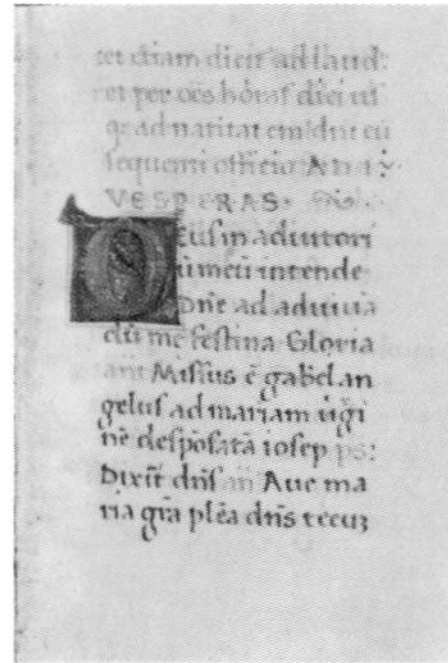

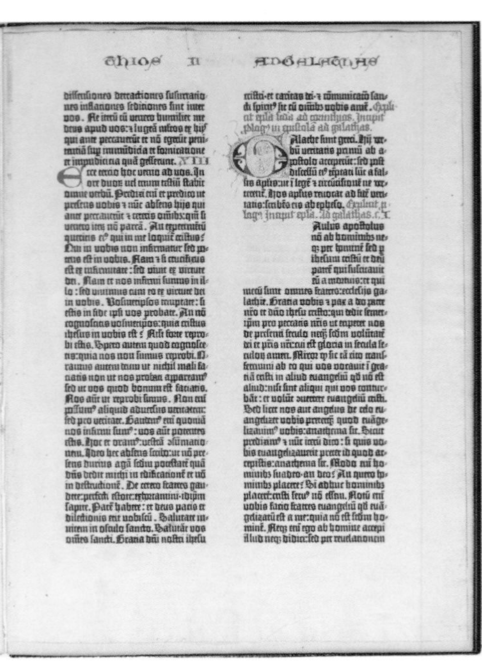

13A
***Horae Beatae Mariae Virginis*, 15th century**
Artist unknown
Handwritten text in black, red, and blue ink on parchment, bound in brown leather, 11.0 x 8.0 x 3.4 cm., 4-3/8 x 3-1/8 x 1-5/16"
Lent Courtesy of Special Collections, Thomas Tredway Library, Augustana College

13B
***Biblia*, or 42-line Bible: Galatians I**, ca. 1450–55
Published by Johann (Gensfleisch zur Laden zum) Gutenberg (ca. 1398–1468), Johann Fust, and Peter Schoeffer, Mainz, Germany
Single leaf page printed with moveable-type on paper, decorated by hand in red, blue, and brown (painted initial "G"), bound in modern black morocco, 39.0 x 28.6 cm., 15-1/4 x 11-1/4" sheet mounted on a larger sheet
Lent Courtesy of Special Collections, Thomas Tredway Library, Augustana College

Twenty-first century readers have become accustomed to the proliferation of information available on demand, but the transmission of information and knowledge has changed greatly over time. Before 1450, most books were handwritten, which meant that they were expensive and time-consuming to produce. Early books, termed manuscripts, are by their nature unique, since only one copy of each was ever made. Because these books were so labor-intensive and costly, they were prized possessions. Often including ornate multi-color and gold leaf decorations, such books are known as illuminated manuscripts. Manuscripts have their own conventions, such as the use of color (often red) or decorated initials to mark the beginning of a new or important section. Because of their great cost and scarcity, illuminated manuscripts were available only to the very wealthy elite. The manuscript seen here (catalogue 13A) is small enough to fit in the palm of your hand, indicating that it was made for personal use, probably for a wealthy woman. This text is commonly known as a "Book of Hours" and contains psalms and prayers written in Latin for Christian devotion.

The invention of moveable type by Johann Gutenberg around 1450 in Mainz, Germany, radically changed book production. Using moveable type and the printing press, more than one copy of a book was created at a time. This reduced the per-book cost, though books would remain too expensive for most individuals until the mechanization of printing in the early 19th century.

The *Gutenberg Bible* (catalogue 13B), or the *42-line Bible*, was the first book printed with moveable type in the West. Early printers designed their books to resemble illuminated manuscripts, including conventions such as decorated initials (see the right-hand column of the Gutenberg page) and typefaces resembling handwritten script. Such flourishes eased the early transition to multiple-copy book production, and gradually books developed their own style and conventions separate from those of manuscripts.

However, printing did not instantaneously displace manuscripts. Intermediate technologies, such as block books (also called *xylographica*), were popular in the mid-15th century. Block books were essentially picture books, usually religious in nature, often aimed at educating the illiterate. There were several

13C

Opera Nova Contemplativa per ogni fidel christiano … or ***Biblia Pauperum***, or **Bible of the Poor**, 1516
Engraved by Giovanni Andrea Valvassori detto Guadagnino (Venetian active 1510–1572)
Woodblock book, or chapbook, printing ink on paper, modern brown morocco binding with contemporary-style blind tooling, 15.8 x 10.5 x 1.4 cm., 6-3/16 x 4-1/8 x 9/16"
Lent Courtesy of Special Collections, Thomas Tredway Library, Augustana College

common texts used in block books, including the Apocalypse, the Dance of Death, and the *Biblia Pauperum* or "Bible of the Poor" (catalogue 13C), a comparison of Old and New Testament stories which was probably intended for less educated clergy. Although the wood used to carve the images and texts was cheaper than metal type, it was also less sturdy, so printers could not produce as many copies of a block book as with moveable type, but it was decidedly more efficient than handwriting individual manuscripts.

These three methods of text production highlight the technological overlap in the late 15th and early 16th centuries. Each of these three books was designed for a different use: the manuscript for personal devotion, the Bible (which is very large) for official use in a church or monastery, and the block book by someone learning or teaching biblical stories. Printers could utilize the different technologies based on the audience, purpose, and value of a book.

Books have continued to play a key role as purveyors of information, from the Renaissance and the Reformation to modern times. But books are also artifacts, providing contextual clues about the society that produced and used them. Looking at these featured texts in their original physical formats is a much different experience than looking at their texts reproduced on a screen, or repackaged in a modern paperback. The materials used and the process of their construction are evidence of the wealth, education level, daily life, and interests of the book's readers.

The three books shown here are among the earliest examples of the materials held in Special Collections—Augustana's collection of rare books, manuscripts, college archives, and local history ephemera. Many of our more "modern" materials are also unique, including letters, diaries, scrapbooks, and photographs which were created by individuals and organizations over the course of a lifetime. Each of these items tells its own story, partly through the recorded text and partly through the surrounding context.

[Sarah M. Horowitz and Jamie L. Nelson,
Special Collections Librarians]

14

Christ on the Mount of Olives from The Passion, ca. 1480
Martin Schongauer (Alsatian ca. 1430–1491)
Engraving, 16.3 x 11.4 cm., 6-7/16 x 4-7/16" image
Paul A. Anderson Chair in the Arts Collection Purchase in Honor of Dr. Mary Em Kirn, Augustana College Art Collection, 2002.11

Printmaking, as an artistic means of expression, appears for the first time in Western Europe in the 1420s in a creative explosion of woodcuts and then engravings that appealed to a broad audience. Creating an engraved image was technologically complex and the delicate lines, subtle shading, textural variations and spatial complexities found in engravings were impossible to achieve in contemporary woodcuts.

Martin Schongauer was the most important engraver in northern Europe during the third quarter of the 15th century and his work was greatly admired (Landau & Parshall 50-56). We know that the young Albrecht Dürer visited Schongauer's studio in Colmar in 1492, just months after Schongauer's death. Scholars believe that Dürer saw most, if not all, of Schongauer's engravings, including the twelve images from the Passion series. This series begins with *Christ on the Mount of Olives* and ends with the *Resurrection* (Shestack, Nos. 24-35).

In *Christ on the Mount of Olives*, Schongauer exhibited his ability to clearly relate a complex narrative. In the foreground, three of Christ's disciples have fallen asleep despite being admonished by Christ to pray. The bald St. Peter reclines with a sword clasped in his right hand. The young St. John the Evangelist rests his head on his Gospel and St. James, with his dark curly beard, props his head on his hand. They are unaware of Christ's agony as he kneels in prayer behind them. Christ gazes at an angel holding a cloth-covered chalice, referencing his future sacrifice on the cross as well as the Eucharistic wine.

Although Christ is positioned in mid-space, he dominates this composition because he is physically raised above both the disciples in the foreground and Judas and his entourage of soldiers, coming around the tall outcropping of rocks, in the background. Judas clutches a moneybag filled with thirty pieces of silver as he searches for Christ who will be led away to be questioned and tortured in the next engraving in this series of narrative images on the Passion.

[Mary Em Kirn, *Professor Emerita of Art History*]

The Mount of Olives, from Stefan Fridolin's *Schatzbehalter der wahren Reichtümer des Heils.* (Treasury of the True Riches of Salvation), 1491
Workshop of Michael Wolgemut (German ca. 1434/37–1519), published by Anton Koberger (German ca. 1445–1513) in Nuremberg, Woodblock print, 30.9 x 21.7 cm., 12-3/16 x 8-9/16" sheet
Purchased with Gift from Sonja Knudsen, Augustana College Art Collection, 1994.1

After the invention of the moveable type printing press in the 1450s, a new publishing industry sprang up in cities across Europe, with major presses in Augsburg, Basel, Nuremberg, Paris and Venice (Harthan 59-107). Books published between 1455 and 1500 are called *incunabula* or cradle books. Incunabula were often illustrated with woodcuts that would be added to the page after the text was printed. Book publishers hired large numbers of craftsmen to set the typeface, create woodblock illustrations, cut the woodblock designs and, for expensive editions, hand color the woodcut illustrations.

Anton Koberger, Albrecht Dürer's godfather, was the major book publisher in Nuremberg (Landau and Parshall 38). In 1509, he had twenty-four printing presses and employed over one hundred fifty workers. Although these early printed books were expensive, they were within reach of a professional class of lawyers, doctors, scholars and merchants. The number of people who could read in the late 15th and 16th centuries is difficult to determine, but recent studies have suggested that literacy was dependent on a variety of factors including social position, occupation, gender, place of residence, age, and religious beliefs (Houston 116-129).

Michael Wolgemut, one of Nuremberg's most important painters and printmakers, worked closely with publishers like Anton Koberger to supply woodblock illustrations for the books they were publishing. In the late 1480s, Albrecht Dürer was one of Wolgemut's apprentices and probably was aware of the 96 full-page woodblock designs being created for *The Schatzbehalter* (Schatzbehalter SMU.edu).

Written by Stefan Fredolin, a Franciscan friar, the book was intended as a guide to affective forms of personal contemplation. This image of *The Mount of Olives* relates specifically to the book's purpose—the contemplation of Christ's Passion by cloistered nuns.

Stylistically, this woodcut contrasts with Schongauer's engraving (catalogue 14) and clearly illustrates different stylistic approaches to the same subject. The broader lines result in surface textures, spatial development and shaded areas that are less subtle than the more technologically complex engraving.

[Mary Em Kirn, *Professor Emerita of Art History*]

16

The Erythraean Sibyl, after the ca. 1508-12 fresco in the Vatican Sistine Chapel, Rome, early 1570s
After Michelangelo (Italian 1475–1564) by Giorgio (Mantovano) Ghisi (Italian 1520–1582)
Engraving, 56.6 x 43.3 cm., 22-1/4 x 17-1/8" image and sheet
Gift of Thomas E. Rassieur, Augustana College Art Collection, 1996.8.4

Giorgio Ghisi's engraving of the *Erythraean Sibyl* is a copy after Michelangelo's figure of the same name, one of twelve seers painted in the famous Sistine Chapel from 1508 to 1512 at the Vatican in Rome. The seers were sibyls and prophets, individuals who were said to be inspired by the gods or God. Although such images were quite popular, one could only see them in the Sistine Chapel. Ghisi shrewdly determined to make prints of many popular images within the chapel. He thus enabled people to essentially have the Sistine Chapel in their own homes. Artists also benefited from such imaging as it was easier for them to study portable versions in their own studios, freeing them from the burden and expense of traveling to various sites in order to see them in person. Since copying the masters before them was considered one of the best methods for learning art techniques, such multiple images were crucial toward their education.

By the turn of the sixteenth century, the output of engravings increased dramatically. Like many engravers of his time, Ghisi was considered a reproductive engraver, copying other artists' works and reproducing them so they could reach a wider audience (Landau and Parshall 167). *The Erythraean Sibyl* was one such print. The term, *sibyl*, comes from the ancient Greek word *sibylla* which means "prophetess." Sibyls were often isolated from society so they could receive new prophecies which they would then share with the people. The *Erythraean Sibyl*, was so named because she prophesied from a cave in the town of Erythrae. At the end of the Middle Ages, the Catholic Church adapted these Classical sibyls by accepting them as twelve pagan prophets who foretold the coming of Christ, counterparts to the Old Testament Prophets. They thus linked the ancient Greco-Roman world with the Christian era.

Michelangelo portrayed *The Erythraean Sibyl* as a young, idealized and somewhat masculine woman, typical of High Renaissance standards combined with the artist's own style. What makes this print appear so remarkable is all the detail that was put into it, not to mention how three-dimensional it looks, similar to the Sistine Chapel. Such reverence for masters like Michelangelo, so soon after his death, demonstrates the sixteenth-century elevation of the position of artists. Michelangelo, as a High Renaissance artist, enjoyed acclaim and was considered a genius in his own lifetime. Unlike the generally subservient roles for medieval craftsmen, artists were now appreciated as educated and talented individuals, well-versed in such fields as anatomy, theology and science, as well as artistic techniques. Michelangelo was a poet as well, illustrating the new concept of the Renaissance man, a genius with expertise in many fields. Artists like Ghisi effectively furthered Michelangelo's position for history by making his masterpieces from the Sistine Chapel more accessible to the public and future generations.

[Amanda Nordstrom, *Class of 2008*]

17

School of Athens, after the ca. 1509 fresco in the Vatican *Stanze della Segnatura*, Rome, 18th century
After Raphael (Sanzio) (Italian 1483–1520) engraved by Joannes (Giovanni) Volpato (Italian 1735/40–1803), drawn by Joseph (Giuseppe) Cades (Italian 1750-1799)
Engraving, 56.7 x 75.0 cm., 22-5/16 x 29-7/16" image
Gift of Mr. and Mrs. Edward Hoban, Augustana College Art Collection, SDC1997.27.18

Augustana's image of Raphael's *School of Athens* is as much a product of eighteenth-century Rome as it is of Raphael's sixteenth-century Rome. What you are looking at is a print made from an eighteenth-century engraving by Giovanni Volpato, who based his engraving on a drawing of Raphael's fresco by Giuseppe Cades, a well known eighteenth-century Italian painter. Prints such as these were common souvenirs for eighteenth-century tourists, and it is likely that our piece started its journey to Augustana in just such a context (Wölfflin 62).

Dominating the fresco from its center, though they stand in the background, are Plato and Aristotle; both are identified by the books they hold: an elder Plato, on the left, holds his dialogue titled *Timaeus*, while his student Aristotle, on the right, holds a work titled *Ethics*. With what are these characters so passionately engaged? A simple answer can be given in one word: learning. But, I propose, the sort of learning depicted here is of a specific variety, and that variety of learning in fact explains both the design of the composition as a whole, and also its purpose: my argument is that the artist's design was inspired by Book 7 of Plato's *Republic*, a book which depicts education as a journey from the shadows of the Cave into the light of the Sun, with the caveat that those who have glimpsed the Sun must return to the Cave to assist those still trapped therein. Raphael's *School of Athens* is a fine example of mimetic art; that is, art that is meant to engender in its viewers what it depicts. The *School of Athens* depicts philosophers in intense and serious discussion for the sake of learning. By not naming any of the philosophers in the composition, the artist compels those studying his work to do exactly what those in the fresco are doing: to discuss and debate what, exactly, something is—in other words, to engage in dialectics. So, while it is impossible to identify with certainty all of the philosophers in the *School of Athens*, the artist wanted us to try. The *School of Athens* is like Plato's dialogues: it does not answer all of the questions it poses, but it compels us to think, and that is its point.

[Emil A. Kramer, *Associate Professor of Classics*]

18

St. Christopher, Facing Left, 1521
Albrecht Dürer (German 1471–1528)
Engraving (Meder A quality), 11.7 x 7.5 cm., 4-5/8 x 3" image
Purchased with Funding Assistance from A. Ben Jasper, Mr. and Mrs. George and Pat Olson, Mr. Thomas E. Rassieur, Dr. Erick O. Schonstedt, and Jane Finnicum in Memory of Marian E. Finnicum, Augustana College Art Collection 1993.36

Albrecht Dürer was a German artist who became one of the most important figures of the Northern Renaissance. Though he also painted and worked in watercolor, Dürer was most famous during his time for his woodcuts and engravings. He created this engraving, *St. Christopher, Facing Left*, in 1521. The subject of the engraving is St. Christopher, a third-century saint who became popular during the Middle Ages and Renaissance. St. Christopher was the patron saint of travelers, and therefore an appropriate subject for Dürer, who created the print after returning from a year-long journey to the Netherlands. The engraving depicts a popular episode from Christopher's life, in which he unknowingly carried the Christ child across a river. Christopher had decided to serve Christ by helping travelers cross the dangerous river, and was one day approached by a child. He took the child on his shoulders and began to cross the river, but the child grew heavier and heavier as Christopher went along. When they reached the other side of the river, the child told Christopher that he had just carried Christ and the weight of the world.

St. Christopher was traditionally shown as strong and masculine, so he would be physically able to carry the weight of the world. Dürer's Christopher is no exception. Dürer usesd delicate horizontal lines in the landscape and sky to lead the viewer's eye to the larger-than-life saint. In contrast, Christopher is composed largely of diagonal and vertical lines, which cause the eye to travel up to the Christ child. Dürer alludes to the Christ child's holiness by surrounding him with a white halo, created through the absence of line in the sky. Dürer is known for his manipulation of line to make shadows and light. The folds of Christopher's cloak, the bark on his staff, and the waves in the water are created by many individual lines contrasting with the whiteness of the empty space. Dürer often signed his engravings and woodcuts by working his monogram into the image. In this engraving, the monogram and the date, 1521, are visible on a rock in the lower right.

[Helen Reinold, *Class of 2011*]

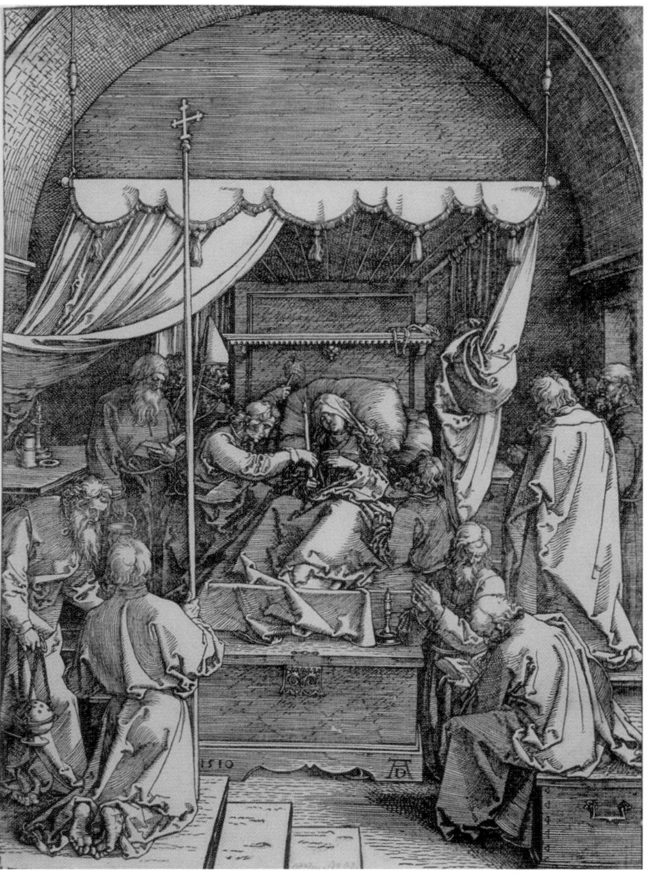

Death of the Virgin from **Life of the Virgin,** 1510
Albrecht Dürer (German 1471–1528)
Woodblock print, 29.3 x 23.3 cm., 11-1/2 x 8-1/4" image
Purchase with Gift of Augustana College Art History Alumni in Honor of Dr. Mary Em Kirn, 2003.7

The 1510 *Death of the Virgin* was one of twenty woodcuts in Dürer's *Life of the Virgin*, which he published in book form for the first time in 1511. Benedictus Chelidonius, a Benedictine monk and member of the Nuremberg society of humanist scholars, joined Dürer in this enterprising venture, providing poems in classical Latin verse to accompany the nineteen narrative images in the series. It has been noted that the large, folio format with text and image opposite each other across the binding, as well as the high quality of Dürer's *Life of the Virgin* series and other religious prints, would have made them an excellent means for classroom instruction or for private devotional use (Hutchison 54).

The legendary account of the Virgin Mary's death and subsequent Assumption is drawn from various apocryphal books dating to the 2nd and 5th centuries. These earlier sources were condensed and popularized in the thirteenth century by a Dominican friar, Jacobus de Voragine, in his so-called *Golden Legend*. By Dürer's time, it was no longer customary for *Death of the Virgin* imagery to include Christ and the heavenly host at her bedside. In Northern Renaissance art, the Virgin Mary is generally shown holding a candle, in accordance with established Christian death ritual (Binski 33-47 and Wieck 109-119), which recommended placing a candle in the hands of a dying person as a symbol of his or her faith, as she rests on a canopied bed set within a domestic interior.

What set Dürer's composition apart from those of his predecessors was his innovative narrative style—in particular, his sophisticated use of one-point perspective (invented in the previous century) to draw in the viewer, to focus the eye on the central figure of Mary, and to map out the interior space in a clearly legible, realistic manner. Dürer employed a more sophisticated tonal system in his woodcuts, allowing him to impart an even greater sense of naturalistic light and shadow to the final three prints of his *Life of the Virgin* series, as we see here (Gunter 13).

[Paul Bacon, *Class of 1990*]

20

The Child (Job xiv, 1 and 2) from **Dance of Death**, first published in 1538
Hans Holbein the Younger (German 1498–1543)
Woodblock print in *Les simulachres et historiees faces de la mort, autant elegammēt pourtraictes, que artificiellement imaginées* [sic], (Images and illustrated facets of death, as elegantly depicted as they are artfully conceived), 6.5 x 4.9 cm., 2-5/8 x 1-15/16" image
Augustana College Art Exhibits Purchase, 1991.72.a and b

In his fascinating and imaginative *Dance of Death* woodcuts, Holbein transformed a traditionally well-known medieval art form to a new vehicle for his own Renaissance time period. Previously the theme had always represented Death's arrival as a punishment for a person's sins. It was during the Renaissance period that the *Dance of Death* moved away from this theme of retribution to focus instead on the state of humankind, frequently with mocking undertones (Collins 29). A *memento mori* (reminder of death) generally appeared as the familiar skeletal form of Death, who served to remind people of the frailty of their passing life in comparison to the eternal life for which their soul was destined. People of the time believed that after death all would be judged by God.

With the woodcut of *The Child*, Holbein depicted a living drama, showing Death's sudden intrusion into everyday life. This monochromatic woodcut shows Death, in the form of a skeleton, leading a young child away from his mother while she prepares dinner over an open fire. With one hand, the mother clutches her cooking pan and with the other holds her head in horror. Another child behind her also grabs at his hair as he watches, with panicked eyes, his younger sibling being wrenched away from their home. By placing this scene in a common house with a family performing the familiar task of preparing a meal, Holbein created a picture of an immediate reality, of an innocent child being taken away by death from a mother who, contrary to her maternal instincts, cannot save him. *The Child* was first published as part of *Les simulachres & historiees faces de la mort* in 1538, a book containing forty-one of Holbein's woodcuts (Clark 71). With the Renaissance invention of the printing press and its facility to produce multiple copies of books, rather than the medieval tradition of the handmade illuminated manuscript (catalogue 12), books became more accessible to larger audiences.

[Jessica Feinman, *Class of 2008*]

Augustus and the Tiburtine Sibyl, ca. 1528
After Parmigianino (Italian 1503–ca. 1540) by Antonio da Trento (Italian ca. 1508–ca. 1550)
Chiaroscuro woodblock print in brown and olive inks, shield watermark, 34.6 x 26.8 cm., 13-5/8 x 10-9/16" image
Gift of Harris Schrank in Tribute to Dr. Catherine Goebel, Augustana College Art Collection, 2007.3

In the late 1520s, the Emilian painter Parmigianino provided drawings to the woodcutter Antonio da Trento to be translated into prints. The *chiaroscuro* woodcut is a printmaking technique that attempts to transfer the tonal effects of painting and drawing to the printed medium. Instead of using a single block to create the entire image, artists making a chiaroscuro woodcut employ a different woodblock for each variation of tone or color (Wechsler 24 and 787). In the Parmigianino print, the line block bearing the basics of the design of figures and architecture was laid down first in dark olive ink. The block bearing the middle gray tone, which covers almost the entire composition, followed. To form the highlights, Antonio da Trento left the white color of the paper exposed (Harris Schrank).

Sibyls held great interest during the Renaissance as humanists sought to reconcile the glories of the pagan past with the Christian present. Clairvoyant women of the ancient world who predicted future events, sibyls were recast by early Christian scholars as foreseers of the coming of Christ, a role they continued to play in the Renaissance. According to legend, when the Emperor Augustus approached the Tiburtine sibyl about his deification, she revealed to him a vision of the Virgin and Christ child in glory to alert him to a deity higher than any pagan god. The classical architecture of the scene in Parmigianino's print recalls ancient Rome, but the plants overtaking the columns on the right imply the impending decline of the pagan world, trounced by a new religious era signaled in the sibyl's vision.

The artistic collaboration between Parmigianino and Antonio da Trento was short lived. The artist and biographer Giorgio Vasari (1511-1574) recounts that the woodcutter stole all of the drawings, engravings, and woodcuts stored by the painter in a trunk and was never seen again. While Parmigianino retrieved the actual metal plates and woodblocks, his drawings were gone for good. Vasari goes on to suggest that the event irrevocably damaged Parmigianino and caused him to abandon printmaking altogether, but the painter continued to produce drawings, many of which were transferred into prints after his death (Vasari Volume 3: 787).

[Margaret Morse, *Assistant Professor of Art History*]

22

Allegory of the City of Nuremberg with Justice, Peace and Prosperity, 1564
Monogrammist M.S. (German active 1545–1580)
Woodblock print,
26.6 x 16.2 cm., 10-1/2 x 6-3/8"
Gift of Drs. Mary Em and Michael Kirn, Augustana College Art Collection, 2007.26

In the 16th century, Nuremberg was a major center of Christian humanism and one of the most important free Imperial cities in the Holy Roman Empire. The city was home to Albrecht Dűrer and to a major publishing industry led by Dürer's godfather, Anton Koberger. In 1525, the Nuremberg city council eliminated the practice of Catholicism and abolished all of the city's convents and monasteries. Church leaders were told to conduct services in accordance with Protestant practices. This change to Protestantism led to shifting perceptions of the relationship between secular and spiritual authority (Witte).

In 1564, a revised and updated civic legal code, *Der Stat Nürmberg verneute Reformation*, was published by the Nuremberg printer Valentin Geissler (British Museum). Its importance is based on the clarity of the legal language and its rational organization into three major parts: court and procedural law, contract law and inheritance law. At the beginning of the book is a full-page woodcut by an artist known as the Monogrammist M.S. Attempts to identify him have not been successful.

Monogrammist M.S.'s fascinating woodcut focuses on a personification of the city of Nuremberg. Resting on her lap is a personification of Peace holding an olive branch. Nuremberg is flanked on her right by Justice, holding a sword that denotes her power and a balance scale that indicates her impartiality. On the left of Nuremberg is Prosperity holding a bowl filled with coins and an upturned moneybag from which coins are flowing. A swarm of bees is identified as Harmony. Above these four personifications, God the Father appears among the clouds and holds his arms out in blessing. In the background, parts of the the walls and towers of Nuremberg are visible.

Clearly, this image provides a message to the legal scholars, lawyers, judges and clerks who would have used this book. They were to remember that the honest administration of the city's new civic legal code would result in justice, peace and prosperity for the town's citizens. But most important, this image emphasizes that God rules the world and supports and blesses civic laws based on human rationality.

[Mary Em Kirn, *Professor Emerita of Art History*]

23

***Justicia* (Justice)**, 1559
After Pieter Bruegel (the Elder, Flemish 1537–1612) by Philip Galle (Flemish 1537–1612)
Engraving, Gothic "P" watermark, 22.6 x 29.2 cm., 8-15/16 x 11-1/2" image
Purchase in Honor of President Steven C. Bahls, Made Possible by the Paul A. Anderson Chair in the Arts, Sonja Knudsen, Mr. and Mrs. George and Pat Olson, with Courtesy of Mr. Harris Schrank, Augustana College Art Collection, 2005.10

Pieter Bruegel's complementary sets of drawings, *The Seven Deadly Sins* (anger, sloth, lust, gluttony, avarice, pride and envy) and *The Virtues* (prudence, charity, justice, faith, hope, temperance and fortitude), became models for his two most popular series of engraved prints. In both series, a central allegorical figure is surrounded by other characters in a way designed to cause the viewer to think more deeply about sin and virtue. The allegorical figure at the base of the landscape in *Justicia* is Iusticia. She is the Roman equivalent of Hellenic Themis. The imageries of Iusticia and Themis have been combined to create a symbol familiar to all, Lady Justice, who hovers over scores of courthouses around the United States.

Around the pedestal which elevates Iusticia a mere step above her surroundings, a riot of official violence is being played out: a tortuous rack, a beheading, a flogging and a hand being cut off are sufficiently graphic that gallows and torture wheels on the horizon seem somehow less chilling by comparison. Each of these acts is committed by self-righteous persons, seemingly in the name of justice. Iusticia is oblivious to the world around her. Aloof and blindfolded, she stands as a statuesque symbol of justice, who neither sees nor understands the horrors done in her name. That Bruegel would surround Iusticia with such horrors is not surprising given the artist's time. *Justicia* was completed in about 1560. It was in 1547 that Henry II, King of France, tried heresy cases by setting up special courts, colloquially called "Burning Chambers."

Though Bruegel might have seen Iusticia's blindfold as allowing her to turn such a "blind eye" to the horrors wrought in her name, contemporary notions of Lady Justice view the blindfold more positively. Today, "Justice is blind" has a positive connotation, indicating that neither worldly wealth nor position can create advantage in her presence. Likewise neither race, gender nor creed should put one at a disadvantage when justice is blind.

[Steven C. Bahls, *President*]

24

Luther Bible: Tower of Babel, ca. 1565, German edition ca. 1597
Hans Bocksberger (Austrian ca. 1510–1569)
Woodblock print, 11.0 x 15.5 cm., 4-5/16 x 6-1/8" image
Purchase with Gift of Augustana College Art History Alumni in Honor of Dr. Mary Em Kirn, Augustana College Art Collection, 2006.15

As citizens of the Information Age, it is impossible for us to imagine a day when everyone did not have access to a printed Bible. Until the invention of the Gutenberg Press in 1455, all books were written or copied by hand and were affordable only to the wealthiest individuals or, in the case of the Bible, the Church. That one of Martin Luther's greatest achievements was the translation of the Bible into his native German fits his egalitarian principle that we are all part of "the priesthood of all believers" and ought therefore have equal access to the Bible.

Exiled to Wartburg Castle by his followers in 1521 for fear of his life, Luther took a mere eleven weeks to complete a translation of the New Testament.

He worked directly from the original Greek text and was aided by notes from the recent Latin translation by Erasmus and by advice from Philip Melanchthon, Luther's closest disciple and a Greek scholar. He completed a translation of the Old Testament in 1524 and was constantly revising his work up to 1546, the year of his death.

Luther's work is by all accounts a free translation of the original, concerned to set the text into vernacular German, that is, to make the text speak to the reader with the same expressions that were used in common discourse. He complained, for instance, about the Latin translation of Psalm 63 that "No German can understand that," so that in his translation, "We now speak clear German." When translating Paul's words about being saved by grace, Luther added the word *alone*, as in "by grace alone," insisting that this was Paul's intent, even if the word was not in the original.

All translation is thus *interpretation*, despite protestations by the translator that he is just reproducing the text word-for-word from the original into the vernacular. It is understandable, therefore, that visual art would be paired with the written word in Luther's Bible, as it was from the earliest editions. This woodcut, possibly designed by Hans Bocksberger for the 1597 Luther Bible, is a visual translation of the story from Genesis, chapter 11, that emphasizes the audacity of human striving. The archetypal warrior and king Nimrod (who is not in the Biblical text!) dominates the landscape, literally as tall himself as the Tower behind him, which reaches almost to the clouds. Luther was fond of the medieval aphorism, *Quod supra nos, nihil ad nos*, "What is above us is none of our business." "Let God be God," he asserted; our proper task is simply to trust God and to love our neighbor in need.

Both in Luther's translation of scripture and in the artist's "translation" of the text, we see the folly of trying to "be like God" (Gen. 3:4) and are encouraged to be human, no more, no less.

[Richard Priggie, *College Chaplain*]

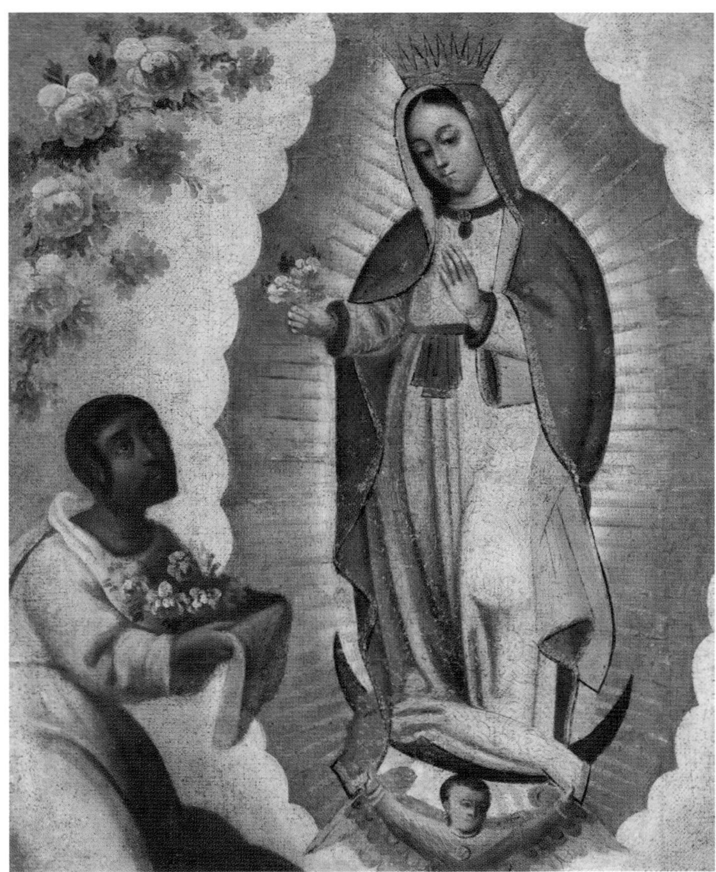

Our Lady of Guadalupe, early to mid 19th century
Artist Unknown, Mexican Colonial
Oil on canvas on masonite, 36.9 x 29.8 cm., 14-1/2 x 11-3/4"
Augustana College Art and Art History Department Purchase in Honor of the Sisters of the Visitation, Villa de Chantal, with Conservation Services Donated by Mr. Barry Bauman, 1991.80

This painting is a typical one of colonial Mexico and depicts the apparition of *la Virgen de Guadalupe* to Juan Diego. The colorful details tell the story of the December 1531 apparitions: the Castillian roses in the upper right-hand corner symbolize the roses that *la Virgen* caused to grow outside Mexico City and which Mexican peasant Juan Diego scooped up in his maguey cactus fiber robe *tilma* to take to Bishop Zumarraga of Mexico City to prove the authenticity of *la Virgen's* apparitions to him. For his part, Juan Diego is depicted as a dark-skinned Indian peasant, and the legend is that *la Virgen* spoke to him in his native *Nahuatl* language. He genuflects before her to honor her, and his open *tilma* holds pink Castillian roses.

La Virgen in this painting resembles the typical colonial Mexican depiction of her. She is darker-skinned than other colonial-era Virgins, she holds some of the roses as a way to acknowledge her powers as a heavenly mediatrix, and around her waist we see a sash which indicates she is pregnant. Gold rays extend from her figure and gold traces the edges of her headpiece, indicating her heavenly identity. Moreover, she wears a golden crown, indicating her place as Queen of the Heavens. Her mantle is blue and embedded in it are 46 stars. The angel who lifts her up is interpreted by most scholars as the angel of Revelations and she is seen by some as the Woman of the Apocalypse. The Virgin of Guadalupe's primary identity in New Spain was that she was the patroness of a colonized people. Her pregnancy, darker-colored skin, and use of Juan Diego's native language when addressing him are all cited as her place as "mother" of the Mexican people. As a *mestiza*, she marks the birth of Mexico and the *mestizo* identity of Mexicans.

The now-standard story of the apparitions are that the Virgin appeared to Juan Diego three times and that it was on the third visit that he took the roses to the bishop and upon opening his tilma, the roses became embedded, along with the image of la Virgen, on the robe. Notably, *la Virgen* has darker skin than Spanish national Virgins and is called "*la Morena*" and "*la Morencita*" by her millions of devotees around the world.

[Kristy Nabhan-Warren, *Associate Professor of Religion*]

26

Christ Preaching, or ***La Petite tombe***, ca. 1652
Rembrandt van Rijn (Dutch 1606–1669)
Etching and drypoint, 15.4 x 20.7 cm., 6-1/8 x 8-1/8" image
Paul A. Anderson Chair in the Arts Collection Purchase, Augustana College Art Collection, 2001.12

Rembrandt Van Rijn is generally regarded as the most significant printmaker of all time. He grew up in Holland during the seventeenth century, the era of the Dutch Baroque, which represented a great change from the established Italian Baroque style. The Dutch began to create more secular works of art in response to the taste of the growing middle class, who wanted more comprehensible themes.

Rembrandt was an extremely religious man, reflected in his preference for Biblical themes. Mirroring Mennonite beliefs of his time, the theme of Rembrandt's work often focused on the "poor in spirit" over "the worldly wise and learned" (White 41). His imagery is filled with ordinary people expressing sorrow and joy; characters with whom everyone can relate. Christ in this etching is seen speaking to the poor in a small, yet comfortable area that appears similar to seventeenth-century neighborhoods found in modern Holland, in order to help his audience relate to the idea. The viewer's focus is drawn to Christ since He is the central and brightest figure in the print. Only the faint halo above His head, symbolizing religious light, distinguishes His holy lineage. Christ stands upon a small platform separating Him from the rest of the public. This example of hierarchic scale enables the viewer to understand the importance of the figure, not in a symbolic, but in a more human manner. Visible to the left are a few wealthier men, probably Pharisees, with finer clothing and hats, however, Jesus is focusing his attention on the poor and sick, grouped to the right in the print. Everyone is captivated by what he is saying. People are leaning forward as if straining to make sure they do not miss a single word (Boon, xxxiii). Rembrandt clearly defined the rules of etching. He was able to bring to life such etchings by using *chiaroscuro*, a sharp contrast between light and shadow, very difficult to achieve with prints. Through the print medium he reached a vast new audience with a quiet but powerful religious message.

[Cristy Martinez, *Class of 2008*]

27

Rembrandt and His Wife Saskia, 1636
Rembrandt van Rijn (Dutch 1606–1669)
Etching, 10.6 x 9.5 cm., 4-3/16 x 3-7/8" image
Gift of Augustana College Class of 1951, Augustana College Art Collection, 2001.19

While Rembrandt created numerous self-portraits and regularly depicted his wife Saskia van Uylenburgh (1612-1642) in both his prints and paintings, this etching is one of only two images where they appear together. The other instance is Rembrandt's boisterous painting *Self Portrait with Saskia in the Guise of the Prodigal Son* (1635, Gemäldegalerie, Dresden) where Rembrandt and Saskia are shown in a tavern with Saskia seated on Rembrandt's lap while Rembrandt gaily turns to the viewer and raises his drink.

This etching of Rembrandt and Saskia was created two years after they married. In stark contrast to the *Prodigal Son* portrait, Rembrandt portrays himself as an artist—working in his studio and engrossed in his art—with his supportive wife, model, and muse firmly behind him. Rather than wearing contemporary seventeenth-century clothing, Rembrandt and Saskia don fancy costumes from the sixteenth-century, which were perhaps props found in Rembrandt's studio. By selecting this setting and placing them in costume, Rembrandt ignored the well-established conventions of Dutch marriage portraiture where artists formally placed couples in contemporary and comfortable domestic spaces. Instead, it is possible that Rembrandt was alluding to a popular Dutch motto, "*Liefde baart kunst*" or "Love brings forth art." Given the numerous representations of Saskia in his oeuvre, Rembrandt's relationship with his wife was likely a significant source of inspiration and this etching might be a representation of her important role in his art and life.

In this etching, Rembrandt dominates the composition and radiates confidence. He appears to relish his increased prosperity and growing social position, some of which was due to Saskia's prominent family and significant dowry. He is seated at a table with his wife—his arm positioned prominently in the foreground holding an etching tool, but at rest. He places Saskia behind the table and deep in the composition; however, Rembrandt draws the viewer to her because she is so brightly illuminated and has an almost other worldly appearance. Like her husband, she looks out to the viewer, but Rembrandt stands between his wife and audience. In this intimate setting, Rembrandt stands as the gate-keeper to his wife and muse and we only approach her through him.

[Kathryn Hannen Walker, *Class of 1993*]

28

The Hunt of the Hippopotamus and the Crocodile, after 1615-16 painting, ca. 1650
After Peter Paul Rubens (Flemish 1577–1640), by Willem Pietersz De Leeuw (Flemish ca. 1603–1665)
Engraving, 45.3 x 63.5 cm., 17-13/16 x 25" image
Augustana College Art and Art History Department Purchase, 1995.10

Peter Paul Rubens is generally regarded as one of the greatest and most influential artists in history. The intricate Mannerist style of such greats as Raphael Sanzio and Michelangelo Buonarroti was replaced around 1600 by the less symbolic and more realistic pieces of the emotionally charged Baroque era with which Rubens is directly affiliated. Rubens' artistic popularity grew immensely while he produced many religious masterpieces, landscapes and secular hunting scenes including *The Hunt of the Hippopotamus and the Crocodile*. These highly emotional and intense subjects in nature appealed to his audience who sought empathetic, rather than thoughtful, responses.

This print after Rubens' famous painting *The Hunt* (1615–16), was engraved a few years after the artist's death, attesting to the continued popularity of the painter and this particular piece. Rubens' *The Hunt of the Hippopotamus and the Crocodile* captures the spirit of the Baroque era with its fascination for exotic cultures. The observer is taken to the climax of struggle between five men, a crocodile and a hippopotamus, the moment before the prey is stabbed to death by three of the men on horseback. These turbaned and bearded men were considered *exotic* by their European audience, as were the crocodile, hippopotamus, and location, which included a palm tree in the background. The figures are draped in various fabrics and armed with spears and swords. The foreshortening effect on the hippopotamus and crocodile make them appear to be leaping out of the marshy tropical environment and into the viewers' space. *The Hunt* captures intellectual and emotional tensions. Viewers are left in suspense, not knowing the fate of the man lying on the ground, perhaps about to be devoured by the lunging crocodile. This active overall composition is characteristic of Rubens' distinctive style, effectively capturing all of the climactic action that occurs throughout the piece.

[Kaitlin Bradley, *Class of 2008*]

29

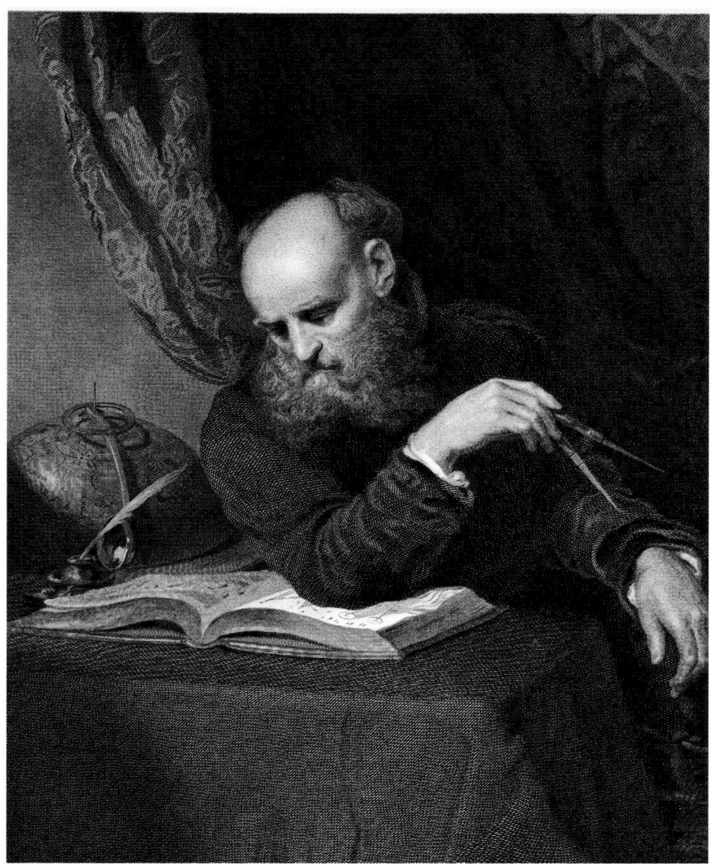

Galileo: The Astronomer, after 1832 painting, n.d.
After Henry Wyatt (British 1794–1840) by Robert Charles Bell (Scottish 1806–1872)
Engraving, 24.4 x 19.6 cm., 9-5/8 x 7-11/16" image
Paul A. Anderson Chair in the Arts Collection Purchase, Augustana College Art Collection, SDC2010.10

Galileo (born, 1564) learned to experiment with his father, a musician who worked with string lengths and tensions. He studied at Pisa, where he was appointed professor of mathematics. No record survives of his legendary study of speed of fall, involving objects of different weights dropped from the Leaning Tower, but it is the kind of thing he might have done. In 1592 Galileo moved to Padua, where he discovered the ratios that govern falling bodies, using inclined planes and rolling balls as his primary means of investigation. He found that as a descending body accelerates, speed is proportional to time of descent and distance covered to the square of the time. Galileo thus created a new method of science, the use of experiment and precise measurement to validate conclusions. For this reason he is often regarded as the father of experimental science.

In 1609 he heard about an optical instrument that made distant objects appear close. With high quality Venetian glass, he succeeded in improving the optics of the telescope, and in 1610 (*Starry Messenger*) he published his astonishing results: contrary to Aristotle, the Moon is not a polished sphere but is instead very much like the earth topographically; there are multitudes of stars never before seen; Jupiter has satellites of its own. He began to argue for Copernicus and against Aristotle. By 1615 this brought him into conflict with the Church, in the person of Cardinal Roberto Bellarmino, who in 1616 informed Galileo that Copernican theory could be used but not taught as truth, owing to conflicts with the Bible.

Seven years later a good friend and supporter of Galileo's, Maffeo Barberini, was elected Pope Urban VIII. Overjoyed, Galileo went to Rome and secured permission from Urban to write a book on Copernicus. The two men seem to have misunderstood one another. Urban expected that the book would be even-handed and would draw no firm conclusions—an exercise in assessing the evidence. Galileo wrote a pro-Copernican polemic (*Dialogue on the Two Chief World Systems*). Urban was enraged at this, and at the discovery that Galileo had treated some of his own suggestions with apparent contempt. Galileo was called to Rome, tried, and convicted of disobedience and vehement suspicion of heresy. He spent the rest of his life under house arrest, and is variously thought to be a martyr to science or an ingrate who betrayed his own patron.

[David Hill, *Professor of Philosophy*]

30

Marie de' Medici, 1631
Attributed to Anton (Anthony) van Dyck (Flemish 1599–1641)
Oil on oak panel, 25.4 x 19.8 cm., 10 x 7-3/4"
Gift of Professor Irma Adelman, Augustana College Art Collection, 2004.25

Marie de' Medici (1573–1642), the 58-year-old Queen Mother of France, gazes stolidly at us from this small oil sketch. She wears a black oval cap preferred by widows (her husband Henri IV was assassinated in 1610) (Saward 98-99). Her dress, with its stiffly starched white band collar, features fashionably slashed, wide puffed sleeves that end in double cuffs at her wrist (Gordenker 83). The tight bodice is held together with pearl buttons and adorned with a brooch, her only jewelry. Cupped in her hand are flowers similar to those held by women in van Dyck portraits. Marie's features are not idealized as evidenced by her prominent nose, pursed lips and jowly jaw. On a shelf, next to Marie, rests a crown topped with a *fleur-de-lis* design that references her relationship to the French royal family. Although this oil sketch is not signed by the artist, the thick impasto dots and small slashes of white paint evident on the curtain and Marie's right sleeve and bodice are visual signatures of a painting style associated with van Dyck.

The early 1630s were watershed years for both Marie and Anthony van Dyck. In 1631, Marie and her son Gaston had been expelled from the French court by her oldest son King Louis XIII for plotting to overthrow his major advisor, the Cardinal Richelieu. They initially took refuge in Antwerp (Barners 332-333). Just five months after Marie's visit to van Dyck's Antwerp studio in the fall of 1631, the artist moved permanently to England and by 1632 had become principal painter to King Charles I and his wife Henrietta, one of Marie's daughters. Some scholars have even speculated that van Dyck's move to England could have been facilitated by Marie, who might have recommended van Dyck to her daughter Henrietta (Wheelock 76).

Also in the early 1630s, van Dyck initiated a project known posthumously as the *Iconography*—a contemporary "who's who" (Depauw and Luijten 75). Because of Marie de' Medici's status as a patron of the arts, her engraved portrait is included in both early editions. In all, van Dyck is associated with over sixty grisaille oil sketches that were used by engravers as models for the *Iconography* (Spicer 357–363). *Grisaille* refers to images dominated by tonal ranges from white to black, a technique that can be traced back to medieval manuscripts and Renaissance panel paintings (Baer 32). Scholars disagree about the level of van Dyck's direct participation in the creation of these small oil portrait sketches and many believe that at least some of these images were done by his pupils (Depauw and Luijten 81–82). Clearly, the spontaneity of the paint application is evident in this *grisaille* oil sketch of Marie de' Medici. The incompleteness of the sketch results in forms that are suggested and surfaces that are not precisely delineated. As in some modern paintings, we have to use our imagination to fill in these surface details. In this portrait sketch of Marie de'Medici painted over 370 years ago, we are still able to envision the creative skill of the artist.

[Mary Em Kirn, *Professor Emerita of Art History*]

31

Nell Gwyn, after the 1675 painting, 1793
After Sir Peter Lely (b. Dutch, active England 1618–1680), drawn by Sylvester Harding (British 1745–1809) engraved by Sheneker
Engraving, 12.5 x 10.0 cm., 4-15/16 x 4" image
Paul A. Anderson Chair in the Arts Collection
Purchase, 2011.9

"Portrait painting has ever been the art most appreciated in England—the most appreciated and yet the most neglected." (L.C. 111)

Sir Peter Lely was one of England's most famous seventeenth-century portrait painters, living and working through some of the country's most uncertain times. He began working as King Charles I's court painter until Charles' beheading in 1642, contributed to Oliver Cromwell's dour Puritan-influenced portraits (Knoppers 1282), and served as King Charles II's official court painter when Charles was "restored" to the throne in 1660.

The portrait was considered a sign of social status, and Lely's studio was popular with both aristocrats and members of the new middle class. After Lely would paint a subject's head, his students would finish the portrait, choosing from an array of pre-determined poses. Among Lely's most famous contributions were the "Windsor Beauties," ten portraits of women from Charles II's court, including Barbara Palmer, one of Charles' mistresses. These portraits, "handsomely déshabillé and languorous," conveyed the hedonistic, libertine spirit of Charles II's court (Rodgers). Charles' mistresses were not confined to the aristocracy; a lover of the theatre, Charles had affairs with at least two actresses, including Nell Gwyn.

This portrait demonstrates the dual nature of Nell Gwyn's image by 1675. Gwyn was born into abject poverty and worked in one of London's seediest brothels before getting her start as one of England's first actresses. By 1675, however, Gwyn was retired from the stage and enjoying life as Charles II's mistress. Her hair is styled in the latest fashion and she wears the indicators of her material wealth, an expensive strand of pearls, in her hair and around her neck. In that respect, the painting is of a moneyed woman, worthy of respect and titles in English society.

There are marked differences, however, between this portrait and those of the Windsor Beauties, which all indicate Gwyn's "base" background. Her clothing is not elaborate and lush; rather, it appears as if Gwyn is wearing a nightgown and is in a state of partial undress. As a subject, she is captured raising a cloth over what the viewer can imagine are her exposed breasts. These details demonstrate that Gwyn is also a lower class woman, the property of any man who desires her.

The portrait is a realistic portrayal of Nell Gwyn at this point in her life, as a woman in a liminal position: both lady and kept woman, moneyed and in need of protection, demure and sexual, base-born but intimately connected to the monarch. She was a woman situated between two oppositional social positions, incapable of fully occupying either.

[Jennifer Popple, *Adjunct Instructor of English and Liberal Studies*]

32

Epigonation, early 16th century
Artist unknown (Italian), Venice
Embroidered vestment fragment: silk, gold and silver fibers, emerald, 30.0 x 30.0 cm., 11-7/8 x 11-7/8"
Gift of Dr. Paul Plante, Augustana College Art Collection, 2008.33

This embroidered panel came to the Augustana collection identified as a sixteenth-century Venetian work. Such a classification may seem strange given the Greek inscription that runs along the border, but works of art bearing Greek letters or executed in a Greek manner would have been entirely common in Renaissance Venice, as that city had long political and religious ties with the Byzantine empire as well as colonies in Greece and the Aegean. The diamond-shaped textile is most likely an *epigonation*, a stiff fabric panel bishops and other high-ranking church officials of the Orthodox church hung over their belt to rest on their right thighs (Woodfin 305 and Johnstone 18-19). If this *epigonation* is from Venice, then it probably came from the church of San Giorgio dei Greci, the Orthodox church (completed 1573) that served the large Greek population that resided in the city during the Renaissance.

The inscription, a verse from Psalms (45:3), reads, "Gird Your sword upon Your thigh, O Mighty One, With Your glory and Your majesty." These words allude to the origins of the *epigonation* (Father Papanikolaou). Byzantine emperors bestowed on their military commanders ceremonial swords, usually accompanied by thigh shields suspended from the belt, to honor their bravery and feats in defending the empire. Over time, clergy also received this imperial tribute, but were granted only the thigh shield, which eventually morphed into a common liturgical vestment that symbolizes defense of the faith (Johnstone 19).

A half-length image of Christ occupies the center of this *epigonation*, identified by the Greek abbreviation for the name Jesus Christ—ICXC—and the gold nimbus that frames his head. Surrounded by swirls of floral patterns, he raises both hands in a gesture of benediction, and is dressed as an archbishop while wearing the crown of an emperor, a reference to his power over both spiritual and worldly affairs. Textiles were costly items and critical to the liturgical context as they enhanced the visual and material magnificence of church interiors. This example is no exception, despite its worn condition. Made largely from silk, it was embroidered with gold and silver threads as well as jewels, evidenced by the one emerald that still adorns Christ's crown.

[Margaret Morse, *Assistant Professor of Art History*]

33

Mercury Attaching his Wings, after 1741 terracotta, n.d.
Jean-Baptiste Pigalle (French 1714–1785)
Cast bronze, 57.0 x 27.7 x 32.5 cm., 22-1/2 x 10-7/8 x 12-7/8"
Paul A. Anderson Chair in the Arts Collection Purchase,
Augustana College Art Collection, SDC2000.37

Pictured here, is a bronze replica of Jean-Baptiste Pigalle's eighteenth-century statue of Mercury. As the god of trade and trusted messenger of the mythological pantheon, he appears anxious to take flight as he twists to attach his winged sandal. His winged hat or *petasus*, and the *caduceus* (a staff with entwined snakes) that lies at his feet, further identify the figure as Mercury.

The original statue was created during the Neoclassical period in France. During this period, artists derived inspiration from the artistic traditions of the Greek and Roman past, denying the superfluous aesthetics of the Rococo. Art of the Rococo favored curvilinear lines, pastel colors, and subject matter that frequently depicted the elite engaging in trivial activity (catalogue 38 and 40). Emerging from the Rococo was a philosophical movement that dissented from the aristocratic mores. Known as the Enlightenment, this movement promoted science and rationality and looked to Greece and Rome as ideal civilized societies. This invariably influenced artists' awareness in depicting classical motifs and subject matter.

Interest in antique art was furthered by several other factors such as the *Grand Tour*. The Grand Tour was popular throughout the eighteenth century, and involved touring many European countries, sometimes over the course of several years, while learning about each country's history, politics and culture. Italy in particular was a popular destination. It was upon returning from Rome, that Pigalle created his initial statue of Mercury. The Grand Tour, along with the contemporaneous excavations of Pompeii and Herculaneum, fueled a public interest in the classical past.

Also influential was the German philosopher, Johann Joachim Winckelmann, who is often considered the first modern art historian. In his most notable work, *Thoughts on the Imitation of Greek Art in Painting and Sculpture*, he purported that Greek art had created an ideal aesthetic, based on the harmonious composition of parts. He theorized that Greek artists had developed an imaginative method of extracting the most beautiful parts of nature, to create an ideal, harmonious whole. Pigalle, clearly inspired by the antique past, represents an idealized nude in a posture that serves to enhance the figure, underscoring the perfection of form that is derived from nature. The twisted position of the figure enhances the muscular physique of the youth, as his muscles flex to support his posture. The polished bronze adds a sensuous element to his naked form, which juxtaposes the rigid folds of the swirling drapery. When considered independently, the nude form, the youthful appearance and the textured bronze incite mediocrity—but when combined, they create a harmonious, idealized whole.

[Megan MacCall, *Director, Digital and Visual Resources, Department of Art History*]

34A

Page from the work titled *Madarik al-Ahkam* by Muhammad al-ʿAmili, (d. 1600), ca. 1800
Artist and calligrapher unknown
Casein on vellum, 23.1 x 14.9 cm., 9 x 5-7/8" image and text within framing lines
Lent Courtesy of Private Collection in Memory of Reverend E. A. O'Connor

Depicted in these illustrations is a marriage of two worlds: Islamic jurisprudence and the court of Qajar Iran. The Qajars, fond of paintings depicting hunting scenes, also had a pragmatic interest in a particular method of interpreting Islamic law. This interpretive school, the Usuli School, emphasized rational derivation of law from scriptural sources, and it had only recently emerged triumphant after over a century of contending against a traditionalist school that frowned upon the use of individual reason in determining law, namely, the Akhbari School. The authors of the two books subject to illustration here epitomize this rationalist approach to Shiʿi jurisprudence.

While the content of the discussions depicted (divorce and ritual purity) might seem technical or even bland, the victory of their legal approach might have been exciting enough to warrant the production of such books. It is interesting that the authors of these texts represent bookends, in a way. The first author, Muhammad al-ʿAmili (d. 1600), is earlier and emphatically rational. His more well-known name, "Author of the Madarik," derives from the work depicted here. The second, ʿAli Tabataba'i (d. 1815), lived either during or near the time of this production. While Tabataba'i was centered in Karbala, ʿIraq, his following as a doctor of law extended all the way to India, affirming the scope of influence such scholars had acquired by this time.

The illustrated manuscript echoes a time when book-making was not an industry, but an art. These lengthy productions were written entirely by hand, and beautifully so. One of these two compositions, in a contemporary printing, can span eleven volumes, which suggests the amount of work that went into their production. The

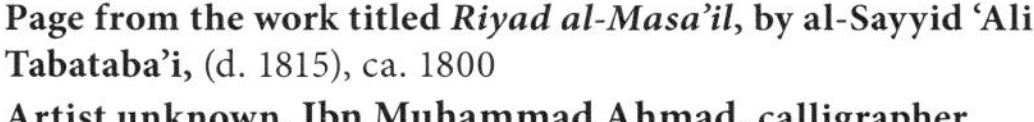

Page from the work titled *Riyad al-Masa'il*, by al-Sayyid ʿAli Tabataba'i, (d. 1815), ca. 1800
Artist unknown, Ibn Muhammad Ahmad, calligrapher
Casein on vellum, 24.6 x 16.5 cm., 9-13/16 x 6-1/2" image and text within framing lines
Lent Courtesy of Private Collection in Memory of Reverend E. A. O'Connor

calligrapher signs off at the end of this section that he wrote the manuscript "with my sinful, ephemeral hand, and I am the base servant Ibn Muhammad Ahmad, serving with pleasure." The calligrapher's signature at the end of one section or "book" signifies that, by this time, the artist as an individual has come to replace the artistic anonymity of the past. Working with a reed pen, the calligrapher aims to have a sense of regularity in the length and style of letters, to project beauty yet also lucidity, and, clearly also, to make a name for himself.

That a team of calligraphers, illustrators, paper-makers, and book-binders were commissioned to do projects of this sort is nothing new. It seems distinctive of the Qajar period, though, that they exerted such efforts for works of Shiʿi religious law, as opposed to epic poetry, for example. It is intriguing that the images truly have nothing to do with the text at all. They are simply adornments indicating the quality of production. These manuscripts were likely produced for the Shah's court, so they needed regal pictures to make them suit their elitist audience, an audience that was probably not all that interested in the content of the text itself. Thus these illustrated manuscripts stand as visual representations of the intertwining of courtly and clerical interests, in a not-so-distant age when rulers relied on religious scholars for authority and even legitimacy.

[Cyrus Ali Zargar, *Assistant Professor of Religion, Islamic Studies*]

35

Sahasrabhuja Avalokiteshvara, n.d.
Artist unknown (Chinese attribution)
Cast bronze, 37.3 x 21.7 x 12.1 cm., 14-11/16 x 8-1/2 x 4-3/4"
Augustana College Art Collection, 1993.3

Sahasrabhuja Avalokiteshvara (Chinese *Qianshou Guanyin*; Japanese *Senju Kannon*), or the thousand-armed lord who looks down with compassion, is one of the Buddhist figures known as *Bodhisattvas* (Enlightenment Beings). In early Buddhism, the term Bodhisattva refers to the historical Buddha (*Siddhartha Gautama/Shakyamuni*) before his enlightenment as Buddha. In later Buddhism, a Bodhisattva often refers to any being who takes a vow to delay his or her own enlightenment in order to save all beings from *samsara* (the cycle of rebirth and redeath).

The concept of the Bodhisattva became prominent in Pure Land Buddhism, where the Bodhisattva Avalokiteshvara is associated with the Buddha Amida (*Amitabha*). According to Pure Land Buddhism, beings that have faith in Amida and recite his name are automatically born into his Pure Land also known as the Western Paradise. Beings reborn in the Pure Land are assured liberation from samsara. The Bodhisattva dwells in the Pure Land of Amida and assists him in ensuring the salvation of beings.

According to the Buddhist texts, *Sahasrabhuja Avalokiteshvara* has one thousand arms with eleven small faces (each is a transformed Buddha form) on top of the main head. The Bodhisattva's immense compassion and capacity, represented by the vast number of arms, are believed to save all sentient beings from perils in this world and the next. Some of the painted or sculpted *Sahasrabhuja Avalokiteshvara* images have one thousand arms, but most have forty-two, with two principal palms pressed together in supplication, and twenty arms each on the right and left sides. Each of these forty arms symbolizes twenty-five arms (forty times twenty-five equals one thousand), and holds an attribute (item) that has a symbolic meaning.

Augustana's *Sahasrabhuja Avalokiteshvara* is of a further abbreviated form: it has only sixteen arms and four faces in addition to the main head. It still carries some typical attributes of *Sahasrabhuja Avalokiteshvara*; for example, a skull for subjugating evil spirits, and sun and moon disks for curing blindness and fever. It is distinctive of this statue to have a large *mandorla* (halo surrounding the figure). In the Indian texts, Avalokiteshvara is male, but in China Guanyin, also known as the Goddess of Mercy, is more often female than male. In Japan, Kannon's gender is ambiguous. Although the origin of Augustana's sculpture is unknown, it was probably produced in China.

[Nirmala Salgado, *Professor of Religion* and
Naoko Gunji, *Assistant Professor of Art History*]

36A&B

36A

Landscape with Waterfall and Figure on a Rocky Path, 18th–19th century
Artist unknown (Japanese)
Ink drawing on scroll, 109.8 x 39.0 cm., 43-3/16 x 15-5/16" image
Paul A. Anderson Chair in the Arts Collection Purchase in Honor of Cyrus and Mildred Churchill, Augustana College Art Collection, 2007.23.a

36B

Landscape with Waterfall and Figure on a Bridge, 18th–19th century
Artist unknown (Japanese)
Ink drawing on scroll, 110.7 x 38.9 cm., 43-1/4 x 15-1/4" image
Paul A. Anderson Chair in the Arts Collection Purchase in Honor of Cyrus and Mildred Churchill, Augustana College Art Collection, 2007.23.b

This pair of hanging scrolls of landscape paintings depicts a so-called *monumental landscape*, a style that originated in Song China (960-1279). The style typically portrays a grand-scale mountain with subordinate, small-scale streams, rocks, trees on slopes and paths for travelers, representing not an actual view of nature but a conceptual vision of the macrocosmic universe. In Japan, where it was executed almost exclusively with monochrome ink, its popularity grew in the Muromachi period (1333-1573) and onwards.

The scrolls at Augustana depict tiny architectural structures—from the foreground, a bridge, pathways, buildings that may be a restaurant and a pavilion, and a Buddhist temple sanctuary—against dominant mountains in the background. From the cliffs of the mountains, two waterfalls flow down to a river. Trees are shaped with strong brushstrokes as if projecting from the surface of the paintings. Travelers in the foreground are taking pilgrimages to the temple.

It is unknown how Augustana's landscape paintings were used, but they may have served as part of an architectural setting in which a viewer could identify him/herself with depicted pilgrims and undergo a spiritual journey to the sacred temple, by shifting his/her perspective from the bottom corner, where a traveler and his attendant are crossing over the bridge, to the top, where the temple stands at the peak of the sacred mountain.

Landscape is one of the most significant and enduring subjects in the East Asian tradition, and embodies a spiritual essence of the universe. The term *san/sui*, the Japanese equivalent of the western "landscape," is composed of two characters for mountain and water—two opposite elements, mountain for yang and water for yin—thereby epitomizing a perfect balance of the entire universe. By uniting him/herself with the depicted vast universe as if he/she were traveling in the mountain, the viewer could purify and nourish his/her mind and spirit, in the same way a pilgrim could through ascetic religious practices in a sacred mountain.

[Naoko Gunji, *Assistant Professor of Art History*]

37

Jacob's Dream, ca. 17th century
Artist unknown
Carved ivory relief, 2.6 x 7.2 x .7 cm., 1-1/16 x 2-7/8 x 5/16"
Paul A. Anderson Chair in the Arts Collection Purchase, Augustana College Art Collection, 2000.57

The piece shown here is an ivory relief carving. The subject of the carving is one of the most popular stories in the Old Testament—Jacob's dream at Bethel, which is narrated in Genesis 28. The carving is quite small (it barely measures 7 cm on its longest side), but it contains a wealth of detail. The piece is unsigned but it is definitely modern, and it can be dated to the seventeenth century on the basis of stylistic features.

Seventeenth-century art was characterized by a number of styles, including Baroque, classicism, realism, and naturalism. Landscapes, portraits, and still lives were common; classical themes, which had dominated the Renaissance, continued to be popular. Religious subjects were also popular, and painters such as Caravaggio, Georges de La Tour, Rembrandt van Rijn, and Peter Paul Rubens set biblical stories to canvas. Not all religious art produced in the seventeenth century was Baroque, and not all Baroque art was religious. However, a good deal of Baroque art was religious in content, and several features of *Jacob's Dream* suggest a Baroque influence. For example, the gestures of the angels exhibit a melodrama that is found in Baroque paintings such as Guercino's *The Resurrection of Lazarus*—the gestures of the angels, like the gestures of Christ and Lazarus in Guercino's painting, are exaggerated and striking, and they draw the viewer into the scene. Furthermore, the movement of the angels in *Jacob's Dream* exhibits a dynamism that can be found in Baroque paintings (catalogue 28) such as Rubens' *Deposition from the Cross* (Giorgi 84-89, 126-129). One scholar describes Baroque dynamism: "The new compositions were asymmetrical, with wide use of diagonals and sinuous forms that did not entangle forms, but rather freed them into the so-called open form that helped project a sense of boundless space, of a yearning for the immense" (Giorgi 126). These words can be accurately applied, I think, to the angels on Jacob's ladder. Melodrama and dynamism were not just found in Baroque painting—they were common in Baroque stucco relief, which was frequently used in Baroque architecture (Giorgi 119-20). The creator of *Jacob's Dream* may have been influenced by Baroque stucco relief, though we cannot know this for certain. At any rate, he certainly seems to have been influenced by Baroque art.

The story of Jacob's dream at Bethel has fascinated Jews and Christians for centuries. Several features of *Jacob's Dream* suggest that it was created by a Christian artist. For example, Christian writers (including St. Paul) have long referred to the Cross as a tree, and the carving represents Jacob sleeping under a large cruciform (cross-shaped) tree. The image of the tree would naturally be interpreted as a reference to the Cross in the seventeenth century, and it is difficult to imagine that the artist did not intend the viewer to interpret the piece in this way. Still, the shape and placement of the tree may be purely coincidental. Again, we cannot know for sure. What we do know is that *Jacob's Dream*, like the biblical story on which it is based, offers rich possibilities for interpretation.

[Leslie Wolf, *Fellow of Philosophy*]

***Les Hazard Heureux de L'escarpolette* (The Happy Accidents of the Swing or The Swing),** after the 1767 painting, 1782
After Jean-Honoré Fragonard (French 1732–1806), engraved by Nicolas DeLaunay (1739–1792)
Engraving, 59.7 x 44.6 cm., 23-9/16 x 17-9/16" image
Paul A. Anderson Chair in the Arts Collection
Purchase, Augustana College Art Collection, 2010.3

Producing art in an age of frivolity and decadence, Jean-Honoré Fragonard showed a deep understanding of the style widely accepted by the French public in the eighteenth century. The aesthetics of the Rococo movement exemplify the vices of debauchery and excess quite present at the time, a lifestyle King Louis XV brought to the limelight with his royal succession in the mid eighteenth century. Consequently, popular artists of the time felt a need to produce lavish pieces to adorn the ornate residences of French aristocrats. As a result, artists such as Fragonard may have never truly found their full creative potential as they instead subscribed to the style they knew patrons and consumers desired (Sheriff 2).

The Swing is no exception to the sumptuous subject matter practically synonymous with the Rococo movement. This eighteenth-century engraving is a mirror image of the original oil painting. The omnipresent eroticism mixed with lush surroundings hints at indulgence and flirtation, both between humankind and nature. We see a nymph-like maiden being pushed on a swing by an older man, presumably her father or husband, into the gaze of a young boy who has positioned himself so as to see the girl's undergarments with the undulation of the ropes (Cuzin 97).

Viewers are entranced by the juxtaposition of the Utopian surroundings and provocative gestures. The woman seems pleased with her admirer, tossing her dainty shoe as an act of flirtation, or invitation of sorts, which either the boy will have to return or she will have to fetch, inevitably causing an interaction. We delight in the playfulness of the vignette-like snapshot, yet we sympathize for the poor man unknowingly, and literally, pushing his daughter or mate into impious arms. Even the young cupid sculpture on the right has his finger to his lips, as if to warn of the repercussions of lust. In this way, the work encapsulates the strains of primitive desire, as human desire is often a negative thing, even when placed in such a quaint setting. The twisting of branches and billowing of leaves leads the eye upwards at which point we notice natural light, perhaps a hint at what is to come from the heavens if these mortals continue with their impurities. Originally painted in 1767, this piece commemorates the height of Fragonard's artistic career as a painter of eroticism, or more broadly the Rococo, as his wealthy clientele specifically requested amorous scenes packed with splendor and lust, truly validating the time period as one of a celebration of earthly delights in which the patron and viewer can revel (Cuzin 97).

[Katherine E. Goebel, *Assistant Editor*]

39

Portrait of a Lady in a Blue Gown, ca. 1748
Attributed to John Hesselius (American, born to Swedish immigrant, 1728–1778) [Carlton Neville and Stephanie Strass]
Oil on canvas, 119.9 x 89.5 cm., 47-1/4 x 35-1/4"
Gift of Neville-Strass Collection to Augustana College; Conservation Funding Assisted by Mr. and Mrs. George and Pat Olson, Mr. Dan Churchill, and Gift of Services by Mr. Barry Bauman, 2004.4

In eighteenth-century American portraiture, definitive attributions are rare. Such is the case with this portrait of a lady in a blue gown. Although the attribution to John Hesselius remains tentative, it is extremely persuasive. It was first suggested when the painting was sold at auction in 1988 (Sloan's 1988). Since that time the donors conducted extensive research and located a similar portrait of a female member of the Byrd family, likewise attributed to John Hesselius (*Antiques* 1962). The woman in the Byrd picture is wearing an almost identical blue gown with white trim and a cord tied loosely around her waist. Both women have silk drapes, loosely slung around their backs, folded in identical patterns. The compositions are also similar. Several elements are quoted nearly verbatim, such as the pose of the women, the placement of the pedestals and the backgrounds. Since the two portraits appear to be by the same artist, we can likewise consider this painting to also be by John Hesselius.

Hesselius was one of the first successful native-born American portrait painters. He most likely received his earliest training from his father, the Swedish born painter, Gustavus Hesselius (1682–1755), known principally for church painting. Like most colonial artists of the time, the younger Hesselius absorbed influences from a variety of sources, such as fellow native-born artist Robert Feke and English artist John Wollaston. If this picture is indeed the work of John Hesselius, then it may date from the early 1750s, when he first began mimicking Wollaston's emphasis on luxurious fabrics with rich folds, while simplifying decorative patterns. Augustana's portrait foreshadows the impact Hesselius would have on the younger generation of American colonial portraitists. The woman's solid mass, inescapable presence and direct gaze are traits that Hesselius's student, Charles Willson Peale (1741–1827), would incorporate into his own portraits, including those of George Washington (Saunders and Miles 251-253).

Because Hesselius was one of the most mobile colonial portraitists, the identity of this woman remains a mystery. Hesselius traveled to Philadelphia, to Maryland and to Virginia, fulfilling commissions. As a result, this woman could have been from any of those cities or any community in between. Although her costume clearly indicates she hails from a wealthy family, there is nothing shown in the painting that could elucidate her identity. She is not wearing jewelry. Nor is she holding a book or musical instrument and is not wearing a specific uniform. The absence of these details maintains this woman's anonymity.

Despite the fact that this painting perhaps encourages more questions than it answers, it is an example of a particularly dynamic period in American history. It illustrates the emergence of a powerful middle class that is simultaneously exuding its British colonial pride, while creating strong, independent communities, economic markets and individual identities. Moreover, this portrait was created when the status of painters was shifting from practical craftsmen to learned gentlemen. The work of Hesselius and this painting specifically embody this new American spirit.

[Emily Vokt Ziemba, *Class of 1998*]

Hebe, attributed to mid 18th century
Artist unknown
Oil on canvas, 38.3 x 32.9 cm., 15-1/16 x 13"
Paul A. Anderson Chair in the Arts Collection Purchase, Augustana College Art Collection, 2004.10

In the eighteenth century, French art evolved through various styles to gradually meet new demands. Painters began to depict the elitist pleasures found within the sumptuous lifestyle of the French aristocrats during this period. The Rococo style, in fact, was based upon the priorities of royalty and the aristocratic class in France, molded by eighteenth-century *feminine* taste and influence.

Hebe is a French Rococo painting created within this context. In reaction to the previous Baroque style, Rococo taste shifted from masculine pieces based on the past, to lighter subjects that were tasteful to the eighteenth-century female eye. In this particular painting, the female subject is portrayed as the beautiful *Hebe*, the mythological goddess of youth and the cupbearer to the gods (Reid 490). Although the identity of the artist remains unknown, it is most likely based on Jean-Marc Nattier's *Madame de Caumartin as Hebe* from 1753, although the female sitter is different. Similar to Nattier's piece, the woman holds a pitcher and cup in her hands in order to serve the gods. The vessel's form resembles, and was probably inspired by, the ancient cups that were unearthed at the excavations of the lost Roman city of Pompeii, rediscovered in the early eighteenth century after long being buried beneath the erupted rubble of Mt. Vesuvius. Hebe was the daughter of Jupiter and Juno, the king and queen of the gods, and was said to have married the great Hercules when he ascended to Mount Olympus. The bird flying through the pastel sky is either Jupiter's attribute or the personification of the god himself, disguised as an eagle.

This painting carefully balances its dual purpose of depicting an actual portrait of a Rococo woman and illustrating a classical goddess. The pastel colors of light pinks and blues, representing delicacy and feminine taste, are typical of the Rococo style. Attention is drawn to Hebe's face through minute detail and brilliant lighting. Rather than showing her rank or position, the artist concentrated more on the subject's expression, gesture and individual personality, inviting the viewer to consider her thoughts.

[Erin Reeverts, *Class of 2008*]

41A

Cupid Disarm'd by Euphrosine. Metastasio, Vol. 7, 1784
After Angelica Kauffmann (Swiss 1741–1807) by Thomas Burke (Irish 1749–1815)
Stipple etching, 35.4 x 39.0 cm., 13-15/16 x 15-3/8" sheet
Lent Courtesy of Private Collection

Swiss painter and etcher Angelica Kauffmann was a major Rococo/Neoclassical artist who achieved remarkable success for a female artist of her time. She was accepted into the Accademia de S. Luca in Rome at the young age of twenty-three; she was one of two female founding members of the British Royal Academy in 1768; and she garnered the patronage and support of international royalty, including the family of Britain's George III, Russia's Grand-Duke Paul and Prince Nikolay Yusupov, Poland's Stanislav II Poniatowski and Stanislav Kostka Potocki, Naples' Queen Caroline, and Austria's Emperor Joseph II (*Grove Art Online*). As a Classicist with an interest in Women's and Gender Studies, I was initially drawn to Kauffmann's work because of her use of Classical themes. In researching her life and work further, however, I was intrigued at more pervasive connections with the Classical world as well.

While the appearance of Classical subject matter in art of the 18th-century Neoclassical period is not unusual, it was unusual for a woman of the time to specialize in subject pictures because of the prejudice against women studying anatomy (*Grove Art Online*). Nonetheless, by her mid-twenties, Kauffmann became determined not to confine herself to the portraiture more accepted for women artists and she began to study Classical sculpture. Today, Kauffmann is best known for the small Neoclassical scenes she subsequently produced and which were disseminated through engravings. The two works featured here, *Cupid Binding Agalia to a Laurel* (41B) and *Cupid Disarmed by Eiphrosine* (41A) are typical, focusing on scenes including the god of love and two of the three *Kharites*, or Graces. In addition to mythological subjects like these, Kauffmann also drew from literature, as with her *Hector and Andromache* and *Penelope at*

41B

Cupid Binding Aglaia to a Laurel, 1784
After Angelica Kauffmann (Swiss 1741–1807) by Thomas Burke (Irish 1749–1815)
Stipple etching, 35.0 x 38.8 cm., 13-3/4 x 15-1/4" sheet
Lent Courtesy of Private Collection

her Loom, and history, as with *Cleopatra Adorning the Tomb of Marc Antony* and *Virgil Reading the "Aeneid" to Augustus and Octavia*. While she continued to earn most of her income from portraiture, she incorporated her interest in history paintings by overlaying them with Classical allegories: for instance, in her *Marchioness Townshend and her Son*, the subjects are portrayed as Venus and Cupid, and her *Frances Hoare* includes a sacrificial offering to a statue of Minerva (ibid.).

There has been, in addition, suggestion that Kauffmann's interest in Classical subjects stemmed from more personal connections: in an article on Kauffmann's 1775 *Sappho (Burlington Magazine* Vol. 113 no. 818: May 1971), Peter A. Tomory notes "considerable similarities in the shape of the head, the mouth in particular and the eyes" between the image of Sappho in this piece and in Kauffmann's two self-portraits (275). As a pioneering female artist of her day, Sappho might well have had a particular appeal to Kauffmann, who in addition, as Tomory points out, includes in this painting lines from Sappho's *Ode to Aphrodite*, in which the poetess is "sorely troubled" due to problems with love, much as Kauffmann herself would have been around the time of its production (275). Others have likewise suggested that in a broader sense, Kauffmann's heroines represent the artist herself in a similarly personal way (Fuseli noted in Tomory 1971.275). Kauffmann's connections to the Classical world are also reflected in her connections to Rome, where she spent much of her career, and where her final tribute was paid with a triumphal procession of two of her works, emulating the funeral of Raphael, but also a clear nod to the Classical tradition.

[Kirsten Day, *Assistant Professor of Classics*]

42

A, B, C...Sampler, 1789
Zerviah Crocker (American, born ca. 1781)
Embroidered, hand-woven linen sampler, 32.0 x 23.5 cm., 12-5/8 x 9-1/4"
Paul A. Anderson Chair in the Arts Collection Purchase, Augustana College Art Collection, 2000.3

Zervia Crocker's *A, B, C...Sampler* is a charming piece of needlework that gathers together the various details of a world that is far distant from us today. Like the pages of an old manuscript, Zervia's stitches provide us with a glimpse into history—and the educational practices of the late 1700s. At first glance, the virtue of this particular sampler is characterized by an ornamental band of letters and numbers, three houses with French pane windows, and a lovely, undulating hand-stitched border. A more purposeful examination of the needlework reveals the stitcher's name, age, town, and date. An even richer analysis brings us back to eighteenth-century colonial America when education for young women was limited to skills that would make them good wives and mothers.

This enchanting peek into the past was completed by Zerviah Wednesday Crocker. Zerviah was born circa June 26, 1781 to Alvan Friday Crocker and Sylvia Thatcher Crocker of Barnstable, Massachusetts (Cifelli). The Crockers, a very prominent family in the early 1600s, were one of six founding families located on the cape of Massachusetts. Zervia was the youngest of their seven children (Ring). Her cross-stitched sampler displays remarkable skill for a young child. The fancy letter "A," the gabled doorway, the latticed fence, and the intricate chain stitches and flowers around the houses show meticulous artistry. After completed, a superior sampler such as hers might have been hung in the home to impress prospective suitors when they came to call (Cleaveland). Darning, mending, and marking fine linens were extremely important tasks in the home and girls were not considered marriageable until they had mastered the art of stitchery (Ulrich).

Samplers were more than an elegant pastime or means of self-expression. They are also enduring examples of what the school experience looked like in the late 1700s. The embroidered display of letters and numbers was used as a teaching tool and memory aid—to assist Zerviah and other young girls with the alphabet and numbers (Hlebowitsh and Tellez). This *curriculum* was considered a most fit and proper form of education for women during the late 1700s. Later (*since Zervia's future dominion would be the home*), these skills could be used for marking fine linens and clothing, since it was important that any homemaker keep track of her most valuable household goods.

As the nation entered the 19th century, educational reforms diminished the importance of the *domestic curriculum*. The country began to develop as a national entity and the *public school* was conceived as an agent that could provide social and economic opportunities to all (Hlebowitsch and Tellez). This common national experience (which has evolved into a push towards high-stakes testing, state-mandated directives, and federally imposed sanctions—aka *No Child Left Behind*) will call for new forms of female expression. One can only hope that the memories stitched into the samplers of tomorrow commemorate quality, equity, and community.

[Deborah Bracke, *Assistant Professor of Education*]

A Night Piece, 1795
Margaret Williamson
Embroidered, silk thread, hand-woven linen sampler, 40.6 x 41.3 cm., 16 x 16-1/4"
Paul A. Anderson Chair in the Arts Collection Purchase, Augustana College Art Collection, 2000.5

Margaret Williamson is identified only through her needlework. Her biography remains unknown. However upon examination of her sampler, *A Night Piece*, much can be deduced about this artist.

Upon initial examination, one might conclude that this 1795 sampler is of British origin because of the soft, pastel colors embroidered on hand-woven ivory linen. Note, however, that a basket of flowers is stitched onto the bottom left of the sampler. This basket motif was typically sewn into samplers by an eastern Massachusetts sampler school (Goebel 70). Margaret Williamson must have therefore attended this New England school and she was not English but American.

After the American Revolution and the emergence of the new federal government, "artists devise[d] a distinctive nationalistic culture around neoclassical principles, looking to the ancient republics of Greece and Rome for inspiration for their new Republic" ("The United States"). Margaret Williamson's sampler, *A Night Piece*, exemplifies this cultural influence through her choice of poetry which records lines 687-698 of the *Translation of Homer's 'The Iliad'* by Alexander Pope (1688-1744) (Mack). Although orthodox moral or religious texts were frequent choices in compositions for many samplers of this time, Williamson's selection of *A Night Piece* conveys not only her identification with contemporary social currents, but also her sophisticated ability to read, understand and illuminate this English version of *The Iliad*.

Late eighteenth-century samplers are generally characterized by depictions of genre scenes, houses and farm buildings, as well as flocks of animals with shepherds (Bolton and Coe 20). Williamson's sampler incorporates such a typical pastoral scene of a man playing a piped instrument accompanied by a shepherdess, dog and several sheep at the bottom of the poem. All are framed by a border of vines and flowers. Utilizing the embroidery techniques of chain stitches and French knots, the sampler is constructed with top quality linen and silk thread that would infer Williamson's financial ability to secure the finest.

Although we can only surmise that Williamson was an educated, fairly wealthy, American; her needlework remains her legacy. And as in so many cases of female sampler artists, "these small bits of embroidered cloth are often all that remains to testify to the otherwise unrecorded lives of their makers" (Peck).

[Deann Thoms, *Class of 1990*]

44

The Exhibition of the Royal Academy, 1787, 1787
Drawing by Johann Heinrich Ramberg (German 1763–1840), engraved by Pietro Antonio Martini (Italian 1739–1797)
Engraving, 35.5 x 49.5 cm., 14 x 19-1/2" image
Paul A. Anderson Chair in the Arts Collection Purchase, Conservation Funding Assisted by Professor Adrian R. Tió, Augustana College Art Collection, 2004.9

The Exhibition of the Royal Academy, 1787 is an engraving that was based on the original painting created in the same year by German artist, Johann Heinrich Ramberg. Ramberg, who was born in 1763, pursued most of his career in Germany, but spent some time in England studying from 1781 to 1788 under the great Neoclassical American expatriate and future President of the Royal Academy, Benjamin West (Turner 871). It was during this period in London that Ramberg created this piece. Pietro Antonio Martini was the engraver who reproduced Ramberg's artwork and translated it into a print.

This print's subject matter does not stem from history or tales of the gods, but instead illustrates real contemporary life in London. There is not much movement or action in the scene, since people are focused on verbal discourse and studying art. This particular work of art was made to celebrate the Prince of Wales' visit to the Royal Academy's exhibition. The prince's portrait by Sir Joshua Reynolds, the current President of the Royal Academy, hangs in the center of the back wall in the print (Rosenthal 602). The engraving shows many different social classes wandering about the gallery. Some people seem to belong to the middle class while still others are clearly aristocratic, such as the man standing front and center dressed in light clothing. There appears to be a clergyman to his left. Dogs are surprisingly roaming and playing freely in the academy exhibition.

The Royal Academy was established in 1768 in England as a vehicle for artists to display their works. These exhibits were the first large-scale non-commercial art exhibitions held in England (Turner 677). The Great Room at Somerset House, the headquarters for the Academy then and now, which is depicted in this print, was a massive space that could hold between two and three hundred oil paintings on its walls. Somerset House opened in 1780 and held the Academy's annual summer exhibitions. The institution quickly became a great success, as evidenced in the fact that during the first two months of its opening, over 61,000 viewers made their way through the exhibit (Turner 603). The most interesting aspect to this work is perhaps the method of exhibiting a massive number of works within a relatively limited space. The paintings are hung so close together that there was little room for explanation or identification. Paintings at the highest level are four or five times higher than the people in the picture. Exhibition techniques have clearly changed over the years .

[J.D. Rotzoll, *Class of 2008*]

Marriage A-la-Mode: The Marriage Contract, Plate I, 1745
William Hogarth (English/British 1697–1764)
Etching with engraving, from series of six plates, fourth state of seven, 38.4 x 46.8 cm., 15-1/8 x 18-1/2" image
Paul A. Anderson Chair in the Arts Collection Purchase, Augustana College Art Collection, 2000.22

Hogarth's general philosophy was that art should not be extremely fancy. He rebelled against the feminine frills and idyllic scenes of the contemporary French Rococo style. He believed paintings should instead be didactic and deliver a message, often deeming that several moralistic scenes would more accurately tell the story, rather than limiting himself to just one. For instance, *Marriage A-la-Mode* (1743), a series of six images, makes a mockery of the wealthy upper class and their extravagant lifestyle. In traditional English manner, he advanced the storytelling potential of his art. Hogarth drew the faces of the characters in the original painted scenes himself, both since he was an experienced portrait painter and also because he understood, like a novelist, that proper character sketches made the scene palpable.

The Marriage Contract is the first of the six plates in this series. The setting is the home of Lord Earl Squanderfield, who is the father of the groom. He is seated to the left and holds a document containing a family tree which traces his family's aristocratic lineage back several generations. At the beginning, at the tree's base, is William the Conqueror, thus attesting to the Earl's long line of royal blood. In the background, through the window, a large building is under construction. This palace alludes to the reason why the marriage is taking place. Lord Earl Squanderfield is building a new home with such extravagant plans that it has put him into debt. He has no money left, only his noble title. The father of the bride, however, has made a great deal of money from his employment as a merchant, yet he is still not considered a member of the socially elite. Through this union, Lord Earl Squanderfield will acquire needed funds and the father of the bride will elevate his family's status through his daughter's new position (Cowley 29-30). The prospective bride and groom are located on the right side of the engraving. Although physically seated together, they display absolutely no psychological interest in one another.

[Kristin McLinden, *Class of 2008*]

46

Miniature Portrait of a Young Girl, early 19th century
Artist unknown
Watercolor on ivory, 8.0 x 6.5 cm., 3-1/8 x 2-1/2"
Paul A. Anderson Chair in the Arts Collection Purchase in Memory of Dr. Michael P. Nolan, Augustana College Art Collection, 2000.4

The nineteenth-century American *Miniature Portrait of a Young Girl* is heir to a long tradition. Miniatures grew from earlier forms of art, such as illuminated medieval religious manuscripts. Illuminated manuscripts often included a small painting showing the person who had financed the manuscript's reproduction, in prayer or handing the sacred text to a saint.

A second type of early influence—ancient portrait medallions, coins, and cameos—suggests a more public emphasis. Painted on vellum, early miniatures portrayed the kings, queens, and nobles in European courts. Miniatures came to the American colonies from Britain in the 1700s. At first those with political prominence were painted, such as the Revolutionary War heroes and early presidents. Upper and middle-class Americans became enamored with miniatures, commissioning them for life's signal moments, including births, engagements, marriages, and deaths.

The *Miniature Portrait of a Young Girl* was painted by an unknown American artist, most likely self taught, given the uneven technique. There is evidence of painterly skill: the girl's tousled hair is handled with finesse, set down in fine lines creating feathered locks that fall with a naturalness over the forehead. Refined brushwork creates the delicately blended hues of the girl's face. But there is awkwardness in the girl's hands, and neither the flowers nor clothing are represented with equivalent vividness. Does the miniature memorialize a dead child? Nineteenth-century iconography of death typically shows flowers with closed blooms. In the nineteenth-century "language of flowers," sweet peas were associated with "departure." But other pea blossoms were associated with the "everlasting, an appointed meeting, and lasting pleasure." If the flowers have a language, they offer us contradictory advice.

Whatever its intent, the portrait conveys strong affection for the child. The miniature's size and rectangular shape suggest that it was not carried or worn, but displayed. Perhaps the portrait was more akin to a studio photograph, meant, of course, to be a likeness, but also to capture something particular about the child. Today nearly 180 years later, it is hard not to be intrigued by the image, to wonder who the child was and who loved her enough to have her painted.

[Michael Nolan, *Adjunct Instructor of English*]

Miss Constance Malford, n.d.
Artist Unknown
Oil on wood panel
36.8 x 25.5 cm., 14-5/8 x 10-1/8"
Paul A. Anderson Chair in the Arts Collection Purchase,
Augustana College Art Collection, 2000.33

This oil painting illustrates a loose, painterly style similar to that of eighteenth-century English artist, William Hogarth, known for his effective images of children. This work perhaps reveals a slice of the lives of eighteenth and nineteenth-century working class children. It depicts a young girl, most likely dressed in secondhand clothing, common among poor families at the time. Perhaps she is wearing shoes too large, or maybe none at all (Mitchell 137). Holding what appears to be a full basket, she is probably following in her family's footsteps, helping with agricultural work.

For the majority of the nineteenth century, there were no laws regulating child labor, so children worked as much as adults and were often treated harshly. They started working regularly around the age of seven or eight, and sometimes as early as three or four (Mitchell 43). They would labor long, grueling hours, sunrise to sunset, and often walk miles to work. Children were ideal for urban factory work (catalogue 146) for several reasons: they did not need great strength because machinery provided most of the power, they had small hands and fingers to operate the equipment, and they were employed cheaply (Mitchell 2). Yet, even though they earned very little, their families, often large, depended on their earnings for daily survival. In rural society, large families provided more laborers for the family farm. Boys usually were put to work earlier than girls because they were physically stronger. Young children aided in tasks such as tending cattle or picking weeds, as they grew older, they helped with duties that required more strength such as plowing or mowing (Hopkins 12).

Another interpretation of this piece might be that this young girl is an aristocrat, *playing* at being a lower class rural child. Since the eighteenth-century example of Queen Marie Antoinette in her hamlet at Versailles, the social elite was fascinated with going back to nature and living *the simple life*. At this time, English artists like Thomas Gainsborough and Sir Joshua Reynolds depicted many upper class patrons, including children, in more relaxed and natural settings. The fact that the back of this piece is labeled: *Miss Constance Malford*, suggests that this young lady had some status during her lifetime. In addition, the gilt frame, if original, is an indication that this was deemed an important work of art. Constance may simply be carrying fruit or vegetables while dressed in *play clothes*, still rather ornate by our standards, but much more appropriate to the task than those she would have worn for high tea. The sparkling brushwork and the beautifully modeled face indicate a master's touch to this painting.

(Lauren Habenicht, *Class of 2001* and Catherine Carter Goebel, *Editor*)

48A&B

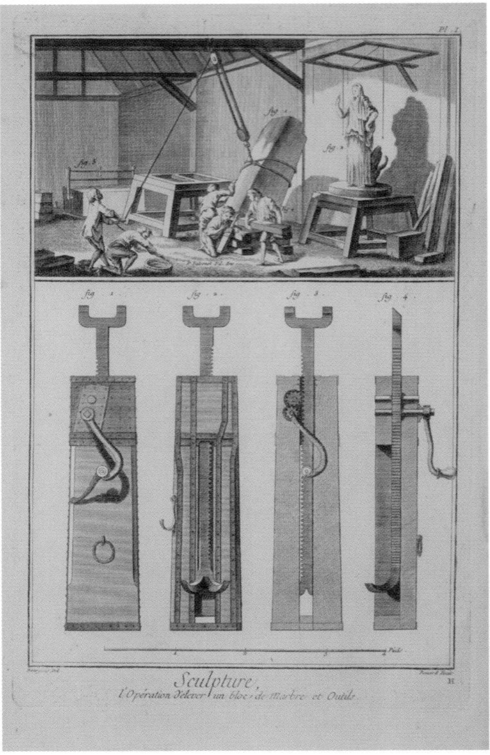

48A

48B

Encyclopédie of Diderot and d'Alembert
Robert Benard (French b. 1734, fl. 1750–1785), 1751-72
Engravings, 35.8 x 22.8 cm., 14-2/16 x 9" image, ***(A) Sculpture, l'opération d'élever un bloc de marbre et outils, Planche 1ère*** (Sculpture, Operation to Lift a Block of Marble and Tools. Plate One), ***(B) Antiquités, Planche IV*** (Antiquities, Plate IV)
Purchases with Gift of Elizabeth and John Ducey, Augustana College Art Collection, 2001.35. k, c

The *Encyclopédie,* edited by Denis Diderot and Jean d'Alembert, was developed by a large variety of contributors from many different backgrounds, from doctors and priests to nobility and merchants. Containing 72,000 articles, it represents one of the most important historical artifacts toward technology education (Wernick 72-80). The *Encyclopédie*, with its detailed illustrations of the mechanical arts, allowed industrial knowledge to be available to many people. This created a potential shift towards a liberal economic strength based more on the individual's self-interest. It also created a shift that minimized the amount of control the state and government had on industrial aspects. This particular plate (48A), engraved on laid paper, introduced a jack mechanism used for lifting marble blocks (*L'operation d'elever un bloc de marbre, & outils*) (ARTFL Project).

Featured at the top of the plate is a diagram (top Figures 1-5) that illustrates a situation where this tool would most commonly be used. At the bottom of the plate (Figures 1-4), the tool is depicted in four different views in order to communicate its constructive attributes. The contributors to the *Encyclopédie* developed an accurate integrated language that could be digested by the largest variety of people and paved the way towards approaches used in modern education.

[Jeffrey Weiland, *Class of 2008*]

The *Encyclopédie* reflected the basic philosophy of the European Enlightenment and the growing interest in intellectual pursuits, especially in the arts and sciences which are referenced within. The point of this work was to summarize contemporary knowledge and offer people a new way to look at the world. It was written by more than 140 contributors, many of them the *great thinkers* of the Enlightenment, with some of the more famous names being Jean-Jacques Rousseau, François-Marie Arouet de Voltaire, and Jean-François Marmontel (ARTFL).

[Katie Otter, *Class of 2008*]

Antiquitiés Planche IV (48B) was engraved by Robert Benard, a prolific engraver who was most active during the 1770s and 1780s. Ancient architecture as is depicted on this page, *Antiquitiés*, was extremely influential both culturally and artistically as the modern European world looked to its enlightened past for inspiration. As Pompeii and Herculaneum were being unearthed, students completed their Grand Tour and intellectuals fawned over the grandeur of the past. The architectural wonders of Rome particularly attracted many admirers. This specific engraving depicts three ancient structures in Rome, the Circus of Caracalla (or Circus of Maxentius), the Theater of Marcellus and the Forum Nerva. (ARTFL). Such imagery inspired many enthusiasts of antiquity to take the Grand Tour and visit these sites in person in order to experience firsthand the wonders of ancient Rome.

[Andrea Ritchie, *Class of 2008*]

49

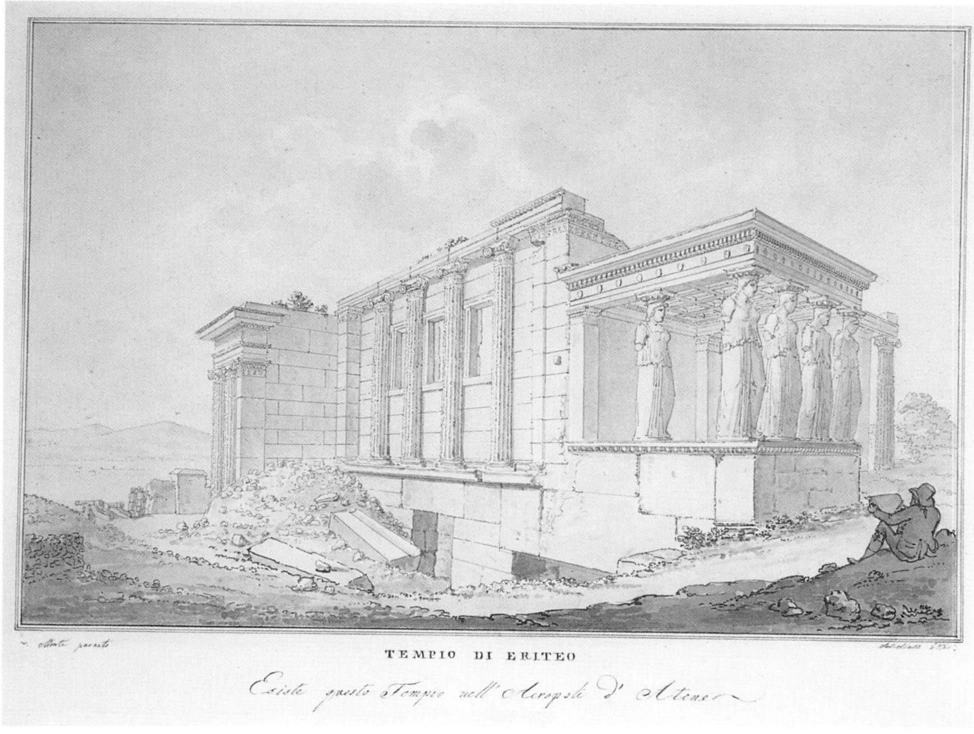

Tempio di Eriteo **(Erechtheum Temple)**, ca. late 18th century
Sebastiano
Pen and ink drawing, 15.7 x 23.3 cm., 6-1/4 x 9-1/4" image
Paul A. Anderson Chair in the Arts Collection Purchase, Augustana College Art Collection, 2000.36

Today's culture is accustomed to taking photographs of events that occur throughout our lives that we wish to capture and remember forever. Even more recently, with the advent of the computer age and digital photography, we take for granted the instantaneous record that we might capture and transmit to others. This wish to preserve and share an experience is not a newly developed concept. Sebastiano's *Tempio di Eriteo* demonstrates similar interests in response to the international Neoclassical movement.

The *Tempio di Eriteo* is a *snapshot*, of sorts, of one of the most revered stops along the *Grand Tour*. This Grand Tour consisted of extensive travel, primarily in Greece and Italy, often culminating with Rome, the Eternal City and a center for classical culture. It drew people from all over the United States and Europe, attracting a variety of devotees seeking intellectual and cultural enrichment. Many young gentlemen who embarked in their early to mid-twenties on the Grand Tour, considered it a final step in their formal education before taking on the responsibilities of manhood. The Neoclassical movement fueled this desire to directly confront the past and to seek inspiration from the classical cultures of ancient Greece and Rome.

The *Tempio di Eriteo*, one of many temples on the Acropolis in Athens, is distinctive for its caryatids (vertical supports carved into female figures) making up the *Porch of the Maidens* seen on the right side of the drawing. Sebastiano drew a picturesque atmosphere and applied the same compositional characteristics to paper that tourists today capture in a photograph, and in the same manner, this portable art could be taken anywhere to be admired by anyone. It is quite simple in format, yet very detailed in the ruin itself. The figure sketching in the lower right corner establishes scale and invites the viewer of this drawing to also study the ruins and develop an even deeper appreciation for its grandeur.

The *Tempio di Eriteo* and other such Grand Tour drawings were not just memories captured for an eighteenth-century audience. They have also become modern culture's *snapshots* from the past, and even though they do not reflect our own personal memories, we can appreciate and enjoy the drawings since they enable us to experience the ruins within their historic context. This drawing reveals to us in the twenty-first century, just how people over two centuries ago revered great monuments erected some twenty-three centuries before their time. In this manner, such images allow us access both to the ancient as well as the more recent past and seem to invite us to also visit the Erechtheum in order to construct our own context for such ancient wonders.

[Jennifer Windmiller, *Class of 2007*]

50

The Boston Massacre, 1770, 1970 restrike from original
Paul Revere (American 1735–1818)
Engraving, 20.5 x 23.0 cm., 8-1/16 x 9-1/16" image
Paul A. Anderson Chair in the Arts Collection Purchase, Augustana College Art Collection, 2010.45

On March 5, 1770, a mob hurled insults, snowballs and rocks at British troops stationed at the State House in Boston, Massachusetts. Threats came at the soldiers from all sides, including jeers daring them to "Fire!" At some point the troops mistakenly heard an order to fire and shot into the crowd, ultimately killing five persons and injuring eleven more. Captain Thomas Preston and his troops were arrested, but all but two were acquitted after a vigorous defense by none other than John Adams.

This depiction was printed from an original plate by Paul Revere, the silversmith and colonial patriot who became a revolutionary hero for his mythologized "midnight ride" of April 18-19, 1775. Revere copied extensively from a drawing by artist Henry Pelham, *The Fruits of Arbitrary Power* (Casper 22), without his permission (Kellogg 385-386). Revere's print, colored by Christian Remick, was included with an incendiary pamphlet prepared by Boston's town committee entitled *A Short Narrative of the Horrid Massacre in Boston*.

The print takes liberties with the historical truth of the event in order to amplify its impact as propaganda. Note how the British troops stand in single-file formation, releasing their fusillade upon the order of Captain Preston, whose sword arm is raised in command. Such an orchestrated attack never took place. The original print also displays the spewing blood of the victims in a vivid red, a sharp contrast to the otherwise muted hues of the colonists but a perfect match with the red coats of the death-dealing British troops. The death of Crispus Attucks, lionized as the first American casualty as well as the African American hero of the revolution, is depicted as the reclined head in the lower-left corner. However, his biracial identity is elided by the white skin tone. In the original pamphlet, the print is accompanied by a poem likely written by Revere. It begins:

> Unhappy Boston! See thy Sons deplore.
> They hallow'd Walks besmear'd with guiltless Gore.
> While faithless P-------n [Preston] and his savage Bands,
> With murd'rous Rancour stretch their bloody hands;
> Like fierce Barbarians grinning o'er their Prey,
> Approve the Carnage, and enjoy the Day
> (qtd. in Kellogg 383).

The word "propaganda" derives from the Latin *propagare*, to spread or disseminate, as one would spread seeds that take root, flower, and produce their own seeds which are propagated in turn. It is important for students of American history to remember that the power of propaganda has been a driving force of American political culture from the very beginning.

[Stephen A. Klien, *Associate Professor of Communication Studies*]

51

Declaration of Independence, after ca. 1786–1794 painting, ca. 1832
After John Trumbull (American 1756–1843) by Illman and Pilbrow (firm active circa 1829–1836)
Hand-colored engraving, 13.0 x 19.9 cm., 5-1/8 x 7-7/8" image
Purchase with Gift of Adam J. DeSimone and David A. DeSimone, Augustana College Art Collection, SDC2005.19

In 1817, President James Madison was given the authority by the United States Congress to hire an artist to create four paintings for the Rotunda of the Capitol Building in Washington D.C. President Madison designated John Trumbull to carry out this first official art commission awarded by the government. Following much discussion, they settled upon four important events from the American Revolution: *The Surrender of General Burgoyne*, *The Surrender of Lord Cornwallis at Yorktown*, *The Resignation of Washington*, and most importantly, *The Declaration of Independence*.

Trumbull decided that rather than fictionalizing and dramatizing the stories surrounding these events, he would create a straightforward American rendition. The men in the scene were not dressed in elegant clothing fit for a royal ceremony or papal benediction, or even in the classical drapery currently in vogue, they were instead represented in authentic American fashion. The room was decorated in plain, Classic Ionic form, providing the painting with a true sense of American simplicity and realism.

The brave men involved in signing *The Declaration of Independence* were not depicted as idealized warriors, but as real life farmers and lawyers of the Revolution. The understated heroes, according to Trumbull, were Thomas Jefferson, John Adams and Benjamin Franklin. Jefferson, the tallest member standing in the center of the group, presents the document to the President of the Continental Congress, John Hancock (Jaffe 77-78), who would release it with his signature on July 4, 1776. John Adams, a lawyer from Massachusetts who helped with the drafting, appears to Jefferson's right. Benjamin Franklin, standing to Jefferson's left, is depicted as older and perhaps more weathered than the other members of the Continental Congress.

Trumbull distinguished these men by placing them in the center of the painting. The other forty-seven members of the Continental Congress surround them in parabolic formation, sitting or standing in various groups. There is a mood of somber purpose as they reflect upon the historical significance of this event. Their faces reveal no emotion, suggesting a reverential silence in anticipation of this important moment.

Trumbull's realistic representation was conceived during a time of transition from the propagandistic European tradition to the modern American hero. Trumbull presented his champions as common working men who came together for the greater good rather than for the promotion of any single person. The painting suggests a true sense of *republic* in the act of many men working together for a common purpose, perhaps the crowning achievement of the Enlightenment.

[Thomas J. Goebel, *Class of 2008*]

THE Independent Chronicle: AND THE UNIVERSAL ADVERTISER.

VOLUME XIX. NUMBER 982.

THURSDAY, August 23, 1787.

BOSTON: Published by ADAMS and NOURSE, Printers to the Honourable GENERAL COURT, of the Commonwealth of *Massachusetts*, at their Printing-Office, opposite the new Court-House, Court-Street.

From the HAMPSHIRE GAZETTE.

POLITICAL and MORAL ENTERTAINMENT.

NUMBER II.

The Independent Chronicle—Thursday, August 23, 1787,
(Notice of the American Constitution), 1787
Published by Adams and Nourse, Boston
Printed newspaper, 48.7 x 30.0 cm., 19-1/4 x 11-3/4" sheet
Paul A. Anderson Chair in the Arts Collection Purchase,
Augustana College Art Collection, SDC2010.46.a, b, c, d

Newspapers assume many things about their readers. They may assume that their readers are members of a community and therefore part of an on-going conversation. Their readers share certain needs, values, and interests, and a common body of knowledge. When we, as students, pick up a newspaper more than 200 years old, we can be sure that many of those assumptions do not apply to us. We struggle to make sense of the text, reading carefully and drawing on what we know, or think we know, about the historical context.

This newspaper in Augustana's collection was published in Boston in August of 1787. It contains an early report of the completion of a proposal for a new constitution for the United States. Indeed, the report, filed by an unnamed correspondent in New York but reporting events in Philadelphia, anticipates the actual completion of the work of the constitutional convention by a month. The report warmly endorses the proposal, though the author could not have yet seen the final document.

The newspaper containing the report is more akin to a present day journal like the *New Yorker* than the *New York Times*. It is a mixture of literary writing, social commentary, current events, and, of course, advertising. The political upheavals of the new American republic, as experienced in Massachusetts, are a prominent theme, and the inclination of the paper is clear. In the traumatic aftermath of Shays' Rebellion, the paper sides with the state government against the rebels. On the front page is an extended essay asserting that demands for radical democracy will only lead us back to monarchy and tyranny.

The reporter's favorable expectations for the new constitution stem from his belief that a stronger national government is needed to serve national purposes adequately. To a readership personally familiar with the original "Boston Tea Party," the author asserts, "It is undoubtedly the duty of a free people to be tenacious of their liberties and guard against encroachment—but does it follow that we should be suspicious of every public measure or character?"

The author reports that the next step is submission of the proposed constitution to the state legislatures for ratification. This was a matter of concern because the state legislatures were the very bodies that stood to lose power if a stronger national government was created. What the author did not know is that the politically astute founders had anticipated that problem and provided, as part of the constitution itself, that it be ratified by the people through special conventions called for the purpose, rather than by the incumbent legislatures. That plan, we know, carried the day.

[David M. Dehnel, *Professor of Political Science*]

George Washington (The Athenaeum Portrait), after 1796 painting, 1852
After Gilbert Stuart (American 1755–1828), by Thomas B. Welch (American 1814–1874)
Engraving, 67.2 x 50.6 cm., 26-1/2 x 19-7/8" image
Purchase with Gift of Adam J. DeSimone and David A. DeSimone, Augustana College Art Collection, SDC2005.23

This particular nineteenth-century engraving of Washington is based on Gilbert Stuart's most famous portrait of the *father of our country*. The so-called *Athenaeum Portrait* was known during Stuart's lifetime as one of a pair of *Mount Vernon Portraits* (Miles 43), commissioned by Martha Washington to be hung at Mount Vernon in commemoration of Washington's retirement from public life. Unfortunately, however, Stuart never delivered the promised works, and instead kept them, making multiple copies of George's likeness for an endless number of responsive patrons.

Stuart rose to the challenge and effectively captured a straightforward depiction of the former general and statesman. The dark background, contrasted against the warm flesh tones, blue eyes and simple powdered hair, lent an air of intimacy and dignity to the composition. In this particular likeness, Washington posed to face the viewer's left, in order to balance Martha's mirrored position to the viewer's right, as it was anticipated that the two paintings would ultimately hang together. The squared jaw and bulge around Washington's mouth in this version were likely owing to a new set of dentures that the president complained to his dentist sat "uneasy in my mouth" (Barratt and Miles 152).

The real genius in this work rests in its balance of portraiture, a popular type of painting in America since Colonial times, and history painting, considered the most elevated form according to European academic standards. Artists like John Trumbull, one of Stuart's competitors, actively pursued history painting in the wake of the American Revolution, as in his famous image of *The Declaration of Independence* (catalogue 51). Although this work hung in the Capitol Rotunda, the market for large, expensive history paintings was more problematic in this new republic than in the traditional patronage system of European popes and monarchs. Stuart, on the other hand, shrewdly perceived that just the right portrait of the first American president could astutely blend the popularity of portraiture with the elitist status of history painting. In the *Atheneaeum Portrait*, he thus successfully combined the two in order to create an icon for American history.

This engraving, similar to those hanging in schools across America, is easily the most recognizable symbol within a flood of modern imagery. After all, what person in the United States has not held the miniature of this image that is on every dollar bill? It was, and remains, the consummate image of promise and achievement for this country.

[Thomas J. Goebel, *Class of 2008*]

54

***Serment des Horaces* (Oath of the Horatii),** 1815 drawing after 1784 original painting
After Jacques-Louis David (French 1748–1825), draftsman undetermined
Charcoal drawing, 53.0 x 69.6 cm., 20-7/8 x 27-3/8" image
Paul A. Anderson Chair in the Arts Collection Purchase, Augustana College Art Collection 2010.52

Few painters have had the level of precision Jacques Louis David exemplified in his work. He possessed a rare ability to paint a story that enthralls the viewer into its historical narrative, while simultaneously pleasing the eye with its visual acuity. One of his most famous works, *The Oath of the Horatii*, painted in 1784, presents a theatrical scene from which much can be drawn. It was originally painted for King Louis XVI during an extended stay in Rome with his esteemed pupil Jean-Germain Drouais (Schnapper 73).

The story of the Horatii is one of tragedy and honor. Dating from 669 BCE, the cities of Rome and Alba were at war, the victor of which was to be decided by six choice warriors, three Horatii brothers from Rome and three Curiatii brothers from Alba. The heartrending spin to this conflict lies in the right side of David's composition, as the mourning women represent Sabina, a woman married to a Horatii and the sister of the Curiatii, and Camilla, engaged to a Curiatii and sister to the Horatii (De Nanteuil 90). Consequently, the viewer mourns for the women who will inevitably lose a loved one over a petty quarrel.

While the right half of the canvas occupies a feminine, emotional quadrant, the left, on the other hand, illustrates a sense of honor and valor as the three Horatii brothers pledge to their father their safe return, thus deeming the Horatii the victorious side. David was particularly vigilant about the portrayal of the warriors as their stance quite obviously dominates the composition, echoed by the three Roman arches in the background, whose blackness makes the oath stand out quite vividly. The three arches could also perhaps comment on the three levels of human emotion visible in the work. On the left, we see three brawny, determined men eager to please their father and defend their good name. In the center, we see Horatius, a father proud of his sons' loyalty, yet also anguished by the fact that their lives are at great risk. And, on the right, we view the women immobilized by dread and grief as they know they will soon mourn either a brother or lover's death (De Nanteuil 90). In this way, the three archways, divided by immense columns, precisely relate to the three levels of passion we recognize in David's figures (De Nanteuil 90). The Horatii brother in the forefront is based directly on artist Nicholas Poussin's seventeenth-century painting, *Rape of the Sabine Women*.

The juxtaposition of heroism and tragedy along with an immense focus on lavish drapery can be similarly seen in David's *The Death of Socrates*, 1787 (Schnapper 75). The overall tone of condemnation and vigor as the men prepare for battle is softened by the vulnerability of their loved ones. The shadow that bathes the background of the composition is likewise balanced by the soft hues that cover the figures in the forefront, again setting a stage-like scene from which the viewer can easily read the narrative.

[Katherine E. Goebel, *Assistant Editor*]

Allegorical Figure of Painting, ca. 1768–1785
Gavin Hamilton (Scottish/British 1723–1798)
Pastel, 102.4 x 74.1 cm., 40-1/4 x 29-1/4"
Paul A. Anderson Chair in the Arts Collection Purchase, Augustana College Art Collection, 2000.67

The *Allegorical Figure of Painting*, a large pastel by Scottish artist Gavin Hamilton, appeared at the dawn of the Neoclassical period. Hamilton was a key figure in both founding and defining this important movement in art history and was celebrated as a major European tastemaker of the time. Through his passion for the study and collecting of Classical antiquities, he advanced a revival of the characteristics of ancient art which appropriately helped generate Neoclassicism. Spurred on by the rediscovery of the lost Roman cities of Pompeii and Herculaneum (buried by the volcanic eruption of Mount Vesuvius in 79 CE), Neoclassicists rejected the previous *feminine*, decadent Rococo style in favor of a return to ancient Greco-Roman ideals, which they perceived as demonstrating such noble attributes as honor, loyalty and intelligence.

Hamilton's *Allegorical Figure of Painting*, represents the discipline of painting, symbolized by the painter's palette and brushes that have been cropped off from view. She is looking at a canvas covered with a preliminary sketch of figures that she will presumably finish in oil. This pastel is packed with classical references and represents many ideals of Neoclassical art, such as the use of the ideal figure of a woman with a calm, rather expressionless demeanor. This work helps to create a peaceful, serene image to represent the art of painting. Both her demeanor and her clothing are typical of Neoclassicism. The adornments in the woman's hair and her classic Greek profile further reinforce the classical basis for the depiction. The woman also stands in a typical classical *contrapposto* position with her hip jutting forward and her arm propped against her side. This is a natural stance, based on Classical sculpture, which illustrates an even, natural weight distribution in the figure. The contrapposto pose as well as proper anatomical proportion reflect the artist's clear understanding of the form of the human body, fundamental in classical portrayals of figures.

[Chris Johnson, *Class of 2007*]

56

Femmes en révolte (Women in Revolt), ca. late eighteenth century
Philibert-Louis Debucourt (French 1755–1832)
Watercolor, 23.1 x 37.0 cm., 9-1/16 x 14-9/16" image
Gift in Honor of Dr. Thomas William and Mrs. Barbara Lee Carter, Augustana College Art Collection, 2004.23

Femmes en révolte is a watercolor attributed to French artist Philibert-Louis Debucourt by Parisian art dealer, Pierre Jonchères, from whom the painting was purchased. In attributing this painting to Debucourt, Jonchères referenced the artist's work titled *Almanach National* (Goebel 96). Debucourt is cited frequently in discussions of eighteenth-century French genre painting and color printmaking; however, literature on the artist's work and career is not extensive. Debucourt worked throughout the Revolution and is known for his skill in a variety of printmaking methods often combining several techniques in the same design (Taws 170-71). The *Gazette des Beaux-Arts* compared Debucourt to Jean-Honoré Fragonard (catalogue 38) as he retained the rose, blue, and gold palette of Rococo-era painters like Fragonard (Goebel 96). This palette is abundant in *Femmes en révolte.*

This watercolor depicts a mob of women rioting in a street amongst tall buildings suggesting an urban location. The windows of these buildings are filled with onlookers. The loose, flurried lines used in the painting suggest the crowdedness and frenzied movements of the scene. In the foreground, one can see toppled baskets of food as well as women who have been knocked over in the revolt. The fact that women are rioting amidst overturned food seems to suggest that this may be a subsistence riot.

Information from Bohstedt's essay seems to support this theory as he notes that when women revolted, they tended to be involved in food riots (29). In pre-Revolutionary Europe, food riots were significant as were women's roles in them (Bohstedt 21). Bohstedt reports that 1000 riots took place between the years 1790-1810 because they were often successful and forced authorities to respond (Bohstedt 24). Objectives of these riots were local and concrete: women taking over food markets to stop profiteering through local export of grain in times of famine (Bohstedt, 24); their motivation was hunger and the need to feed their children (McMillan 21) as well as to gain constitutional rights (Levy and Applewhite, "Popular Classes" 27).

While this painting may or may not depict a particular riot, the presence of women in bread riots and in the politics of subsistence has been documented through the seventeenth and eighteenth centuries (McMillan, 20). The year 1775 recorded the "flour wars" in Paris after which fourteen women were arrested for protesting against steep rises in the price of flour and bread (McMillan, 21). In October 1789, a group of 7000 women marched fourteen kilometers to Versailles, armed with pikes, clubs, knives, swords, and muskets in the rain while crying out against the scarcity of bread. One group demanded that King Louis XVI's verbal promises of wheat supplies for Paris be put into writing. Another group marched on the National Legislature and demanded a guaranteed supply of affordable bread (Levy and Applewhite "Militant Citizenship" 83). In April 1795, women protested again for food shortages. When their pleas went unheeded, they protested by sacking shops, seizing grain, and kidnapping officials before launching a May 20th uprising when women descended on the Convention to plead for bread and democracy (McMillan 24-25).

[Angela Granet Lynch, *Class of 2001*]

Self-portrait, n.d., after 1790 painting
After Marie-Louise-Elisabeth Vigée-Le Brun (French 1755–1842)
Oil on linen, 58.8 x 42.8 cm., 23 x 16-7/8"
Paul A. Anderson Chair in the Arts Collection Purchase, Augustana College Art Collection, SDC2004.11

This painting, done with oils on linen, is a nineteenth-century copy of Vigée-Le Brun's original *Self-portrait* created in 1790. Copies of the Old Masters were often painted by students and followers in order to improve techniques and teach subtleties in application. The fact that this piece was copied in the nineteenth century provides evidence that this painter was greatly respected by subsequent generations.

This self-portrait reveals Vigée-Lebrun's mature painting style, with its almost invisible brushstrokes and fine academic finish. It seems to capture a moment as the artist, in the middle of painting Marie-Antoinette's image, turns to pose for her own portrait. The subject of her canvas, the queen of France, reinforces the painter's important status. The almost monochromatic background is interrupted only by the faint outline of a canvas and the face of Marie-Antoinette, but essentially serves as a backdrop for the main subject. Vigée-LeBrun's face appears flawless and her eyes reflect an engaged intellect. It is this perfect, finished expression that led many critics to unfairly call her portraits "vacuous" (Opfell 42). The artist's use of black and white with a touch of red, as well as the sophisticated play of light and shadow, lends the painting drama and purpose, reflecting her own independent nature and never-ending drive to succeed.

As with many successful portrait painters, Vigée-Le Brun was known to flatter her subjects, even herself, when she painted. In this image, she would have been thirty-five years old, but painted herself looking much younger, possibly in her twenties. Her clothing is simple and unembellished. She did not wear the elaborate styles of dress, hair and makeup in vogue at the time, but insisted on simple gowns without lavish makeup or wigs. She also often wore a turban on her head, as seen in this painting. In addition to her not being bound by fashion, she often insisted that her subjects also not wear fashionable makeup and wigs (Opfell 41). She likely wanted to get at the heart of the person and not allow props to overshadow the personality.

[Jennifer Johnson, *Class of 2006*]

58

Minerva, n.d.
Ernesto Gazzeri (Italian 1866–1965)
Carved marble sculpture, 107.8 x 29.1 x 21.3 cm., 42-3/8 x 11-1/2 x 8-1/2"
Paul A. Anderson Chair in the Arts Collection Purchase, Augustana College Art Collection, 1999.21, pedestal not original to piece, SDC1999.23

According to ancient mythology, Minerva (the Roman version of the Greek goddess Athena) was the goddess of wisdom, institutions for the arts and higher learning and the defender for just causes in war. Believed to have been born out of Jupiter's head fully grown and in full armor, Minerva had domain over wisdom and defensive war. She was not considered bloodthirsty like Mars, the male god of war, and therefore better remembered for her wisdom and knowledge.

As the goddess of just war, she is usually depicted in full armor looking thoughtful and prepared. She was Jupiter's favorite child and therefore she was given some of his armor, which she often wears in depictions (West 633). Minerva's main attribute is not sensuous beauty like Venus, the Roman goddess of beauty and love (equivalent to the Greek Aphrodite), although Gazzeri's version seems to portray her in that idealized role as well, perhaps inspired by the famous Hellenistic sculpture of *Venus de Milo*.

Her helmet is the only symbol that clearly identifies her as the goddess of defensive war. The crown on her head possibly symbolizes her general status as a goddess. This version does not include an owl, which in other depictions is often perched near her atop a stack of books, reinforcing her connection with learning. Minerva was also known for her virginity (West 633), although she did have suitors. Gazzeri likely preferred to focus on her wisdom and purity rather than her prowess in warfare, thus depicting her as a graceful young idealized maiden instead of a keen warrior ready for battle.

Gazzeri sculpted Minerva in a more active position than would be typical for Classical Greek art. Her left foot rests on the helmet, while she shifts her weight firmly onto her right leg, creating a dramatic shift in the rest of her body. The *contrapposto* pose combined with the wet drapery, firmly bent knee and turned head give the sculpture a sense of liveliness reminiscent of the later Greek Hellenistic period (Lopez 58).

[Jennifer Bock, *Class of 2008*]

Portland Vase, limited edition originally released 1791
Wedgwood (Josiah Wedgwood, English/British 1730–1795); figural modeling by Henry Webber (British 1754–1826)
Ceramic, 26.6 x 20.1 x 20.1 cm., 10-1/2 x 8 x 8"
Paul A. Anderson Chair in the Arts Collection Purchase, Augustana College Art Collection, 2000.66

Webster's dictionary defines Neoclassicism as a revival of classic style and form in art, literature, etc., a description which exactly fits the basis for Wedgwood's *Portland Vase*. When Josiah Wedgwood first began to work with the idea of constructing pieces such as the *Portland Vase*, he was definitely inspired by the contemporary revived interest in early Greek and Roman artwork. Wedgwood also knew that most people could not afford to build collections of authentic ancient Classical pieces. He thus determined to create objects that resembled such antiquities, but were affordable and accessible enough that more people could have them in their own homes.

His most famous and celebrated piece was known as the *Portland Vase*. The original Roman *Portland Vase*, also called the *Barberini Vase*, was made from deep blue-black glass with an engraved overlay of white glass. It dates from around 25 BCE, early in the so-called *Golden Age* of Caesar Augustus. It traveled through the hands of many owners including the family of Cardinal Francesco Barberini (hence the title, *Barberini Vase*), Sir William Hamilton (a close friend of Josiah Wedgwood) and eventually the Dowager Duchess of *Portland*, giving it the name by which it is most commonly known today (Keynes 237). Wedgwood borrowed the vase for a year from the Third Duke of Portland, the son of the late Duchess, in order to copy the designs and reproduce the vase in his new ceramic invention, *jasper ware*. The process of creating the actual vase took much longer than he anticipated, however, and after multiple experiments and trials, a final perfected copy was produced three years later, four years after he first obtained the original (Keynes 240).

Although the exact meaning of the scenes on the vase is still debated by scholars, a popular theory relates them to the myth of Peleus and Thetis, the parents of Achilles, the great Greek hero of the Trojan War, celebrated in Homer's Classical masterpiece, the *Iliad*. It has been determined that the original shape of the vase was an *amphora* (meaning *to carry on both sides*) with a foot that has since been broken and replaced with a circular disc made about a century later. Wedgwood did an amazing job of reviving and advancing the early Greco-Roman style in his own time period.

[Johanna Voorhees, *Class of 2008*]

60

Homer Invoking The Muse, 1805
William Blake (British 1757–1827), with John Flaxman (British 1755–1826)
Engraving, 25.3 x 35.4 cm., 9-15/16 x 13-15/16" image
Inscription: *"Achilles wrath to Greece the direful spring*
of woes unnumberd heavenly goddess sing!
Pope's Homer's Iliad"
Paul A. Anderson Chair in the Arts Collection Purchase, Augustana College Art Collection, 2010.4

Today we view William Blake as one of the central figures in British literature, but he was virtually unknown during his life. His illuminated books of poetry didn't sell, and his gallery openings attracted little attention. A painter, illustrator, engraver and, especially, a poet, he died poor. Lucky for him, he'd cultivated a close friendship with John Flaxman, one of England's greatest sculptors and illustrators, internationally famous at the time of the friendship for his drawings devoted to the ancients like the one featured here. Flaxman helped Blake earn a living as an engraver by continually referring clients to him (Bentley volume 12), and the esteem was mutual. Upon Flaxman's death, Blake called him a "Sublime Archangel" (Keyness 51). Like many visionaries, Blake was too strange for his contemporary audience. His religious views were unconventional (William Wordsworth considered him mad); his politics were radical. He was once tried for high treason for allegedly speaking against the king (Gilchrist 195). By contrast, Flaxman devoted his art to Christian and ancient mythological subjects, work that would have been deemed appropriate to eighteenth-century English society.

It is appropriate to represent Blake with this particular engraving. In it, we see Homer, the ancient Greek poet credited with writing the *Iliad* and *Odyssey*, invoking one of the Muses, goddesses who inspired creativity in literature and art. Notice that the Muse's lute is more ornate than the poet's, her superior position looking down on him. It may have been a combination of modesty and true belief that compelled poets such as Homer to give most of the credit of their work to the Muses. A convention of epic poetry and other long forms of literature was to begin by asking the Muses for inspiration, often requesting both content (sometimes accessed through memory) and the ability to write it. "O Muses," wrote Dante Alighieri in Canto II of *The Inferno*, "O high genius, aide me now! / O memory that engraves the things I saw, / Here shall your worth be manifest to all!" (13). Considering Blake's body of work, we know that he was no stranger to the muse, that is, to artistic inspiration. Some might say he'd have been better served invoking Ploutos, the Greek god of riches. But for reasons we'll never know, William Blake didn't use his talents for personal gain; he chose greatness over wealth.

[Kelly Daniels, *Assistant Professor of English*]

Death's Door, from **The Grave,** a poem by Robert Blair, 1813
William Blake (British 1757–1827), etched by Luigi Schiavonetti (Italian 1765–1810), published by Rudolph Ackermann (1764–1834), printed by Thomas Bensley (1760-1835)
Etching, Plate III, 29.7 x 17.5 cm., 11-11/16 x 6-7/8" image
Inscription: "'*Tis but a Night, a long and moonless Night, We make the Grave our Bed, and then are gone!*"
Paul A. Anderson Chair in the Arts Collection Purchase, Augustana College Art Collection, 2009.5.c

Hardly any of the work for which we now consider William Blake a major Romantic poet and artist was widely known in his own time. His illustrations commissioned for an 1808 luxury edition of Blair's "The Grave" are an exception. This large and expensive book was dedicated to the queen, and had hundreds of wealthy, well-connected subscribers. It was Blake's most conspicuous success.

"The Grave" is a long meditation on death as a fearsome, gruesome leveler, and on the pains of suffering, loss, and grieving. Blair was a clergyman, and just before the poem's end he makes the turn one still hears at funerals toward the idea that death is an exit but also an entrance, and a new beginning. Blake's twelve illustrations focus on this last portion of the poem. Though the images are linked to specific lines, there is much more of Blake than of Blair in them.

In "Death's Door," for instance, both figures are versions of human forms Blake had drawn and engraved before, though never together on the same page. What do they represent? A now/then, body/soul narrative? The aged man entering the tomb certainly looks to be an image of mortality, and the youth above the door surely can be seen as the same man's immortal soul rejuvenated as it will be after his death.

But for prophetic, visionary Blake, eternity and immortality could suddenly be, at any moment, *here* and *now.* And the stages Blake was most careful to define and explore were not episodes in time but attitudes: ways of seeing and being, states of understanding and comprehension, parts of what he called Vision.

What attitudes do these two figures embody? The aged man looks strikingly like several other figures in Blake's poetry and art who bend, lean, or look down, in fear, despair, or denial, preferring darkness to light, down to up. And the nude male above belongs to a large family of Blakean figures who are radiant and new, arising, awakening, emerging like newborns, or opening like flowers. We might call such figures opposites; Blake's preferred word was "contraries." Innocence and Experience, he said, were "contrary states of the human soul," and "without contraries there is no progression." A more deeply Blakean response to "Death's Door" should perhaps notice tensions between the two figures, should see them as contraries, contending for our attention and empathy. Seen together in this way, the two figures may be drawing us into a kind of *progression* or expansion of perception, toward increasing identification with the open, bright youth who so obviously sees better, sees farther and more, . . . and not later, but immediately, right *now.*

Walt Whitman first saw "Death's Door" when he read Alexander Gilchrist's *Life of William Blake* in 1881. A decade later it was still in his mind, and he left instructions that his own tomb be made in its image. When he died, it was (Ferguson-Wigstaffe).

[Don Erickson. *Professor Emeritus of English, Dorothy J. Parkander Professor Emeritus in Literature*]

62

No hay quien nos desate? (Will No One Untie Us?),
from ***Los Caprichos*** (The Caprices), etched 1793–1798,
published 1799, posthumous printing
Francisco José de Goya (Spanish 1746–1828)
Intaglio, 21.4 x 15.1 cm., 8-1/2 x 5-15/16" image
Paul A. Anderson Chair in the Arts Collection
Purchase, Augustana College Art Collection, 2000.20

While there is an undeniable streak of cynicism in even the lightest and most frivolous of Francisco de Goya's works, it is in his etchings and aquatints where we can find his most direct and powerful critiques of society and its foibles. This print, "*¿No hay quien nos desate?*," or "Is there no one who can unbind us?," demonstrates a trademark scorn for both superstition and unchallenged tradition in Spanish society which define the series of prints called *Los Caprichos* (the Caprices). While not as overtly anticlerical or critical of political structures as many of the *Caprichos*, this image of a man and woman bound together, seemingly tied to a tree as prey for the bespectacled owl above them, strikes at one of the principal social norms of the time: arranged marriage.

The theme of marriage, and, in particular, the difficult cultural transition from a model of marriage as economic or familial contract to an act of love entered into willingly by young paramours rather than through parental directive, was very much a contentious issue at the time of this work, first published in 1799. One of the most influential playwrights of the time, Leonardo Fernández de Moratín, depicted the same sense of tragic misfortune as Goya's aquatint in his most famous work, the 1801 satirical drama "*El sí de las niñas*" or "The Maidens' Consent," a play which draws attention to the role of parents in matchmaking and the often undesirable pairings created for economic or social gain.

Both Goya and Moratín stressed the impact on the young woman, in the case of this print, with the ill-fated bride, tied at the waist and ankles to her equally unhappy husband, suffering both his struggles to move or free himself and the ominous talons of the owl. Rather than struggle herself, she seems to take on a pose of despair or futility, perhaps foreshadowing a life of abnegation, a term often used to describe the role of the ideal wife and mother whose identity becomes defined as one of service to her husband and children. Though we might certainly look at the male figure, straining against the ropes around them both, as a victim as well. And then, there is the owl. As with many of Goya's *Caprichos*, animal imagery highlights the absurdity of both superstition and tradition. In this case the owl's odd spectacle eyes reflect the *wisdom* of the ages, a wisdom Goya rejects as irrational folly. While not as powerful as the animal imagery in a work such as "*El sueño de la razón*" ("The Sleep of Reason"), the owl effectively emphasizes the irrationality of blind tradition which Goya, among many, lambastes at the dawning of the 19th Century.

[Allen Bertsche, *Director, International and Off-Campus Programs, Professor of Spanish*]

63

El sueño de la razon produce monstrous (The Sleep of Reason Produces Monsters), from ***Los Caprichos*** (The Caprices) etched 1793–1798, published 1799, posthumous printing
Francisco José de Goya (Spanish 1746–1828)
Intaglio, 21.6 x 15.1 cm., 8-1/2 x 6" image
Paul A. Anderson Chair in the Arts Collection Purchase, Augustana College Art Collection, 2000.21

Goya's *Sleep of Reason* has generated varied interpretations. Of particular interest are those analyses that look within Goya's own psyche to examine his personal "demons" (e.g., despair over his failing health and disaffection with society) or generalize his work to the deeper content of the human mind (Dowling 331-332). Alford notes that "[t]he successful, aesthetic artifact, so successful that we call it a work of art, serves as a bridge between the artist and ourselves" (483). In this way, art may be seen as a statement of universal human experience.

Sigmund Freud, the founder of psychoanalysis, proposed that people are motivated by innate, unconscious desires, just as instinctual drives guide the behavior of animals (*Freud: A Life 35-36*). Humans differ only in their ability to restrain and channel their instincts in acceptable directions, such as artistic expression ("The Origin" 214). Freud would agree with Goya that these animalistic or "monstrous" tendencies lie close to the surface of awareness, threatening the individual's sense of reality and self-control. Sometimes, however, unconscious impulses manage to slip into consciousness, as they do in dreams (201).

For Freud, dreams are "the *via regia* [royal road] to the interpretation of the unconscious" ("The Origin" 200). He believed that all dreams symbolically fulfill and partially satisfy the most basic wishes that people have learned to deny. Individuals remember only the dream's façade (what Freud called the *manifest dream content*), a disguise that hides the raw desires that churn within the unconscious. Freud referred to these unconscious desires as *latent dream-thoughts* ("Consciousness" 8-18). Although an ordinary dream signifies that these urges have been disguised successfully, "dreams which are apparently guileless turn out to be the reverse of innocent. . . they all show 'the mark of the beast'" (*The Interpretation of Dreams* 86).

It is not known whether Goya intended the night creatures to represent the artist's dream itself or to establish the dream's ominous mood. Either way, Freud would find the image closely tied to the primitive nature within all humans that constantly threatens to express itself—and sometimes succeeds.

[Ruth Ann Johnson, *Professor of Psychology*]

64

Mother and Child, late 18th–early 19th century
Artist unknown
Terra cotta, 13.9 x 7.5 x 8.3 cm., 5-1/2 x 2-7/8 x 3-1/4"
Paul A. Anderson Chair in the Arts Collection Purchase, Augustana College Art Collection, 2000.56

Little background is known about this small, delicate terra cotta sculpture. Its medium consists of clay that is suitable for shaping and firing in a kiln or by direct sunlight. Terra cotta is generally brownish-red in color and consists of combined earth products. Its natural tonality and required shaping and modeling, lend itself to tactile surfaces that invite the viewer's examination and touch. The surface indeed reflects that this is a sculpture that has been lovingly touched by admirers over the years. It has a tradition that can be traced back to early history in both the east and west and continues to be widely used by sculptors and potters today.

The subject portrays the popular *mother and child* theme that appears throughout various periods and cultures in art history. Probably the most common western tradition for this theme is the Christian subject of Madonna and Christ child. Yet these terra cotta figures wear no halos, symbolizing light emerging from the holy heads of saints. Instead, as is typical of this subject by the late eighteenth to early nineteenth centuries, the period to which this piece is traced, religious subjects became less popular in Europe and were increasingly replaced by secularized versions of maternal bonding. Stylistically, this piece reflects the quiet elegance and classicism of Greek and Roman precedents in vogue during the Neoclassical period.

This sculpture appears to have been carefully hand-crafted rather than mass-produced, as evidenced in the subtle, modeled curves, particularly in the dominant figure's arm as well as in the fine details in general. The drapery of the female figure with its sweeping classical line and interest in the body beneath are beautifully conceived. Note the subtle and carefully crafted anatomical details of the child and the doting attention offered by his mother. She displays an idealized classical profile and her sense of support and touch, reflect the sense of *bonding* typical of late nineteenth-century works by Mary Cassatt (catalogue 95, 101 and 102). The unknown artist has aptly captured the physical as well as psychological truth of the scene, reflecting a fine master's touch.

[Robert Lopez, *Class of 2001*]

65

Study for the Highlander, ca. 1835
Sir David Wilkie (Scottish/British 1785–1841)
Graphite and watercolor study for ***General Sir David Baird Discovering the Body of the Sultaun Tippoo Sahib after having Captured Seringapatam, on the 4th May, 1799***, painting ca. 1835-1838
25.3 x 19.9 cm., 9-15/16 x 7-13/16" sheet
Lent Courtesy of Dr. Thomas B. Brumbaugh Art History Collection

The great Scottish painter, David Wilkie (1785–1841), first studied under John Graham in Edinburgh and later trained at the Royal Academy, elected a full academician in 1811 (Chiego xvii). Wilkie primarily created genre paintings, which established his reputation, and reflect the British love for storytelling and character sketches. Wilkie also produced a large number of history paintings. These works, considered by academics to be more elevated in stature than genre, probably better reveal his Romantic temperament. In such works, he employed rich color and drama, often reflecting his strong interest in exotic lands—particularly evident in the subject of one of his last great history paintings, *Sir David Baird Discovering the Body of Sultaun Tippoo Saib* (1839), for which this drawing is a study.

The rising interest in exotic people and places greatly affected Romantic artists like Wilkie. This exquisite study, made of graphite and watercolor, is a portrait of the face of the Scottish torchbearer. It is mostly sketched in black, but enriched by the subtle hint of red outlining the eyes, nose, mouth and jaw in order to emphasize his facial features. The angle of the man's head adds dimension to the piece in that he looks as if he is coming out at the viewer and at the same time looking down at the defeated enemy.

In a letter to Lady Baird, Wilkie described this character as "the Highlander stooping with the torch" (Chiego 254). And when the painting was exhibited at the Royal Academy in 1839, the catalogue further defined the importance of this figure in the overall composition: "...in front, on the General's left hand, bending forward with a torch is a Highlander, a McLeod of the old 71st [the Highland Light Infantry] who, with his comrades on leaving the trenches, were reminded by the General of the old scores they had now to settle for the severe imprisonment they had formerly endured as captives at Seringapatam" (Chiego 256).

The great care that Wilkie took in capturing the personality and physical appearance of his subject is sensitively rendered in this drawing. Examining such sketches reveals the artist's steps and invites the viewer to make connections between the study and the final piece, much like fitting the pieces of a puzzle together. In this manner, drawings help viewers see the breakdown of an artist's thought process as well as the time and planning that went into each work of art.

Wilkie, along with landscape painters, John Constable (catalogue 67) and Joseph Mallord Turner, was estimated in his own time as one of the *three* greatest Romantic British artists of the first half of the nineteenth century. He was a close friend to Constable and a more distant acquaintance and competitor to Turner. His own short life likely best exemplifies Romantic myth—dying young on his return from the Middle Eastern journey on which he embarked the year after exhibiting this painting.

[Lisa Johnson, *Class of 2008* and
Catherine Carter Goebel, *Editor*]

66

Study of Lion Heads, ca. 1832–1861
Ferdinand-Victor-Eugène Delacroix (French 1798–1863)
Graphite drawing, 24.2 x 31.3 cm., 9-1/2 x 12-3/8" sheet
Gift of Mr. and Mrs. Michael Moss, Augustana College Art Collection, 1995.26.2

This drawing illustrates Romantic fascination not only with nature as observed in landscape, but with exotic and dangerous animals that inhabit such environments. The potential drama offered by such subjects challenged the privileged position of humans as defined in the classical tradition and reinforced by the Neoclassicists of the previous generation. While Delacroix was universally celebrated for his rich and innovative use of color, his talent is immediately apparent in his sketches as well. The *Study of Lion Heads* was most likely undertaken during a journey to Morocco and Spain, where he saw a variety of such animals (Wellington 56). Another influence for the subject would have been seventeenth-century Peter Paul Rubens' *Lion Hunt* (1617–1618).

Within the overall *Study of Lion Heads*, there are seven smaller sketches, all unfinished, five of lions and two of lionesses. The lions speak to anyone viewing them; the graphite pencil effectively contrasts the harsh, dark lines of the lions' eyes with the lighter, wispier lines of their manes. Since most of the lions' heads are unfinished, they take on an even more mysterious look, as if they are camouflaged and fading back into the paper itself. They are all sketched in graphite with the power and force of this medium beautifully capturing their essence. This sketch exemplifies the type of careful preliminary consideration Delacroix took in preparation for his final paintings, demonstrating how the foundation, the armature beneath the color, was just as important to him as the finished canvas.

Delacroix was truly swept up in Romanticism and advanced its cause through his new techniques, subject matter and overall artistic ability. Like most Romantics, he emphasized nature and its intriguing potential for danger. This sketch demonstrates the versatility of Delacroix's artistic talents, far beyond his celebrated use of color, within the more restrictive medium of graphite.

[Regina Gorham, *Class of 2006*]

Study for Landscape: Boys Fishing, related to 1813 painting
John Constable (English/British 1776–1837) [M. Robinson]
Oil on canvas, 44.7 x 63.6 cm., 17-5/8 x 25-1/16"
Lent Courtesy of Private Collection in Honor of Dr. Gary James Goebel

Though he was not a formal student of science, the English landscape painter John Constable (1776-1837) took justifiable pride in his painstaking and careful observations of nature (Bailey 2007). He spent countless hours in the field, using tube oil paints so that he could paint while there, rather than from sketches in his studio. He is known for accurate details, like the bend of his trees matching the direction of prevailing winds, and nowhere is this understanding of nature clearer than in his treatment of clouds. Constable also adopted the new scientific vocabulary (e.g., cumulus, cirrus) to describe clouds. He often went *skying* (sky watching) and resisted the advice of patrons to replace his sometimes dark skies with clear blue backdrops.

Constable's philosophy is well-expressed in lectures he gave a few years before his death for the Royal Institution, an important promoter of science. Audiences flocked to R. I. lectures to hear new ideas, and to also see flamboyant chemistry demonstrations by the likes of Humphrey Davy and Michael Faraday (the latter of whom attended Constable's talks). Although Constable was clearly Romantic in his perspective (he wrote that "painting is feeling"), he also argued that a painting could be like a scientific experiment. The dominant philosophy of science in his day, *inductivism*, stressed the need for thorough observations of nature and the avoidance of speculation until theories presented themselves from the amassed facts (Bowler 1989). Likewise, Constable believed that direct observation of nature, rather than the mere imitation of past masters, was the key to good landscape painting.

Although Constable sometimes painted seascapes, he loved inland waters best and many of his paintings feature the interactions of humans, both at work and play, with rivers. Through most of his career, Constable struggled with his relative lack of recognition in England. However, his paintings of the rural landscapes of his boyhood homeland in the Stour Valley eventually won him a seat in the prestigious Royal Academy. The region he painted is still often referred to as "Constable's Country."

[C. Kevin Geedey, *Professor of Biology*]

68

John Philip Kemble as Hamlet, ca. 1801
After or by Sir Thomas Lawrence (English/British 1769–1830)
Oil on canvas, 79.0 x 54.1 cm., 31-1/8 x 21-5/16"
Purchase with Gift of Dr. Karin Youngberg,
Augustana College Art Collection, SDC2005.24

The present image is a version of Sir Thomas Lawrence's *Portrait of J. P. Kemble as Hamlet* (1801). The original painting is one of four massive canvases, each focusing on Kemble in one of his famous tragic roles. Through this group, Lawrence hoped to infuse portraiture with a new dignity and importance by merging the portrait with the widely admired genre of historical painting.

Lawrence's ambition to elevate the genre of portraiture by combining it with the dignity and power of theatrical performances was furthered by the stature of his model, the English actor John Philip Kemble (1757–1823). Kemble specialized in serious dramatic roles that required a kind of aristocratic grandeur.

The Lawrence painting is identified in the Tate catalogue with Hamlet (V. i), the famous Graveyard scene in which Hamlet with his friend Horatio engage in a darkly comic conversation with two grave-diggers. At one point Hamlet picks up a skull which the digger's spade has unearthed and contemplates fragile human mortality which this *memento mori* (reminder of death) recalls. But when the grave-digger identifies the skull as belonging to Yorick, a court jester and Hamlet's childhood playfellow, Hamlet throws down the skull in horror and disgust. In Lawrence's image, only the skull, and the faint outline of grass and gravestone in the front left corner suggest the graveyard. Instead Hamlet stands inert and serene against a largely dark background into which he seems to melt. Even his feathered hat and the crimson lining of his fur-lined cloak are nearly swallowed up by the darkness.

Lawrence's painting is perhaps best seen, not as an evocation of a particular scene, but as a kind of epitome in the sense of a summary or abridgement of the entire play. His black clothing denotes both his mourning for his father and his melancholic, introverted disposition present throughout the play. But the focus of the painting is Hamlet's luminescent face, framed from below by an open white collar. His features reflect the serene calm of the last soliloquy, "There is a special providence in the fall of a sparrow. . . the readiness is all" (V. ii).

[Karin Youngberg, *Professor of English, Conrad Bergendoff Professor of Humanities*]

69

Burial of Atala, after 1808 painting, n.d.
After or by Anne-Louis Girodet de Roussy-Trioson (French 1767–1824)
Oil on canvas, 48.9 x 66.1 cm., 19-1/4 x 26"
Purchase with Gift of Adam J. DeSimone and David A. DeSimone with Framing Assistance from Lisa M. Jacobson '92
Augustana College Art Collection, SDC2005.18

Originally a pupil of the Neoclassicist and Revolutionary painter Jacques Louis David (catalogue 54), Anne-Louis Girodet de Roucy-Trioson diverged early and dramatically from the work and politics of his mentor (Antal 19). This work is an especially interesting transitional piece. We can still see some striking links to David's Neoclassicism in the anatomically detailed and idealized vision of the human body, the sense of wet drapery in the elegant lines of the figures' "poor" clothing, and the contemplative facial expressions of the dead girl and even of her bereft lover.

Artistically innovative but politically conservative, Girodet was attracted by the emotional neo-Catholicism of early Romantic writers like François-René de Chateaubriand. While previous paintings, notably his 1806 *Flood*, suggest links to Chateaubriand by their extravagant "natural" settings and emotionally charged subject matter (Antal 22), this painting is an explicit reference to one of Chateaubriand's most famous works, his novella *Atala*. Set in a still appealingly wild North America and peopled with Christianized Native Americans who become star-crossed lovers, *Atala* had all the elements that would seize the imagination of that first generation of Romantics: an exotic setting and cast of characters, an idealized vision of "primitive" humanity, and a tragic love story laced with religious mysticism.

Girodet's painting is a somewhat free interpretation of one of the closing scenes of the novella: the burial of the heroine, Atala, who has committed suicide rather than give in to her passion for the young hero, and has learned too late from the hermit priest that the vow of chastity she took on her mother's deathbed was not required of her by God. Although Chateaubriand describes other scenes from Atala's final hours in great detail, he tells us of her burial only that he and the hermit "carried the beautiful one to her earthen bed" (Chateaubriand 74). Girodet's envisioning of the scene, in which the young Chactas is seen desperately clutching Atala's legs rather than actually assisting in the burial, is certainly true to the spirit of the character, who is portrayed throughout the tale as more passionate than functional.

[Taddy R. Kalas, *Professor of French*]

70

Cypripedium Elliottianum (lady's slipper orchid), late 19th to early 20th century
Artist unknown
Color lithograph or chromolithograph, 28.1 x 21.2 cm., 11-1/16 x 8-3/8" image
Gift of Mr. and Mrs. Martin Barooshian, Augustana College Art Collection, 1994.14.7

In an 1861 letter to his friend Sir Joseph Hooker, then assistant director of the Kew Gardens in England, Charles Darwin admitted that "I never was more interested in any subject in my life than that of orchids." Indeed, so keen was the interest of the great biologist in orchids that he published a book on them in 1862 entitled *The Various Contrivances by Which British and Foreign Orchids are Fertilized by Insects*, and he continued to study and include them in his writings until the end of his life in 1882. In focusing on the orchid family, Darwin had chosen one of the most specialized but at the same time diverse and species rich groups of flowering plants. Botanists estimate that the family Orchidaceae may contain 20,000 to 25,000 species or more in most terrestrial habitats although the great majority are concentrated in tropical rain forests. A guide along a Costa Rican river once identified for me seventeen species of epiphytic orchids on one fallen tree. By contrast, all of Illinois contains only four dozen species of native orchids.

The orchid in the accompanying print is a lady's slipper orchid. The genus name of this orchid *Cypripedium* is Greek for "slipper of Venus" or simply "lady's slipper." The slipper-shaped flower petals vary from yellow to white to pink or other shadings in various species. These are among the best known of native Midwestern orchids and are sought out by casual hikers and plant lovers alike. These rare wildflowers should never be picked, however, or transplanted to a garden because they rarely survive removal from their specialized habitat.

[Bohdan Dziadyk, *Professor of Biology, Director of College Field Stations*]

Whippoorwill, 1830
John James Audubon (b. Saint-Dominique, now Haiti, American 1785–1851)
Hand-colored engraving, 66.4 x 53.0 cm., 26-1/4 x 20-1/8" image
Gift of Audubon Elementary School, Rock Island-Milan School District Number 41, Augustana College Art Collection, 1996.24

The Audubon engraving, like all of Audubon's works in *The Birds of America,* attempts to portray the Whip-poor-will in its natural habitat, which is hardwood deciduous forest (Chancellor 30). Also depicted are examples of its behavior. Audubon did a fine job depicting an individual on the fly hunting moths. Below this is another, probably a female, in a pose which biologists have interpreted as *copulation solicitation*, with wings elevated (as if fluttering), head positioned as if looking up, and tail high. The last individual—far left—appears motionless on a tree branch suggesting a roost or resting position. All content in the engraving accurately portrays the detail in color and pattern, including a *Cynthia Moth* (top) and *Io Moth* (bottom). Presumably, the moths are included to suggest that Whip-poor-wills are active mainly at night, which may have been difficult for Audubon to draw.

How lucky for Audubon to have actually seen individual Whip-poor-wills behaving in the field. To date, ornithologists know relatively little about this bird because of its secretive habits, nocturnal way of life, and very cryptic coloration and behavior (Cink 1). Biologists suspect that there are actually two species of Whip-poor-wills, both of which are North American (or short distance) migrants. One population breeds in the northeastern quadrant of the U.S. The other population breeds in the desert southwest. Thus, there is very little contact between these two groups. Evolution has selected for differences in the males' song and in egg characteristics. Indeed, luck and perseverance is what one needs to see this bird. Audubon's "luck" was augmented by dispatching individuals and mounting them in species-appropriate postures and positions for his paintings. Those methods notwithstanding, his painting displays the beauty and elegance of the Whip-poor-will. Without this work of art and other illustrations by a very small number of observers, I would have no real idea what this bird actually looks like!

[Stephen Hager, *Associate Professor of Biology*]

72A

Tiger Hunt, 19th century
Artist Unknown, Mughal (or Mogul) style, India
Gouache or casein on fabric, 29.5 x 21.8 cm., 11-5/8 x 8-5/8"
Paul A. Anderson Chair in the Arts Collection Purchase, Augustana College Art Collection, SDC2011.2.1

The Mughal dynasty ruled over the Indian subcontinent from the sixteenth century to the mid-eighteenth century. This dynasty was founded by Babur who belonged to the house of Timur and was a descendant of Genghis Khan. Babur came to the Indian subcontinent from the small Central Asian state of Fergana (modern Uzbekistan). He began his travel to the east in 1504, and after a long and enduring conquest of India, by 1527 Babur was able to lay the foundation of what was to become the Mughal empire. Babur's grandson Akbar, known as the architect of the Mughal empire and its greatest emperor, fortified this empire by gaining control over northern, western and central India and securing the northwestern border (modern Afghanistan) which had been the gateway to India for many previous invasions (including those led by Alexander the Great and Genghis Khan). Akbar established a strong civil administrative system, was extremely tolerant of other religions and is considered the first great Mughal patron of the arts (Department of Islamic Art). His son Jahangir ascended the throne after Akbar's death and continued to patronize the arts, adding his own unique and strong artistic preferences. Jahangir's son, Shah Jahan, ascended the throne in 1628 and continued the patronage of the arts, and is best known for his architectural accomplishment, the Taj Mahal. Shah Jahan's reign was forcibly ended in 1658 by his son Aurangzeb, who followed extremely orthodox religious beliefs, and his reign saw the beginning of the decline of Mughal patronage of the arts and ultimately the decline and demise of the Mughal empire which was succeeded by the British empire in India (Sarder).

Babur's son, Humanyun, introduced the Mughal style of painting to India that was inspired by Persian art but (over time) incorporated Indian and Islamic styles and added new themes and colors. Mughal paintings often depict historical events, court life, stories and legends, hunting scenes, wildlife and portraits. Most Mughal paintings were commissioned and were confined mainly to book illustrations and miniatures. Earlier periods of Mughal paintings used a team of artists, similar to Western workshops, where each artist played a different role in the process of completing the work

72B

Krishna, Radha and Women, 19th century
Artist Unknown, Mughal (or Mogul) style, India
Gouache or casein on fabric, 25.0 x 35.2 cm., 9-3/4 x 13-7/8"
Paul A. Anderson Chair in the Arts Collection Purchase in Honor of Dean Pareena Lawrence, Augustana College Art Collection, SDC2011.2.2

of art, such as determining composition, coloring, and delineating distinctive faces. Later, individual artists were commissioned to complete an entire painting. Artists were Persians as well as Indian Muslims and Hindus. This collaborative process helped to foster the development of a specifically Mughal style of painting distinctly different from the Persian style (Sarder). This style of painting was further developed and refined during the reigns of Akbar's heirs. In many Mughal paintings, a single frame could depict multiple scenes and narrate different events. In the later phase, Mughal art was influenced by Western art and started using light and shade to create the illusion of space and volume (Beach 39-110).

The two 19th-century Mughal paintings that are part of the Augustana collection are on silk and each narrates a single event. The borders are painted in gold with a floral motif. The first of the two paintings (72B) represents Hindu Lord Krishna, characteristically blue-skinned, and his consort Radha in conversation with three women who are carrying water on their heads at dusk. The artist(s) have used bright blue and pink colors and paid attention to details such as necklace, anklets, bangles, earrings, head jewelry and eyelashes.

The second painting (72A) depicts a tiger attacking an elephant during a tiger hunt in the semi-arid setting of Western India. The action is furthered through the incorporation of three men armed with spears as well as one with a bow and arrows. The colors chosen by the artist(s) reflect earth tones and show exceptional details in the facial features, clothing and jewelry worn by the soldiers and royalty. These works eloquently illustrate the later phase of Mughal art, evidenced by traditional Eastern subject matter as it was impacted by Western illusionistic characteristics and the Rajasthani style of painting that became increasingly dominant in north India in the eighteenth and nineteenth centuries.

[Pareena G. Lawrence, *Dean of the College and Professor of Economics*]

73

The Voyage of Life—Youth, 1849
After Thomas Cole (American 1801–1848) by James Smillie (Scottish American 1807–1885)
Hand-colored engraving, 50.8 x 67.4 cm., 20 x 26-1/2" image
Purchase through Gift of the Reynold Emanuel and Johnnie Gause Leak Holmén Endowment Fund for the Visual Arts, Augustana College Art Collection, 1998.12

Immediately following the American Revolution, the art scene in America was focused primarily on portraits and history paintings of such notable heroes as George Washington and Paul Revere. However, a new and independent America needed a revised national art identity, something distinctly American. Such an identity was found in the vast wilderness and rugged landscape that stretched within the boundaries of this young country. International Romanticism fostered appreciation for nature that America, with its untouched and unspoiled wilderness, seemed to fulfill. America's most important landscape painter was truly Thomas Cole, who combined the modern interest in nature with tradition.

In 1839, Samuel Ward commissioned Cole to paint a four-part, allegorical series called *The Voyage of Life: Childhood, Youth, Manhood, and Old Age*. He wanted these paintings to convey a basic Christian moral dealing with the journey of life and the passage of time. Cole developed the paintings specifically to be exhibited side-by-side in order to emphasize the chronological stages in life of the main character, complimented by the corresponding changes in the seasons as time passed. The second painting, *Youth*, represents confidence and expectation. It is the most optimistic scene of the series, and was therefore the most popular.

The hand-colored engraved version, pictured here, was part of a print series, commissioned by a minister in 1849, the year after Cole's death. This patron recognized the greater didactic potential that multiple affordable images offered a larger audience, toward further spreading their "pure moral tone and Christian sentiment" (Kasson 42-56). In *Youth*, the infant has become a young man. Although still inexperienced, he now holds the rudder and steers the small craft into the waters ahead, as his guardian angel watches from the bank. The stream is very clear, and the towering trees on the riverbanks and rich, green foliage of summer represent a youthful life full of promise. Cole painted a late morning summer scene in order to convey a feeling for the climax and full fruition of life.

[Julius Gylys, *Class of 2008*]

Youth depicts a young man in a golden boat floating calmly down the river. The most critical part of the print hangs in the misty clouds above the mountains in the sky. An elegant castle erupts out of the clouds, clearly the pride of the Heavens. In partnership with this *castle in the sky* is a woman, a guardian angel, near the bank of the river acting as the young man's mentor, urging him to continue along the path of life. This represents the point in our lives that college students have reached. Students at Augustana are attending college because they have some inkling of a dream they want to achieve. All of us can place ourselves in such a boat aimed toward reaching our goals. Students today can thus directly relate to this work of art created, as was Augustana College, over 150 years ago.

[Alexis Long, *Class of 2014*]

74

The Voyage of Life—Old Age, ca.1850
After Thomas Cole (American 1801–1848) by James Smillie (Scottish American 1807–1885)
Hand-colored engraving, 38.3 x 57.8 cm., 15-1/16 x 22-3/4" image
Purchased through Gift of the Reynold Emanuel and Johnnie Gause Leak Holmén Endowment Fund for the Visual Arts, Augustana College Art Collection, 1998.13

The fourth and final painting in the series *The Voyage of Life—Old Age*, commissioned for Samuel Ward in 1839 (Kasson 42-56), reflects the conflicting motifs of life and aging that were present during the mid-nineteenth century. At the beginning of the century, attitudes toward aging tended towards *gerentophilia*, or the valuing of old age. Those few who survived to old age were considered wise men and women. As late as the early 18th century, most wealth and power was still held in the hands of the elders. But industrialization, migration, and capitalism let to declining power among seniors, just as more and more people were living longer (T. R. Cole 55-56). Ironically, as life expectancy rose from approximately 40 years of age at midcentury to the current age of 80 (United States Bureau of the Census, 45), *gerontophobia*, the fear of old age, emerged and today dominates. Simultaneously, attitudes shifted from aging as something ordered by the Divine to something mortals, or at least science and medicine, could control. Oliver Wendell Holmes' poem "The Deacon's Masterpiece or The Wonderful One-Hoss Shay" first published in 1858, highlights this shift.

Cole's painting contains elements of both gerontophilic and gerontophobic views. The old man no longer guides his boat, now damaged and missing the hourglass so prominent in the three earlier canvases. He does not control the direction of the craft. He sits in the boat, rather than stands. He is stooped, diminished, and frail; clearly at the end of life. But his face is hopeful and alert as he gazes upward. There is no sign of senescence in his eyes. In fact, he does have control of his future. He lifts his countenance and hands to the bright, immortal, heavenly skies. He now is able to see his guardian angel, and is intent on leaving behind the stark, grim, barren landscape of old age. Cole himself wrote about this in his poem about the series. His "voyager, an ancient man, withered and blighted by the frosts of time...knew 'his Angel'; ne'er before discerned...And he soars—away—away!" (T. Cole).

[Marsha Y. Smith, *Professor of Sociology*]

75

La Galerie Notre Dame (Notre Dame Passageway), 1853
Charles Meryon (French 1821–1868), printed by Auguste Delâtre (French 1822–1907)
Etching and engraving on chine-collé, 28.3 x 17.5 cm., 11-1/8 x 6-7/8" image
Paul A. Anderson Chair in the Arts Collection Purchase, Augustana College Art Collection, 2000.29

Despite his color blindness, Meryon clearly possessed a unique sensitivity to subtle variations in shades of certain colors and the delicate gradations of light and dark, making the primarily black-and-white medium of etching a perfect choice (Southgate 105). He embraced the technique wholeheartedly, focusing his attention on medieval Gothic architecture. This choice of subject was inspired at least in part by the current Parisian reconstruction initiated by French ruler Napoleon III, who hoped to improve the poor living conditions of lower class sections of *old Paris*. The streets there were narrow, dark and dirty, as they were arranged like a labyrinth, making travel difficult and ultimately promoting disease through lack of ventilation. Meryon and some of his contemporaries openly objected to this plan for demolition and to the advancement of progress in general. His primary means of protest was recorded in his series of etchings of sites in old Paris that were slated for destruction. He identified with the spirit of these old Gothic buildings in an intensely personal manner, indicative of a Romantic temperament, beyond what other artists ever achieved. His accurate, highly-detailed renderings of architecture and use of careful preliminary drawings, reflect the influence that traditional academic classicism had on his technique.

La Galerie Notre Dame is one of six etchings by Meryon of the impressive Parisian Cathedral of Notre Dame, also a source of inspiration for Victor Hugo. Meryon typically coupled his bold *chiaroscuro,* contrast of light and shadow, with painstakingly accurate attention to detail that earned him much praise. The shadows are strongly emphasized, almost exaggerated, for effect. He also employed his own brand of iconography in many of his works, such as the crows added here, some flying in the background sky, and others landing within the passageway, which smoothly connect interior and exterior spaces. Since Meryon held a rather high-minded, rigid sense of morality (Bradley 31), they may also have represented the degraded moral state of Paris as he saw it, perhaps symbolizing that old Paris, in its current state, had effectively "gone to the birds" (DeLamoreaux 88).

[Alisha Boley, *Class of 2006*]

76

Black Lion Wharf, 1859
James Abbott McNeill Whistler (American 1834–1903)
Etching and drypoint, from *A Series of Sixteen Etchings of Scenes on the Thames and Other Subjects* or *"The Thames Set,"*
15.2 x 22.4 cm., 6 x 8-3/4" image
Paul A. Anderson Chair in the Arts Collection Purchase, Augustana College Art Collection, 2002.16

The year 1859 found American expatriate artist, James Abbott McNeill Whistler, sketching in the East End of London along the Thames River amongst the working class. Here he gained material for *A Series of Sixteen Etchings of Scenes on the Thames and Other Subjects*, a series that would come to be known as *The Thames Set*. In this set, he recorded the colorful haunts along the Thames, soon to be erased through modernization that entailed building an embankment. Similar views in Paris, recorded by Charles Meryon, likely inspired Whistler to similarly immortalize such traditional scenes before they disappeared. This set of etchings was completed in 1861 and was positively received by critics of the time, who appreciated Whistler's evident skill in the medium (MacDonald, de Montfort, and Thorp). *Black Lion Wharf* has become one of the most popular etchings in the series and must have been a favorite of the artist's in that it was included in the background of his iconic painting, *Arrangement in Grey and Black: Portrait of the Artist's Mother* (1871).

In *Black Lion Wharf*, Whistler effectively captured the essence of the gritty, grimy dock areas that he experienced while immersed in this environment along the Thames River. He utilized his skill in etching to convey a sense of space and depth in *Black Lion Wharf*, as evidenced by his using different techniques to separate the foreground and background. The main subjects, a seated man and his surroundings, are boldly outlined in the foreground. His size suggests both his importance and his proximity to the viewer, and the sketchy quality of the lines may indicate movement or action. Conversely, the detail and definition of the buildings in the background provide a sense of permanency, while their diminished scale indicates visual distance.

Very little definition was included on the water's surface which thus affords a visual break in the work. The figures in the middle ground are represented in less detail to suggest that they are of lesser importance to the main figure. When viewed as a whole, the delicate details such as smoke from a chimney in the background offset the bold, dark lines in the foreground and make a cohesive composition. In combination, the effects of these various elements communicate the picturesque nature of everyday scenes. Whistler ultimately came to be regarded as the greatest etcher since Rembrandt van Rijn (catalogue 26 and 27).

[Margaret Maksimovich, *Class of 2010*]

77A&B

77A

Nadar élevant la photographie à la hauteur de l'art (Nadar Raising Photography to the Height of Art), 1862
Honoré Daumier (French 1808–1879)
Lithograph, published in *Le Boulevard,* 28.8 x 22.1 cm., 11-3/8 x 8-11/16" image
Paul A. Anderson Chair in the Arts Collection Purchase, Augustana College Art Collection, 2000.28

77B

Portrait of Honoré Daumier, 1877
Gaspard-Félix Tournachon (Nadar) (French 1820–1910)
Woodburytype photograph from a ca. 1865 negative, published in *Galerie contemporaine, littéraire, artistique, année 2*, Paris, 12.0 x 8.4 cm., 4-3/4 x 3-5/16" image
Paul A. Anderson Chair in the Arts Collection Purchase, Augustana College Art Collection, 2007.4

Honoré Victorin Daumier was a French artist who delighted a mostly *bourgeois* audience with his illustrations. Daumier turned his drawings into prints by producing them as lithographs. He enjoyed using this medium because it effectively captured the immediacy of his sketches. Daumier's chosen technique enabled him to reach a larger audience through multiple prints drawn on the lithographic stone—a democratic approach to patronage. During his lifetime he created nearly six thousand lithographs. His early works were characterized by a revolutionary spirit with biting illustrations for *La Caricature* and *Le Charivari*, popular journals of the day.

Nadar Raising Photography to the Level of Art (77A) is a piece that really defines Daumier's mature style. It portrays a single subject, as most of his illustrations do, and the drawing is further animated through Daumier's signature lively and energetic lines. As with most of his lithographic production, this work was printed in black and white. It illustrates a gentler side than his earlier political cartoons. Here, he explores the world of modern life, with its innovations and foibles. This lithograph, like most of his illustrations, was published in the press, in this case in *Le Boulevard* (1862).

An innovative photographer, Nadar was struggling to have his photographs, such as his portrait of Daumier (77B) seen as real works of art. He believed that art could be expressed in many ways, including photography. Nadar would also take *bird's-eye view* photographs from his hot air balloon in order to achieve the vantage points he desired, in this case, of the city of Paris.

Daumier here illustrates Nadar in his familiar hot air balloon which he dubbed the *Giant* (77A). He appears as an awkward bourgeois entrepreneur, with hat flying and topcoat disheveled. The windblown effect illustrates the excitement of the aerial feat depicted. The double meaning of this lively cartoon is evident—Nadar is raising photography to the height of art—both physically through his bird's-eye view as well as symbolically with his advocacy for photography's being considered a major art medium, like painting and sculpture.

[Matthew Brownley, Class of 2005 and Catherine Carter Goebel, *Editor*]

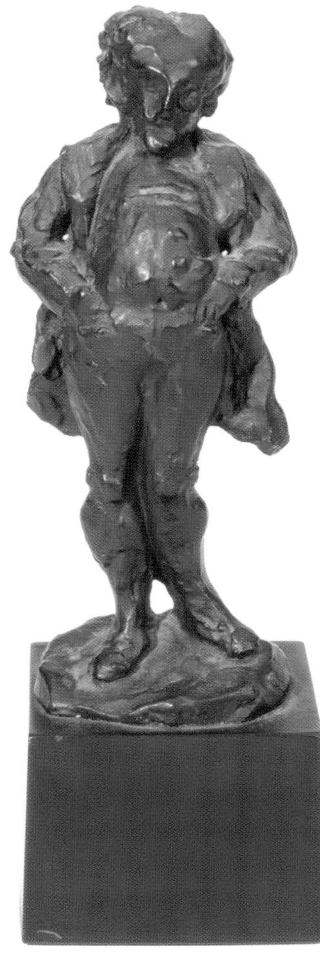

***Le Monsieur qui ricane* (The Scoffer)**, terra cotta original dated ca. 1849–1850
Honoré Daumier (French 1808–1879)
Cast bronze , 25.4 x 7.9 x 7.9 cm., 10 x 3-1/8 x 3-1/8" with base
Lent Courtesy of Private Collection in Honor of Dr. Thomas B. Brumbaugh

Most of his contemporaries had no idea that Honoré Daumier was one of the first French artists to experiment with modern Realist sculpture. Famous as a lithographic illustrator for the popular press, his sculptures were a means by which he could study character and form, in three dimensions, which he would then translate onto the lithographic stone. Daumier's art as a whole does not have an elevated idealistic vision, unless this was defined as truth to nature in depicting the dignity of the common person, like many Realists of his time. His works appealed to the general eye—one did not need to have a background in the Classics, history, theology or literature to appreciate them. In an age dominated by the *bourgeoisie*, these elements appealed to an audience that preferred recognizable and easily comprehensible imagery.

Le Monsieur qui Rican (The Scoffer), was named by Maurice Gobin in his catalogue raisonné (Gobin 47) of Daumier sculpture. The movement of the coattails and hair are similar to the portrayal of the photographer in Daumier's lithograph of Nadar (77A). The artist used a rough-modeled realism to detail the character of his subject. With the elderly man's receding hairline and his modeled flesh, a finer sense of variation is revealed which gives him a distinctly caricatured face.

Dressed in outmoded frock coat and trousers streaming over his protruding belly, the subject projects a mix of self-confidence within a smug posture. The sweeping diagonals revitalize the figure. His gaze looks off into the distance, balanced by his shoulders and chest which propel him forward as he arches his back in a dramatic curve, thrusting his hands solidly into his pockets. This model clearly shows Daumier's skill in sculpting, delineating the figure's dramatic expression which has been described as *Goyaesque* (catalogue 62 and 63) (Wasserman 231). Although it may not be his most famous piece, *Le Monsieur* demonstrates Daumier's masterful ability to take a seemingly immobile model and make him tell a thousand words.

[Aron Lees, Class of 2008 and Catherine Carter Goebel, *Editor*]

79

The Army of the Potomac—A Sharpshooter on Picket Duty, 1862
Winslow Homer (American 1836–1910)
Magazine wood engraving, from 15 November 1862 *Harper's Weekly*, 23.3 x 34.9 cm., 9-1/8 x 13-3/4" image
Gift of Mr. and Mrs. George and Pat Olson, Augustana College Art Collection, 1999.1

As a correspondent-artist for *Harper's Weekly*, Winslow Homer recorded the lives and adventures of Northern soldiers in camp, on reconnaissance, in battle, and in this case, on sniper duty. While certain images served to valorize wartime activities, many also pointed to the horrors of modern warfare with its distanced, impersonal killing fostered by rifled muskets, telescopic sights and flesh-shredding bolts (Hess 197-217). This tension can be seen in "The Army of the Potomac—A Sharpshooter on Picket Duty.-[From a painting by W. Homer, Esq.]," which appeared in print on 15 November 1862.

A wood engraving on newsprint, this particular image was based on Homer's first oil painting of the same name, which was based on camp sketches he made while imbedded with the Army of the Potomac during the Peninsula Campaign of 1862. By the time the painting was exhibited in January 1864, the horrors of war first seen during this operation were being regularly reported on and printed in image form. Nevertheless, several people both in the public and in the army still viewed Berdan Sharpshooters as heartless killers. Years later even Homer remarked, "I looked through one of their [sharpshooters'] rifles once when they were in a peach orchard in front of Yorktown in April 1862" and it "struck me as being as near murder as anything I could think of in connection with the army & I always had a horror of that branch of the service" (np).

Homer's close-up on this "Dead Eye for the Union" is composed in such a way that it is as if the viewer is sitting in the adjoining tree, partaking of this isolated life. Particularly interesting is Homer's use of line to draw attention to the shooter's eye as it stares down the barrel of the telescopic scope, drawing a bead on another unsuspecting kill that could be as far as one mile away. As Nicolai Cikovsky, Jr. notes, "Homer's image of the sharpshooter is all the more forceful and meaningful because of the extraordinary visual and symbolic compactness of its form that makes the subject not an incident or episode of the war, but an emblem of what is essential in and special to it" (22).

[Scott Irelan, *Assistant Professor of Theatre*]

80

1861 The War for the Union 1865/Photographic War History, 1078. The Ambulance Corps, ca. 1892 print after 1864 photograph of ambulance drill at Headquarters, Army of Potomac, Virginia
Taylor and Huntington, The War Publication and Exhibition Co.
Albumen stereoview photograph, 8.2 x 16.1 cm., 3-3/16 x 6-3/8" image
Paul A. Anderson Chair in the Arts Collection Purchase, Augustana College Art Collection, 2010.18

This image appears to show wounded men on a Civil War battlefield being loaded into a wagon. Closer examination, however, reveals that the wounded are neatly arranged for the composition and, though bandaged, have no bloodstains. What the image actually records is an ambulance drill taking place sometime between 1861 and 1864.

The Union's Ambulance Corps shown here was new, organized due to public pressure over the lack of trained ambulance crews (Wagner). The Ambulance Corps would first be put to the test at the Battle of Antietam in 1862 (Dearth).

A few men are wearing baggy trousers and turbans—not the standard Union uniform. This costume reflected the "Zouave craze" that saw some American troops emulate the light infantry regiments of the French Army serving in North Africa ("The 5th"). The drummer at right may have been a bandsman pressed into ambulance service, as frequently happened.

Technology had advanced sufficiently by the Civil War to make it possible for photographers to capture events as they unfolded, although the work of hauling bulky equipment and chemicals in the field was difficult. Their plate glass negatives could make prints like this one using albumen, a substance found in egg whites. It was the most popular and inexpensive method of printmaking from about 1850-90 ("Albumen Print").

To produce a stereoview, a camera with two lenses takes two images about 2.5 inches apart (about the distance between our eyes). Even though they appear the same, the images are slightly different. When we look at the images through a stereoviewer, our brains put the two images together as a 3D picture.

Stereoviews were enormously popular before and after the Civil War, documenting everything from tourist sites to historic events. Families commonly had a stereoviewer and collection of photos they used for entertainment and education, and photographers leapt at the chance to provide this market with Civil War images.

Although the demand for war photos diminished after the war ended, stereoviews like this one were used as a sort of 1860s slideshow. The War Publication and Exhibition Co., which produced this print, sold a complete setup—stereoviewers, images and notes—to anyone who wanted to go on the lecture circuit (Gleeson).

[Leslie Dupree, *Director of Web Services and New Media*]

81

Woman Sewing Amongst Cows, mid 19th century France
Attributed to Barbizon School (follower of Camille Corot [French 1796-1875])
Oil on linen, 39.3 x 53.5 cm., 15-1/2 x 21-1/8"
Purchase with Gift of Mr. Dan Churchill, Augustana College Art Collection, SDC2004.12

Woman Sewing Amongst Cows is a beautiful nineteenth-century landscape scene with all the necessary elements. From the babbling brook to the background filled with an open field, the artist clearly knew how to construct a pleasing piece. This painting originated from the French Barbizon school, which bridged the Romantic Movement with Realism.

The Barbizon was the first major organized group of nineteenth-century landscape painters, centered in the village of Barbizon, located within the verdant Forest of Fountainebleau. The woods around Barbizon were kept in their pristine condition for the pleasure of the king, since they surrounded the Palace of Fountainebleau, the hunting palace for French royalty. This area thus provided artists with unspoiled natural scenery to inspire them with subjects for their artwork.

At first glance, viewers might note the deep shade that the trees cast over the foreground, enveloping the woman and the cows. She sits peacefully as she quietly works, presumably sewing, while tending the herd. Barbizon artists were often called *Romantic Realists*, to acknowledge that although like Realists, they focused on everyday observed reality, they often included a slight interpretive sense of Romantic grace. As in many of Camille Corot's paintings, the cows are given more attention than the woman.

This is not a work of history or mythology, but instead, represents the present in a prosaic manner. There is no great action or moral, simply a normal day in everyday modern life. In the distance, the light rakes across the field, revealing more cattle as well as buildings. The style of brushwork is lively, yet gentle. This is consistent with nineteenth-century Barbizon landscapes by Corot, who generally did not reveal every detail, yet managed to communicate the story of his figures within their environment. The cows here appear to be comfortable with the woman's proximity as they graze, and one meanders to the creek. The artist might be painting something with which he was familiar and had directly observed from life, undoubtedly in the Barbizon environs.

[Brian Allured, *Class of 2005* and
Catherine Carter Goebel, *Editor*]

La Bouillie **(The Baby Gruel),** 1861
Jean-François Millet (French 1814–1875)
Etching, 16.1 x 13.3 cm., 6-3/8 x 5-1/4" image
Paul A. Anderson Chair in the Arts Collection
Purchase, Augustana College Art Collection, 2008.11

How do we represent mothers and children, in art, in politics, in everyday conversation? Who can be called a good mother, and why? This wonderful nineteenth-century print can begin such conversations about social relationships. Millet is known as a Realist, preferring practical scenes of the everyday lived experience. Later artists would take a turn toward more Impressionistic, sometimes idealized maternal scenes. Viewing representations of mothers and children in art can help us begin to uncover hidden messages about good motherhood—messages and rules that change over time, but that always are considered important to the functioning society.

In public discourse, mothers both matter and don't. Motherhood may be portrayed as the single most important role in any society and simultaneously devalued in public and private discourse about *success*. Motherhood is intensely political, with all of a culture's most cherished values bound up in how we define families. Current conversations about *good* motherhood include heated debates pitting *working mothers* against *stay-at-home* mothers, with stereotypically narrow views of care and love within each category. Having only one represented view of honorable motherhood can hurt all mothers, and in so doing, hurt children and families as well. In spite of the easy narratives of a simpler past, we always have had multiple ways of mothering our children, of caring for them, of defining family and *motherwork*. And yet the battle for representing good motherhood is fierce.

At a time when most scholarly analyses place the United States dead last among industrialized nations in terms of support for working families (without the guarantee of even unpaid leave, demand for affordable daycare far outpacing the supply, and contestation about the merits of universal healthcare that would cover stay-at-home parents and children), this lovely little print based on a pencil drawing could and should spark firestorms of debate about what we think of and how we value family and caring practices. Do we value those who care for our sick and nurture our children? Are they even visible at all?

Millet has given us a window into one story of motherhood, of childhood, of care and of work. To be true to Millet, perhaps our job now is to ask the tough questions about our own cultural stories of motherhood and care, and, to act upon those questionings with our own best gifts and skills.

[Sharon Varallo, *Associate Professor of Communication Studies, Violet M. Jaeke Chair of Family Life*]

83

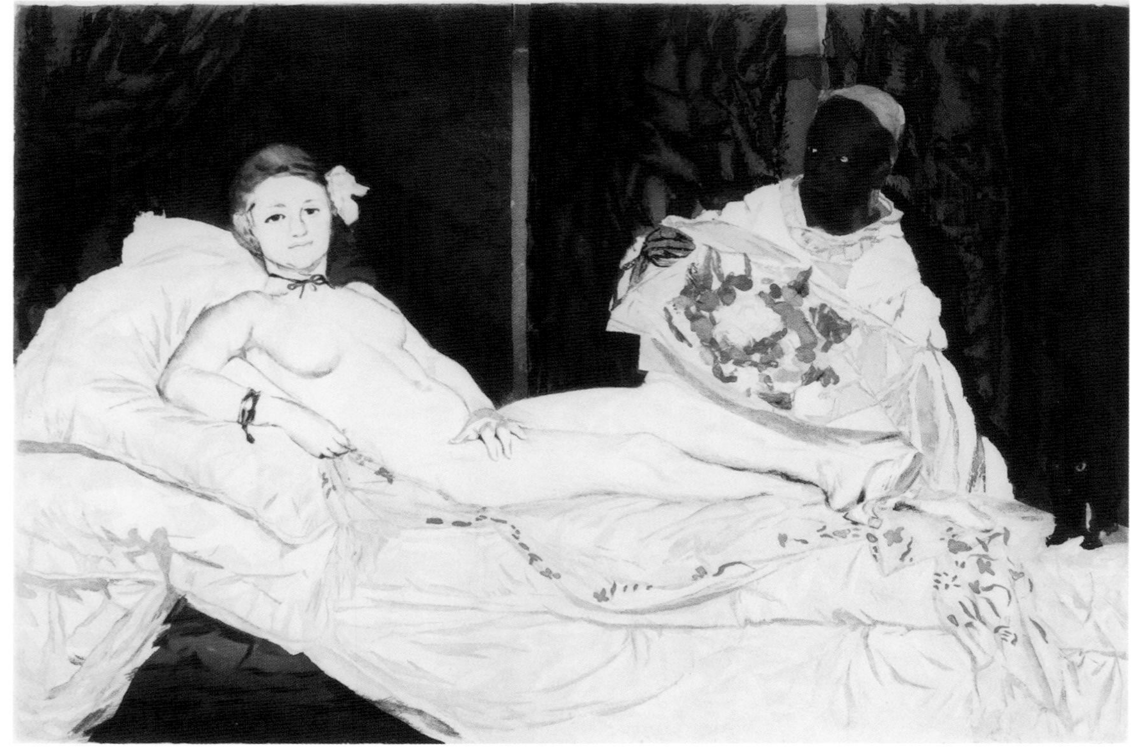

L'Olympia, after 1865 painting, 1926
After Édouard Manet (French 1832–1883) by Jacques Villon (French 1875–1963)
Aquatint in colors, backed with parchment paper, 47.4 x 58.5 cm., 16 x 23" image
Gift of Private Collection of Luis R. Ubillus and Alex M. Adelman, Augustana College Art Collection, 2010.54

Often deemed the "Father of Modernism," Édouard Manet played a pivotal role in transitioning the Western art world from one of academic traditions and standards to one of individual direction and interpretation (Rabinow). His painting, *Olympia* of 1865, is an exceptional example of deviation from the art historical canon. With a recognized prostitute set as the main attraction, the composition makes no apologies for the lifestyle portrayed. Being served flowers from a gentleman caller as she strikingly challenges the viewer's gaze, we are abruptly aware not of the classical nudity before us, but of the nakedness this common woman splays.

Her pose heavily recalls Renaissance painter Titian's *Venus of Urbino* of 1538, deeming this painting as, at the very least, in conversation with past masters. However, we are not looking at a goddess, or admiring the beauty of the female form. Instead, we are peering at the modern Venus' vulnerable flesh, a human form not being recognized for its splendor, but rather as a means of sustenance for the prostitute. The painting caused a great scandal upon being accepted into the Paris Salon in 1865 because of its blunt sexuality and frank portrayal.

This painting, along with his controversial *Luncheon on the Grass* of 1863, gave Manet a great deal of recognition, be it positive or negative. He situated himself as a deviant in terms of his original, unconventional subject matter. Prostitutes, seen as practically bottom rung on the ladder of social classes, had infiltrated the decadent Salon, walls normally adorned with conservative academic paintings. Thus, Manet had made his mark, inspiring future generations of artists with his nonstandard tactics and innovative style.

One of these artists is quite obviously Jacques Villon, a French painter and printmaker, who chose to copy *Olympia* in the form of a color aquatint. Artists such as Manet, Edgar Degas and Henri de Toulouse-Lautrec initially inspired Villon's artistic career, before he later opted for the Fauvist, Cubist and Abstract Expressionist movements. Aquatint is a medium that belongs to the intaglio family of printmaking. It serves as a variant of etching in which the printmaker makes marks on a copper or zinc plate to which the ink may then be transferred. The flatness and broad planes of color evident in Olympia translate quite nicely to Villon's aquatint, deeming the later version both a nod to the successes of Manet, the legacy he left behind and its ability to remain relevant long after its birth.

[Katherine E. Goebel, *Assistant Editor*]

84

Charles Baudelaire, Full Face III, dated 1865 but prepared 1868 for 1869 publication
Édouard Manet (French 1832–1883), printed by Atelier Salmon
Etching and aquatint, 9.5 x 8.2 cm., 3-13/16 x 3-1/4" image
Paul A. Anderson Chair in the Arts Collection Purchase, Augustana College Art Collection, 2002.5

During the course of their friendship, Charles Baudelaire and Édouard Manet were pioneers for artistic modernity, in part in reaction against the belief that art should be timeless and classical. Such traditional conservative views discouraged artists from creating contemporary subjects in their paintings which might specifically date them, presumably rendering them meaningless to future generations. This etched portrait of Baudelaire by Manet is the fourth state of four, entitled *Charles Baudelaire, Full Face III.*

Manet began this etching in 1865, while Baudelaire was still in Brussels, and he completed the fourth state in 1868, following his death. The first state of the etching is unadorned, and Baudelaire's face is clearly lit and visible. Manet completed the second two states during Baudelaire's mental decline. They predict the impending sense of loss, evident in the inclusion of memorial scrolls, inscribed with Baudelaire's name and embellished with flowers. Manet also added dramatic *chiaroscuro* (contrast of light and shadow) to the image which caused Baudelaire's eyes to appear shrunken, emphasizing his skull-like forehead. In this fourth and final state, published after Baudelaire's death, viewers sense the *memento mori* (reminder of death) tribute through which Manet commemorated his close friend (Harris 187-190).

The fourth state etching was exhibited at the Salon of 1869 and published in the same year in a biography on the poet (Harris 190). The final version of Manet's portrait of Baudelaire effectively communicates the deep-thinking theorist whose life ended far too soon. He wears the topcoat and cravat of the *bourgeoisie* (middle class). His influence was immense as his criticism fueled the Realist and Impressionist movements and his controversial book of poems, *Les Fleurs du mal* (1857), helped inspire late nineteenth-century Symbolism.

[Nikki Kromphardt, *Class of 2005* and Catherine Carter Goebel, *Editor*]

The history behind this piece illustrates the relationship between the artist, Édouard Manet, and the poet and critic, Charles Baudelaire. Both of these men pioneered artistic modernity through their respective artwork. Most artists of this time aimed for timeless depictions. Manet and Baudelaire, on the other hand, saw the value of depicting their own environs. In an 1846 Salon review, Baudelaire urged his contemporaries to note the world around them, suggesting they should *be of their time*: "Parisian life is rich in poetic and wonderful subjects. The marvelous envelopes and saturates us like atmosphere; but we fail to see it" (Baudelaire 52-53) Manet responded to his friend's advice and displays the writer, in *bourgeois* attire, with deep thought and emotion carved into his face. This is perhaps owing to the fact that this final state was completed following the death of Baudelaire, as a sort of posthumous tribute, and thus also demonstrates the deep loss felt by Manet.

[Amanda Greenlee, *Class of 2014*]

85

Early Morning, 1878
James Abbott McNeill Whistler (American 1834–1903)
Lithotint, 16.7 x 26.0 cm., 6-9/16 x 10-1/4" image
Paul A. Anderson Chair in the Arts Collection Purchase, Augustana College Art Collection, 1999.22

The gentle lithotint, *Early Morning* (1878), is a highlight in the advent of modernity in nineteenth-century art. Its artist, the eccentric American expatriate, James Abbott McNeill Whistler, was an inimitable figure in his day. Throughout his career of painting and printmaking he acted as an individual, freely associating with various art movements of the late 1800s.

Whistler's interest in harmonious aesthetics, in coordinating all the elements of a work, led him to explore the artistic manipulations possible with printmaking. Once the image is etched into the metal plate, and the ink is wiped into the depths created by the acid treatment, the areas meant to be blank must be wiped clean of excess ink. Lighting effects can be accomplished by doing this selectively, creating an effect of dramatic contrasts in tone called *chiaroscuro* (Lochnan 60-61). Whistler also varied the hue of his inks from dark browns to blacks, and the quality and effect of his papers.

In 1878, Whistler began collaboration with the printer Thomas Way to use the relatively untested technique of the *lithotint*, a form of lithography that employed special solvent and pigment washes applied selectively by brush. The result had the fluid gradations of hand-painted monochromatic watercolor, a smoothness comparable to the luxury of velvet. *Early Morning* is one of six lithotints Whistler completed for publication.

Many of the design elements of *Early Morning* are shared among Whistler's prints. The simplicity and subtle abstraction of form in this riverside landscape were more typical of his later, more understated works, although early in his career he made a departure from over-embellished Victorian print styles. Also notable for *Early Morning* is the hazy, passive, rather than didactic, impression of the scene, expressing Whistler's preference for design over content. The elegant balance between positive and negative space, between the inked shorelines and the almost blank sea and sky areas in the distinctly horizontal composition, mimics the design virtues of Japanese woodblock prints and porcelain, which Whistler collected throughout his life (Goebel 19).

[Carol Marquardsen, *Class of 2006*]

86

The Beach at Trouville, ca. 1864
Louis-Eugène Boudin (French 1824–1898) [R. Carta]
Oil on canvas, 24.1 x 35.3 cm., 9-1/2 x 13-7/8"
Lent Courtesy of Private Collection in Tribute to Steven C. Bahls, President, Augustana College

The Beach at Trouville (1864) is attributed to Louis-Eugène Boudin and is likely a smaller version of the published oil on panel of the same scene (Jean-Aubry and Schmit 41). It demonstrates the robust impression of nature gained through *plein-air* painting, to which Boudin introduced Monet six years earlier. The location at Trouville, a popular beach resort with the *bourgeoisie*, as well as Empress Eugénie and Napoleon III, provided a constant source of inspiration for the artist. Of the eleven works that Boudin exhibited at the Paris Salon between 1864 and 1869, seven were beach scenes from Trouville (Hamilton 63).

By 1864, Boudin had already painted such views for at least two years and had derived a basic formula whereby the sky consumes nearly two-thirds of the composition and the beach and sea together make up the other third. Also typical is the horizontal orientation with bands of sky punctuated with clouds, sea with boats and bathers, and the beach as stage-set for various diverse figures on holiday, seemingly unaware of the artist's presence.

In this beach scene, the viewer's eye is inevitably caught by the pair of women on the right, whose fashionable hoop skirts billow in the breeze. A quizzical dog seems to interact with these self-absorbed women, his tail ably suggested by the thinnest brushstroke. A *bathing machine*, off center to the left, provides a changing place to take refuge from the elements, its geometry at odds with the organic flow of the various figures that enliven the beach. Two women seem to brace themselves against the wind to its right, while a couple interacts at left. A group of three women further left appear to gossip as they react to the shore breeze, as does a gentleman to the far left, who gazes toward the far right at the two approaching women, effectively holding the composition together.

The distant spaces are beautifully and subtly rendered while the atmospheric perspective cools the colors as they retreat. The facility of the brushstroke, quickly noted, effectively indicates the figures in the distance: the boaters at left, the bathers just off center and the seated figures within the concave bay at right. In closely examining such consummate *plein-air* painting, viewers can appreciate the enthusiasm with which Claude Monet embraced Boudin's philosophy: "...My eyes were finally opened, and I really understood nature. I learned at the same time to love it...I was governed by the advice of Boudin" (Nochlin: 37-8).

[Dana Ziganto, *Class of 2007* and
Catherine Carter Goebel, *Editor*]

87

Pont Neuf, late 19th century
Albert Charles Lebourg (French, 1849–1928)
Oil on wood panel, 22.2 x 27.0 cm., 8-7/8 x 10-5/8"
Lent Courtesy of Private Collection

Impressionism, originating in Paris and rising to prominence in the 1870s and 1880s, is characterized by visible brushstrokes, ordinary subject matter, unusual visual angles, and emphasis on light and movement. Albert Charles Lebourg (1849-1928) is recognized as a French Impressionist for his skilled use of these techniques in his paintings. His early interest was architecture, but he developed a passion for art that flourished under the tutelage of the landscape painter, Victor Delamarre (1811-1868). Lebourg decided to give up architecture and enrolled in the *École Municipale de Peinture et de Dessin* in Rouen under Gustave Morin (1809-1886). He obtained the post of professor of drawing at the *Société des Beaux-Arts* in Algiers and remained there from 1872 to 1877. Here he began experimenting with depicting a single site in a variety of different lights, in a manner similar to works by Claude Monet (1840-1926) (Lebourg askart).

In 1877, Lebourg left Algeria and returned to Paris where he studied in the atelier of Jean-Paul Laurens for two years. It was here that he became aware of Impressionism and became friendly with Edgar Degas (1834-1917), Claude Monet and Alfred Sisley (1839-1899) (Lebourg FADA). The influence that this exposure to Impressionism had on his art is visible in his painting of the Pont Neuf, the oldest standing bridge across the river Seine in Paris. The informal vantage point Lebourg used in this work creates the impression that we are viewing the bridge through trees that line the bank of the river. It is seemingly an ordinary day with just a few people visible on the Pont Neuf. Lebourg's impressionistic brushstrokes blur the scene like an out-of-focus camera lens. Through this effect, we are given the sense of a moment that was captured in time but quickly moved on with the people bustling across the bridge.

Lebourg first exhibited his work at the *Salon de la Société des Artistes Français* in 1883 and again in 1886. Three years later he began exhibiting at the foundation of the *Société Nationale des Beaux-Arts* and exhibited there regularly from 1891 to 1914. Lebourg spent several years living and working in the Auvergne region and northern France before continuing his travels in the Netherlands and then Britain. His time spent in Britain confirmed his love of works by Romantic landscape painters such as Joseph Mallord William Turner, John Constable (catalogue 67), and Thomas Gainsborough. Lebourg continued working in a lucid Impressionist style up until 1921 when he was paralyzed by a stroke.

[Elizabeth Jakaitis, *Class of 2014*]

Pont des Arts, attributed to ca. 1860–1870
Charles Camille François Pécrus (French 1826–1907)
Oil on canvas, 33.0 x 46.4 cm., 13 x 18-1/4"
Lent Courtesy of Private Collection

French Impressionist Charles Pécrus' main subjects in painting were genre scenes and landscapes. In this pursuit, he was encouraged by friends such as Louis-Eugène Boudin (catalogue 86), the pivotal landscape painter who mentored Claude Monet. Although Pécrus often worked alongside Boudin, their styles differed. Boudin's "touch was more nervous and sometimes even jerky," and Pécrus "painted more gently while giving a light impression of blurriness" (Pécrus and Pécrus 4). Pécrus' oil *Pont des Arts* (Bridge of the Arts—completed in 1804) is an example of his combining his interests in genre and landscape. Many important Parisian figures crossed this centrally located historic bridge. Its wood and steel construction (the first of its kind in Paris) connected the Louvre on the right bank to the Institut de France on the left.

The building and reconstruction of this bridge hailed Napoleon III's innovative modernization of Paris, undertaken by Baron Haussmann during the mid-nineteenth century. Many Parisians felt that "Balzac's Paris—crumbling with age, slum-ridden, unsanitary, prone to cholera epidemics, over-crowded—was to be brought up to date" (Jones 214). Artists captured the renewed intimacy Parisians now felt toward their capital city. The depiction of such architectural achievements reflected Pécrus' homage to the newly renovated bridge, a magnificent example of French engineering within its urban environment. In this painting, Pécrus created a modern urban landscape, including genre scenes at the city's center. Parisians are portrayed in a variety of poses and locations along the Seine. Some are in the foreground engaging in daily activities accompanied by their dogs, others are strolling along the river and a few in the distance are crossing the Pont des Arts. Portraying these figures together in this scene demonstrated that Paris enjoyed much active life and leisurely flow.

Upon analyzing the technical aspects of Pécrus' brushstrokes, one notes that the lack of sharpness around the edges of the figures and the seeming blurriness of atmospheric perspective combine to give the painting that unfinished look for which the Impressionists are famous. Pécrus' interesting mix of colors is evident in his shades of black in the dog and owner in the foreground and in the famous bridge behind them. This specific technique was probably learned from Boudin who mixed shades of black in a similar fashion in his figures. In terms of stylistic composition, it is interesting to note that although this is an *urban* landscape, nearly two-thirds of the painting depicts the vast sky, river and trees lining the walkway. In fact the balance of nature and figures is quite similar to that achieved by Boudin in his Trouville beach resort depictions. With his Impressionist love for landscape, this painting also clearly reflects Pécrus' growing tendency to dedicate his work solely to nature.

[Colleen Jaycox, *Class of 2006*]

89

Le Jardin des Tuileries (The Tuileries Gardens), n.d.
Emma Ruff (French b. 1884)
Oil on canvas, 33.0 x 41.2 cm., 13 x 16-1/4"
Lent Courtesy of Private Collection in Honor of Thomas James Goebel

In *Le Jardin des Tuileries*, as in *Le Jardin du Luxembourg* (catalogue 90), Emma Ruff depicted a scene from everyday life, an afternoon at the popular Parisian park. An attentive young man in soldier's uniform converses with the object of his attention, a young lady, possibly the distracted nanny for the children playing in the sand below. Upper class and *bourgeois* Parisians stroll through the park in the background but are not necessarily the focal point. Small in scale and generally scattered throughout the painting, they share the spotlight with the gardens. The background apartment buildings are distanced through the use of atmospheric perspective, the cooler colors effectively convincing the viewer that they actually recede in space beyond the flat picture plane.

Located in the heart of Paris, the Tuileries have a long history, having been first constructed under Catherine de' Medici as private gardens next to the palace. They were later opened in the center to form an axis that projected outward, culminating in a boulevard leading to the Arc de Triomphe. When the city underwent its nineteenth-century renovation by Napoleon Bonaparte, and the palace was declared a public art museum, this became the grand axis of Paris that was used as the base for the new ground plan (Turner). People could escape the hectic city life in the parks and gardens, if only for a short while, and effectively get back to nature. Both young and old, wealthy and working class came to wander in these beautiful gardens.

This piece is very Impressionistic in the sense that Ruff used small dots of color to create a larger picture, revealed upon closer examination of the flowers and trees. Characteristic of Impressionism, the overall conception becomes more comprehensible when viewed from a distance. The Impressionists aimed not to paint a particular object, but instead to paint the light reflecting off that object. In doing so, they employed new theories on the physics of light, published by Eugène Chevreul, whose recent scientific theories established the color wheel, still accepted today. Shadows were no longer considered black but became the darker complementary colors to light, such as blues and purples opposite the warmer colors of orange and yellow. Light was broken into a myriad of hues and shades depending on the time of day, the weather and the angle of light.

[Beth Gilmartin, *Class of 2008*]

90

Le Jardin du Luxembourg (The Luxembourg Gardens), n.d.
Emma Ruff (French b. 1884)
Oil on canvas, 33.0 x 41.2 cm., 13 x 16-1/4"
Lent Courtesy of Private Collection in Honor of Katherine Elizabeth Goebel

Emma Ruff's style clearly reflects Impressionist roots. Her paintings are full of color and beauty, much like these works, yet there are some distinct differences. Her brushstrokes are much tighter, especially when depicting figures, a tendency also apparent in Impressionist Edgar Degas' beautifully drawn pieces (catalogue 98 and 106). Ruff's painting is oil on canvas. There are no existing records to indicate its exact date or if it was exhibited. It comes from a private collection and was likely meant to be paired with Ruff's other painting, *Le Jardin des Tuileries* (catalogue 89). Ruff's style might properly be called *conservative* Impressionism. It was probably painted *en plein air*, in open air on site, rather than in the studio. Most of the composition is bright and colorful, and you expect to see a blue sky with puffy, billowing clouds, but instead it is a subtle color, tinted with shades of gray above, perhaps hinting at a more romantic side to the artist or simply reflecting an overcast day.

The composition depicts the Luxembourg gardens in Paris. This location is indicated by the two shaded pathways and the sculpture and fountain. These beautiful gardens and their sculpture surround the Luxembourg Palace, once home to Marie de' Medici (catalogue 30), but now the headquarters for the French Senate. During the nineteenth century, as well as in our present time, these gardens seemed to belong to the people of Paris. They remain a favorite meeting place for Parisians during the milder seasons of the year. Throughout the garden, people from different walks of life gather: a family, a soldier, a young couple, the wealthy and the working. It is a place to relax and to play. Beyond the trees and the fountain, the *mansard* roofs which visually defined modern Paris tower over the gardens, evidence of the many recent changes sweeping away old Paris and replacing it with modern boulevards and buildings. But here in the park, one could still catch a glimpse of nature and retreat to a simpler world, seemingly far away from, but actually within the more complex city (Tinterow and Loyrette 142-143).

[Courtney Olson, *Class of 2007*]

91

Lilas (Lilacs), n.d.
Victor Bussière (French 1836–1905)
Oil on canvas, 55.0 x 38.0 cm., 21-3/4 x 15"
Paul A. Anderson Chair in the Arts Collection Purchase, Augustana College Art Collection, 2000.35

Little is known about Victor Bussière. So little, in fact, that he seems only to be mentioned as father to his better known painter-son, Gaston Bussière (1862-1929). We do know, however, that this work was probably atypical of Victor Bussière's repertoire since he was trained and worked as an interior mural painter in Paris and Macon during the mid-nineteenth century (Bussière 22). We can assume, then, that Victor probably painted *Lilacs* during or near the end of his apprenticeship. Given this, it is quite possible that this painting may have determined the direction of Victor's career.

Lilacs was painted at a time when still life subjects were still considered the lowest form of artistic representation by the French Salons. In 1840, still life was even mockingly described as "the hors d'oeuvre of painting" for its use of flowers and fruit as subject matter (Hardouin-Fugier 97). Paintings like this were purchased frequently to adorn dining rooms and were rarely hung in gallery exhibitions. Still life artists of the time, however, heralded the genre as a combination of the studies of nature, reality and light. Eventually this genre began to gain popularity and was increasingly shown in Salons. The French term for still life, *nature morte*, literally meaning *dead nature*, appropriately names the art form for its fixation on transient and decomposing subject matter.

Perhaps, then, *Lilacs* represents Victor Bussière as a still life artist-to-be who chose another path in his artistic career to avoid the difficulty of establishing himself in a genre surrounded by much criticism and debate. Yet Bussière successfully mastered the play of light on nature in this work, showing the effect of sunlight as it hits the plant's shiny green leaves. He also made use of still life's fundamental quality of decay by representing the flowers in different stages of growth—displaying both buds and full booms. Particularly beautiful is Bussière's use of *trompe l'oeil* (illusionism) and atmospheric perspective, making the flowers look almost as if they are growing into the viewer's personal space through an open window. The blossoms have such tactile quality that they offer their audience a visual bouquet.

[Amy DeLamoreaux, *Class of 2001*]

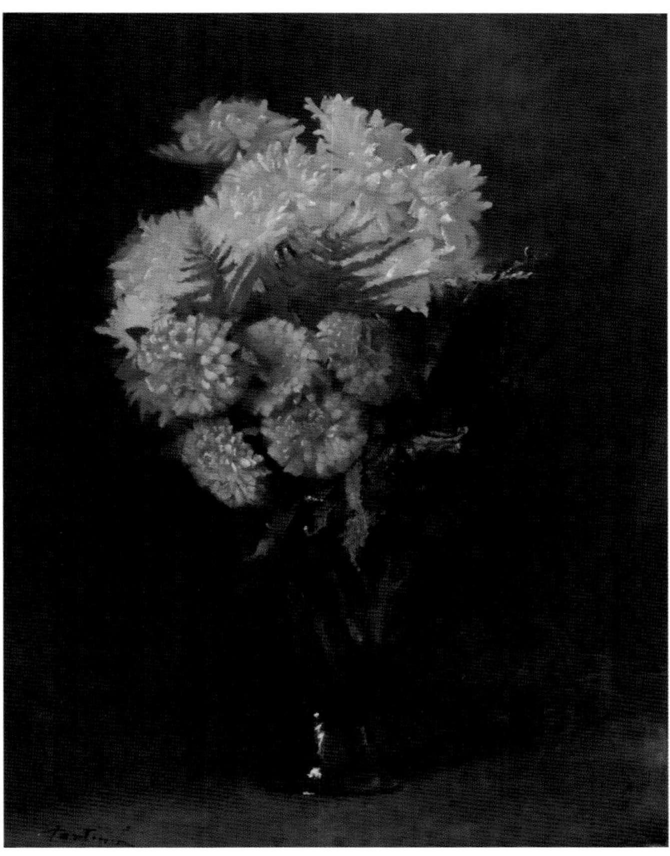

Floral Still Life, n.d.
Ignace-Henri-Jean-Théodore Fantin-Latour (French 1836–1904)
Oil on canvas, 51.5 x 40.8 cm., 20-1/4 x 16"
Lent Courtesy of Private Collection in Memory of Dr. Thomas William Carter

Perhaps the most formative influence in the development of Henri Fantin-Latour was the training he received not in an art school but in the Louvre where as a young artist he spent eighteen years copying the masters (Druick and Hoog 12). Here, Fantin observed, honed his technique, and steeped himself in the great tradition of art. In the halls of the Louvre, too, Fantin met fellow artists who were to shape his career, especially James McNeill Whistler (catalogue 76, 85, 103, 115 and 125) who more than anyone else was instrumental in promoting Fantin as a painter of still life.

Born in 1836 in Grenoble, the only child of an artist, Fantin learned early to draw and paint under his father's tutelage and later to paint from memory. Although well known as a painter of portraits and fantasies, subjects Fantin hoped would earn him lasting respect, it was as a painter of still life, especially flowers, that Fantin earned a reputation and a living, especially in England where Whistler introduced him to Mr. and Mrs. Edwin Edwards who for three decades successfully marketed his still life paintings to an eager English market.

Although acquainted with the Impressionists, Fantin didn't like to work in "the sun and the shade" (Lucie-Smith 22) outdoors, preferring to arrange a bouquet of flowers from his wife's cottage garden in Buré and paint it in the studio. His rendering of chrysanthemums in the painting here reveals his typical muted background (Poulet and Murphy 73), his attentiveness to the lush and elegant flower shapes, and his delight in a restrained reflection of light on glass and leaf, creating a charming effect of "hushed silence" (Bailey and Rishel 29).

Throughout his life, Fantin was ambivalent about still life, at times reveling in it as a "marvellous thing" (Druick and Hoog 113), and at others, distrusting its popularity, marketability, and repetitiveness—"Never have I had more ideas about art in my head, and yet I am forced to do flowers. While painting them—standing before the peonies and roses—I think of Michelangelo. This cannot go on" (Druick and Hoog 113). Yet, even when he didn't have to, "the visual poet of flowers" (Druick and Hoog 114) went on painting them for the rest of his life.

[Margaret Rogal, *Reference Librarian and Assistant Professor*]

93

Young Woman and Child in a Garden, ca. 1888–94
Berthe Morisot (French 1841–1895)
Oil on canvas, 35.9 x 21.7 cm., 14-1/8 x 8-9/16" sight
Lent Courtesy of Private Collection in Honor of Patricia Carter Deveau

This painting attributed to Berthe Morisot (1841-1895) is signed "BM" which was often the way Morisot acknowledged her smaller works. The subjects closely resemble those in other Morisot paintings such as *Young Woman and Child on the Isle* (1888) and *Young Woman and Child Avenue DuBois* (1894). Stylistically, the painting includes many of the elements typical of Impressionism. Morisot incorporates the *plein-air* technique that she first learned as a pupil of recognized landscapist Camille Corot.

The short, full brushstrokes establish an immediacy to the piece, while the size of the subjects in relation to the surroundings pulls the viewer close to them. The conversational moment is created as the woman with the wispy veil on her stylish hat bends toward the child. The facial features of the child are not clearly articulated, suggestive of the viewer's brief glance at the two. The pops of yellow and red, and the vibrant green background illustrate the Impressionist interest in bright color.

Everyday domestic life was frequently captured in Morisot's work, scenes suitable to a woman artist of her social class and time, and typical for Impressionists who wanted to avoid the more iconic images of the Academy. Morisot often used friends and family as subjects for her work, featuring harmonious scenes in parks and countryside. Even though widely exhibited and acclaimed, Morisot was often categorized, as were other women of the era, as an amateur. With her first solo exhibit in 1892, and the 1894 purchase of *Young Woman in a Ball Gown* by the French government for display at Luxembourg Palace, Morisot was able to shed this label and is today recognized as one of the leading artists of the movement.

[Ellen Hay, *Professor of Communication Studies*]

Child on Second Empire Balcony, 1872
John Dabour (b. Turkey, American 1837–1905)
Pastel, 76.4 x 63.5 cm., 30-1/8 x 24-15/16"
Paul A. Anderson Chair in the Arts Collection Purchase, Augustana College Art Collection, 2004.14

Child on a Second Empire Balcony is a beautiful pastel created by John Dabour in 1872. The date indicates that this work was completed at the dawn of the Impressionist movement in Paris (the first Impressionist exhibition occurred two years later in 1874). The image depicts a charming young child posing along the edge of a balcony while she stands directly in front of a room framed by curtains. Although the date, in French terms, indicates the early beginnings of Impressionism, it was created when Dabour was working in the United States, developmentally far behind contemporary European movements. American Impressionism began long after the Civil War.

Dabour's image reflects the Impressionist immediacy of capturing a specific moment in time as well as the sweet innocence of childhood that Mary Cassatt would establish as her hallmark (catalogue 95, 101 and 102). Like Cassatt, an American working in Paris, Dabour presented this child in a believable and sympathetic manner at eye level. One cannot help but be intrigued by her expression, and wonder, exactly what is the focus of her gaze? She seemingly looks out toward the audience, yet beyond us as well.

This image reflects elements of both modernism and tradition. We are presented with seemingly contradictory characteristics, such as an industrial wrought iron railing behind which a beautiful child in classical-revival dress stands. The metal factory-made floral patterns contrast with the natural delicate flower she holds. We are confronted with the immediacy of a sort of photographic zoom-lens view of a balcony in a modern apartment building yet softened by the traditional beauty of the pastel medium.

Most likely, this child spies an inviting distant garden (catalogue 89 and 90) and longs to go there. The pink flower she holds is a trumpet petunia, a native flower of France. This bloom seems to have been plucked from the vine or ivy entangled around the wrought iron railing of the balcony. A repeated pattern of this vegetation is seen throughout the image. Floral patterns are apparent in the lace sheers, the flowers on the vines and on the bottom section of the railing as well. This repeated three petal design might represent the insignia of France, the *fleur-de-lis*, or lily flower, symbol for the king. By the time Dabour created this image, the emblem was adopted and incorporated into most French architecture as was the use of wrought iron (Goebel).

[Michael Skelton, *Class of 2005*]

95

The Manicure, ca. 1908
Mary Cassatt (American 1844–1926)
Drypoint, 20.8 x 14.7 cm., 8-1/8 x 5-3/4" image
Purchase through Gift of the Reynold Emanuel and Johnnie Gause Leak Holmén Endowment for the Visual Arts, Augustana College Art Collection, 2001.27

The Manicure (1908) is a typical mother and child portrayal by Mary Cassatt. The purpose of such subjects, for which she was famous, is open to interpretation. In 1902, the Symbolist Camille Mauclair termed Cassatt a "painter of childhood," adding that "To paint an adult is to record a state of mind; to paint a child is to record the foreshadowing of a soul…Cassatt may be the only painter today to have given us an interpretation of childhood that is contained within the child itself" (Pollock 185-86).

The subject of *The Manicure* is enthralling. The mother and child interaction reflects the warmth of their relationship. Although Cassatt never married or had children of her own, she instinctively perceived the psychological *bonding* between mother and child. At a time when British Victorian subject matter was laden with saccharine sentimentality, Cassatt delved beneath the surface to create remarkable images that have truly stood the test of time.

Cassatt sensitively captured her models' outward appearance, as well as inner feelings, through subtle drypoint lines scratched on the copper plate. It is remarkable how the shading around the mother and child frame them, adding focus and tenderness to the composition. The manner in which the mother continues to work as the child's hand touches hers, reflects the subtle and tender feelings of blissful motherhood.

An interesting feature of this drypoint is the models' anonymity. Cassatt often used her own family and friends in such scenes. When she hired models, she preferred peasant women who were comfortable with handling their own children. There are many possible theories as to Cassatt's focus on the theme of mothers and children. Perhaps as a woman, she was more at home in the traditional domestic sphere and possibly, because she did not have children of her own, she longed for the emotional attachment that is shared only by a mother and her child. She was deeply rooted in her larger family and enjoyed painting her nieces and nephews. Impressionism was the "first avant-garde movement in the history of art in which women were significant members" (Slatkin 111), since artists like Edgar Degas (catalogue 98) recognized that Cassatt possessed "infinite talent" (Slatkin 109).

[Gayln Landem, *Class of 2007* and
Catherine Carter Goebel, *Editor*]

Jeune fille au chat, or **Girl with a Cat**, 1889
Berthe Morisot (French 1841–1895)
Drypoint, 14.8 x 12.1 cm., 5-7/8 x 4-3/4" image
Paul A. Anderson Chair in the Arts Collection Purchase in Honor of Professor Ellen Hay, Augustana College Art Collection, 2010.5

The print *Girl with a Cat* (1889) is from a drypoint etching by Berthe Morisot (1841-1895) of her daughter Julie Manet. The punch holes at the top and bottom indicate the print was made from a plate that Morisot had cancelled. Reminiscent of a painting that Morisot and her husband, Eugene Manet, commissioned from Pierre-Auguste Renoir in 1887, it was done at a time when her friend Mary Cassatt urged Morisot to study printmaking. Morisot also produced the image in pastels. Her friendships with artists such as Renoir, Cassatt, brother-in-law Édouard Manet, Claude Monet, and Edgar Degas place Morisot at the center of an artistic movement, *the Independents*, that resulted in the first Impressionist exhibit in 1874. While she had successfully shown paintings at the prestigious Salon, she actively encouraged her contemporaries to stage a rival exhibit that challenged the capricious juries of the Salon system.

The works of the Impressionists (a name derived from Monet's painting *Impression: Sunrise*) were markedly different than those favored by the French Academy of Fine Arts in their execution, subject-matter, and use of color. These alternative exhibitions allowed Morisot to escape the rigid parameters and show in an array of different media, ranging from oil paintings to watercolors to prints. Morisot submitted works to all but one of the eight Impressionist exhibitions, only missing the year Julie was born. She seems to have participated freely and frequently in the milieu of late nineteenth-century Paris. Morisot's upper middle class parents were not bound by conventions, and provided Morisot and her sisters with excellent instruction in the arts. She and her sisters were featured in each others' works and also included in paintings by Manet, Renoir, and Degas. Recognizing that women were not able to participate in the intellectual café life that typified the era, her mother, and later Morisot herself, hosted weekly soirées that brought together influential artists, writers, and thinkers.

[Ellen Hay, *Professor of Communication Studies*]

97

Courtesan with Umbrella, ca. 1840s
Keisai Eisen (Japanese 1790–1848)
Color woodblock print, 68.0 x 23.2 cm., 26-3/4 x 9-1/8" image
Lent Courtesy of Dr. Thomas B. Brumbaugh Art History Collection

By the nineteenth century, *ukiyo-e* (pictures of the floating world) focused on "the world of fleshly pleasure centering in the theater and the brothel" (Takahashi 9) and revealed a new "mature femininity, full of worldly wisdom" (Neuer and Yoshida 329). Such woodcuts created a modernist revolution in the second half of the nineteenth century, freeing Impressionists, Post-Impressionists and others from traditional illusionism established during the Renaissance.

Keisai Eisen's *Courtesan with Umbrella* represents one of the "decadent, coquettish women" (Neuer and Yoshida 330) typically depicted by this artist. Originally influenced by Katsushika Hokusai, Eisen ultimately developed a personal style based on new innovative color printing techniques (Takahashi 145). He was a court painter who is thought to have fallen from grace, and perhaps found his female models by running a brothel (Goebel 56). This particular woman is a well dressed courtesan in lavishly patterned clothing consisting of four different colors, necessitating multiple blocks for printing. She is likely holding an umbrella, not to protect herself from the rain, but more as a fashion statement. Her pose is complex, as she turns backward to view something behind her. As many ukiyo-e prints, Eisen's work projects an ideal beauty rather than a particular figure. The woodblock-print designers did not attempt to capture real likeness of models, but they created idealized women who were fully aware of the gaze of male audiences in the pleasure quarters which were secluded and different from the ordinary world.

The vertical format, often showing a single posed figure set against a blank background, developed from the traditional Japanese hanging scroll or *kakemono-e* (Wichmann 170-177). Unlike Renaissance one-point perspective, which draws the viewer's eye into the piece, the Japanese version leads the eye upward, as it was translated to the woodblock as a vertical pillar print. The effect was bold and unsettling to the establishment, but revealed new viewpoints to the avant-garde.

[Joe Marusarz, *Class of 2005* and
Naoko Gunji, *Assistant Professor of Art History*]

***Au Louvre, la peinture, Mary Cassatt* (Mary Cassatt at the Louvre),** ca. 1879–80
Edgar Degas (French 1834–1917), published by Vollard, Paris
Etching and aquatint, 21st state after cancellation, 30.1 x 12.5 cm., 11-7/8 x 5" image
Lent Courtesy of Private Collection

Edgar Degas was one of the few French Impressionists who found it difficult to abandon old academic traditions. He embraced the quick snapshot moments of this group, but seemingly could not resist delving deeper into the personalities of people. *Mary Cassatt at the Louvre* was based on a series of sketches that Degas undertook between 1879-80, depicting his good friend and colleague, Mary Cassatt, with her sister, Lydia.

Cassatt stands poised and confident, leaning on her umbrella, as she gazes at the artwork in the Grand Galleries of the Louvre. Lydia sits behind her, presumably reading a guidebook. Cassatt was one of the few active women in the Impressionist movement. In this particular print, Degas shows Mary turned away from the viewer while Lydia, with head tilted downward, looks up at the art on display as if she has just consulted her booklet. Degas' innovative view of Cassatt from the back was encouraged by critic Edmond Duranty, who had described Impressionism as the *new painting* and encouraged artists to depict subjects from the back as well as various other angles. In this manner, he argued, they could subtly demonstrate their "age, temperament, and social position" (Pollock 23 and 119). Yet Cassatt seems oblivious to her observers. Although prominent and fashionable, she is primarily concerned here with studying the art of the past, an important source even for modernists. The artwork on the wall is unidentifiable and fades into contrasting shapes and shadows against an abstracted flat background. The scene is framed by the door jamb, and the floor dramatically angles upward, presenting a dramatic *bird's-eye view*. The *chiaroscuro* (contrast of light and shadow) is sensitively accomplished through the printing technique.

The tall, cropped composition of this print was no doubt influenced by the recent flood of Japanese artwork and prints into France (catalogue 97), due to the reopening of Japan to Europe. Degas had collected several Japanese woodblock prints and like many of his contemporaries, practiced *Japonisme*, adapting characteristics of Japanese style. He was probably the finest draftsman of his generation. His talent here is illustrated by his ability to capture figures so elegantly with merely a few lines and shapes. He also, however, accomplished much more in this image, by announcing the position of the new woman in modern art.

[Megan Crandall, *Class of 2005* and
Catherine Carter Goebel, *Editor*]

99

The Letter, from the 1890-91 original
Mary Cassatt (American 1844–1926)
Color intaglio—aquatint and drypoint, published 1991 by the Bibliothèque Nationale, 34.2 x 22.7 cm., 13-3/8 x 8-15/16" image
Purchase through Gift of Lynn Jackson, Augustana College Vice President of Advancement, Augustana College Art Collection, 2010.16

In 1890 Paris hosted a major exhibition of Japanese art featuring hundreds of woodblock prints. Here were "scenes of everyday Japanese life, usually in bold color and design" (Mathews 194). The prints mesmerized the American expatriate Impressionist Mary Cassatt. "I dream of doing it myself," she wrote after viewing the prints, "and can't think of anything else but color on copper…" (Mathews 194). Cassatt had already won accolades for her drypoint prints, using only black ink, and she knew the challenges involved in the medium. Needle on copperplate allows for no mistakes, no corrections. "In drypoint," she said, "you are down to the bare bone, you can't cheat" (Sweet 117). But to advance to color affected both design and printing techniques—problems she solved with her usual ingenuity.

The famous color prints which wonderfully attest to her success are known as *The Ten*. Each of the ten compositions she inked by hand, and each, hand-inked, was duplicated twenty-five times (Mathews 196). Her friend and fellow impressionist Camille Pissarro, seeing her prints, was eloquent in appreciation: "…the tone even, subtle, delicate…adorable blues, fresh rose, etc…" (Sweet 119). *The Letter*, one of *The Ten*, must surely have been in Pissarro's memory when he wrote of "adorable blues," for the color irresistibly invites the viewer to closer scrutiny. In a perceptive and stimulating appraisal of Cassatt's art, critic Frank Getlein comments, "In several important ways Mary Cassatt did in painting what Jane Austen did in prose fiction" (32). This insightful comparison offers a key to some of the delights to be discovered in this particular print.

The young woman here is not sitting for a portrait. She is authentic, she is herself, caught in a "private moment" (Getlein 82), a privacy which the enclosed space with its one-dimensional effect emphasizes. Desk and chair and close background wall secure her. The scene is internal in both physical and mental environments. But despite the secure enclosure, the lady's freedom is not restricted. Rather, the enclosure gives her power. In the very act of sealing her letter, she hesitates. Has she said what she intends in the way she intended to say it? She is not anxious or agitated, simply reflective. She seems to indulge in a personal assessment. Whatever her answer, she controls the choice as, in the social act of writing, she controls the discourse. Here is no mannequin but rather an Austenian woman—an Elizabeth Bennett, an Elinor Dashwood— a vital personality capable of trusting her judgments. Like Austen too, Cassatt gives precision of focus, no detail wasted or excessive. The blossoms on the lady's dress and on the wallpaper behind her—part of the Japanese influence—add a graceful, appealing femininity which softens the rigidity of vertical line and enclosure and lends the character charm as well as strength. And, of course, these details suggest the social class to which the letter-writer belongs. Cassatt chooses to depict, as Austen does, the world she knows. Her vision, like Austen's, is unsentimental, probing, and wholly engaging.

[Dorothy Parkander, *Professor Emerita of English and Conrad Bergendoff Professor Emerita of Humanities*]

100

Actor Iwai Hanshirô VI as Rikijirō's Wife Hikite, 1852
Utagawa Kunisada II (Toyokuni IV) (1823–1880), carved by Shoji
Color woodblock print, vertical ôban, from the series *From the Tales of the Eight Dog Heroes (Hakkenden Inu no sōshi no uchi),* published by Tsutaya Kichizō, 35.6 x 24.7 cm., 14-1/16 x 9-3/4" image
Augustana College Art Collection, 1982.17

The woman holding a torch in the dark woods is Hikute, a beautiful, chaste, brave young widow of a samurai. She lives with her sister Hitoyo and her mother-in-law Otone in the mountains, hiding, to assist the grand scheme of the heroes in the story of *The Eight Dog Chronicles* (*Nansō Satomi Hakkenden*).

The Eight Dog Chronicles, the popular historical novel of 106 volumes, was periodically published between 1814 and 1842. It was written by Takizawa Bakin (1767-1848), a famous fiction-writer of early-modern Japan. The novel is an adventurous story of eight samurai heroes who are mysteriously born from Fusehime, a daughter of the Satomi clan, who is impregnated by a dog's spirit. Though the eight heroes are raised in different places, a supernatural force gathers them and together they assist the Satomi clan to reestablish the household. Each hero represents a Confucian moral, and the story is full of virtuous and courageous men and women, as well as violence and gore.

The novel was an instant success and remains as one of the most influential literary works in Japanese society. In the early 19th century, different authors contemporaneously adapted the novel in different media. Some adapted the novel for Kabuki theaters; some published the abridged versions adding illustrations; some *ukiyo-e* masters made prints highlighting certain scenes and characters. In more recent times, the novel has been adapted into movies, TV dramas, manga, anime, and video games.

The ukiyo-e portrait of Hikute that Augustana possesses is one of the fifty prints included in a set of ukiyo-e portraits entitled *From the Tales of the Eight Dog Heroes* (*Hakkenden Inu no sōshi no uchi*). The set was created by a famous ukiyo-e master Utagawa Kunisada II and printed by a successful publisher Tsutaya Kichizō in 1852. The commercial success of the ukiyo-e set was assured not only by the big names of the artist and the publisher and the popularity of the novel, but also by the fact that Kunisada II incorporated likenesses of popular Kabuki actors into the portraits of the *Hakkenden* characters. The portrait of Hikute is, for example, also a portrait of the Kabuki actor Iwai Hanshirō. Ukiyo-e prints were cherished by both the prospering townsmen in the city of Edo and the visitors from the countryside alike. Later when Japan opened its ports to the West, the prints proved to be an attractive souvenir from Japan. Having bid farewell to the other forty-nine characters, Hikute, a supporting female character from the *Hakkenden*, journeyed to Augustana in 1982 with her story.

[Mari Nagase, *Assistant Professor of Asian Studies*]

101

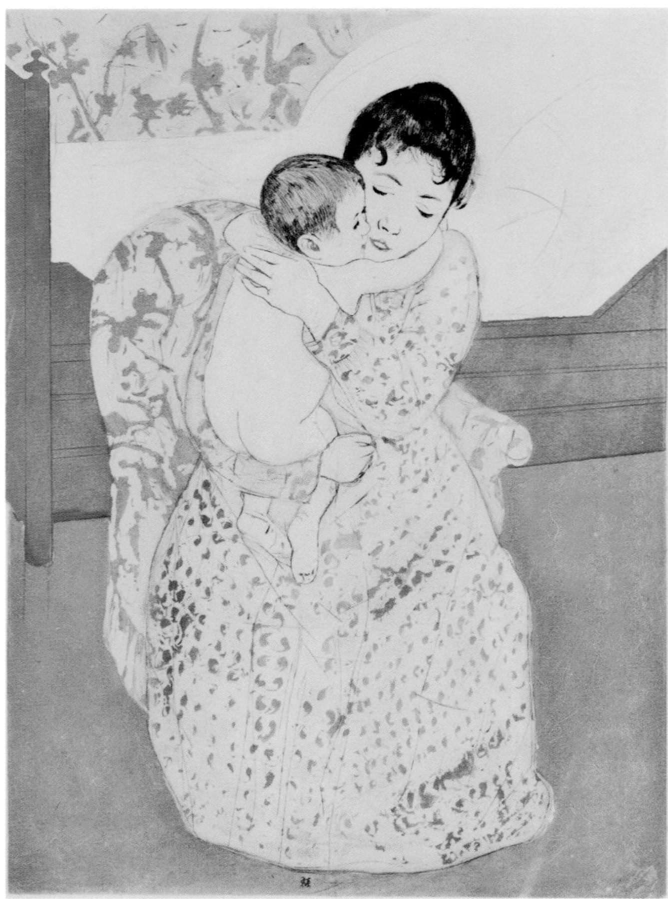

Maternal Caress, from the 1890-91 original
Mary Cassatt (American 1844–1926)
Color intaglio—aquatint and drypoint, published 1991 by the Bibliothèque Nationale, 36.6 x 26.5 cm., 14-1/2 x 10-1/2" image
Lent Courtesy of Private Collection

Mary Cassatt, an American expatriate artist, is one of the best known female artists in all of Art History. Born into a wealthy family in 1884, she quickly became a lover of art and had a passion for depicting relationships between mothers and their children. Cassatt moved to Paris and became part of the Impressionist movement, making friends with well-known French Impressionist artists such as Edgar Degas. She changed the way women were represented in art, believing that "women should be *someone*, not *something*" (Yeh 363).

While images of mother and child are not uncommon, Cassatt brought in new techniques to emphasize their relationships. She depicted women who were emotionally attached to their children and showed their connection and enjoyment of being together. *Maternal Caress* demonstrates this idea. The embrace of the mother shows the love she feels towards her child. The mother is gentle and affectionate. Images like this would have reinforced to women the joys of motherhood. Cassatt once said, "To us the sweetness of childhood, the charm of womanhood, if I have not conveyed some sense of that charm, in one word, if I have not been absolutely feminine, then I have failed" (Broude 36). While never a mother herself, Cassatt used what she knew from her childhood and the lives of her friends and family to create such images.

Cassatt was heavily influenced by Japanese *ukiyo-e* woodblock prints. While in Paris, she attended many different exhibitions of Japanese art. At these exhibits, Cassatt and fellow Impressionists directly confronted Japanese prints and paintings. The influence of Japanese art and its aesthetics on European and American art, called *Japonisme*, became more popular at this time. Japanese art had not been seen until Japan was re-opened to trade with the west in the mid nineteenth century and began exporting items. The style was different from what western artists knew from the traditions of illusionism inherited from the Old Masters, and they were fascinated by this *new*, provocative style. This image, *Maternal Caress*, comes from a print series of ten works that Cassatt designed based on Japanese art. She created this series using drypoint and aquatint techniques to masterfully imitate and even enliven the effect of Japanese woodblock prints. *Japonisme* is demonstrated in the flattened space; emphasis on pattern through the wallpaper, chair, and clothing; and the cropping of the image.

[Amanda Miller, *Class of 2012*]

Mother's Kiss, from the 1890-91 original
Mary Cassatt (American 1844–1926)
Color intaglio—aquatint and drypoint, published 1991 by the Bibliothèque Nationale, 33.8 x 22.6 cm., 13-5/16 x 8-15/16" sight
Lent Courtesy of Private Collection

So familiar are Mary Cassatt's idealizations of mother and child that her paintings can seem natural. Docile, selfless, middle-class—this is what motherhood looks like, isn't it? But of course, artists don't just reflect reality; they help create it. And at the turn of the century, Mary Cassatt helped promote and shape changing attitudes towards motherhood.

In the nineteenth century, attitudes towards motherhood and childhood underwent a dramatic shift. As men followed the new manufacturing *jobs* of the Industrial Revolution, women, who had once worked alongside their husbands on family farms and shops, got new jobs as a new standard of womanhood—called the *Cult of True Womanhood*—came to the fore. According to the Cult of True Womanhood, all women were naturally pure, pious, and domestic, and thus, ill-suited to the business world. Reassuring men that while they confronted the materialism and competition of the industrial economy, their women were back at home rearing the children in the morals of western civilization and providing a cheerful place to which the men could return, the Cult of True Womanhood helped ease men's entry in the business world. Meanwhile, because large numbers of children were no longer necessary to work the fields, nineteenth-century women also started having fewer children ("quality, not quantity" was the motto of the day), and as advances in medicine meant more and more children were surviving past infancy, parents came to invest more emotionally in their children. The result was a redefinition of childhood. Where children were once viewed as mini-adults ready for work, they came to be viewed after the Industrial Revolution as precious innocents to be petted by their selfless and virtuous mothers.

The mother and child in Mary Cassatt's *Mother's Kiss* give form to these beliefs. With everything around them erased, Cassatt's mother and child exist in a domestic sanctuary, and sharing a common border (neither possesses her own space), merge into one unified shape. Still, other details in the print raise questions about this maternal ideal—are these skies blue or grey? is the home really a sanctuary? who is the child looking at? are these two safe? Here, Cassatt thoughtfully questions the images of the maternal she helped reproduce.

[Meg Gillette, *Assistant Professor of English*]

103

The Music Room, 1858
James McNeill Whistler (American 1834–1903)
Etching on cream laid paper, 14.4 x 21.6 cm., 5-11/16 x 8-9/16" image
Gift of Mr. and Mrs. Michael Moss, Augustana College Art Collection, 1996.17.9

The medium of etching first distinguished James McNeill Whistler in his career. *The Music Room* is an early work, centered on a table lamp set within the warm, comfortable domestic interior of the London residence at 62 Sloane Street. Dr. Seymour Haden and his wife Deborah, Whistler's older half-sister, lived here with their daughter Annie. The subject simultaneously illustrates typical French Realist and English Victorian subject matter which both focused on everyday life. This atmosphere provided Whistler with *bourgeois* relief when he needed a break and family support during his tumultuous *bohemian* student days in Paris. In fact, soon after this etching was completed, Whistler moved his artistic base from Paris to London. This was due to his perceived promise for success through the acceptance of his related painting, *At the Piano* (also staged in this music room), for exhibition at the Royal Academy. Haden, in addition to having a solid career in medicine, was an accomplished artist who reinforced Whistler's printmaking by installing a printing press in his home to enable collaboration. With time, however, this artistic linkage was broken through competitive egos and viewpoints, resulting in a falling-out that prohibited Whistler from further visiting Deborah and Annie.

Whistler demonstrated his early mastery of etching in this work, ultimately earning him a reputation as the new *Rembrandt*, the most celebrated *Old Master* in this medium. The lamp provides a central axis from which the figures revolve as each responds to the welcome light. Deborah, mainly cast in shadow at right, focuses on her needlework in traditional female role-play. Seymour, in contrast at left, appears relaxed as he stretches outward in the glow to read his newspaper, thus portrayed as a *man of the world*. Behind the lamp, slightly left of center, Haden's partner, Dr. James Traer, examines a book at the table, demonstrating his continuing education. The complexity of *chiaroscuro* (contrast of light and shadow) is beautifully captured via the various perceptions of light as it filters throughout the room and between the various figures and objects it illuminates. Whistler would later evolve away from such complexity toward a simpler *Art for Art's Sake* aesthetic.

[Catherine Carter Goebel, *Editor*]

104

The Lamp, from the 1890-91 original
Mary Cassatt (American 1844–1926)
Color intaglio—aquatint, drypoint and soft-ground etching, published 1991 by the Bibliothèque Nationale, 32.4 x 25.3 cm., 12-3/4 x 10" image
Paul A. Anderson Chair in the Arts Collection Purchase in Honor of Hollis Clayson, Professor, Northwestern University, Augustana College Art Collection, 2010.32

In 1890, Paris was dazzled by a large exhibition of Japanese graphic arts at the *École des Beaux Arts*. After viewing the exhibition, Mary Cassatt excitedly wrote to her friend and fellow female Impressionist, Berthe Morisot: "Seriously, *you must not* miss that. You who want to make colour prints you couldn't dream of anything more beautiful...You *must* see the Japanese—*come as soon as you can*" (Mathews 214). Cassatt was not only interested in Japanese items depicted within the works but in the style, composition and technique used.

Cassatt soon embarked on the creation of her own set of color prints *à la japonaise*. She was enthused by the bold linearity of the compositions and simple flat areas of evocative color. She was also inspired by the subject matter of the woodblock prints—the daily lives and ordinary activities of Japanese women. This focus on women in a domestic setting was not seen in European art at this time. The work of eighteenth-century Japanese master, Kitigawa Utamaro (1753-1806) who portrayed the lifestyle of courtesans in a series of prints titled *The Twelve Hours in the Pleasure Quarter of Yoshiwara*, might have been a conceptual and stylistic model for Cassatt's first set of prints. *The Lamp* is a print from this series entitled *The Ten*.

As with other prints in this set, elements of *Japonisme* appear in details such as the lamp table and the porcelain pottery arranged on it; the elegant angle of the nape of the woman's neck, a symbol of beauty in Oriental art; and the Japanese fan, a stylish fashion accessory. In addition to reflecting Japanese influence, *The Lamp* offers a glimpse into the intimate *daily life* experienced by late nineteenth-century women in simply depicting a woman at ease within her own home. Cassatt's focus on the normal everyday activities of women set her apart from other artists working in France at the time who reveled in the lavish entertainment culture of *bourgeois* Paris.

In addition to *Japonisme*, the organic curves of *Art Nouveau*, a popular turn of the century decorative style, might also be traced in the arc of the lampshade, bend of the chair, and turn of the fan. The lamp itself dominates the upper half of the print and evidences innovations in the late 19th century. Artistic response to new technological advances with lamplight in the *City of Light* bears further examination as illustrated in the 2010 Augustana guest lecture by Professor Hollis Clayson, Northwestern University, in whose honor this work was dedicated.

Edgar Degas, frequently a harsh critic but also a mentor, acknowledged Cassatt's success in this series by stating: "I will not admit that a woman can draw so well" (Gunderson 24). Indeed, this set demonstrates Cassatt's range of abilities as an artist as well as her perseverance in becoming a great and celebrated printmaker—not an easy task for a woman at the time. Her influences, including the Impressionists and Japanese *ukiyo-e*, allowed her to expand and grow into a modern and continually influential artist whose prints are still heralded today as a printmaking *tour de force*.

[Emily Cox, *Class of 2011*]

105

Study for "Shuttlecock," ca. 1868–1870
Albert Joseph Moore, R.A., R.W.S. (British 1841–1893)
Black and white chalk drawing, 32.9 x 16.2 cm., 13-1/16 x 6-7/16" image
Paul A. Anderson Chair in the Arts Collection Purchase in Honor of Martha Tedeschi, Curator of Prints and Drawings, The Art Institute of Chicago, Augustana College Art Collection, 2002.6

Albert Moore began his life surrounded by a family of landscape painters. He synthesized many influences in his art. His Classical roots were evident in his detailed and structured compositions, emphasizing the mathematical linearity he employed in his architectural studies. He had in fact copied many Classical works of art, including the famous *Elgin Marbles*, sculptures from the Greek Parthenon temple in Athens that were brought to England by Lord Elgin in the early nineteenth century. Similar to these figures, Moore's females are clothed in *wet drapery*, with delicate folds that subtly reveal idealized bodies beneath.

Along with Classical sources, Moore revered nature, which resulted in his initial admiration for the powerful Victorian art critic, John Ruskin, who encouraged artists to replicate nature (Prettejohn 118). To this end, Moore generally worked from a live model for his studies. He, however, never fully adhered to slavishly copying nature, but ultimately moved toward the opposite camp of *Aestheticism*, which encouraged interpretation. Advocates of *The Aesthetic Movement*, or *Art for Art's Sake*, believed in the artistic liberty to manipulate nature in order to improve it. Opposing these ideas were those who felt, as Ruskin and many conservatives did, that true art was edifying if it followed nature.

In 1865, Moore forged a very important friendship with American expatriate, James McNeill Whistler, perhaps the most vocal leader of *The Aesthetic Movement* in England. Both artists were fascinated by the possible aesthetic analogies between music and painting and were strong advocates for *Aestheticism* (Prettejohn 127). In this particular sketch, Moore has drawn a figure that is supposed to be playing badminton, but by looking at the dress and stance of the figure, it would be difficult to discern this recreational aspect, her quiet beauty being the more evident theme.

This *Study* is one of many preliminary sketches for Moore's painting, *Shuttlecock* (1868–1870), which was commissioned along with another work, *Battledore*. In his biography of Moore, Baldry related that Moore "set his models for some hours to play the game of battledore and shuttlecock, watching them and sketching each attitude that struck him as presenting pictorial possibilities" (Asleson 112). In this chalk sketch, Moore's preoccupation with drapery is evident. The contrasting vertical and horizontal lines of the cloth seem to be the focus, rather than the figure whose head and foot are lightly sketched and whose arms are only suggested by means of a few dark lines.

This sketch clearly reflects the artist's love for Greek idealism gained through his thorough academic training. The drawing was done in chalk with beautiful detail and no smudging. Lone Classical Greek figures are generally the focus in Moore's works. This work, as a study, better reveals the true artist as he searched for his essential form, demonstrating Moore's idealism at its very best.

[Meghan O'Brien, *Class of 2005* and Errin Copple, *Class of 2005*]

106

Le Bain (The Bath), 1889
Edgar Degas (French 1834–1917) and Georges William Thornley (French 1857–1935) printed by Atelier Becquet
Lithograph from *Quinze lithographies* (Fifteen Lithographs)in brownish bistre ink on chine-appliqué, 20.3 x 20.2 cm., 8 x 8" image
Paul A. Anderson Chair in the Arts Collection Purchase, Augustana College Art Collection, 2001.17

Le Bain (The Bath), or *Woman Bathing in a Shallow Tub*, was originally completed in 1886 by Edgar Degas. The image was later made into a lithograph through collaboration with Georges William Thornley in 1888. This bather was part of a collection of two hundred images of bathing woman completed by Degas in the 1880s. Most of the bathers began as multiple views in charcoal sketches, ending as pastels on heavily woven paper.

Le Bain was part of a series of seven genre scenes of the same woman bathing in a boudoir. These seven portraits fit in a sequence of images as though a photographer rotated around her, shooting consecutive snapshots from various angles. This composition provides evidence of Degas's geometric drafting skills. He commonly used diagonal lines to show body structure and zigzag lines to add presence to items in his backgrounds. In this print, diagonal lines are the basis for the principal axis of the figure, which includes the spine, legs and especially the arms. The action of the bather is geometric in its portrayal of the balancing act necessary for her position, as she uses the sponge in her hand and is framed by the circular tub. Her hand and feet are the most detailed elements of the piece.

The main significance of these depictions stems from the overall statement that Degas was making with such new portrayals of the female nude. When first publicly displayed, his bathers received negative reactions. Many found them distasteful, and some determined they were completely revolting. It was obvious now that Degas constructed an original approach to the female nude. He had left the academic standard of women portrayed as goddesses and mothers.

Degas could have designed this woman in one of two ways. He may have planned her to be a simple middle class woman. Degas' bather reveals an intimate look into a candid moment of a faceless woman. With this direction, many today interpret the scene in a broader modernist sense, as a *bourgeois* woman taking a bath, a fresh approach to depicting a real nude, in line with the larger subject of Impressionism: everyday people participating in common activities. On the other side of the spectrum, however, many interpret her as a prostitute bathing in a brothel, between clients, in order to ward off venereal disease.

[Joseph Scurto, *Class of 2008*]

107

Where Do Fairies Hide Their Heads?, mid-late 19th century
Artist unknown, American folk artist
Oil on canvas, 68.8 x 55.9 cm., 27-1/8 x 22"
Paul A. Anderson Chair in the Arts Collection Purchase, Augustana College Art Collection, 2002.7

The tradition of American portraiture had been affected by the Enlightenment thinkers John Locke and Jean-Jacques Rousseau. Their ideas about childhood emphasized children's natural gifts—the capacity to learn and the innocence that precedes experience of social relations outside the family (Brant and Cunningham 4). This departure from a Puritan ideology that viewed children as flawed by original sin led to changes in the portraiture tradition of stiffly positioned, properly dressed figures featured early in the 1800s. The girl in this portrait, apparently starting adolescence, seems to exhibit a more innocent and free nature than children from earlier eras in American painting.

The paper or magazine in the girl's hands is quite possibly the most interesting part of the portrait. Children in earlier portraits usually held a toy, a flower or an unidentifiable book. These objects signaled family status and values. The papers in this portrait bear the heading "Oh where do fairies hide their heads?" The girl is thus linked to a world beyond the United States; she is a reader—or perhaps a musician—who participates, like many other anglo-Americans, in the popular culture of England and Ireland. Although no author and date is given in the portrait, a poem with this very title was written by Thomas Haynes Bayly in 1797. Bayly was a British songwriter and dramatist who, inspired by a visit to Dublin, wrote many ballads still sung today. The ballad about the fairies hiding their heads was circulated as both a song and a poem; one printing of the poem appeared in 1895 in *A Victorian Anthology* (Stedman) and it also appeared in earlier collections designed for girls (www.english).

Bayly's poem suggests that the "little spirits" of the fairies appear in our world only when "green leaves come again." In times of frost and snow, the fairies may hide in coral caves of the sea, or even set up winter parties in "red Vesuvius." Once they return in the spring, nothing can stop their music and mischief, and "The maids, to keep the elves aloof/ Will bar the doors in vain; /No key hole will be fairy-proof/ When green leaves come again." This assertion that fairies can't be kept away in spring is a hint that girls will share their mischief and freedom. While the question of where fairies hide their heads in winter is an early version of Holden Caulfield's preoccupation with how fish survive New York cold as well as how children can be saved from adulthood, the poem and portrait do not share this later American literary lament about inevitable loss of innocence. The young girl we see in the painting seems steadfastly and cheerfully situated in her late childhood.

[Nancy L. Huse, *Professor Emerita of English* and Anne Motto, *Class of 2008*]

Children Blowing Bubbles, mid 19th century
Artist unknown, Italy
Oil on linen, 81.1 x 65.3 cm., 31-15/16 x 25-5/8"
Purchase with Gift in Memory of Mr. James Fletcher and Paul A. Anderson Chair in the Arts Collection Purchase, Augustana College Art Collection, SDC2004.13

This charming oil painting on linen is likely from nineteenth-century Italy. The artist and title are unknown, but the loose brushstrokes and subject matter relate to nineteenth-century Impressionism. This image of *Children Blowing Bubbles* is a *genre* scene, meaning that it captures a slice of everyday life. Such scenes were popular with the growing *bourgeoisie* who valued straightforward representations of the real world. Following the Enlightenment, and with the advent of Romanticism, the state of childhood was elevated. As a result, fairytales were collected and beautiful illustrated children's books were published to reinforce the wonder of childhood and that children should be allowed to be children, and enjoy themselves with leisure activities. Specific colors of this piece stand out, for example the bright red color on the young girl's bandana and the rosy pink in their cheeks. The bubbles are painted in *trompe l'oeil* (trick the eye) manner, with amazing translucence, making viewers believe they are real and possibly coming out of the artwork itself. The manner in which the bubbles and children seem to extend from the frame reinforces this illusion.

Displayed are a young boy, perhaps four or five years old, and most likely his older sister who appears to be around ten years of age. The girl seems to be taller and in older sister fashion, she shares the cup of bubbles with the boy. It seems reasonable to conclude they are siblings because of their similar facial features. Also, their proximity reflects a comfortable familial relationship, similar to those depicted by Mary Cassatt between mothers and their children (catalogue 95, 101 and 102). The dark background prevents the audience from being distracted from the subject at hand.

Middle-class children were now allowed more freedom and the ability to play. Although slow to change, efforts developed to ultimately abandon child labor, acknowledging the importance of childhood development. Parents began to provide a separate space within the home in which their children could play, called the *nursery, indoor play area* or *day nursery* (Foy and Schlereth 84). Family time was not taken for granted and capturing such subtle nuances of everyday activities was natural for nineteenth-century Impressionists, aided by photography. This work is thus not merely a genre scene, but a document that reflects the changing role of childhood in the nineteenth century. This artist has effectively captured a quick, lively moment in history, perhaps as fragile and transient as the very bubbles depicted.

[Jessica Whetzal, *Class of 2007*]

109

Macaw, Love Birds, Terrier and Spaniel Puppy/The Property of Her Majesty, after the 1839 painting, **Islay, Tilco, a macaw and two love-birds,** 1877
Sir Edwin Landseer (British 1802–1873)
Engraving. 65.1 x 38.0 cm., 25-5/8 x 15" image
Paul A. Anderson Chair in the Arts Collection Purchase, Augustana College Art Collection, 2010.29

"Landseer gives his beloved animals soul, thought, poetry, and passion. He endows them with an intellectual life almost like our own," stated Théophile Gautier (Casteras 345). An important French critic of Landseer's time, Gautier appreciated Landseer's intense fondness for animals and impeccable gift for portraying them. Edwin Landseer was not alone in his affection for animals. England traditionally exercised a great deal of respect for living creatures. Animal rights had been actively discussed through legislation in England since the 1820s (Casteras 345). In English society, animals were appreciated and enjoyed, especially by Queen Victoria herself. During Landseer's era, art in Victorian England was very realistic and narrative (Brake 412). Landseer successfully combined this English love of animals with the realist narrative theme of art by anthropomorphizing animals in his paintings in order to tell a story.

Landseer's work for royalty began with a portrait commission for Queen Victoria and Prince Albert. The couple loved the painting and determined to hire him as their court's official animal painter. His first animal portrait was of Victoria's favorite King Charles spaniel named *Dash*. The princess was very pleased with the painting and this paved the way for Landseer in the court. Landseer began to paint groups of the royal pets in scenes that told a story. The most famous of these playful paintings is *Islay, Tilco, a macaw and two love-birds*, the beloved pets of Queen Victoria herself.

This image shows a macaw, new to the royal family but fitting in rather well. The painting is hierarchical; closer to the top represents the animal with the most power. The parrot clearly has the two love birds and Skye terrier, named Islay, completely captivated by the cracker he is holding in his claw. *Islay* was Victoria's favorite dog at the time and she taught him to beg for treats in this manner. The Sussex spaniel puppy, the mischievous *Tilco*, is chewing a letter and clearly physically the lowest of the order as he is not even aware of the opportunity above to gain control of the cracker.

During the mid-nineteenth century, in response to Victorian taste, England's art world was experiencing a movement in Realism. The Realists had a way of telling stories through detailed narrative that entertained and paralleled literary style. Sir Edwin Landseer was remarkable at painting such Realist paintings. He had an amazing ability to tell a complicated story without words but instead through paint and canvas. He would either portray a previously told story or make up his own. Sir Edwin Landseer was a very talented animal painter who successfully pulled at the heartstrings of his fellow countrymen through a subject they loved.

[Brooke Bryant, *Class of 2011*]

Children Playing by the Haystacks, ca. 1890
Samuel S. Carr (born England 1837, active America–1908)
Oil on canvas, 30.7 x 40.8 cm., 12-1/8 x 16"
Paul A. Anderson Chair in the Arts Collection Purchase, Augustana College Art Collection, 2000.34

Little is known about Samuel S. Carr, who was born in England and moved to the United States at the age of twenty-eight. Carr lived in Newark, New Jersey and Brooklyn, where he resided from 1870-1907, painting children in outdoor settings, many along the Brooklyn coastline. His beach scenes date from around 1880 and beginning in the 1890s, he painted many pastoral views, popular subjects at the time (Gerdts 143). Carr's paintings are warm and charming, often portraying happy activities, a typical title being *Children's Parade*, date unknown.

Carr enjoyed painting children and their different pastimes, reflecting the interest in family and children that characterized the nineteenth century. He painted at a time when the United States was experiencing many important changes. The country's population was increasing at a rapid pace and an industrial and urban society had all but replaced an agrarian nation. Americans had a strong sense of national pride and looked optimistically to the future. In looking forward, however, it also became imperative to turn their attention toward the children who would inherit that nation. Children's literature of the time expressed an interest in teaching morality, considered essential for the country's future success (MacLeod 87). Training and socializing became key aspects of raising children.

Carr successfully created a believable sense of life in his works. In his many images of children in outdoor settings, he accurately portrayed the innocence of childhood and the importance of setting examples for children. In *Children Playing by the Haystacks*, Carr captured the joys of childhood and the simpler life that many Americans had by this time long given up. The young boy carries the small child *piggyback* while they and the girl standing next to them face the distant haystacks, presumably the labor of the working adults in the far distance. The cool relief offered from wading barefoot in a pond still appeals to a contemporary audience, even if the haystacks are now a distant memory for many viewers today. Carr's works depict the often sentimentalized joys of childhood, which become lost and forgotten as naive children, so easily influenced, grew into adults with children of their own.

[Erin Granet, *Class of 2001*]

111

Chronic!, 1884
Charles Keene (British 1823–1891)
Ink drawing, published in *Punch, or the London Charivari*, 1 November 1884, 20.2 x 13.9 cm., 8 x 5-3/8" image
Lent Courtesy of Private Collection in Honor of Dr. Thomas B. Brumbaugh

Charles Samuel Keene (1823–91) was a talented English artist whose works, including this drawing, were frequently published in *Punch,* a popular Victorian journal of the day. Respected as one of the finest draftsmen of his era, Keene illustrated modern life. As he described: "If you can draw anything, you can draw everything" (Pennell 34).

His beautiful drawings were originally glued to wood blocks to be engraved for multiple printings and thus destroyed in the carving process. However, a new photographic transfer method was developed that allowed drawings, such as this one, to be spared. Keene could then keep the original drawings, reproduced for publication, often giving them to grateful friends and colleagues. His work related Victorian storytelling in true form.

In *Chronic!,* a man makes a selection at a drugstore counter. Across from him stands the druggist, who appears aged and experienced. The dignified gentleman placing his order is perhaps knowledgeable in the ways of modern medicine and has the means of purchasing the latest drugs and remedies. His attire displays his wealth. He wears a long coat and a top hat, a symbol of affluence. His rotund figure also demonstrates that he is well-fed. The man shows his authority by leaning over the counter towards the druggist, demanding his attention.

The customer and chemist share a regular conversation about a common illness. It was these types of interactions that appealed to Keene's audience. People felt they could relate to the characters in his drawings because they were so realistic since they were generally observed and sketched directly from life. Unfortunately, due to their publication via wood engravings translated by other artists, his general audience did not get to see the sparkling superior beauty of his original drawings.

Keene's biographer, George Somes Layard, probably best summarized his contribution to his time: "Keene's humour was the humour of observation rather than the humour of invention. An acute observer of Nature, an eager spectator of the passing expressions and moods of his fellow-creatures, an impressionist of the finest quality, given a subject which he could fully appreciate, and he would picture it with an unerring certainty, an uncompromising realism" (204).

[Katie Arnold, *Class of 2008*]

Man Reading a Newspaper in Crowd, 1896
Philip (also Philipp) William May, called *Philmay* (British 1864–1903)
Ink with graphite under drawing, 26.7 x 15.5 cm., 10-7/16 x 6-1/8" sheet
Lent Courtesy of Private Collection

Philip William May (*Philmay*) was an English caricaturist for the escalating production of newspapers and magazines. "Draw firm and live jolly" (Fox 166) was his work-life attitude. At the time of this illustration, he was primarily working for the comic periodical, *Punch*, in the tradition of Charles Keene and George du Maurier. Like Keene, May's illustrations generally portray single situations, forcefully and economically conveyed without moral overtones. Situations are taken from the stage, sporting events and London street life.

May's illustrations are more complex than the apparently simple, seemingly spontaneous appearance they suggest. He made and revised many pencil sketches prior to "taking down the scaffolding," (Fox 166) as he called it. He paid little attention to background details. He would strip any elements that were unessential before tracing what remained with ink. The resulting illustration is a striking composition of bold black lines and stark white open spaces.

Man Reading a Newspaper in Crowd demonstrates May's distinctive pen-and-ink style. Like a photograph, it crops the edges and accurately captures a typical London street of the day. In the foreground, we observe a heavily outlined figure of an apparently intelligent, upper-class, worldly man intent on reading the newspaper before him. He seems completely uninterested in the bustling street scene around him. A young boy with rosy cheeks in the foreground seems immersed in his own thoughts and equally disinterested in the hustle and bustle.

A woman in the middle ground gazes toward the man and the boy as she advances along the walkway. She is also clearly intent on her own daily agenda. Directly behind her is a concert sign, suggestive of refined London city life. Less immediate are the faint suggestions of a man and his horse on the right and a figure far off in the background. May used the tree line, along with atmospheric perspective through fading ink color, to gently draw the viewer to the distant white background. The faint graphite outlines suggest this illustration is unfinished, since May generally erased such lines upon completion.

May suffered with fragile health throughout his life, further compromised by his bohemian lifestyle and alcoholism, tragically leading to consumption and his death before age forty. His brilliant, striking pen-and-ink illustrations established his reputation as one of the most talented illustrators of nineteenth-century city life. Deriving his style from Keene's beautiful hatching and detail, he filtered these qualities into a more reductive and modernist aesthetic.

[Kim Weidner, *Class of 2006* and
Catherine Carter Goebel, *Editor*]

113

Metropolitan Railway Types, 1891
George Du Maurier (French 1834–1896)
Sepia ink drawing, published in *Punch, or the London Charivari*, 10 January 1891, 14.6 x 18.4 cm., 5-1/4 x 7-1/4" image
Lent Courtesy of Private Collection

George Du Maurier had spent more than three decades reading the classic Victorian novels, and illustrating other writers' works, before he embarked on his own authorial career. Yet that movement from one kind of pen stroke to another wasn't such a giant step for him. He'd been creating his own world of character and story in cartoon engravings for *Punch*, the British humor magazine, since his twenties. *Metropolitan Railway Types,* a *Punch* production, demonstrates this close connection between cartoon and story. The two side-by-side panels reward careful scrutiny for their visual details. Such details define character. And because, as his friend Henry James contended, you can't have character without story, and you can't have story without character, the result is an invitation to explore the stories it expresses.

In this cartoon two contrasting women travelers are pictured on a railway platform. Both are wealthy, dressed in rich furs and fabrics. Both sport flat hats crowned with a small bow and carry similar traveling accoutrements: umbrella and muff. But the party on the left is cumbered with her gear: high-shouldered cape with thick fur lining, muff like an overgrown dandelion gone to seed, square heavy purse, large umbrella with hooked handle. She occupies—commandeers, rather—most of her space. Does she fear losing a privileged position long held or newly gained? In contrast, the fit of the other woman's clothing, her slender figure, the turn of her head, the contours of her face, the shapely delicacy of her hand, all suggest an inborn gentility, a gracefulness bred in the bone, a grace that expresses itself in appreciation for courtesies received. There's a visual harmony about the way she's rendered, yet her expression may call into question this external poise. Does the wistfulness, almost the sadness, with which she gazes past the present moment, suggest sorrow? Regret? Yearning? Has she, also, lost something in the rush and roil of the changing Victorian world?

Many of the novelists Du Maurier loved were posing questions about those seismic changes. As wealth and political power shifted from agrarian to industrial centers, traditional social markers lost their authority. Thoughtful writers like Dickens, Thackeray, Eliot, and Trollope were asking what constitutes true gentility. Is it an innate quality, conferred at birth by long generations of breeding, or can it be practiced and learned? To what degree do social behaviors reflect or even shape who we are? What, finally, do we mean by the terms *lady* and *gentleman*?

It may be no accident that Du Maurier chose a railway station as his venue for examining two modes of behavior—for the railway both created and expressed the swift movement of a culture from rural to urban. Social mobility, both literal and metaphoric, whizzed along like the landscapes outside a train window, ever shifting. In this unstable world the ultimate question may be: where does real power lie? In assertion or surrender? In standing fast or discovering how to move with grace? Indeed, such an illustration continues to "haunt the memory" (Du Maurier) with both the chuckle and the questions it raises. Maybe even more than some novels.

[Ann Boaden, *Adjunct Associate Professor of English*]

114

The Railway Station, 1866
After William Powell Frith (English/British 1819–1909) by Francis Holl (British 1815–1884)
Engraving, 51.9 x 111.4 cm., 20-7/16 x 43-7/8" image
Paul A. Anderson Chair in the Arts Collection Purchase, Augustana College Art Collection, 2000.12

The Railway Station depicts the hustle and bustle of the newly emerging upper middle class in England, a country that was at that time arguably the richest and most powerful country in the world. The railway itself was a symbol of the rising prosperity of the nation.

The Paddington railway station, originally the London terminus of the Great Western Railway, was designed by Isambard Kingdom Brunel and his associate Matthew Dingy Wyatt and built in 1854. The glazed roof, supported by wrought iron architecture, created vast interior spaces but still let in abundant natural light. The same techniques had recently been pioneered by architect Joseph Paxton and proved successful in the design and construction of the Crystal Palace, which housed the Great Exhibition of 1851 in Hyde Park, London.

The image was a collaborative effort designed from the start to make money. Art dealer Louis Victor Flatow (depicted in the picture as a small figure chatting with the conductor of the train) commissioned the oil painting and paid Frith then the stunning sum of about £9,000. Frith in turn commissioned Samuel Fry to take photographs of the interior of the station to ensure an accurate rendition, and William Scott Morton was taken on to paint the architectural structural details. A year later Flatow sold the painting and the rights to make prints for more than £16,300. In the meantime over 20,000 people paid a shilling each to see the painting. Francis Holl made a steel engraving and Henry Graves sold the prints. The confluence of the art world and entrepreneurship was a success.

The commotion of over one-hundred figures fills the lower half of the scene. As the people go about their lives, some with tearful goodbyes and others looking forward to seeing family and friends again, they seemingly ignore the very technology that makes their enriched society possible. Frith, however, placed a small boy in the center, gazing upward in awe and wonder, perhaps to remind us all to take a moment and appreciate the bigger picture.

[Thomas Bengtson, *Professor of Mathematics, Earl H. Beling Chair in Mathematics*]

115

The Long Gallery, Louvre, 1894
James Abbott McNeill Whistler (American 1834–1903)
Transfer lithograph on ivory wove paper, published in *The Studio*, 15 September 1894, 21.9 x 16.0 cm., 8-5/8 x 6-3/8" image
Gift through Dr. Thomas B. Brumbaugh, Augustana College Art Collection, 2001.31

The Long Gallery, Louvre, depicts a central location for nineteenth-century artists. This former Parisian palace for the French monarchy was converted to a public museum in the wake of the French Revolution. From this point onward, it became a hub for art students like James McNeill Whistler, who in the 1850s first met his close friend, Henri Fantin-Latour, in this very hall. Fantin often sketched in this Long Gallery, a typical contemporary means toward a young artist's education through learning by replicating the Old Masters. This practice also resulted in marketable copies of masterpieces which provided welcome revenue for *starving artists* at the time. The friendship that resulted from this chance meeting not only introduced Whistler to the world of French Bohemia through Fantin's considerable connections, but also benefitted Fantin through Whistler's English ties which provided him with a market for his beautiful still life paintings (catalogue 92).

Whistler thus returned to this great landmark of his youth when he and his wife Beatrix moved to Paris in 1892. His prints during this time were produced in lithography, a medium that Beatrix encouraged and which he valued for its ability to capture the immediacy of the artist's sketch. Through his mature, reductive style, subtleties of spatial illusionism are rendered through subtle strokes of light and shadow. Although the flickering effects seem similar to French Impressionism, his *Art for Art's Sake* philosophy behind them differed. This work also contrasts with his earlier Realist etching style (catalogue 76 and 103). With the slightest masterful stroke, the viewer's eye moves down the corridor toward the adjacent gallery in the distance. The figures appear abstracted, yet are complete in essence. Perhaps he also reflected nostalgia with the artist depicted in the middle ground, painting on canvas after an original as Fantin did when they first met here. As audience, we in turn consider the spectators in this print, examining the artwork that embellishes the museum walls. This motif of depicting visitors studying artwork dates back to at least the eighteenth century. Whistler also continued his current practice of layering space through doorways. This image reached still further audience through publication in the journal, *The Studio*.

[Catherine Carter Goebel, *Editor*]

James McNeill Whistler, 1897
William Nicholson (British 1872–1949)
Woodblock print, 24.5 x 22.6 cm., 9-5/8 x 8-7/8" image
Lent Courtesy of Private Collection

In 1897 William Nicholson, at that time an artist for *New Review* magazine, was commissioned by his editor to deliver a portrait of noted artist, James Abbot McNeill Whistler. The result was this stunningly elegant depiction of the contemporary tastemaker, generally considered one of Nicholson's greatest works (Schwartz 66). The manner in which this piece portrays Whistler is very intriguing. His image, as it emerges for the viewer, is submerged in darkness, as if the black background completely absorbs him. Staged on a warm horizon, he holds his signature cane as he proudly displays his ribbon signifying the honor he received in being awarded the French Legion d'Honneur. The fine attire that he wears recalls his appearance in 1885 when he delivered his famous *Ten O'Clock* lecture.

Nicholson presented the artist wearing his trademark monocle and a pompous expression on his face, which is further emphasized through the dramatic use of *chiaroscuro*. Whistler's arrogant and refined appearance was fitting considering the brilliance he exuded. *James McNeill Whistler* acts as a tribute piece to Whistler's reputation as one of the leading artists of the *Aesthetic Movement*, an art era that emphasized the aesthetic beauty of art over any implied story or moral. Nicholson, along with many younger artists of the day, revered Whistler as a great master. Even as a teenager, Nicholson was infatuated with the artist and his paintings. At the time of this portrait's publication, Whistler was at the height of his fame, being as well known as his work, if not more. Aside from his artistic talent, his outlandish behavior assisted in promoting his image and his art. Whistler had a penchant for effective use of the media, and the critics were clearly aware of his potential for selling newspapers and magazines. He was truly an original character, which made him a very memorable celebrity. Whistler supported such imagery with his 1892 release of his autobiographical book, *The Gentle Art of Making Enemies*. In this publication, he dedicated a chapter to venting frustrations based on his career (and certainly enlivened beyond reality) about the nature of art critics.

[John Regan, *Class of 2008*]

117A&B

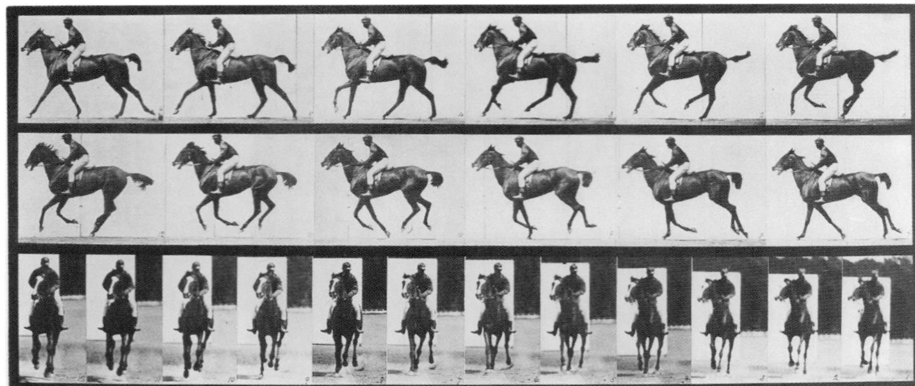

117A

117B

The Galloping Horse, Animal Locomotion. Plate. 621, 1887
Eadweard Muybridge (born England, American 1830–1904)
Collotype, 17.9 x 40.7 cm., 7 x 16" image
Purchase through Paul A. Anderson Chair in the Arts, and through Gift of the Reynold Emanuel and Johnnie Gause Leak Holmén Endowment Fund for the Visual Arts, Augustana College Art Collection, 2006.18

The Running Man, Animal Locomotion. Plate. 61, 1887
Eadweard Muybridge (born England, American 1830–1904)
Collotype, 17.9 x 40.6 cm., 7 x 16" image
Purchase through Gift of the Reynold Emanuel and Johnnie Gause Leak Holmén Endowment Fund for the Visual Arts, and through Paul A. Anderson Chair in the Arts, Augustana College Art Collection, 2006.19

Eadweard Muybridge (1830–1904) was an innovative nineteenth-century photographic artist who passionately pursued his obsession to freeze time and capture the body in motion. A British-born photographer, he advanced photography as a tool for demonstrating the mechanics of human and animal locomotion (Strosberg 225).

In 1872 the former California governor, Leland Stanford, had a question that he wanted answered through photography. Stanford believed that there was a point in a horse's gallop when all four hooves were off the ground and he wanted scientific proof of this. Muybridge unsuccessfully attempted to photographically document this action several times. However, by 1878 he finally succeeded in photographing a horse in fast motion (117A). Muybridge placed fifty cameras at equal distances along a track parallel to the running horse, controlled by a trip wire which, when triggered by the horse's hooves, set off the shutters in sequence as the horse passed. Each image was recorded sequentially at 1/200 of a second (Solnit 62).

Muybridge proceeded to take many photographic sequences of humans and animals in motion. People were often photographed doing various activities with little or no clothing (117B). These studies were undertaken in order to more accurately study the human body.

The images indicate an artist committed to the emerging culture of modern science—understanding through controlled observation and rational analysis of the world, using the potential of technology to surpass the limits of our own senses in order to enhance our powers of perception (Kerr 5-6). The proliferation and ubiquity of visual media today operates simultaneously with expanding technological precision in the production of visual tools. There is an unquestioned faith in, and reliance upon, the machinery of viewing, be it through the detail-capturing capability of digital cameras, the craze for high definition televisions, or the sophisticated computers and other machinery which allows scientists and physicians to see inside the human body (Barenscott 10). This reliance can be seen to originate with Muybridge.

[David Freeman, *Class of 2006*]

Moonrise from the River, ca. 1899
Theodore Roussel (French 1847–1926)
Softground etching on Japan tissue, 5.6 x 9.8 cm., 2-3/16 x 3-7/8" image
Lent Courtesy of Dr. Thomas B. Brumbaugh Art History Collection

"At last, I have found a follower worthy of the master."—James Abbott McNeill Whistler, ca.1885 (Getscher 148-149)

There is a subtle but pressing tension present in Théodore Roussel's soft ground etching *Moonrise from the River* between painstakingly meticulous skill and what appears to be fleeting, near-whimsical—if quiet—artistry. Its spareness, its broad, yet focused pastoral scene, and its subtle intensity bring to mind Post-Impressionist painter Vincent van Gogh's *Wheatfield with Crows.* Roussel, a mostly self-taught printmaker and painter, was French-born (Anderson 2011). He served in the Franco-Prussian War, but, due to poor health, gave up military service in favor of pursuing art (Getscher 148-149). And, in 1878, when he moved to England, his work met quick and enthusiastic acclaim.

In 1885, Roussel was introduced to artist James Abbott McNeill Whistler (Anderson 2011). Having seen some of Roussel's paintings on display, Whistler asked the gallery director to make the introduction, noting some of their common interests: boats, factories, children, nocturnes (Getscher 148-149). A lifelong friendship resulted (Anderson 2011). To be sure, Roussel's head was often bare when he was in Whistler's presence, a sign of respect (Getscher 148-149). Roussel was an enthusiastic disciple of Whistler's style, and was also among the few contemporaries Whistler recognized as possessing great artistic skill (Wilcox 317). Whistler would go on to introduce Roussel to the dual engraving media of drypoint and etching (Anderson 2011). And although Roussel often claimed he was a "pupil of Whistler"—his paintings do tend to echo Whistler in both style and subject matter—his routinely distinct style, namely found in his etchings, suggests otherwise.

Roussel would pursue etching and drypoint throughout the rest of his life, even going so far as to fashion his own frames, like Whistler, for each individual work (Anderson 2011). Like Whistler, too, Roussel regularly chose paper and ink with exacting care (Getscher 148-149). And, like abstract painter Vasily Kandinsky, Roussel was endlessly fascinated by color theory, which led to regular experimentation with color, and, eventually, to pioneering the technique of color etching in England (Anderson 2011). Around the year 1894, Roussel began experimenting with lithography (Getscher 148-149). His impassioned commitment to his work even led him to experiment with textile and celluloid plates, in addition to, near the end of his life, creating a new ink-substitute paste, dubbed the Roussel medium (Wilcox 317).

Moonrise from the River, however, is a *black and white* etching, a work that does not rely on color but merely suggests it with its low, rising moon, its tall grasses likely swaying on the riverbank, and its languid water reflecting the moon on its dark surface.

[Erin Bertram, *Fellowship Instructor in English*]

119

Red Snapper and Still Life, (ca. 1884-1915)
William Merritt Chase (American 1849–1916)
Oil on canvas, 74.3 x 91.9 cm., 29-1/4 X 36 1/4"
Anonymous Gift in Memory of Lewis J. Stone (Augustana 1965), Augustana College Art Collection, with Conservation Services Donated by Mr. Barry Bauman, 91.16.1

William Merritt Chase was an American still life painting master. In this image, the assembled objects allowed for a virtuoso tactile rendering of slippery fish set against hard reflective metal surfaces. We can appreciate the varieties of paint layering and the architectural balance of forms. The composition is not as busy as those in the European tradition that burst with foodstuffs and flowers, yet it is livelier than the subdued works of fellow American still life practitioner Emil Carlson (1853–1932).

Chase took up still life painting in 1869 while a student at the National Academy of Design (Pisano 1910:4). His earliest known fish still life, very reductive in scope, is dated to circa 1884 (Pisano 1910:14). His still life approach was influenced by Hans Makart and Munich circles (Bye 201-202). He excelled in rapid brushwork that both articulated a surface and reposed on the canvas as beautiful paint strokes, a verve matched only by his contemporary John Singer Sargent (1856–1925). Chase was known to finish a fish still life in one day, propelled by his use of siccatif (drier composed of metallic salts) and varnish as a medium that required quick execution (Bye 203-204).

It is difficult to date the Augustana oil because Chase continued throughout his career to paint comparable compositions of shimmering fish in dark kitchen settings. His style was not so consistent for other subject matter. During the 1880s, Chase gravitated toward the Impressionist brighter palette colors and landscape subjects. Although he is now better remembered for his shore scenes and portraiture, there is evidence that Chase's fish still life paintings were during his lifetime his economic success, his trademark (Burns 1996:16). In a 1915 article, Chase was quoted as saying "It may be that I will be remembered as a painter of fish" (Pisano 1979:82).

Chase marketed himself as a vibrant personality, a refined gentleman who courted the emerging American upper middle class that was becoming affluent enough to collect art. He was a renowned teacher, associated with the Art Students League of New York, the Shinnecock Summer School of Art, and the Chase School (now Parsons School of Design, New York), among others. Counted among his pupils are Charles W. Hawthorne, Georgia O'Keeffe and Edward Hopper.

[Sherry C. Maurer, *Director, Augustana College Art Museum* and Dr. Alex B. Stone]

Durham, 1892
Albert Goodwin (English/British 1845–1932)
Oil on canvas, 65.5 x 141.5 cm., 25-3/4 x 55-5/8"
Purchase with Gift through Paul Arnell, A Friend of Augustana College, and the Paul A. Anderson Chair in the Arts, Augustana College Art Collection, 2002.15

This is a painting of light and shadows.

It is often said that Albert Goodwin, the artist of this piece, lived in the shadows of the Romantic artistic legacies of Joseph Mallord Turner and John Constable as well as more popular artistic voices of his day such as John Ruskin and James McNeill Whistler. He was indeed influenced by the Impressionists and Pre-Raphaelites, but he also broke somewhat from their aesthetics and ethos. For example, he disliked the "flinging about of crude paints" that he often saw in others' works (Barker 8), and instead of celebrating bright colors like many Impressionists, spent a career exploring the depths of the interplay between shadow and light. Indeed, as his aesthetic evolved, the most important color in his palette became grey (Barker 8).

This painting, simply entitled *Durham*, is typical Goodwin. He often painted landscapes and dramatic architecture, and "his chief interest was the mood of clouds and the sinking sun" (Barker 9). Although Goodwin is known more for his use of watercolors, he occasionally dabbled in oils (Smith 14). In this painting, the city of Durham, with its thousand-year-old castle and cathedral at its center, is draped in mist, fog and smoke. However, the shadows are penetrated by the sunset on the horizon. The orange and red light reflects off the River Wear and provides the last moments of daylight for the fieldworkers in the foreground.

I happen to know this place well. As a student at the University of Durham, I walked along this same path to attend classes. My wife learned to row crew along this bend in the river. I walked through the cobbled streets of Durham on my way to the library where the Norman cathedral and castle loomed overhead, and it was in the Cathedral where I graduated. So, while much more could be said about this painting and Goodwin himself, sometimes art thrills us because of the way it throws light onto the shadows of memory.

[Adam Kaul, *Associate Professor of Anthropology*]

121

Forest landscape Study, n.d.
Attributed to Paul Cézanne (French 1839–1906)
Oil on board, 15.7 x 28.4 cm., 6-3/16 x 11-3/16"
Gift of Professor Irma Adelman, Augustana College Art Collection, 2006.43

In such beautiful examples as *Forest Landscape Study*, one might discern the manner in which Paul Cézanne increasingly separated himself from past artists, as well as his contemporaries the Impressionists, and elevated his style into an original realm of its own—perhaps defining the most influential and powerful force on twentieth-century modernism. Cézanne's oeuvre is difficult to arrange into chronological order because he often did not date his works (Kendall 15). By investigating subtle clues within this composition, however, it is evident that this study was painted early in his career, most likely during the 1870s. This conclusion is consistent with Cézanne's style at this time, as well as his technique of applying paint very thickly with a palette knife (Kendall 9).

The loose and fluid brushstrokes that define this piece are also typical of Cézanne's early work, which was based in Impressionism (catalogue 86). Cézanne's attempt at this style is demonstrated in his aim to capture the fugitive manner in which light played across the scene at a specific moment in time. However, even at this point in his career, Cézanne was already reinvesting greater solidity into the landscape, very different from the ultimate dissolution of form achieved by Impressionist painters such as Claude Monet (1840-1926).

The manner in which the trees spread across the panel also reinforces the dating of this piece, as Cézanne was guided at this time by Impressionist Camille Pissarro, whose compositions often include a similar veil of trees (Cachin 212). Although Cézanne's trees do not cover the entire foreground of the piece, as they might with Pissarro, the idea of peering through a grouping of trees is similarly conveyed to the viewer. During the 1870s, Pissarro and Cézanne often painted together *en plein air*, directly before nature. Scholars attribute Cézanne's deep reverence and affinity for landscape painting to this early influence and mentoring from Pissarro (Kendall 10). Although Cézanne lived during a time of rapid industrial growth, his art recorded the simple and infinite beauty of nature as seen in *Forest Landscape Study*. Yet his nature represents the perfect bridge between nineteenth and twentieth-century modernism.

[Megan O'Connor, *Class of 2009* and
Catherine Carter Goebel, *Editor*]

122

Arundel Park, n.d.
Henry Charles Clifford (British 1861–1947)
Oil on canvas, 38.8 x 46.3 cm., 15-5/16 x 18-1/4"
Lent Courtesy of Private Collection

Impressionism in Great Britain followed behind France and continued well into the twentieth century. Henry Clifford captured a picturesque moment in Arundel Park on a lovely summer day. The lower center focuses on six figures, separated into two groups of three. Two women supporting a young child approach a boat in which two men sit with another child between them, highlighted in red and facing the approaching figures. The fashionable white dresses appear light blue as they reflect the water below.

The painting illustrates Clifford's interest in capturing the color, light and beauty of the English rural landscape. The people are secondary. Loose brushstrokes subtly depict the small figures as they emerge at the end of a very long pathway lined with trees in full bloom. The foreground opens onto the water with a cropped boat at right, as well as the center boat around which the activity takes place. The stream bends and inspires viewers to imagine a far-off point toward which the boaters will embark. The trees are subtly painted in the water. Judging from the length of the shadows, the time of day is either early morning or late afternoon.

The painting crops the edges of the trees, zooming into the scene like a close-up camera lens. The scene reflects the Impressionist quest for the good life: the promise of a day filled with conversation and leisure. The linear perspective seems to break into two directions. It leads viewers up the path to the right, through the trees, into a world with which they might be familiar. And it also follows to the left, where they might find themselves in a boat venturing through the bend in the brook, either on the popular Swanbourne Lake or the Arun River at Arundel Park, toward something yet unknown. The whole illustrates a world filled with opportunity and abundance. The atmospheric perspective, which recedes to cool, grayish-blue colors in the distance, reflects recent theories on the physics of light.

Clifford's *Arundel Park* resonates from its historic location at the turn of the century into our present day. The soft brushstrokes inspire the observer to seek out peaceful moments in the scene. As with most Impressionist paintings, this landscape suggests a consummate harmony between painter and viewer. It takes us around the river bend into a world still filled with Impressionist style and grace.

[Beth Luebke, *Class of 2005* and
Catherine Carter Goebel, *Editor*]

123

Harmony in Grey, n.d.
Eliot Candee Clark (American 1883–1980)
Oil on academy board, 40.5 x 50.8 cm., 16 x 20" sight
Lent Courtesy of Private Collection

Favorite paintings are like old friends—it's good to see them again and again. One of my favorite paintings is *Harmony in Grey* (circa 1912) by Eliot Candee Clark (1883-1980). Depicting an autumn landscape in the gray light of evening, it captures the eye as the viewer visually walks through the various layers of the painting. In the foreground is a stream with slender trees along its banks. The trees have lost most of their leaves. Across the stream is a field with two cows grazing near a small white house with a brown roof. I don't know who lives there. The house does appear to be inhabited. If you look carefully, you can see a wisp of smoke rising from the chimney. In the distance are tree-covered hills, with many of the trees wearing their autumn colors.

An American impressionist influenced by the work of James McNeill Whistler and John Henry Twachtman (who was a family friend), Clark excelled in the use of chromatic grays, achieved by mixing together complementary colors. The son of landscape painter Walter Clark and Jennifer Woodruff Clark, who was a student of psychic phenomena, Clark was a precocious artist who by the age of thirteen exhibited with the National Academy of Design and the New York Watercolor Club. In 1897, he studied with Twachtman at the Art Students League in New York City, which was his only formal training. In 1904, Clark left for Europe, where he spent two years painting and traveling. He was not yet thirty when he won the first of many national awards for his artwork. In 1915, President Woodrow Wilson purchased one of his paintings. Clark served as president of the American Watercolor Society from 1920 to 1923, as president of Allied Artists of America from 1948 to 1952, as an ex officio trustee of the Metropolitan Museum of Art, and as president of the National Academy of Design from 1956 to 1959. After living in New York and Connecticut for nearly fifty years, he moved to Virginia in 1933, where he continued to paint landscapes until shortly before his death in 1980 at the age of 97.

[Daniel Lee, *Professor of Religion and Director, Center for the Study of Ethics*]

124

Winter Landscape, n.d.
Theodore Butler (American 1861–1936)
Oil on canvas, 33.0 x 40.9 cm., 13 x 16-1/8"
Lent Courtesy of Mr. and Mrs. Michael Moss

The American Impressionist, Theodore Earl Butler (1861–1936) painted this beautiful *Winter Landscape*. The town is viewed from above, the typical *bird's-eye* perspective preferred by Impressionists. There seems to be a distinct foreground and background, but very little middle ground, evidence of the abstract influence of Japanese woodblock prints that were currently being imported.

The piece evokes a sense of quiet, reinforced by the winter whites and soft tonality, which could be disrupted at any moment. Winter scenes were popular with the Impressionists because they offered opportunities to contrast clear and diffused light, an atmospheric challenge these artists embraced. They also effectively reduced forms to simplified shapes that worked well with the Impressionists' quick and loose brushstrokes. The atmospheric perspective, achieved through the beautiful background tones of blue and purple, produce an illusion of depth and ambience. One of Butler's goals was to capture the essence of the place, which he achieved in this painting. Like most Impressionists, Butler painted *en plein air*, meaning outdoors, in front of the subject, rather than in the studio. This was now possible due to the invention of portable oil paints. Such painting better enabled artists to capture the immediacy of a certain time and place.

Winter Scene is most likely one of Butler's earlier Impressionist paintings, painted between 1888 and 1889. Butler's talent and painting were often overlooked in favor of the more famous Impressionists of his era, such as Claude Monet and Mary Cassatt. He ventured to Giverny, a small village about forty-five miles northwest of Paris along the Seine River. Here he worked under the influence of Monet. As this painting demonstrates, he was an innovative artist of his time and a sensitive practitioner of the beautiful naturalism of Impressionism. He was the only early American Impressionist in Giverny who remained there throughout his career. In this position, he became an important "conduit for Americans in Giverny" (Gerdts 75) and thus facilitated the spread of Impressionism to America.

[Kate Felde, *Class of 2006* and
Catherine Carter Goebel, *Editor*]

125

***Tête-à-tête* in the Garden**, 1894
James McNeill Whistler (American 1834–1903)
Transfer lithograph on laid paper, 19.9 x 16.6 cm., 7-13/16 x 6-9/16" image
Paul A. Anderson Chair in the Arts Collection
Purchase in Honor of Darlene Link, Controller,
Augustana College Art Collection, 1997.9

James McNeill Whistler composed the original drawing for this transfer lithograph using inspiration from his own backyard. When Whistler and his wife Beatrix moved into their Paris home at 110 Rue de Bac, they focused their time and energy on making the garden the focal point of their property. It was here where they hosted many friends and family, which is likely why Whistler chose to commemorate these visits artistically. This particular work shows Beatrix's sister, Ethel Birnie Philip, with Ethel's husband, Charles Whibley, in the very same garden in which they took their wedding photos.

Here, they are enjoying a convivial picnic among prevalent flora and fauna in typical nineteenth-century fashion. This generally included a linen tablecloth, crystal, silver, china, fine wine and food. Like Whistler's scenes from the Luxembourg Gardens, the gracious atmosphere created here is truly Parisian. The couple is given no more attention than the objects on the table before them or the trees behind them. The shady relief offered from a summer in the city cools the composition, and the whole speaks of an idyllic environment for the Whistlers and their visiting relatives.

Because there is no discrimination in the amount of attention given to both the people and the garden, this style of portrayal is similar to that of the Nabis movement, well-known for depictions of women in intimate spaces. At times it is difficult to separate the people from their environments. While Whistler applied his immense skill in varying tonalities here, the people themselves are partially obscured by somewhat-abstracted plant-life. Whistler selectively composed outlines of trees and bushes to create varying interest in the work. Although these comprise simple and slightly abstracted forms, there is a certain focal point in the work. Ethel is placed in the center, possibly because she was Whistler's favorite of his wife's relatives. She is encased in a shadow which provides cool and calm to the work and showcases Whistler's talent in this medium.

During this period, Whistler produced a number of lithographs in collaboration with printer Thomas Way. Beatrix encouraged him to pursue this medium and clearly inspired subjects that reflect such domestic bliss. Unfortunately, however, this fragile beauty would soon be shattered by the first symptoms of Beatrix's cancer, appearing during the fall of this year. Following her death in 1896, Whistler never again created lithographs.

[Stephanie Loria, *Class of 2011* and
Catherine Carter Goebel, *Editor*]

126A&B

126A

Au Jardin (In the Garden), ca. 1895
Henri-Edmond Cross (né Henri Delacroix, French 1856–1910)
Preparatory color pencil drawing for *Les Champs-Elysées*, 9.8 x 9.0 cm., 3-7/8 x 3-5/8" image
Paul A. Anderson Chair in the Arts Collection Purchase, Augustana College Art Collection, 2001.25

126B

Les Champs-Elysées, 1898
Henri-Edmond Cross (né Henri Delacroix, French 1856–1910)
Five-color lithograph, published in *Pan* IV, No. 1, "The Color Revolution" 52, 20.3 x 26.2 cm., 8 x 10-5/16" image
Paul A. Anderson Chair in the Arts Collection Purchase, Augustana College Art Collection, 2000.61

Cross became involved in the second phase of the Neo-Impressionist art movement, along with Paul Signac, Charles Angrand, Camille Pissarro, Maximilen Luce and Albert Dubois-Pillet. The *Pointillist* style of the Neo-Impressionists was composed primarily of tiny dots, typically painted in primary colors in order to optically generate secondary colors. The term *Pointillism* derived from the uniform touches of paint employed, called *points* in French (Clament and Houze xv). During his career, Cross evolved from tiny pointillist dots to larger more mosaic-like brushstrokes, akin to *Fauvism* (French Expressionism), which grew out of Pointillism and Post-Impressionism.

This print entitled *Les Champs-Elysées* (126B) is a beautiful Parisian scene reflecting the French *joie de vivre* (joy of living) along the fashionable Champs-Elysées. This street was one of the major boulevards constructed in the newly remodeled modern Paris, lined with fashionable shops and restaurants. It was considered a very chic area by the bourgeoisie. Since it linked the Arc de Triomphe and its turnaround with the Tuileries Gardens and the Louvre at the opposite end, it was utilized as a major thoroughfare for strollers and carriages. A nurse and child are seated in the foreground, simplified into abstracted shapes. In the background, there are many additional figures, including other seated women and a pair of horses pulling a carriage. The vertical tree trunks balance the curvilinear masses of rounded figures in order to produce compositional unity. The bright shades suggest the warm sunlight shining on the women on this idyllic day. Cross added shades of blue to intensify the grass and the trees.

A very rare opportunity presents itself in comparing this five-colored lithograph with one of its preliminary sketches entitled *Au Jardin* (At the Garden—126A). The drawing shows a more detailed study of a woman seated, in nearly the same position and angle as the finished print. The sketch, however, is more detailed and three-dimensional as defined through subtle color gradations and sensitive additions in colored pencil. It is interesting to note that Cross first worked from such beautifully rendered naturalistic studies, which he then abstracted into overall shapes and patterns, arranging the parts into a balanced composition and finishing it in the pointillist technique. This comparison demonstrates his steps in abstracting nature.

[Kelly Volkert, *Class of 2007*]

127

Messe en Bretagne (Mass in Brittany), ca. 1895
Èmile Alfred Dezaunay (French 1854–1938 or 1940), printed by Eugène Delâtre (French 1864–1938)
Etching, aquatint and roulette, 4-color plate, 1/5 proofs apart from edition of 50, 32.1 x 42.1 cm., 12-5/8 x 16-9/16" image
Augustana College Art Exhibits Purchase as a Memorial Honoring William L. Beer, from Betty L. Beer, 1997.11

Dezaunay was among several artists who studied under Paul Gauguin in Brittany, where he developed his etching skills and an understanding of Gauguin's *Synthetism*, which he later applied to his own work, *Messe en Bretagne* (Mass in Brittany). Synthetism aimed at achieving beautiful and powerful artwork through the fusion of nature, artistic training and medium (Bretell 26). Gauguin's theory challenged earlier Impressionist beliefs that one should paint nature just as it appears. Gauguin instead advised his followers that "the synthetist artist must dominate rather than be submissive to nature" (Bretell 26). He further suggested: "Paint in your room; finish it outside" (Hanson 81). His main ideology was to create a direct and bold composition through simplicity and concentrated color (Hanson 82). This artistic approach was one of the most prevalent ideas in art during the latter part of the nineteenth century (Bretell 26-27).

Dezaunay's scene depicts *fin-de siècle* (end of the century) religious practice in Brittany at a peasant devotional site. The people of Bretagne had a very rigorous and full religious life. The young women wore aprons and head coverings, part of their everyday dress, each region distinguished by a unique female head covering. The subject of the painting, according to the title, is a religious service. Young women in traditional costume dominate the foreground while the church and graveyard loom large and imposing in the background. The women appear to be socializing; some whispering to each other, others appear disinterested. One particular young woman leans against a crucifix, her eyes closed and turned away from the church and the doorway which appears dark with doors shut. The juxtaposition of the church, the young women and the graveyard seems to be making a statement about the closeness of life and death, as well as the role of religion in both. The young women are extremely vague and generalized. Only two faces are shown, in profile and without much detail. As a Symbolist, Dezaunay suggests meaning, but does not explain, inviting viewers to interpret. This work might also imply the idea of youth being wasted upon the young. Surrounded by death and spirituality, the women are perhaps no closer to faith in this setting than they would be in their own homes.

[Mikeda Cannon, *Class of 2007*]

128

Gathering Oysters, Low Tide, ca. 1874–1880
Edgar Melville Ward (American 1839–1915)
Oil on canvas, 55.3 x 68.5 cm., 21-7/8 x 27"
Purchase with Gift of a Friend of Augustana College, Augustana College Art Collection, 2003.3.2

For nearly 200 years, Brittany has been a rich artistic source for inspiration. Paul Gauguin was one of the many artists to escape the busy life of Paris to find solace in the rich and vibrant landscapes, colorful costumes, and traditional way of life in Brittany. American expatriate, Edgar Melville Ward, studied with academic French painter, Thomas Gérôme (a former student of Neoclassicist Jacques Louis David—catalogue 54), along with future American Impressionist, J. Alden Weir. Weir accompanied Ward to Pont-Aven where he painted, *Gathering Oysters, Low Tide*. The artist colony at Pont-Aven flourished for twenty years before the arrival of Gauguin.

Oyster gathering, or harvesting, was an important job in the inlet called Cancale Harbor in Brittany. The bustle of this activity created a fertile subject for artists. Stylistically, this is a brilliant and visually stimulating painting. There have been many accounts from artists about the illuminated landscape in Brittany. The color is beautiful, ranging from the intense blue-green of the water and sky and the bright red skirt, balanced by the neutral sandy color of the beach. The painting is Realist in style, however the bright colors may reveal an early Impressionist influence. In this painting, the vibrant colors of Brittany's scenery are beautifully captured. Such peasants in their traditional costumes enticed many artists of the time. The eye never wanders from the well-orchestrated composition: the woman on the right is balanced by the other oyster gatherer who is bending down in a circular pattern. One cannot help but wonder, what is the object of the woman's gaze? She seems to be captivated by someone or something in the distance. Perhaps she is weary of her peasant lifestyle and longs for change. One can only speculate, but it is possible that she is dreaming of a more glamorous and exciting city life, ironically, the very life that artists like Ward and Gauguin chose to flee.

Modernist, Henri Matisse later reminisced about his stay in Brittany, "And soon I was seduced by the brilliance of pure colours. I returned from my trip with a passion for the colours of the rainbow" (Delouche). This painting epitomizes those very colors that Matisse (catalogue 166) and so many others experienced and relished while in this region. Artists like Ward longed for the charm and diversity that this timeless environment offered: a place where they could find nature, spirituality and perhaps even themselves.

[Laura Kurczodyna, *Class of 2007*]

129

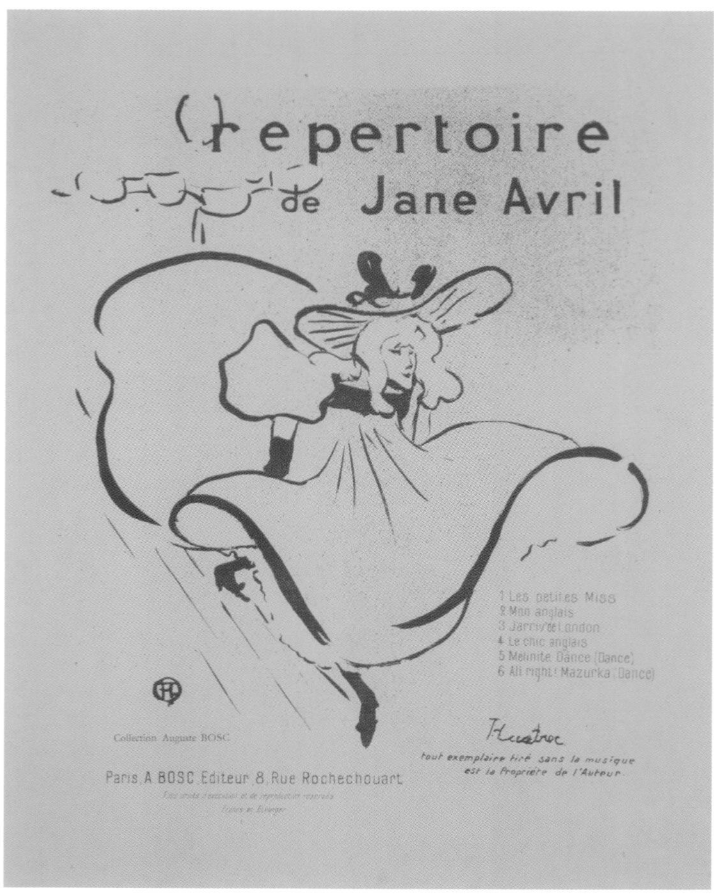

Repertoire de Jane Avril , ca. 1893
Henri de Toulouse-Lautrec (French 1864–1901)
Lithograph in olive green ink, published by Antoine Bosc, 27.7 x 22.5 cm., 10-7/8 x 8-7/8" image
Lent Courtesy of Private Collection

Henri de Toulouse-Lautrec established Jane Avril as a celebrity in Montmartre (the artists' district of Paris). As she later recalled: "It is to Lautrec that I owe my fame, which dates from the appearance of his first poster of me…My dreams were so far removed from reality! I have fluttered my way through our epoch without revealing an inkling of the depths of my innermost soul." She was the pale, elegant, ethereal performer whose enigmatic demeanor intrigued her receptive audiences. Lautrec's friend, dealer and biographer, Maurice Joyant appropriately described: "She dances like a delirious orchid" within the *hothouse* environment of the Parisian café-concert (Huisman and Dortu 108). "Of all the pleasures of Paris—the dance halls, circuses, cabarets, and brothels—it was the café-concert and its stars that cast the greatest spell on Toulouse-Lautrec" (Thomason, Cate and Chapin 137). The art of the modern poster reflected the contemporary shift from artists creating works commissioned by elitist patrons towards *public* works such as advertisements for the cafés and cabarets they frequented. These images now serve as visual records of the microcosm of *fin-de-siècle* (end of the century) Paris.

Toulouse-Lautrec was the finest of these illustrators, a master in the rendering of human emotion through his adaptation of modern life *à la Japonais*. With the opening of trade, Japanese woodblock prints came into vogue in European collectors' circles. Characterized by bold areas of flat color, curvilinear forms and the depiction of genre scenes, the stylistic and iconographic qualities of the printed media became the preferred method for highly trained fine artists. Lautrec was by far the most illustrious of these chroniclers of modern life and his favorite muse was Jane Avril. This single-color lithograph depicting *Repertoire de Jane Avril* demonstrates Lautrec's mastery of caricature and line as well as the popular use of his artwork as illustrations for textual media such as this songbook.

Repertoire de Jane Avril was the cover for a music book, written and edited in Paris by A. Bosc. This particular illustration is organically composed of curvilinear forms in monochromatic olive green ink. The form of Avril is meticulously constructed to produce a character that is both delicate and fluid. Lautrec depicted her celebrated sensuous dance, always alone with lateral movements of her legs, while maintaining a façade of cool detachment. We gaze upward toward the floating figure, delicately lighting on the stage as a butterfly on a flower. Jane Avril was a loyal friend to Lautrec throughout her life, keenly aware that during the course of her career, she "had many a lover, but only one painter" (Huisman and Dortu 108).

[Dana Kau, *Class of 2005*]

130

Moulin Rouge—La Goulue—Tous les Soirs (Moulin Rouge—*The Glutton*—Every Evening), 1896
Henri de Toulouse-Lautrec (French 1864-1901)
Color lithograph, small format version in Maindron's *Les Affiches illustrées*, 20.1 x 14.0 cm., 7-15/16 x 5-9/16" image
Purchase with Gift in Honor of Dr. and Mrs. Thomas William and Barbara Carter, Augustana College Art Collection, 2005.8

Henri de Toulouse-Lautrec's celebrity was not achieved through exhibitions in galleries or commissions from private collectors, but through a single commercial piece publicizing Montmartre's most infamous cabaret, the *Moulin Rouge*. *Moulin Rouge: La Goulue* (1891), a poster reaching nearly six feet in height on public exhibition along the Paris streets, elevated Lautrec and *La Goulue* to overnight celebrity status. As the official chronicler for this popular institution, through his posters as well as smaller journal illustrations such as this one published in 1896, Lautrec exploited the popularity of the Moulin Rouge and established his own position as one of its immortals.

Moulin Rouge: La Goulue was the embodiment of *fin-de-siècle* Parisian society. Paris in the 1890s was coming to terms with a rapidly industrialized world. With censorship laws relaxed, subjects with overt sexual connotations rapidly emerged. The Moulin Rouge became an effective stage-set for performers like La Goulue who epitomized this climate. *Moulin Rouge: La Goulue* embraces what was *modern* for the 1890s. The world which for centuries was agrarian was becoming commodified. The rapidly industrializing city needed an outlet for its workers. The café culture of Paris was at its peak. The former outlying suburb of Montmartre, the artists' district, had recently become an official quarter of Paris, with further latitude granted to media and art. And no artist more shrewdly integrated the two than Lautrec, who effectively defined his persona in the process.

He astutely combined the commercial textual message with large flat outlined forms, here featuring the characters of Valentin le Désossé (*the boneless one*) in the right foreground, cast in purple shadow, and Louise Weber, nicknamed *La Goulue* (*the glutton*), spotlighted at center. The foreground includes Valentin while la Goulue is pushed further back at center, yet highlighted as she teases the crowd with her raised skirts. The *bourgeoisie*, depicted as a black mass defined by elaborate coiffures and top hats, provide a backdrop as well as targets for her performance, since she was famous for kicking off the hats of her spectators. The yellow lamps appear to take on a personality and importance of their own, one particular lamp on the far left seems to illustrate a time sequence as it spins.

[Dana Kau, *Class of 2005* and
Catherine Carter Goebel, *Editor*]

131

L'Estampe Moderne, 1898
Alphonse Mucha (Czech 1860–1939), published by Imprimerie Champenois, Paris
Lithograph in olive green and sienna, 38.0 x 26.3 cm., 14-15/16 x 10-1/4" image
Paul A. Anderson Chair in the Arts Collection Purchase, Augustana College Art Collection, 2010.23

Alphonse Mucha (1860-1939) was born in Ivancice, a small town in Moravia. Today this area is part of the Czech Republic, but Mucha lived there under the Austro-Hungarian Empire. He grew up in the lower middle class from which his family experienced religious freedom to practice Catholicism and developed healthy patriotic ties to their country. As an artist, Mucha always kept his Czech identity placed firmly in the niche of his heart. In 1885 he entered the Munich Academy of Art, but after two years of study, he escaped to Paris convinced that the city of Munich had nothing more to offer him (Ellridge 25).

Working as an expatriate, Mucha brought his skills into the lively art world of late nineteenth-century Paris. Commercial artists who could create advertisements, posters, and magazines were in high demand and Mucha heeded that call. Starting in 1889, after working a series of non-art related odd jobs, Mucha started doing illustrations for books, catalogues and calendars. By 1894, he was a fully-operating freelance graphic artist.

Upon arriving in Paris, Mucha began cataloging photographs of his female models from which he drew his commercial designs. He never scoffed at "producing such objects as minor as magazines that would bring the Mucha chic into everyday life" (Ibid. 82). This cover of *L'Estampe Moderne* is a prime example of his use of a female model to sell a product to mass audiences. Mucha was heavily influenced by the curvilinear forms and close-up viewpoint of religious figures on Byzantine icons and one can see their haunting presence on this magazine. His curvilinear forms also reinforce the *Art Nouveau* movement and its naturalistic abstractions in vogue at the time. Furthermore, the British Arts and Crafts movement argued that art should be accessible to all (Ibid. 54). Since magazines were art forms accessible to ordinary people, it was possible that Mucha was adhering to the Arts and Crafts movement in utilizing the medium of the magazine cover to display his artwork for the public eye.

[Matthew Bowman, *Class of 2012*]

132

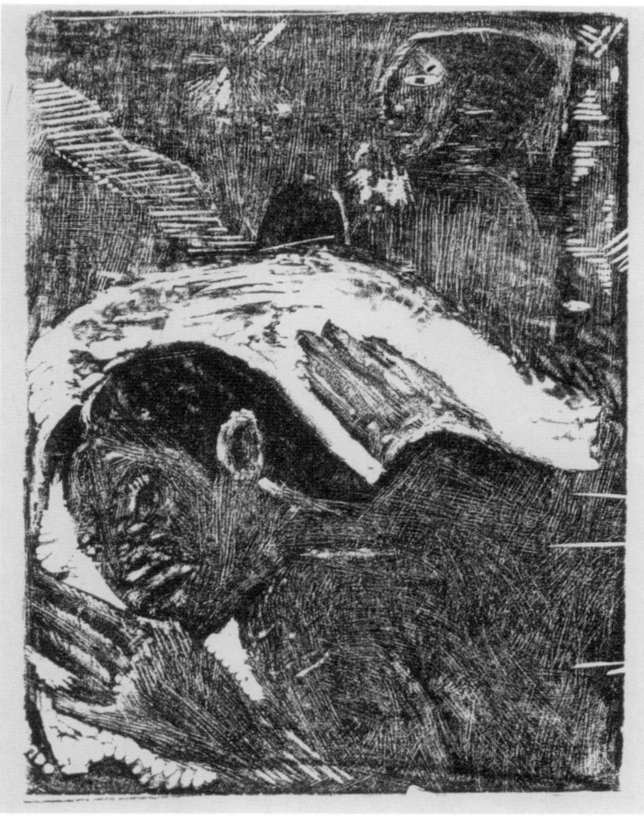

***Manao tupapau* (Spirit of the Dead Watching)**, 1894–1895
Paul Gauguin (French 1848–1903)
Woodblock print, 17.3 x 12.8 cm., 6-3/4 x 5" image
Purchase through Paul A. Anderson Chair in the Arts Collection, Art Exhibits, and Gifts of Dan Churchill, Mr. and Mrs. George and Pat Olson, Mr. and Mrs. Al and Lynne DeSimone, and Dr. Kurt Christoffel, Augustana College Art Collection, 2004.8

This woodcut is a variation on the theme of the *tupapau* (Spirit of the Dead) which Gauguin had already treated in 1892 in an oil painting with the same title during his first sojourn in Tahiti. Among several other versions of the tupapau figure were two *(Te po [Night]* and *Manao tupapau)* of a series of ten woodcuts which Gauguin made in 1893–4 for use as chapter illustrations in *Noa Noa*, his projected travel account of his first stay in Tahiti. This 1894–5 woodcut is similar to the original oil painting in that it depicts an (abbreviated) nude female figure lying on her stomach and peeking fearfully from the shelter formed by her upstretched fingers; the enigmatic figure of the tupapau looms behind her. In both oil painting and woodcut, the tupapau is a forbidding, hooded figure with a piercing almond-shaped eye seen against a shadowy background, although in the woodcut the tupapau is perhaps more menacingly placed almost directly behind the head of the nude woman.

Gauguin's woodcuts are innovative in both technique and subject. Though he may have drawn on a long tradition of French woodcuts or on a growing interest in Japanese woodcuts (catalogue 97 and 100) in *fin-de-siècle* France, Gauguin was a precursor of the revival of woodcuts in the early twentieth century (Goldwater 49).

As regards subject matter, Gauguin was no less a revolutionary. One might compare Gauguin's female figure (seen full length in the original oil-painting and in abbreviated form in the woodcut) with Édouard Manet's *Olympia* (1863—catalogue 83), since in each case the figure is a reclining female nude. However, Gauguin's stated intentions in his letters and journals underline the differences between the Realist Manet and the primitivist, Post-Impressionist aspects of Gauguin's art. They suggest perhaps a greater affinity with artists like Pablo Picasso who drew much of his early inspiration from African masks and the Expressionists of the early 20th century.

[Roger Crossley, *Professor Emeritus of French*]

133A&B

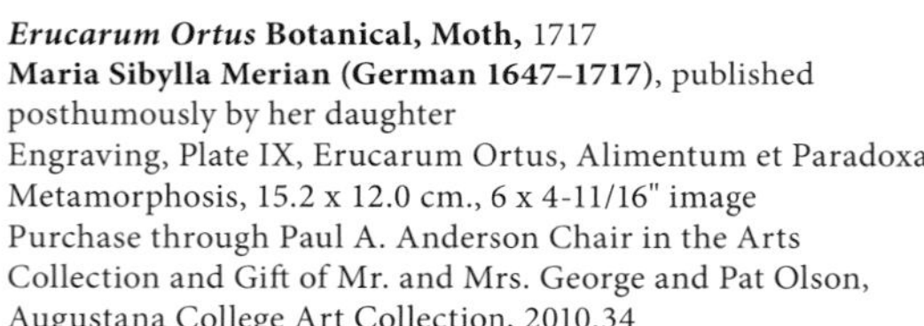

***Erucarum Ortus* Botanical, Moth,** 1717
Maria Sibylla Merian (German 1647–1717), published posthumously by her daughter
Engraving, Plate IX, Erucarum Ortus, Alimentum et Paradoxa Metamorphosis, 15.2 x 12.0 cm., 6 x 4-11/16" image
Purchase through Paul A. Anderson Chair in the Arts Collection and Gift of Mr. and Mrs. George and Pat Olson, Augustana College Art Collection, 2010.34

***Erucarum Ortus* Botanical, Lily**, 1717
Maria Sibylla Merian (German 1647–1717), published posthumously by her daughter
Hand-colored engraving, Plate 50, *Erucarum Ortus, Alimentum et Paradoxa Metamorphosis,* 15.4 x 12.1 cm., 4-3/4 x 6-1/16" image
Purchase through Gift of Mr. and Mrs. George and Pat Olson, and Paul A. Anderson Chair in the Arts Collection Purchase, Augustana College Art Collection, 2010.36

From Antiquity through much of the seventeenth century, it was commonly understood that insects were formed by spontaneous generation in mud, decaying flesh, and other unpleasant substances. It was not until the mid seventeenth century when physicians and naturalists documented insects forming from eggs rather than *abiogenesis* (Reitsma 68). Even so, observations and descriptions of the complete life cycle from egg to adult, including metamorphosis, had only been completed in a small number of insects. Maria Sibylla Merian (1647-1717), an artist and a naturalist, transformed the early field of entomology through her plates and paintings of butterfly and moth life cycles which were based on her personal observations of live organisms.

Merian was trained in engraving and floral still life painting. Yet, from an early age, she was captivated by insect metamorphosis. At age 13, she began raising silkworms from eggs while carefully describing and painting each stage of the life cycle—egg, larva (caterpillar), pupa within cocoon, and moth. She meticulously documented the metamorphosis of hundreds of moth and butterfly species that she caught in the wild and reared in her home and gardens. Her *Study Book* (what we would call a lab notebook or field journal today) even contains records of the number of eggs laid by a mated female (Reitsma 24). These detailed data are all the more remarkable when we consider she collected her data with only the aid of a magnifying glass. While other entomologists documented life cycles of insects, Merian's work is distinctive because of the precision and lifelike detail she captured in her plates. Additionally, she included each phase of the life cycle of the species and the host plant on which the caterpillar feeds in each of her paintings.

The detail and accuracy of Merian's work speak to her keen observational skills. These skills were likely honed as she practiced painting still life in her early years. Interestingly, observational skills developed as an artist are the very skills that make Merian such an important figure in science. Taking the time to be curious, pay attention to detail, and capture the detail for others to experience—this is science. Maria Merian was both an artist and a scientist, and her work is adored in both fields.

[Kristin Douglas, *Associate Professor of Biology*]

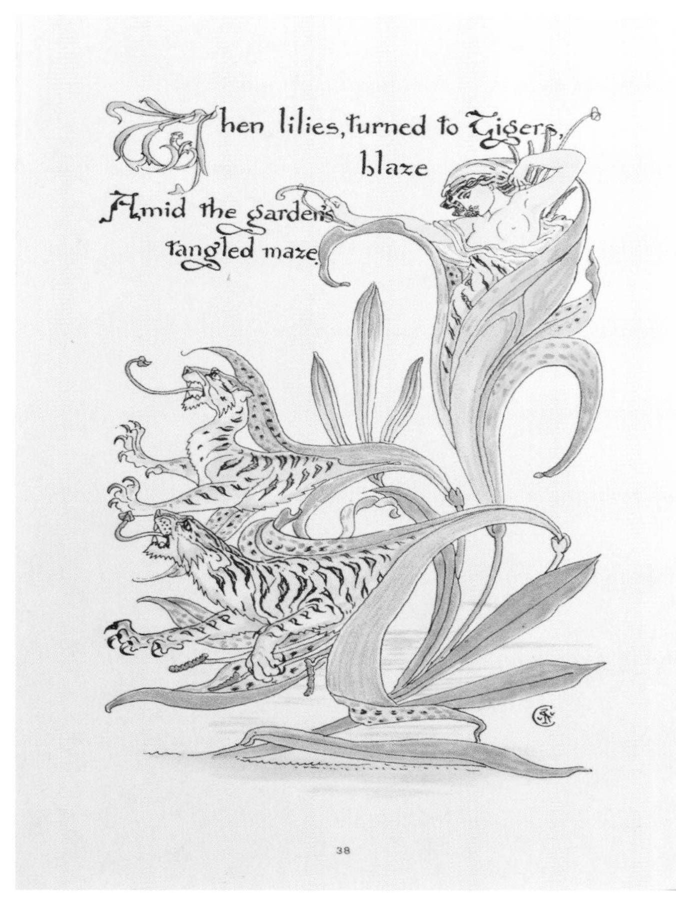

Then lilies, turned to Tigers, blaze
Amid the garden's tangled maze.
38

Flora's Feast: A Masque of Flowers, 1889
Walter Crane (British 1845–1915)
Printed book, Page 38, 25.7 x 19.0 x 1.4 cm., 10-1/8 x 17-3/8 x 5/8"
Paul A. Anderson Chair in the Arts Collection Purchase, Augustana College Art Collection, SDC2010.26

These brilliant orange lilies, tigers literally bursting from their bells, appear as the thirty-eighth of forty colored lithographs which illustrate a pageant of personified flowers called from winter's sleep by their Queen Flora. The procession follows the seasons; early spring flowers like crocuses and daffodils lead while autumn blooms such as tiger-lilies and chrysanthemums conclude. Walter Crane, one of the most prolific illustrators of the late 19th century, composed a couplet for each flower and handwrote it in Gothic characters over its illustration. Lettering and illustration become a coherent design as each text includes initial letters illuminated with aspects of the illustration below. In "Tiger-lilies" the organic curves in the three upper-case letters mimic the curves of lily petals and tiger tongues, and a tiny tiger's head pops from a flower bell in the initial "T."

Crane's life was filled with art and literature from many periods and places. Born in 1845, the second son of a portrait painter, in 1859 he was apprenticed to an influential engraver, William James Linton, who introduced Crane to Pre-Raphaelites and their fascination with nature and medieval culture. He learned to understand illustration and decoration by closely studying such eclectic sources as illuminated medieval manuscripts, Japanese block prints, Persian rugs, Renaissance emblems, Greek architecture, and European cathedrals. Crane often mixed styles within the same book or even within the same illustration. In *Flora's Feast*, characters in the procession wear floral versions of various fashions including classic Grecian drapery, medieval armor, or intricately embroidered Renaissance gowns.

Like other pages of *Flora's Feast*, "Tiger-lilies" includes large amounts of white space while text and illustration are unbound by borders. These are unlike illustrations in most of Crane's books where text appears in boxes or scrolls, and thick, often decorated borders crowd primary characters. Like other *Flora's Feast* illustrations, "Tiger-lilies" exhibits Crane's commitment to strong, repeating lines and graduated color as well as Crane's whimsy seen in the tigers' stamen-like tongues. Still, "Tiger-lilies" is unique. Only domesticated animals appear on other pages. In contrast, here exotic tigers spring dynamically like heraldic creatures rampant with claws raised. Here also unlike the rest, the human figure is minimal; only a quarter of her rather languorous body shows. In this illustration, more than any other, the power of the floral tangle nearly overshadows the human form.

[Virginia Johnson, *Director of the Reading and Writing Center*]

135

The Peacock Skirt. From "Salome," 1894
Aubrey Beardsley (British 1872–1898)
Lithograph, from *Salome: A Tragedy in One Act* by Oscar Wilde and Alfred Douglas, Plate 143, 27.8 x 21.9 cm., 10-15/16 x 8-5/8" sheet
Paul A. Anderson Chair in the Arts Collection Purchase, Augustana College Art Collection, 2009.9

Beardsley, Aubrey. "The Peacock Skirt," illustration to Oscar Wilde's play, *Salome*, originally written in French (1892) and translated by Lord Alfred Douglas into English. The translation (heavily revised by Wilde) was originally published by Elkin Mathews and John Lane, London (1894).

The Peacock Skirt is Beardsley's sly and wicked double parody of two of his era's aesthetic icons. It is, on the one hand, a brilliant black-and-white inversion of James McNeill Whistler's 1863 painting *La Princesse du pays de la porcelaine* (*The Princess of the Land of Porcelain*) which had (and still has) pride of place above the mantle in Frederick R. Leyland's magnificent Peacock Room of 1876-7 (decorated by Whistler). Beardsley has reversed the figure and stripped her of color and most of her feminine attributes, but he has exaggerated the original's skirt with its flamboyant peacock-feather design while simultaneously breaking up the image into its component decorative shapes.

On the other hand, the drawing is also an unnervingly accurate personification of the central motive in Oscar Wilde's play. While Beardsley was not fond of the work or its author, his illustrations soon made both Wilde and *Salome* infamous and unforgettable. At the same time, Beardsley's name became ineradicably linked with Wilde's, and the latter's trial and disgrace in 1895 proved Beardsley's downfall as well. What exactly are we looking at in this image, besides a swirling peacock-feather emblazoned skirt?

The figure on the left is clearly Salome, daughter of Herodias, the wife of Herod Antipas, *Tetrarch* (or ruler of the divided kingdom) of Judea and Salome's stepfather. But to whom is she speaking so earnestly? Most readers assumed that the slight figure on the right must be John the Baptist (called by Wilde *Iokanaan*, the Hebrew form of his name). Yet there is no instance in the play of Iokanaan looking directly at Salome or being in any way cowed by her as he so obviously is in Beardsley's drawing. Indeed, Iokanaan forbids Salome to look upon him and spurns her sexual advances, calling her, among other things, "Whore of Babylon!" But Salome DOES speak intimately, almost hypnotically, to the young Syrian captain, Narraboth, beseeching him to release Iokanaan from captivity: "Thou wilt do this thing for me, Narraboth….I have ever been kind toward thee. Thou wilt do this thing for me." The look of dismay on the young man's face and Salome's aggressive, threatening, demanding posture make it probable that it is this moment in the play that Beardsley is addressing in *The Peacock Skirt*, leaving the confrontation of Salome and Iokanaan for another drawing (*John and Salome*).

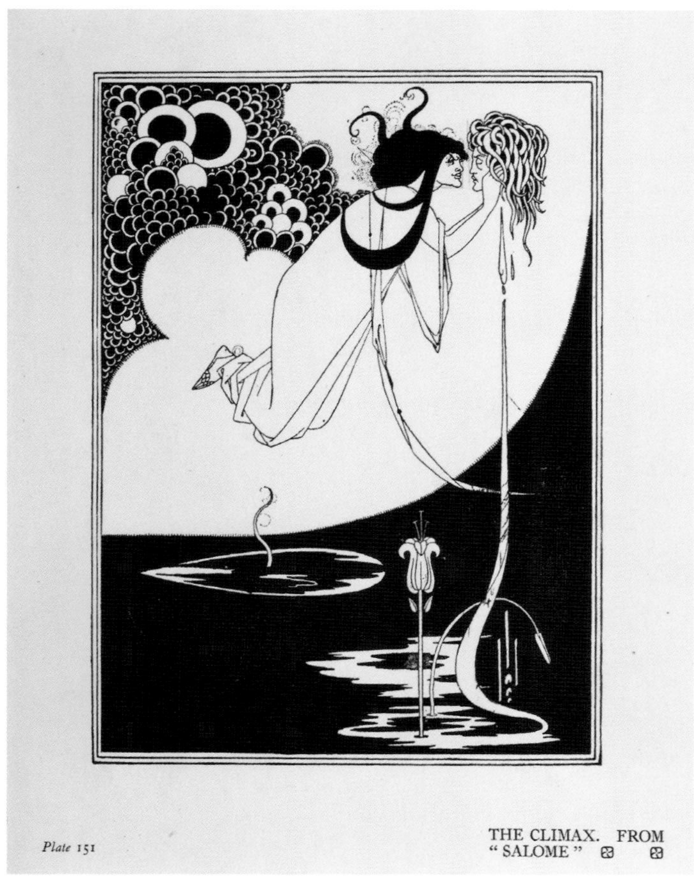

The Climax. From "Salome," 1894
Aubrey Beardsley (1872–1898)
Lithograph, from *Salome: A Tragedy in One Act* by Oscar Wilde and Alfred Douglas, Plate 151, 27.9 x 21.6 cm., 11 x 8-1/2" sheet
Paul A. Anderson Chair in the Arts Collection Purchase, Augustana College Art Collection, 2009.10

But the truly subversive element of the drawing, the element which made Victorian and modern spectators alike uneasy, is the effortless skill by which Beardsley has switched traditional gender roles for both characters. While Salome does wear a beautiful enveloping skirt and an elaborate peacock-feathered headdress traditionally worn by women, her features and posture are anything but feminine. She looms over the hapless Narraboth leering at him and commanding him to do her will. Narraboth—seen fully frontally in contrast to the limited profile view of Salome's face—is as beautiful as Leonardo's John the Baptist. He too wears an elaborate headdress, an elegant sheaf-like dress (with a startling axe-shaped belt and baldric). As Narraboth reels from the forceful overtures of his Princess, he defensively raises his left hand toward—three free-floating black candlesticks! These had quickly become well-known as Aubrey Beardsley's wryly phallic signature: compare it to Whistler's equally famous butterfly-with-stinger. The candlesticks cannot help Narraboth; he is helpless before the force of nature that is Salome. He will release Iokanaan to her and then, quite naturally, perish.

If Beardsley had not allowed us a peep at the unmistakably bony, hairy and knock-kneed legs peeping out from under the inexplicably frayed tunic, we would never dream to consider this character male-gendered at all. Yet that is precisely what Beardsley is doing here. The "perversity" or "decadence" of the drawing (contemporary attributions) lies in Beardsley's unexpected reversal, not merely of gender ATTRIBUTES, but identities as well. The true horror of Salome is the grotesque inversion of sexuality from lust to incest to necrophilia as the thwarted Judean princess—rejected by Iokanaan—enflames the forbidden passions of her stepfather by promising to dance for him if he will grant her a single wish. That desire of course is for the head of the Baptist on a silver charger so that she might finally kiss his lips, captured in *The Climax: Salome with the Head of John the Baptist*. "Ah! I have kissed thy mouth, Iokanaan, I have kissed thy mouth. There was a bitter taste on thy lips. Was it the taste of blood? Perchance it was the taste of love. They say that love hath a bitter taste. But what matter? What matter? I have kissed thy mouth, Iokanaan, I have kissed thy mouth." Herod's final command—"Kill that woman!"—ends the play on an enigmatic note. Wilde's Salome is a female monster ("femme fatale" writ large indeed!), but she is universally recognized (by her beauty, breeding and skills) as a woman. What is Beardsley's Salome? Perhaps we should not ask.

[Larry E. Scott, *Professor of Scandinavian Studies*]

137

N° 77. 2e année. 25 Avril 1896

15 centimes.

Le Rire

JOURNAL HUMORISTIQUE ILLUSTRÉ PARAISSANT LE SAMEDI

Rédaction et Administration : 10, rue Saint-Joseph, Paris. — Directeur : M. F. JUVEN. — Partie artistique : M. Arsène ALEXANDRE

Les pauvres oisifs! Et dire qu'on ne leur accorde jamais la *journée de huit heures!*

Dessin de Vallotton.

Les Pauvres Oisifs! **(The Poor Idlers!)**, 1896
Félix Vallotton (Swiss1865–1925)
Chromotypograph, cover for *Le Rire* , 25 April 25 1896, 22.4 x 19.0 cm., 8-7/8 x 7-1/2" image
Paul A. Anderson Chair in the Arts Collection Purchase, Augustana College Art Collection, 2005.4

Le Rire, or *Laughter*, a satirical humor magazine, published weekly in Paris, debuted in 1894. At this time, with the burgeoning middle class, educated Parisians enjoyed increased income and leisure time. Much like today's news, curiosity toward scandals, government corruption, and performers who appeared in music halls, captured the interest of its readers. *Le Rire* poked fun at the many political and social issues of its day. The *Gay 90's* was a time of crowded cabarets and cafés. A variety of prominent artists illustrated such dynamics via covers and centerfolds printed through *chromotypography* (a relief printing technique, similar to woodblocks, only using metal rather than wood plates).

This particular cover was designed in 1896 by Félix Vallotton. It illustrates an elegant Parisian park and its environs. Here we may study its many varied inhabitants—upper-class men and women who sit and chat or relax for a leisurely smoke while nannies run about and mind their children who play nearby. The caption aptly states: "*The poor idlers! And to say that we have never granted the eight-hour day*!"

Félix Vallotton was a Swiss painter, graphic designer, and writer who admired prints by such Old Masters as Hans Holbein the Younger (catalogue 20) and Albrecht Dürer (catalogue 18 and 19). He joined the *Nabis*, an avant-garde group of young art students from the Académie Julian in Paris, who set the pace for graphic arts in the 1890s. Vallotton formed lifelong friendships with fellow members of the *Nabis*, including Édouard Vuillard (catalogue 138) and Pierre Bonnard, as they pursued the *Synthetist* example in the work of Post-Impressionist, Paul Gauguin. Vallotton illustrated journals alongside such notables as Henri de Toulouse-Lautrec (catalogue 129 and 130), also sympathetic to this group. These artists created their own *Symbolist* movement through simplifying nature to its essential decorative beauty, incorporating elements of *Art Nouveau*. This style was directly influenced by the line as well as flat or patterned areas found in compositions for Japanese *ukiyo-e* prints (catalogue 97 and 100).

In 1891 Vallotton executed his first of more than 200 woodcuts created during his lifetime. He became recognized as an innovative leader in the revival of true woodcut as an artistic medium and would influence members of the twentieth-century German Expressionist movement, the *Bridge* (catalogue 152). His style in all media is characterized by flat areas of color, hard edges, and simplification of detail. Through such graphic design, Félix Vallotton would become an important modernist bridge to the twentieth century.

[Elizabeth P. Ducey, *Graphic Designer*]

138

Figures in a Garden, ca. 1894
Édouard Vuillard (French 1868–1940)
Oil on composition board, possible study for **Public Gardens** series, 1894, 22.7 x 34.8 cm., 9 x 13-13/16"
Lent Courtesy of Private Collection

Figures in a Garden exhibits Édouard Vuillard's *Japonisme* or use of Japanese artistic techniques. This includes flattened perspective, off-centered arrangement, color without shadow and the use of caricature to simplify the features of children. Vuillard witnessed the exhibition of Japanese prints at the *École des Beaux-Arts* in 1890. The publication of *L'Art Japonais* (1883) by Louis Gonse and *Le Japon artistique* (1888-1891) by Siegfried Bing also must have opened up the young artist's eyes to the world of Japanese aesthetics. His fascination with Japanese style can be traced back to his journals; one volume is full of ink drawings done with *Japanesque* techniques—"articulated outlines and dramatic sweeps of the brush" (Easton 46).

Vuillard owned a copy of the *Manga* by Japanese artist Katsushika Hokusai. He may have used its figural sketches and facial models as inspiration. In Japanese art, the simplification of form achieved through caricature is a "powerful vehicle of emotion" (Ives 100). Hokusai humorously showed people on the move, exploring their changing awkward poses (Perucci-Petri 126). While the children in this painting are not moving, they are depicted with mere basic detail. Vuillard preferred not to show their distinguishing features. It is almost as if the individual bodies were of no importance, but rather they join together with the background trees and shrubs to form one single surface texture. The mixing of patterns in the Japanese manner is referred to as "pattern ground technique" and it aims to devalue the individual figure (Wichmann 211-212). Essentially, Vuillard crafted the children as pure decorative motifs.

The park in which they play was not one specific place. Vuillard chose an "amalgam of several public gardens" near his home in Paris. He meant for the park to be a cultural oasis within the increasingly urbanized Parisian environment (Groom 50-51). With that said, this could be a study for his series of *Public Gardens* done in 1894. The Parisian bourgeois ideal was that children be controlled by perpetual parental surveillance, but Vuillard ignored that model here. There appears to be a parent or guardian present, but she is not stifling the children's play in the park. On the contrary, she is allowing them time to engage in recreation.

[Matthew Bowman, *Class of 2012*]

139

Favrile Inkwell, 1899 (marked "K 1901")
Louis Comfort Tiffany (American 1848–1933)
Blown glass and hinged brass lid, 8.2 x 12.5 x 12.5 cm., 3-1/8 x 5-1/4 x 5-1/4"
Erick O. Schonstedt Inkstand Collection, Augustana College Art Collection, 2006.1.202

The inkwell, once a commonplace and often mundanely utilitarian writing tool, was transformed into a rarified, yet functional, *object d'art* by Louis Comfort Tiffany. Heir to Tiffany and Company, he was a talented painter, architect, and decorative artist. Though he designed work in various media, Tiffany is best known as America's premier glass artist. Combining his aesthetic connoisseurship and business acumen with a variety of influences, such as archaeological artifacts, Venetian glasswork techniques, advances in chemistry, and philosophical social theories, Tiffany developed and promoted a new synthesis of American decorative art, as exemplified by this favrile glass inkwell.

Tiffany was foremost a colorist. His earliest experiments were influenced by the coloration of Medieval stained glass windows (Byars 744). His later glasswork, however, such as this inkwell, emulated the quality and color of ancient Syrian and Roman glass, which had deteriorated and become iridescent after long periods of exposure to minerals while buried in soil under alternating wet and dry conditions (catalogue 5A and 5B). Attempting to artificially replicate this effect, Tiffany hired the best glassblowers and chemists to experiment with color, luster, and opacity. In 1881 he patented a type of glass he termed *favrile*, produced by applying metallic oxides directly to the glass or exposing it to metallic oxide vapors which imparted a metallic film either on or within the glass (Baal-Teshuva 26-30). The highly iridescent and metallic luster of this inkwell exemplifies Tiffany's patented process: the body color is solid and slightly opalescent, and the lobed form, while secondary to the color, enhances the reflective quality of the applied decoration by refracting the light hitting the inkwell's surface.

This inkwell reflects not only light, but also Tiffany's fascination with the Arts and Crafts Movement, which advocated economic and social reform and a reevaluation of design standards and labor practices. Complying with the movement's tenets, Tiffany's inkwell was free-formed, not molded, with a hand-painted swirling motif and zipper pattern, thus retaining elements of individual artistic expression. Indeed, the term *favrile*, derived from the Old English word *fabrile*, meaning handmade, further emphasized the connection (Goebel 102). Likewise, advocates of the Arts and Crafts Movement, as well as Tiffany, believed that nature should be the primary source of design. The inkwell's form is naturalistic, but highly abstracted. It also attempts to reintegrate the status of art within utilitarian objects and represents Tiffany's obsession with the *cult of beauty.*

Although this inkwell has much in common with the Arts and Crafts Movement, it also has many conflicting elements that Tiffany was unable to resolve. For example, the manufacturing process for this inkwell, while handmade and not mechanized, was highly industrialized. Contrary to Arts and Crafts principals, Tiffany maintained a division of labor between designer and craftsman: he neither actually made, nor designed this inkwell, but retained artistic control and overriding approval of its creation (Baal-Teshuva 165-68). Though made in volume, Tiffany's inkwell was still a luxury-priced object, making his style of beauty inaccessible to many economic classes, contrary to the Movement's socialistic notion of artist/craftsman. He patented and trademarked his invention, eventually destroying his chemical formulas in 1930 to prevent others from imitating his style of beauty (Byars 744). The accelerated embrace of the Arts and Crafts Movement in America, however, led others to succeed where Tiffany *failed.*

[James Beebe, *Class of 1988*]

Arts and Crafts Inkwell, ca. 1910
Artist unknown
Hammered copper, milk glass insert, 5.4 x 9.0 x 9.0 cm., 2-1/8 x 3-1/2 x 3-1/2"
Purchase with Gift of Mr. James Beebe, Augustana College Art Collection, 2003.15

Since antiquity, inkwells were used to dispense ink until their general disuse by the mid-twentieth century with the invention of reliable pens capable of carrying their own supply of ink (Nickell). Inkwells are single receptacles for the short-term storage of a small amount of ink and to slow its evaporation until its eventual use. Various materials were suited for this task and were fashioned in numerous ways. Hence, inkwells were imbued, not only with ink, but also the aesthetic trends of a particular time and place. This copper and glass inkwell, although not marked or dated, is characteristic of the type of Arts and Crafts metalwork produced in the United States around 1910.

The Arts and Crafts Movement began in England during the nineteenth century as a reaction against rampant industrialization and what was then seen as the undesirable effect it had on the design and manufacture of goods. It was not conceived as a new style, but rather, as a new philosophy for living, working, and making objects. However, a general preference for handcraftsmanship, straightforward construction, design suited to purpose, and (generally) inexpensive materials, created a consistently rustic tone that could be called a style (Fleming and Honour 45-6). Non-precious metals were favored, but copper, in particular, was the preferred metal of choice by Arts and Crafts metalworkers. The use of copper for this inkwell typifies the movement's preference for simple proletarian materials: it was relatively inexpensive, and thus, well aligned with the *democratic* ideals of the Arts and Crafts philosophy.

This inkwell's strong geometric shape upholds the Arts and Crafts' preference for simple forms and straightforward, functional design. Its austerity is softened only by rounded edges, a slightly flared base, and an overall roughly hammered finish. Typically, the surfaces of hand-wrought items were roughly hammered or *planished* to a smooth texture of evenly distributed, yet visible hammer marks. These marks, which generally distinguish Arts and Crafts metalwork, conveyed the imprint of the craftsman as well as the method of manufacture. The hammer marks have not been planished smooth, but are distinctly visible, being uniform in size, of medium depth and evenly spaced. *Patination*, or the chemical alteration of metal to change its color, further emphasizes the character and manipulation of the copper on this inkwell. Unlike the hammer strikes of English copperwork, which were generally restrained, this inkwell's hammer marks are more characteristic of the robust handling of American metalwork. In addition, American Arts and Crafts copperwork was routinely patinated, while English metalsmiths only occasionally patinated their wares. The hammer marks and patination of this inkwell indicate that it is likely of American make. This inkwell seems to be typical of the type of work made by the New York *school* at the height of the movement (Harwood 11).

[James Beebe, *Class of 1988*]

141

Art Nouveau Style Vase in Plum and Yellow, early 20th century
Emile Gallé (French 1846–1904)
Cameo blown glass, 18.5 x 8.9 x 7.5 cm., 7-1/4 x 3-1/2 x 3"
Lent Courtesy of Private Collection

The innovations that Emile Gallé contributed to the Art Nouveau movement came through his manipulation of *cameo*, a technique dating back to ancient Rome. Cameo glass comprises two or more separate colored layers of glass. The top layers are acid-etched, a technique used to remove areas of overlaid glass, in order to create designs in relief on the cameo glass vessels. He transformed formal two-color vases into complex, multilayered compositions. Using combinations of cutting and carving by hand, along with acid-etching, he created organic designs from as many as five layers of colored glass. Gallé also eliminated the sharp color contrasts, preferring to cut away colors at various levels in order to create shading, subtle color gradations, atmosphere and perspective.

Gallé had a close relationship with nature, as a philosopher and as a poet, and he found within the plant world the inspiration for his totally unique glass creations. He felt that beauty was truth and truth lay in nature. In this new era of science and machines, Gallé wanted to get back to the simplicity of nature. The elements of nature that had the most significant impact on Gallé came from the new influence of *Japonisme*.

Japonisme provided Gallé with inspiration, encouraging him to push the boundaries of contemporary glass both in terms of shape and content. He had enjoyed running through the summer fields in Nancy, spotting wild flowers, and sketching their colors and shapes. It was such early experiences with nature that led to his fascination with similar botanical motifs in Japanese art.

Many of these organic Japanese influences can be seen on this particular vase. One of the first points of interest is the winding spiral tree which takes up more than half of the vessel. The curvilinear form is typical of the Art Nouveau movement. Although the line is dramatic, the vase does not lose its organic shape. There is a strong sense that this is not a tree from his local environment, but is reminiscent of an asymmetrical element derived from a distant Japanese garden. By incorporating this exotic addition, the vase gains a mystical, poetic quality which invites the viewer to be contemplative.

[Paul Arnell, *Class of 2006*]

Un Masque à la tenture mauve (A Mask with Mauve Shades), 1907
Fernand-Edmond-Jean-Marie Khnopff (Belgian 1858–1921)
Color crayons, 27.7 x 18.4 cm., 10-7/8 x 7-1/4" image
Gift of Mr. and Mrs. Michael Moss, Augustana College Art Collection, 1993.48.1

Faces dominate the works of Fernand Khnopff, particularly enigmatic feminine faces. Khnopff was a leading artist of the Symbolist movement which emerged during the late nineteenth century. Symbolism was founded on the idea that images hold a power over the mind and convey meaning without being completely specific or rational (Lucie-Smith 15-24). The movement was inspired by the work of French poets such as Stéphane Mallarmé and Paul Verlaine and may be traced in the late works of French artists Henri Fantin-Latour and Paul Gauguin.

Un masque à la tenture mauve exhibits a mesmerizing image of a red-haired woman staring at the viewer against a patterned background. In her right hand she holds a scepter with a blue orb surrounding a small nude female figurine. Introspection and thought are major themes and products of Khnopff's work (Friedman 6). His pieces are known for their sexual appeal and mystery. He was a harbinger of issues concerning the unconscious mind, prior to Sigmund Freud. Freud elucidated the theory that the mind is a complex system and helped to define the concepts of the unconscious, sexuality and repression.

Khnopff used photographs as sources, taking the immediate impression, then altering the background, coloring or other components. These helped to provide the foundation on which he projected his Symbolist images. Khnopff was also very interested in the poetic nature of color, and he combined it with form to create introspective and evocative moods. He sought eternal themes in his works, choosing subjects which embodied such intangible concepts as time, love, death, fate, consciousness, religion and philosophy (Friedman 8). The enigmatic image that Khnopff portrayed was intentional and reflective of the aims of the Symbolist movement.

The Symbolists frequently depicted a new conception of women, which showed them as *femme fatales* (fatal women). Using the word *mask* in the title of the piece allowed Khnopff more symbolic freedom and further confuses the meaning for the viewer. The mask term may apply to the fact that the forehead is missing, and may physically represent the withdrawal of her mind. This also brings more focus on the face, particularly the lips. Khnopff himself described that: "The expression of the mouth is the truest; there it is almost impossible to dissimulate" (Laillet 202). The connotation of a mask with the myriad of other uncertain symbols accomplishes a goal for which Symbolists strove: to challenge the viewer to interpret the work, not for its superficial imagery, but to reflect more deeply on its underlying meaning.

[David Freeman, *Class of 2006*]

143

Immortalité (Immortality), 1898
Ignace-Henri-Jean-Théodore Fantin-Latour (French 1836–1904)
Lithograph, published in *L'estampe Moderne,* 34.7 x 24.7 cm., 13-5/8 x 9-3/4" image
Gift in Honor of Dr. and Mrs. Thomas William and Barbara Carter, Augustana College Art Collection, 2002.10

Immortalité is a work that stylistically parallels artist Henri Fantin-Latour's life. In this beautiful piece, Fantin combined elements of Neoclassicism, Romanticism and Symbolism, but overall, it is based on a very personal imaginative expression. Although Fantin practiced many different styles throughout his career, self-expression was the basis for his work.

Neoclassical elements are apparent in the classical idealism of this female figure, appropriately clothed in *wet drapery* and standing in a typical *contrapposto* position. By this time, Fantin had abandoned his Realist roots, for a more traditional academic approach. Yet his Neoclassical style was infused with romantic mystery and emotion. Aside from the use of this style, this piece is primarily an expression of the Symbolist Movement.

Through the allegorical subject matter, *Immortalité* expresses Fantin's feelings about the importance of the imagination, in a world relying on observed nature through photographic arts. The subject is almost thrust upon her viewers, asking them to think, imagine and interpret. The structure of this work consists of a central idealized female figure with expansive wings. The image evokes a dreamlike aura within a heavenly black and white atmosphere. Rays of light create a miraculous effect as they radiate downward from the upper left corner, originating from an unknown source. Her outstretched wings fade into the background depth. The figure is frontally illuminated, establishing her as an independent light source, reinforced by the star-like form above her head.

The close association of this image with the Romantics—painter Eugène Delacroix and writer Henri Mürger—established Fantin's allegiance to the mysterious world of the imagination, rather than to scenes of modern Paris that surrounded him. Perhaps he typified the modernist crisis of the *fin-de-siècle* (end of the century), in the realization that observed reality was likely not enough, as many wished for deeper elements that lay beneath the surface.

[Katie Gedrimas, *Class of 2007* and
Catherine Carter Goebel, *Editor*]

The Beguiling of Merlin, late 19th century
After Sir Edward Coley Burne-Jones (British 1833–1898) by Adolphe Lalauze (French 1838–1905)
Etching, 26.0 x 15.2 cm., 10-1/4 x 6" image
Paul A. Anderson Chair in the Arts Collection Purchase, Augustana College Art Collection, 2010.57

A careless shoe-string, in whose tie
I see a wild civility:
Do more bewitch me than when art
Is too precise in every part.
—Robert Herrick (1591-1674), *Delight in Disorder.*

King Arthur, if ever there was such an historical figure, flourished between the late 5th and the mid 6th centuries in Romano-Celtic Britain. He won a few battles against the invading Anglo-Saxons, wavered there on the verge of hope, and quickly retreated into song for the next few centuries. We know nearly nothing about that Arthur.

But the Arthur who emerged from obscurity a few centuries later in the Middle Ages quickly became the most talked about figure in Western culture, and his story the most frequently published, of any figure outside of the Bible. Arthur is newly born with nearly each new generation, shouldering the concerns and exemplifying the values of each new generation from about 1115 'til now.

The etching you see here is part of the British Arthur story as exemplified by the nineteenth-century Pre-Raphaelite Brotherhood and its second-generation practitioner, Sir Edward Burne-Jones. It was a world of contradictions: either exciting or terrifying. Britain, at the height of its Empire, was both beguiled by her conquered races and feared them. British society, an impregnable bastion of male privilege and authority, was governed by a Queen. With the Industrial Age raging around them, many British intellectuals sought a reaffirmation of humanity in a return to natural themes and forces. An education which valued pure rationality engendered worries about deeper emotional and erotic roots.

The chaotic age of Victoria sought symbols that would reconcile these disparate characteristics, especially in the realm of the other: the female, the exotic, the romantic, the emotional, and in a false historicity of the past—a phenomenon often referred to as "medievalism," a romanticisation of an era as distant in time as India is in miles.

In this picture we see Arthur's most powerful minister of state, the Druid Merlin, ensnared by the powers that he himself had taught to a trusted devotee. Merlin is captured by the Other in all the ways enumerated above. Does he regret this? Or is his "beguilement" a willing, almost urgent need to sublimate the stated values of his Victorian age? Perhaps there is something guilt-inducing about conquering once sovereign peoples? In ignoring the value of half of our society based only on gender? In pretending that intellect and emotion must be constantly at war? In taking too literally the command that humans must "subdue" the earth?

Finally, it seems to me that this picture illustrates perfectly what an earlier literary age would have called a "wild civility." The images are balanced and the patterns nicely symmetrical. However, there are few right angles or straight lines. All is fluctuating and moving. The patterns are too complex to follow easily and that is, in part, what beguiles.

[Joseph D. McDowell, *Professor of English*]

145

Park Scene with Band, 1909
Ivan Ivanovitch Kowalski (Russian, active in France early 20th century)
Oil on canvas, 46.0 x 33.1 cm., 18-3/16 x 13-1/16"
Paul A. Anderson Chair in the Arts Collection Purchase, Augustana College Art Collection, 2004.15

Little is known of early twentieth-century painter Ivan Ivanovitch Kowalski other than a small citation describing him as a Russian-born painter of landscapes, a watercolorist and pastel artist who lived and worked in Paris. He was sensitive about the changing seasons and liked landscapes with water (Bénézit 18-19). As the international center of the world of art, Paris attracted many other expatriate Russian artists including Bakst, Benois, Chagall and the composer Stravinsky to name a few (White 244).

In *Park Scene with Band* (1909), we see the influences of Impressionism and Post-Impressionist pointillism championed by Georges Seurat. The large tree, the seated girl and the young woman wearing a red dress draw us to the subject of the gathering—the band. A small ensemble is implied and due to the distance, no instruments are displayed. An apparent conductor and sheet music on stands leaves no doubt as to the activity. The festive occasion replete with balloons, likely included orchestral transcriptions of Berlioz, Bizet, Delibes, and Saint-Saëns along with patriotic, revolution-era marches by Gossec, Catel, Jardin and especially the national anthem *La Marseillaise* by Rouget de Lisre.

A moderate temperature allowed this autumnal concert. Since the eighteenth century, the French enjoyed outdoor band performances for any special or historical occasion including Bastille Day celebrations (July 14) or the special performance of Hector Berlioz' *Symphonie Funèbre et Triomphale* (1840), celebrating the tenth anniversary of the July Revolution of 1830. That performance called for a band of over 200 and was witnessed by a crowd so large that it completely overpowered the music (Berlioz 253-255).

The lasting influence of French outdoor band performance on American bands can be first seen immediately following the American Civil War. Large outdoor concerts were "conceived in the tradition of the 'Monster Concerts' of the French Revolution" (Hansen 42). This can be witnessed weekly throughout the summer months in many city or town parks or at the U.S. Capitol steps where one could hear the U.S. Navy Band (Mondays), The U.S. Air Force Band (Tuesdays), The U.S. Marine Band (Wednesdays) and the U.S. Army Band (Fridays).

Yet there is perhaps no finer example than that of the founding of the Sousa Band in 1892. After very successful tours with the United States Marine Band in 1891 and 1892, John Philip Sousa was ordered by the Marine Corps surgeon to recuperate in Europe. The wily entrepreneur David Blakely persuaded Sousa to attend a performance by the Garde Républicaine Band, considered the finest band in the world. After hearing the band, Sousa resigned his commission with the Marine Band and formed his own professional band with Blakely as manager. The initial contract reads: "It shall be the aim and duty of the said Sousa by individual effort, and band rehearsals and practice, and by the preparation and furnishing of music, to make this band equal in executive ability to the band of the Garde Républicaine in Paris" (Bierley 151).

[James M. Lambrecht, *Professor of Music, Director of Bands*]

146

Girl at Loom or **Drawer in Cotton Mill**, ca. 1912
Lewis Wickes Hine (American 1874–1940)
Gelatin silver print, vintage, 11.8 x 13.8 cm., 4-11/16 x 5-7/16"
Purchase through Paul A. Anderson Chair in the Arts, and through Gift of the Reynold Emanuel and Johnnie Gause Leak Holmén Endowment Fund for the Visual Arts, Augustana College Art Collection, 2006.20 © 2011 Artists Rights Society (ARS), New York

Lewis Wickes Hine has been described as a sociological photographer and as such represents, along with Jacob Riis, one of the two most prominent early exponents of "social-documentary" photography—and a precursor to slightly later luminaries such as Dorothea Lange and Walker Evans (Doherty 3). He preferred to describe himself as an "interpretive photographer." Although his politics are not entirely clear, what is certain is that he exhibited a political worldview that made him part of the progressive reform movement of the first half of the twentieth century—a movement that took aim at the exploitation and social exclusion of the working class in the emerging industrial social order. Unsympathetic to radical critics of capitalism, Hine sought to find ways to make the relationship between employers and employees something other than a zero-sum game. Art historians have contended that although work is the central theme throughout Hine's career, one can divide it between an earlier phase, during which the focus was on "negative documentation," and a later phase when he turned to "positive documentation."

With this in mind, how should *Girl at Loom* (which has the alternative title of *Drawer in Cotton Mill*) be located in terms of his corpus? Given that it dates from around 1912 and was produced under the auspices of the National Child Labor Committee, it would appear to be squarely located within the so-called negative documentation period. However, it is difficult to see how the photo in itself could be viewed as a critique of child labor. The girl does not appear to be living in squalor and her work does not appear dangerous. On the contrary, she is neatly dressed, her hair primly arranged in a bun, and she appears to be seated quite comfortably. Given that we do not see her face directly, it is not entirely clear at first view that she is a girl and not an adult. The small hands are perhaps a clue, but it is only because of Hine's title that the matter is certain. Here as elsewhere, the subject is absorbed in the task at hand, but does not appear overwhelmed. Nor is the worker reduced to being a mere appendage of the machine.

[Peter Kivisto, *Professor of Sociology,*
Richard A. Swanson Professor of Social Thought]

147A&B

Crouching Girl, modeled in 1900; cast date unknown
Aristide Joseph Bonaventure Maillol (French 1861–1944), cast by A. Bingen and Costenoble
Cast bronze attached to marble base, 20.2 x 8.0 x 9.8 cm., 8 x 3-3/16 x 3-7/8" without base
Paul A. Anderson Collection Purchase, Augustana College Art Collection 2007.11 © 2011 Artists Rights Society (ARS), New York

The River, modeling begun in 1938; cast date unknown
Aristide Joseph Bonaventure Maillol (French 1861–1944)
Cast bronze attached to marble base, 13.9 x 27.0 x 15.4 cm., 5-1/2 x 10-5/8 x 6" without base
Paul A. Anderson Chair in the Arts Collection Purchase, Augustana College Art Collection, 2007.10 © 2011 Artists Rights Society (ARS), New York

At first glance, one may not understand the message that Aristide Maillol conveyed through sculpture. In this digital era, when maximum pixels and "high res" are prized characteristics of the electronic gadgetry we crave, the more "life-like" or 3D that an image is on our viewing screens, the greater our perception of reality. To appreciate *The Crouching Girl* and *The River*, we must step off the path of "authenticity through minute detail" and consider the larger themes in Maillol's work.

Maillol sculpted during the late 19th and early 20th centuries, using a style uniquely his own but reminiscent of early Greek statues. Maillol, like the Greeks, found the human body the most important subject for artistic expression. Scholars believe the Greeks highly valued the body because they envisioned gods as having human forms, but Maillol's interest seems due to the malleable nature of the thing itself. Not only could the human torso and limbs assume many poses, allowing Maillol to play with positive mass and negative space in his sculptures (e.g., filled vs. open shapes), but the human figure was also an archetype used to express his ideal of beauty in nature. Maillol once said that "The human form is far older than the emergence of man, who had only to mould himself in the image of the primitive creatures swarming around him to give himself an appearance of balance, beauty and harmony" (George 43).

Though Maillol, like most artists, had a favorite model, his sculptures are not depictions of her specifically. In his words, "...a man (or a woman) is no more important, plastically speaking, than any given rock, animal or bush" (Chevalier 29). Faces and other structures are expressionless and anonymous in Maillol's sculptures. Like fellow French sculptor, Auguste Rodin, Maillol sometimes took pieces from one statue to add to another. His work is thus simultaneously abstract and representative. The controlled pose of *The Crouching Girl* is more representative of Maillol than is *The River*, part of a commissioned piece that he chose to finish when funding ceased. The contorted posture of *The River* bespeaks an emotional response requested by the original patron, but is evidence that Maillol could sculpt great detail and emotion, but typically chose otherwise.

[Dara Wegman-Geedey, *Professor of Biology*]

Playdays, 1925 small version from 1923 original model
Harriet W. Frishmuth (American 1880–1980)
Cast bronze with verdigris patina on marble base, 59.6 x 21.2 x 18.6 cm., 23-1/2 x 8-3/8 x 7-3/8"
Paul A. Anderson Chair in the Arts Collection Purchase, Augustana College Art Collection, 2001.40

Harriet Whitney Frishmuth's *Playdays* gracefully captures the exuberant spirit of early twentieth-century modernist sculpture. The playful spirit of the slender nude adolescent girl embodies the signature style of Frishmuth's most notable decorative bronzes and garden sculptures. The young girl's lyrical pose with extended arms and raised tip-toe position reflects Frishmuth's interest in the new free-form dance movement, a style popularized by Isadora Duncan that later became known as *Modern Dance.*

Frishmuth's rendering also typifies her appropriation of the feminine ideal of slender androgyny popular in the 1920s era of the flapper and suffragette. Created in a transitional period for American sculpture, *Playdays'* naturalistic subject also represents the move beyond French academicism toward the modern abstract idiom. The modernist tendencies in *Playdays*—the rhythmic contours of the figure and the slight sleek stylization—reflect aspects of both the curvilinear designs of *Art Nouveau* and streamlined aesthetic of the emerging *Art Deco* movement. Its lighthearted motif with frogs designed to spray water echoes Scudder's *Frog Fountain* of 1901, inspired by Italian Renaissance sculpture. Yet, Frishmuth chose a more naturalistic source—the modern dancer.

Frishmuth first used the motif of a female form teasing a water creature in her small utilitarian bronze *Girl and Frog Ashtray* of 1910, which sold well for many years. Three years later she created *Girl with Fish, Fountain*, in which she also began to explore the use of water sprays as a compositional device. While in demand as a garden sculpture designer, Frishmuth stated she "decided to model small, decorative figures whenever commissions for large pieces allowed me the time. The small pieces were for purposes of bread and butter…." (Arsonson 28). *Playdays*, modeled in 1923 without a specific commission, was intended as a marketable sculpture in the small version.

[Cynthia Wiedemann Empen, *Class of 1992*]

149

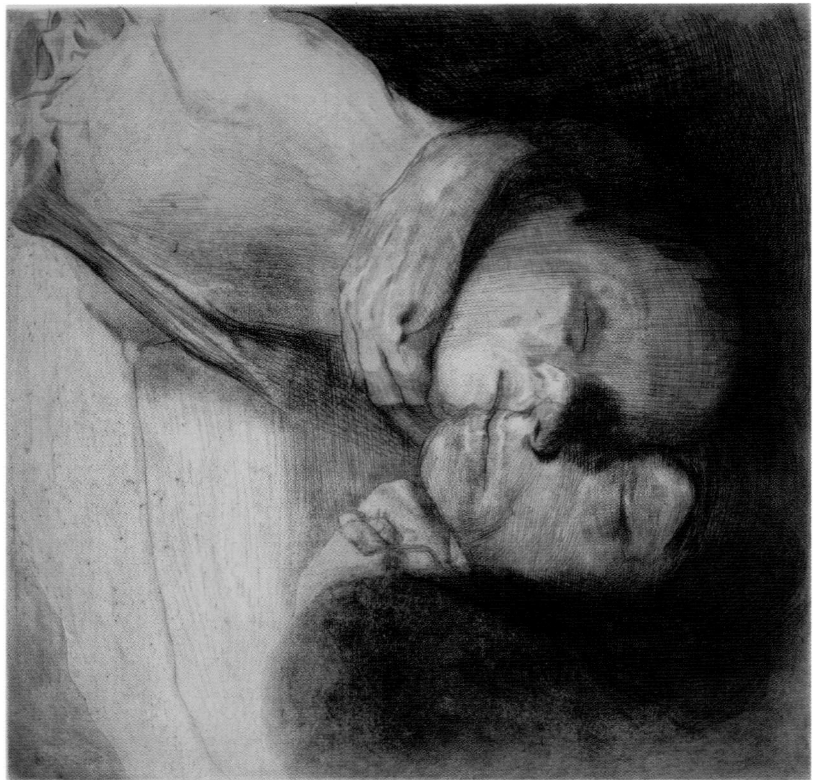

Death, Mother and Child (*Tod, Frau und Kind*), 1910, from Becke edition ca., 1945
Käthe Kollwitz (German 1867–1945)
Etching and drypoint, 39.6 x 39.4 cm., 15-3/4 x 15-1/2" image
Augustana College Art Department Purchase, 1969.24

In her art, Käthe Kollwitz often depicted the working class, whom she considered more beautiful and worthy of artistic representation than the *bourgeoisie* (Kearns 81). For example, various works show a peasants' uprising, families despairing because of their poverty, and mothers agonizing over their children's hunger. Later in her life, she created political posters "to combat injustice, poverty, alcoholism, hunger, infant mortality, and other prevalent social ills" (Bachert 120) and she wanted to have an effect on her era through her art (Prelinger 79). However, even more works depict mothers and children in less clearly defined settings, and for much of her life she was not politically active. This piece, as much of her work, is not a call to political action but a depiction of universal human suffering.

This piece features a motif that was common in her work: a mother mourning a dead child. In this image, we see a mother grasping her child's head to her own. The eyes of both are closed, and one could believe that the image depicts only a tender moment between mother and child, were it not for the skull-like depiction of death in the upper left corner. The two heads pressed tightly together at first glance create a single face; the noses and mouths of mother and child are aligned as the mother clasps her child to her. Beyond the two heads is darkness, and the bodies are barely hinted at. The simplicity of the image is deliberate, since Kollwitz rejected the "use of too much technique as incompatible with the depiction of painful topics" (Prelinger 79). The piece is unsentimental but does not lack emotion: the mother's anguish is evident in her tight grasp of the dead child. Kollwitz produced many such images of loss and mourning, even before she lost her younger son Peter during the First World War; this etching predates that loss by several years. This image gives few hints about the identity of the subjects or of the setting of the scene, leaving only the basics: a mother, a dead child, and grief.

[Lisa Seidlitz, *Assistant Professor of German*]

150

Sitzende Alte (Seated Old Woman), ca. 1900
Paula Modersohn-Becker (German 1876–1907)
Etching and aquatint printed in dark brown, state three of three, 18.8 x 14.5 cm., 7-3/8 x 5-9/16" image
Paul A. Anderson Chair in the Arts Collection Purchase, Augustana College Art Collection, 2000.60

At the close of Part I of Nietzsche's *Thus Spoke Zarathustra,* Nietzsche states: " ...that is the great noon when man stands at the middle of his way between beast and overman and celebrates his way to the evening as his highest hope: for it is the way to a new morning" ("Thus spoke" 78). The artistic and philosophical connections between Paula Modersohn-Becker and Nietzsche are well-known (Diethe). Though Nietzsche died in 1900, Modersohn-Becker's artistic style continued to manifest the key themes of Nietzsche's philosophy for free spirits. Though Nietzsche claimed that free spirits did not yet exist, he maintained: "I see them already coming, slowly, slowly; and perhaps I shall do something to speed their coming if I describe in advance under what vicissitudes, upon which paths, I see them coming?—" ("Human" 6)

Nietzsche's free spirit possessed the "dangerous privilege of living experimentally" ("Human" 8). So, too, did Paula Modersohn-Becker. Not bound by customs and rituals, the free spirit, as exemplified by Modersohn-Becker, was free to create anew—to become master over self and virtue; to stand tall at the great midday and celebrate the possibility of a new dawn, a new way of life. What the free spirit sought—individually, daringly, and painfully—was a direct encounter (an "unmediated" encounter) with *that which is.* This is what others at the time identified as "Being."

Modersohn-Becker's *Sitzende Alte* (ca. 1900), like many of her portrayals of women, children, and peasant life in the often harsh Northern European environs, resonates with the essential form of *being* alive, of life *qua* life. Simplicity and elegance mix with desperation and beauty to form an incomplete vision of what life must have been like for her various subjects. Viewers are inevitably drawn into this incompleteness and forced to co-create answers: Was the old woman tired? Mourning? Fearful? Determined? Why are her hands so pronounced, why so large? Nietzsche, like Modersohn-Becker, understood the effectiveness of the incomplete: "Just as figures in relief produce so strong an impression on the imagination because they are as it were on the point of stepping out of the wall but have suddenly been brought to a halt, so the relief-like, incomplete presentation of an idea... is sometimes more effective than its exhaustive realization: more is left for the beholder to do, he is impelled to continue working on that which appears before him so strongly etched in light and shadow, to think it through to the end..." ("Human" 92). Modersohn-Becker was aware of the risks she bore with her novel approach to a more authentic portrayal of what it was like to be. In a letter to her sister, she claimed: "I can see that my goals are becoming more and more remote from those of the family, and that you and they will be less and less inclined to approve of them...and still I must go on. I must not retreat. I struggle forward...but I am doing it with my own mind, my own skin, and in the way I think is right" (Witzling 199). To create anew—to become master over self and virture—that is Modersohn-Becker's goal in *Sitzende Alte.* This is also what Modersohn-Becker's great friend, Rainer Maria Rilke, honored in his famous *Requiem for a Friend* (1909): "...You set them before the canvas...and weighed out each one's heaviness with your colors....You let yourself inside down to your gaze; which stayed in front, immense, and didn't say: I am that; no: this is. So free of curiosity your gaze had become, so unpossessive, of such true poverty, it had no desire even for you yourself; it wanted nothing: holy" (Rilke 77).

[Heidi Storl, *Professor of Philosophy*]

151

Aufruhr or **Uprising/Revolt,** 1899, Von der Beck edition, 1945
Käthe Kollwitz (German 1867–1945)
Etching, 29.5 x 38.1 cm., 11-3/4 x 12-9/16" image
Art Department Purchase, Augustana College Art Collection, 1969.23 © 2011 Artists Rights Society (ARS), New York

Tumultuously charging forward, the peasants in Käthe Kollwitz's *Uprising*, 1899 (Kearns 105), sweep the viewer up into the chaos. Through this interaction, one relates to the peasants' emotions—anger, fear and anguish line their angular, emaciated faces—and their cause. In presenting their distress, Kollwitz also expressed her early view of revolution and style.

The push for revolt against injustice in Kollwitz's pre-war image was a view held by many of her contemporaries (Moorjani 1110-1111) before the disillusionment of war was thrust into their lives. Clara Zetkin (1857-1933), a socialist leader, said: "We [women] are endowed with the strength to make sacrifices which are more painful than the giving of our own blood. Consequently, we are able to see our own [men] fight and die when it is for the sake of freedom" (Moorjani 1111).

This view is reflected in Kollwitz's print, in which an all-male mob is spurred forth by an allegory of revolution, an image reminiscent of artwork such as Eugène Delacroix's *Liberty Leading the People (July 28, 1830)*, 1830 (Kearns 83). In *Uprising*, the allegory's hair blends into the flag; combining the personification into this banner makes her the essence of revolution.

As Kollwitz strove for Realism, she eliminated this Romantic allegory (Prelinger 33-34) and created the series *Peasants' War* (1899-1908) with the historical figure "Black Anna" from Historian Wilhelm Zimmerman's *General History of the Great Peasants' War* (1841–1842), in addition to her own conceptions of revolution (Prelinger 31, 33-34, 38). *Peasants' War* is the result of her thematic search, as started in *Uprising* (Prelinger 33).

Along with her adjustment in style, Kollwitz's view on revolution eventually was transformed into realistic terms. Six years after the creation of *Peasants' War*, her son Peter died in World War I (Moorjani 1114). Renouncing her earlier views, she reflected, "I have been through a revolution, and I am convinced that I am no revolutionist" (Kollwitz 100). Her Romantic notions of "dying on the barricades" were ruined because she had come to realize revolution's horrific consequences (Kollwitz 100). Though Kollwitz shifted from her Romantic view and style in *Uprising*, she would continue throughout her life to present the proletariat in her unique, expressive style.

[April Bernath, *Class of 2010*]

152

Sächsische Arbeiter (Saxon Workers), 1946
Erich Heckel (German 1883–1970)
Woodblock print, 17.4 x 12.2 cm., 6-15/16 x 4-13/16" image
Gift of Dr. Thomas B. Brumbaugh Art History Collection to Augustana College Art Collection, 2002.18.25 © 2011 Artists Rights Society (ARS), New York

Erich Heckel began his career as an architectural student at the Technical Academy in Dresden, along with his childhood friend, Karl Schmidt-Rottluff. Together, with Ernst Kirchner and Fritz Bleyl, they co-founded the important German Expressionist group *Die Brücke* (The Bridge). All four were self-taught painters and printmakers. Schmidt-Roluff named the association, inspired by a passage from Nietzsche's *Thus Spoke Zarathustra*: "What is great in man is that he is a bridge and not an end: what can be loved in man is that he is a going across and a going under" (Thieme 5).

The *Brücke* kept their artistic styles close to earlier Nordic art, combining influences from the Old Masters as well as *The Fauvist* and *Cubist* movements along with late nineteenth-century expressionist works of Vincent Van Gogh and Edvard Munch. Heckel's works from the early 1920s reflect his dedication to the belief that "the unconscious and the involuntary are the sources of artistic power [and can thus create]...a spiritualized apocalyptic atmosphere" (Baron 250). During this time, he focused on themes that expressed the depression and loneliness of the human condition.

Heckel's 1945 woodcut is a copy of an earlier 1924 oil painting. In these works, Heckel reflected his German heritage by relating a sympathetic view of three working-class German men next to either a doorway or window that is overlooking several pine trees atop the Ore Mountains. The seated man displays a sense of disappointment, based on the empty look in his eyes and the manner in which he supports his head with his hand. The man in the center seems to be in a state of disbelief because his eyes, although wide open, are framed within a blank stare. The third man on the left appears to be deep in thought because of his furrowed brow and gaze. These workers represent a realistic look at the emotional stress felt by German working-class individuals at this time, and the confusion, frustration and emptiness they were consequently experiencing.

As with most avant-garde art of his generation, the Nazis labeled Heckel's works as *degenerate* in 1937. Consequently, his pieces were barred from museums throughout Germany. Furthermore, just before the end of World War II, his studio was bombed in an air raid, destroying much of his collection. His later works were overshadowed by his earlier artistic productions as demonstrated in this woodcut, translated from an earlier oil painting. Heckel simplified his detail and color by using the woodcut medium, which added a more reductive modernist quality to the composition.

[Jason Myers, *Class of 2005*]

153

Improvisation 7, after the ca. 1914 painting series, 1976
Vasily Kandinsky (Russian 1866–1944)
Woodblock print, 19.0 x 12.5 cm., 7-1/2 x 4-7/8" image
Paul A. Anderson Chair in the Arts Collection Purchase, Augustana College Art Collection, 2008.6 © 2011 Artists Rights Society (ARS), New York

Though you may not know it, it is likely that you are a skilled improviser. Furthermore, it is entirely possible that you have participated in the process of improvisation at some time today, given that anyone who has ever been a part of an unscripted conversation has experienced a form of improvisation. By way of contrast, imagine a world where all communication was planned out in advance!

Simply put, to improvise is to spontaneously create with a minimum of planning or preconception. For most of us, this term is typically associated with music, though improvised poetry and theatre maintain active traditions of improvisation (slam poetry and *improv* comedy, for example). Furthermore, to Western audiences, the notion of improvised music calls to mind the style of jazz, due to its association with dazzling displays of virtuosic improvisation. However, every culture that produces music also produces some form of improvised music, and the relationship between improvisation (spontaneous creation) and composition (planned creation) within a culture can reveal a great deal about how its people regard the musical experience.

It is clear that Kandinsky has a typically twentieth-century European view of the notion of improvisation by the way in which he describes two of his creative methods and the importance he places on each. Of one category of work, for which he would use the term "Improvisation," Kandinsky describes as "A largely unconscious, spontaneous expression of inner character, non-material nature." Another method of creation, the "Composition," is described as "An expression of a slowly formed inner feeling, tested and worked over repeatedly and almost pedantically"(77). It is this latter method that held greater significance for Kandinsky, much in the same way that most musicians of his time would typically uphold the virtues of composition as superior to improvisation.

This woodblock print displays the result of Kandinsky's reliance on "unconscious, spontaneous expression." Though abstract, there are clear representations of natural objects as seen in the branches and leaves in the lower half of the work. Yet, the print as a whole has a playful quality to it, as if the artist was completely immersed in the sensation of intuitively filling a two-dimensional space—engaging in creation and reflection as a single activity rather than two separate processes.

[Robert Elfine, *Assistant Professor of Music*]

154

History of Creation II, or **Story of Creation II**, 1914
Franz Marc (German 1880–1916)
Woodblock print in black, yellow and green, 23.9 x 20.4 cm., 9-7/16 x 8-1/16" image
Paul A. Anderson Chair in the Arts Collection Purchase, Augustana College Art Collection, 2000.58

Over time, Marc asserted his personal style through his choice of subject and color. By 1911 he had established subjective symbolism for his color use. Marc viewed certain colors to represent different ideas; blue for spirituality and maleness, yellow for femininity and sensuality and red for terrestrial materiality (Rosenthal 18). While he continued to define his personal style, Marc joined with Vasily Kandinsky (catalogue 153) to form *Der Blaue Reiter* (The Blue Rider) of German Expressionism. This group germinated within the Expressionist movement and was composed of a variety of artists who emphasized a conceptual approach to their work rather than the formalist ideas of Cubism (Selz 206).

Following the formation of *Der Blaue Reiter*, Marc and several other artists, including Kandinsky and Erich Heckel, began a project to represent the books of the Bible through illustrations. Marc chose the *Book of Creation* as his contribution to the project (Myers 228). In 1914 he conceived two woodcuts toward this project, *Story of Creation I* and *Story of Creation II*. Both works are characterized by their use of flowing forms and kinetic lines. The animals and plants depicted in these pieces are embryonic in nature, demonstrating the idea of a beginning rather than an ending. The presence of animals was meant to portray the conceptual post-apocalyptic world, which is free of the *impure* man (Levine 139-140).

Specifically in *Story of Creation II*, we see the moment when God commands: "Let the earth bring forth living creatures," just before its actualization. An embryonic image of some sort of feline creature emerges toward the upper right, beneath the sun. To the left emerges what seems to be a horse or a deer, and in the lower center, there is the genesis of an unidentifiable figure. These images appear to emerge from within the composition. Both the heavens and the earth seem to flow together and converge in the center of the work. Plant life below germinates. We thus see creation occurring in one turbulent moment (Levine 139-142). The scene is likely foretelling the recreation that would follow the apocalypse.

[Beth Cloud, *Class of 2007*]

155

Le Chapeau sur les yeux (Hat over the Eyes), 1923
Marie Laurencin (French 1885–1956)
Etching, hand colored, restrike, 8.6 x 7.1 cm., 3-3/8 x 2-3/4" image
Gift of Mr. and Mrs. LeRoy and Margaret Carlson and Family, Augustana College Art Collection, 2010.63.82

If there was anything Marie Laurencin knew how to do, it was how to shake up the art scene of 1920s Paris.

Laurencin began consorting with the Cubist circle after meeting Georges Braque during their years of study at the *Académie Humbert*. Cubism was a movement that aimed to fuse observation with memory, creating a new perspective reflecting a rapidly changing world. Although Laurencin did not believe her work to be intellectual, echoes of Cubism can be found in *Le Chapeau sur les yeux*. After a few moments of analysis, the viewer realizes that the figure's hat belongs in a work where we are viewing her from above rather than facing her directly, reflecting the intersection of multiple viewpoints inherent to Cubism.

However, Marie was not interested in imitating her peers. In fact, she did not even like them; "Cubism has poisoned three years of my life, preventing me from doing any work. I never understood it... As long as I was influenced by the 'great men' surrounding me I could do nothing" (Laurencin, 134.) In turn, Pablo Picasso once wrote that Laurencin often made "noises like a mythical animal," and his various lovers thought her to be "vulgar" and "ugly" (Broude, 78). Marie's own lover during this time, pivotal writer and art critic, Guillaume Apollinaire (catalogue 156), said that Marie's eccentricities were her "greatest gift." The poet was not speaking only from his heart; Laurencin was the most popular female artist of her time.

Intriguingly, Laurencin did not necessarily believe that she distorted reality drastically in her work or that she was any more peculiar than anyone else. Since her youth she suffered from extreme myopia and relied on emotions to help fill in the blank canvas her sight could not (Sandell, 33). The figure in *Le Chapeau sur les yeux* could be walking through rain or perhaps the abstract patterns surrounding her are an extension of her aura. Laurencin adored walking through the streets of Paris while donning the latest fashions (Laurencin, 47). The woman who appears in this work seems to share her passion. Above all, Marie Laurencin was a woman who loved life for its face value. The figure in this etching is not pondering mathematics or revolutionizing perspective. She is simply taking a walk and enjoying her day.

[Kate McCormick, *Class of 2013*]

156

Apollinaire VI, 1952
Henri Matisse (French 1869–1954), printed by Fernand Mourlot for the book *Apollinaire* by André Rouveyre, Paris
Lithograph, 22.9 x 15.5 cm., 9 x 6-1/8" image
Gift of Mr. and Mrs. Frank Lufrano, Augustana College Art Collection, 1994.10

Guillaume Apollinaire (1880-1918) was a prominent Parisian art critic and writer of the early twentieth century. He and modern artist, Henri Matisse, had a mutually beneficial professional relationship. Although they worked in different fields, the two often influenced each other. Together they helped to define major aspects of modern art. Matisse's portrait, *Apollinaire VI* (1952), survives as testimony to the abiding sympathetic response to modernism that they shared.

Upon their meeting, Apollinaire interviewed Matisse for an article which he published in 1907 in *La Phalange*, concluding that: "We are not in the presence of some extremist venture; the distinctive feature of Matisse's art is its reasonableness" (Benjamin 130). Apollinaire also indicated his frustration with the public for not accepting and supporting Matisse. From this point on, the two maintained a warm friendship, commenting positively about each other's work until the outbreak of World War I when Apollinaire volunteered for the French National Army. While in action, he was hit in the head with a large piece of shrapnel and dismissed, returning home and dying soon after.

Although Apollinaire died in 1918, Matisse later sketched this lithographic portrait in 1952 in memory of his departed friend. When André Rouveyre wrote his book entitled *Apollinaire*, he asked Matisse to do several illustrations of the close friend they had in common. This piece is one of the six that Matisse ultimately drew for this production, entitled the *Apollinaire Suite*. Each is different. Matisse began with near abstraction and ended in this version with a more complete view. The resulting lithographs were printed in an edition of approximately three hundred.

This piece is striking in its bold linear conception. It combines several thin black lines on a white background. It truly shows the ability of the painter to reduce character and mass to the simplest of forms. This work may not be one of his most famous, but the simplicity of its drawing reveals the true talent of Matisse. In contrast to the struggle and time an artist would normally put into an average oil painting, black and white lithographic sketches may have been a great release for Matisse. The depth and character achieved through his masterful and spare use of line and contour allowed him to further refine his drawing skills.

[Gayln Landem, *Class of 2007* and Catherine Carter Goebel, *Editor*]

157

Femme à la cruche (Woman with Pitcher), 1928
After Fernand Léger (French 1881–1955), etched by Jacques Villon (French 1875–1963)
Color aquatint, engraving and roulette, proof aside from the edition of 200, 47.6 x 31.4 cm., 18-11/16 x 12-5/16" image
Paul A. Anderson Chair in the Arts Collection Purchase, Augustana College Art Collection, 2001.18 © 2011 Artists Rights Society (ARS), New York/ADAGP, Paris

Léger's early works had their basis in geometry, while simplifying objects into shapes and dehumanizing people into tubular constructions. After the war, Léger continued with Cubism and applied more industrial themes to his paintings. His subjects took on a machine-like design, almost to the point of seeming robotic. Arthur Danto aptly considered that "...the term 'mechanical' seems fitter than 'cubist' to represent his [paintings]" (Danto).

In *Femme à la Cruche* (1928), it is immediately apparent that each segment of the woman is individual from the next. Each body part is its own shape, except for the continuity of the neck and chest, which is broken up by the yellow necklace. The right forearm is particularly rounded as if a tear was turned horizontally—even the fingers are drawn as being separate from the hand, as though they are an entirely different entity. The face of the figure is nearly expressionless, appearing impassive or trance-like. When this print was created in 1928, industrialization was nearing full swing and some expressed concern as to what the future held for humans.

The vase that she holds represents the strong vertical element that is present in nearly every work by Léger. This is caused by his Cubist influence, which, along with its emphasis on geometry, generally represented the same object from different perspectives (catalogue 158). The color scheme is bold and simple, made up of primary and secondary colors that are outlined in black.

The simplicity echoes the paintings of Paul Cézanne, who often simplified his composition into a few colors—consisting primarily of orange and blue. In his early works, Léger used a wide range of colors, but by 1910 he had begun to limit his palette. Léger's evolution to industrial or *mechanical* art influenced aspiring and upcoming artists who moved into abstraction. The idea that form was more important than color might not continue, but form remained important as artists such as Piet Mondrian composed works in reductive abstractions.

[Dan Pearson, *Class of 2007*]

Sketch for a Cubist Still Life, 1938
Perle Fine (American 1908–1988)
Charcoal drawing, 15.3 x 35.3 cm., 6 x 13-15/16" image
Gift of Dr. Thomas B. Brumbaugh Art History Collection, Augustana College Art Collection, 2002.18.14

In the *Sketch for a Cubist Still Life*, Perle Fine expresses the complexity of playing the violin. One can clearly see the scroll and neck of the instrument in the lower left and the body to right of the neck. On the right side of the sketch, strings are held by a finger and below them a hand is positioned to hold the bow that can be found in the upper left. Sheet music is clearly evident in the background.

Cubism is an early twentieth-century art form that was influenced by analytical processes occurring in science at the same time. In *Analytic Cubism*, the subject is broken up into component parts, analyzed, and re-assembled using a multitude of viewpoints and/or timeframes to represent the subject in a broader context. The result is an abstract image where objects intersect at seemingly random angles. The overall composition thereby loses any traditional western linear perspective sense of depth.

Science was doing much the same thing during this time, trying to tie multiple concepts together within a broader context and unifying conflicting theories. Einstein's *Theories of Relativity* (1905-1916) were examples of defining a broader context within physics. His theory states that the speed of light in free space is the same for all observers, regardless of motion relative to the light source. The result of this prediction led to contradictions in classical physics at velocities close to the speed of light, such as length contraction and time dilation. This reexamination of science aligned with the later development of *Abstract Expressionism*, which Fine interestingly pursued following this Cubist phase in her artistic development.

Although this work was constructed towards the end of the Cubism movement, Fine did a wonderful job in representing fingers rolling up and down the neck as the bow is drawn across the strings that set up the vibrations that we hear as music. It is easy to understand why Perle Fine is considered one of the leading women in Abstract Expressionism of the twentieth century.

[Dell Jensen, *Associate Professor of Chemistry*]

159

Stazione Ferroviara (also titled **Railway Station**), dated 1920
Giorgio de Chirico (Italian 1888–1978)
Oil on canvas-wrapped cardboard, 22.6 x 30.6 cm., 8-7/8 x 12"
Gift of Professor Irma Adelman, Augustana College Art Collection, 2010.58

Giorgio de Chirico was the leader of the Metaphysical art movement and the acknowledged inspiration (although he fervently denied it) for Surrealist painters. He convincingly portrayed a dreamlike world just within the borders of the imagination. Unlike most modern artists who were only appreciated later in life, de Chirico found success early in his career, yet as his style progressed, the seemingly fickle art world no longer approved or understood. His innovative approach was highly influenced by the philosopher Friedrich Nietzsche, who defined art as the "real metaphysical activity of man," and the Symbolist painter, Arnold Böcklin, in his depictions of dreamscapes (De Sanna).

Stylistically, *Train Station Ferroviara* was painted at the height of de Chirico's *Metaphysical* Period. Called Metaphysical because it portrayed a world beyond that of the physical, this art depicted a dream world, ironically rendered in realistic detail. Scenes that could only be constructed in the mind, such as this strange landscape, were put forth on canvas. All the typical de Chirico components of this time are in place—the geometric arches and colonnade, black train and long shadows. De Chirico portrayed an almost uneasy emptiness with a sense of mysterious foreboding.

The deserted city has that quality of a parallel world, where everything looks normal but is far from it. The deep shadows fall at different angles, further altering one's sense of logical reality. Time appears frozen as the puff of smoke lingers in the air above the train. Even the colors, the sharply contrasting blue-green of the sky with the mustard-tan ground, lend to the viewer's discomfort upon examining the piece.

The general locations depicted in these paintings reflect de Chirico's love of Italian architecture and city monuments around the Mediterranean. Ferarra and Turin were two such towns from which he drew inspiration for his *metaphysical* works. Turin was the city Nietzsche loved and Ferrara was the location where de Chirico was stationed with the Italian army from 1915-1918. It was here that he first met Carlo Carrà with whom he would start the Metaphysical group in Italy (De Sanna 69-70). The movement was rather short-lived, essentially lasting less than a year before de Chirico, seeking greater classicism, decided to change his style. However, although not then defined as *metaphysical*, his work from 1912-1917 is now considered to be in this style.

[Errin Copple, *Class of 2005*]

160

Piazza d' Italia (also titled **Italian Plaza—with Beacon**), dated 1921
Giorgio de Chirico (Italian 1888–1978)
Oil on canvas-wrapped cardboard, 24.2 x 33.7 cm., 9-1/2 x 13-1/4"
Gift of Lohrey Family Limited Partnership, Augustana College Art Collection, 2005.22

The landscape of *Piazza d'Italia* was drawn from Giorgio de Chirico's second *metaphysical* Italian city of inspiration, Turin. Turin was important to de Chirico because of its close association with Nietzsche—it was the city Nietzsche loved and the place in which the philosopher suffered from madness the year of de Chirico's birth. The geometry of the streets, piazzas and porticos provided ample space for the young artist's imagination.

The piazza, a metaphysical blend of reality, stands nearly vacant, and long shadows fall at uneven angles. A frozen tableau is again created by the motionless train and the calculated geometry of the archways and columned portico. The insertion of a lone figure, however, adds a new dimension to the scene, raising feelings of isolation for the observer. Within the piece, such elements lead to questions of the enigma of life and the purpose of human existence (De Sanna 68). This inhabitant appears restricted to the limits of the physical world except in his mind.

Striking parallels can be seen between the dream world of Metaphysical art and that of the Surrealists, and indeed de Chirico was considered at the time to be the *Father of Surrealism* with Guillaume Apollinaire (catalogue 156) first calling his work *surréel* in 1917 (De Sanna 280). De Chrico was greatly admired by many of the Surrealists, even considered an inspiration for their works. He joined the group in 1922 at the insistence of its leader, André Breton. However, de Chirico's work by this time had begun to change. He had always professed a wish to return to classicism, often studying and copying works of that period and the Renaissance. The Surrealists considered his new style of painting inferior, and Breton referred to him as a *lost genius* in a magazine article published in 1926 (De Sanna 282). This last act completed his ultimate break with the group and caused him thereafter to vehemently reject the title *Father of Surrealism*, refusing to acknowledge any artistic connection.

A master at creating dreamlike yet realistic scenes, it is de Chirico's deserted cityscapes, frozen in time, for which he is best remembered. Believing that art should be purged of the familar and commonplace, he once wrote, "A really immmortal work of art can only be produced by means of a revelation" (qtd. in De Sanna 66). It is clearly such revelation which has inspired these important works.

[Errin Copple, *Class of 2005*]

161

Cubist Image of Man in a Bowler Hat, 1922
Artist unknown (B.?, Russian)
Watercolor, graphite and litho crayon or charcoal pencil drawing, 22.3 x 15.0 cm., 8-13/16 x 5-11/16" image
Paul A. Anderson Chair in the Arts Collection Purchase, Augustana College Art Collection, 2007.14

Many masterworks are continually investigated because we are intrigued by what we don't know, more than by what we do know.

So what do we know about this piece? We know the work was executed on paper, an affordable and versatile support. We know the subject—a man wearing a bowler hat. Based on formal qualities, we know that this work is Cubist, most likely Russian. We do not, though, know the maker, only the initial "B," though we can presume the date of 1922 is the year of signature and, perhaps, production. While knowing the maker resolves some questions, much can be gleaned from a work by "anonymous."

Cubism developed in France and spread its influence across Europe and into Russia. "B" must have seen Cubist or Russian avant-garde works in order to replicate the style. Cubists focused on the reconstruction of the human figure and objects, employed a muted palette, and typically centered their compositions. The subject is broken up, analyzed, and re-assembled into an abstracted form. This overlapping of parts results in multiple viewpoints and the intersection of surfaces. Here, the man's face is depicted from two points of view. Also, the left side is animated, younger. The right side is shadowed—older—and he appears to be asleep, an intersection of ages and attitudes. The block of orange-red color defines his left shoulder and the three black vertical dots are buttons on his shirt. The rest of the body is subject to interpretation. His right arm is bent, composed of quadrangles and triangles, but we can only assume the presence of hands. As with later Cubist work (catalogue 158), the background is flat and ambiguous, and the random "B" and "5" mimic collage, though, potential meanings are unknown, just like the name of the maker.

For Cubists, particularly Russian avant-garde artists working in the wake of the Bolshevik Revolution of 1917, the stuff of the *everyday*, like common man—rather than royalty—reigned supreme. Prominently featured in this work is the bowler hat (Robinson), worn by both men and women from all walks of life, including the working class.

[Jennifer Jaskowiak, *Class of 1987*]

162

***Le Fils de l'homme* (The Son of Man),** 1964
René Magritte (Belgian 1898–1967)
Twenty-color lithograph on Velin paper, printed by Mourlot of Paris, 48.0 cm. x 35.0 cm., 18-7/8 x 13-9/16" image
Purchase by Paul A. Anderson Chair in the Arts Collection and Augustana College Art Museum, Augustana College Art Collection 2010.24 © 2011 Artists Rights Society (ARS), New York

Whenever I see *The Son of Man* by René Magritte, I immediately think of the remake of the film: *The Thomas Crown Affair* (1999). For his personal amusement, a wealthy financier steals a painting by Claude Monet from a New York museum. At the end of the film, Crown connived the return of the painting to the museum by befuddling police and an insurance investigator with a decoy. During museum hours, a hundred or so men arrive at the museum dressed as Thomas Crown dressed, in the attire of Magritte's *The Son of Man*. During the film, that painting was also spotlighted adorning Crown's residence. Everyone was carrying briefcases; only Crown's contained the Monet. When he deposited the Monet back in the museum and walked away, he became invisible by blending into the hundred others dressed in the black topcoat and bowler hat.

How is it that an extravagantly wealthy man steals? How is it everyone can look the same and yet everyone is different? How is it that a self-portrait doesn't portray the face of the self? These are some contradictions that, in the film, Magritte's painting evokes. I suspect Magritte would have been pleased with the use of his painting in that film. As a Surrealist inspired by the unsettling images of Giorgio de Chirico (catalogue 159 & 160), Magritte similarly created seemingly realistic scenarios that somehow contradict rational *reads*. Contradictions, juxtapositions, ambiguities all deepen the exploration of mystery. "I have painted a thousand paintings but I have only created a hundred or so images. These thousand paintings only come from variants of those images which I have painted; it is a way to better define mystery, to better possess it," Magritte stated (Mundy 411-412).

Philosopher-theologian John O'Donohue invites us to celebrate the contradictions we find in ourselves. He says that they provide the rubbing stones that spark the fires of creative exploration of mystery and the inner landscape of the soul. Magritte's painting invites us to do that; to delve deeply and ask: Who is the real self? Is it what I see or what I don't see? Am I like everyone else? Am I different from everyone else? To each question, Mystery answers Yes!

[Patricia Shea, *Assistant Professor of Education*]

163

Two Women Painting from Plaster Models, ca. 1890–1900
Artist unknown
Oil on canvas, 44.2 x 55.7 cm., 17-3/8 x 21-7/8"
Paul A. Anderson Chair in the Arts Collection Purchase, Augustana College Art Collection, SDC2005.3

Two Women Painting from Plaster Models is unsigned, making it difficult to pin down specific information for research. This challenge, however, encourages us to look deeper into the painting itself, in order to discern clues in its subject and style which can reveal a great deal about its context.

The first immediate clue lies in the subject. Since two women are painting in an academic environment, it seems reasonable to conclude that this painting was completed in the second half of the nineteenth century. By the 1870s in Paris, there were separate alternative classes where women could work from the model. Even the conservative academic *École des Beaux-Arts* (School of Fine Arts) finally admitted women by 1896 (Slatkin 110). In America, artistic opportunities opened sooner for women. Throughout the nineteenth century, girls were increasingly better educated through public schooling and in terms of artistic training, women such as the two pictured here, could study from plaster casts as early as 1844 at the Pennsylvania Academy of Fine Arts. Anatomy classes opened to women in 1860, and by 1868, women could participate in separate life drawing classes (Slatkin 96).

The painting's style provides the second clue for analysis. The artist's brushstrokes are loose and the application fairly broad which suggests Impressionism, likely dating it somewhere between the mid 1870s to the early 1900s. The broken brushstrokes capture the immediacy of the moment as well as the subtleties of color and light. The walls are cropped, as in a photograph, typical of Impressionist viewpoints. The painting still follows traditional Renaissance linear perspective principles, which academic artists were reluctant to abandon.

Along with subject and style, a comparison of contemporary fashion and furnishings can help date the painting. The women's dresses are typical turn-of-the-century design. Their hairstyles confirm this dating. To further the argument, the chair on which the woman on the left is seated is known as *Bentwood.* The bentwood chair was invented in the late nineteenth century, and its back, consisting of curved (bent) wood, repeats the curvilinear line that is a hallmark of the *Art Nouveau* style

It seems logical to date this painting to around 1900. The artist accurately depicted women within the modern art world, where they could now gain the formal education they needed to become professional artists. Considering the evidence, it also seems likely it was painted by an American artist, since Impressionism was passé in Paris at this time but was beginning to blossom in America. Within the context of modernity, this painting records and celebrates the fact that women could now be involved in the arts, not only as models, but as accomplished professional artists as well (catalogue 93 and 99).

[Kate Felde, Class of 2006 and
Catherine Carter Goebel, *Editor*]

Un Crime Allemand qui a indigné la conscience humaine/ L'assassinat de Miss Edith Cavell (The Assassination of Miss Edith Cavell: A German Crime that Outraged the Conscience of Humanity), 1915
Artist undetermined
Newspaper printed in color, back cover of *Le Petit Journal: Supplément Illustré*, 7 November 1915, 44.9 x 31.4 cm., 17-11/16 x 12-5/16"
Paul A. Anderson Chair in the Arts Collection Purchase, Augustana College Art Collection, 2011.12

Nearly a century ago, any educated adult in the western world would instantly have recognized this scene. Most would have been furious. Heroic nurse Edith Cavell, condemned to death by a German military court on October 11, 1915, resolved to face death bravely. Walking to her place of execution, her nerves finally gave out and she collapsed. The captain of the firing squad, disgusted by her weakness and unmoved by her frailty, knelt and fired a bullet into her forehead. Mustachioed, fat soldiers in spiked helmets look on. One soldier, horrified at the event, covered his face with his hand. That act of cowardice later led to his execution.

Cavell's story was a sensation. *The Times of London* discussed Cavell in 45 articles in the three months after her execution. Her life was featured in two films (*The Woman the Germans Shot* and *Great Victory, Wilson or the Kaiser?*) before the end of the war. She was sanctified in two dozen books, bearing titles like *The Martyrdom of Nurse Cavell: the life story of the victim of Germany's most barbarous crime* (1915) and *Nurse Cavell: the story of her life and her martyrdom* (1915). King George V invoked her execution in a plea for more men to enlist; in the three months following, weekly enlistments in the British Army doubled ("Edith Cavell"). Outrage was widespread in Belgium, Italy and France, where posters and series of postcards were issued, depicting the scenes of her arrest, trial and execution. Historians identify this as one of the two stories that most enraged American public opinion against Germany (Kunczik 45).

This image constituted the back cover of *Le Petit Journal: Supplément Illustré* (1915, November). The title, which translates as "The Assassination of Miss Edith Cavell: A German Crime that Outraged the Conscience of Humanity," and the image were both typical of the coverage of Cavell's death. Any reader would immediately fill in the details. The image fit perfectly with what readers already *knew* was true, about German atrocity and about the Cavell case.

What they *knew*, unfortunately, was wrong. Cavell and 35 co-defendants were tried by the Germans for helping 200 wounded Allied soldiers escape German-controlled territory. (Imagine a Confederate court trying the organizers of the Underground Railroad.) Cavell guaranteed her death by volunteering a series of damning details at trial, and agreed that she was aware of the nature of her crime. She was shot by a firing squad, not an officer. She was a nursing school administrator, not an "angel of mercy." She did not faint. She was not a young blond. She did not wear a Union Jack over her heart or a nurse's uniform. The execution was at a firing range, long before dawn. No soldier looked away, none refused to fire, none were disciplined ("The Testimony of Pastor Le Seur").

The art of the propagandist is showing us what we already know to be true. The propagandist does not educate, but instead illustrates and crystallizes. Propagandists need not lie when they can lead us to lie to ourselves.

[David Snowball, *Professor of Communication Studies*]

165

The Amber Necklace, 1907
Charles Courtney Curran (American 1861–1942)
Oil on canvas, 55.5 x 50.9 cm., 22 x 20" image
Gift of Mr. and Mrs. Michael Moss, Augustana College Art Collection, 1996.25.5

What is femininity? Certainly the answer to this question varies with time and culture. Seen time and again, American Impressionist Charles Courtney Curran (1861-1942) unveiled his definition of femininity in many of his paintings. Emerging near the end of the nineteenth century, Curran constructed, what has come to be referred to as "floral-female painting" (Stott 61) with his works of art. Women within these compositions have been manipulated to echo a particular flower's distinguishing features. The development of a *language of flowers* became a pertinent aspect of the Victorian era, during which Curran painted. Regarding life's domestic and social spheres, books were comprised of flowers and their corresponding personified meanings (Rice). In countless displays of artistic expression throughout history, flowers have often symbolized an array of feminine qualities. In certain contexts, biblical references have been attached to specific flowers, such as white lilies, largely regarding spiritual and sexual purity. Flowers have also been used to represent love, a lack of knowledge, fertility, and beauty. Traditionally, femininity was defined in terms of passivity, beauty, and was given an overall more ornamental social role. In an attempt to defuse any growing power women were gaining at the time, as well as reassert a more traditional definition of femininity, floral-female painting portrayed women in delicate and passive terms (Stott).

Pertaining to Curran's *The Amber Necklace* (1907) specifically, he appears to have applied floral-female painting, in a sense, to an upper-class woman, revealed by her flawless complexion and refined appearance. Taking the concept of floral-female painting into consideration once again, moss-roses have been used to portray women in a more fragile manner. Moss-roses were thought to be most beautiful when half unfolded, contributing to a concealment aspect. Similarly, women were often depicted standing or sitting silently peering off, creating an atmosphere of mystery and apprehension (Stott). In this painting, Curran creates a moment in time, an impression, of a woman's gaze enveloped in the confines of her necklace. Anglo-Americans of that time often defined femininity in terms of females' modest and soothing nature, and largely highlighted their pure beauty.

Similar to a flower's inspirational role in floral-female painting, it is possible that the amber necklace depicted in this work serves both decorative and symbolic purposes as well. It has been interpreted in various times and places as having both spiritual and curative powers (Rice). Additionally, the amber necklace reinforces the woman's pure beauty. Even though Curran's definition of femininity in *The Amber Necklace* may be considered stereotypical according to today's standards, chiefly focusing on a woman's beauty as well as her pure and reserved nature, it is important to keep in mind that the paintings of these women were depicted according to the traditional manner of the time.

[Rebecca Hodgson, *Class of 2012*]

166

Odalisque sur la terrasse (Odalisque on the Balcony), 1922–1923
After Henri Matisse (French 1869–1954), etched by Jacques Villon (French 1875–1963)
Color aquatint, 64/200, 48.3 x 60.5 cm., 19 x 24" image
Paul A. Anderson Chair in the Arts Collection Purchase, Augustana College Art Collection, 2001.16

As the leader of the *Fauves (Wild Beasts)* of French Expressionism, Matisse preferred *expression* or feeling versus reality in his drawings and paintings, stating:"...one cannot do successful work which has much feeling unless one sees the subject very simply...." (Elderfield 50-51). He used space and color to create images that would ultimately please the viewer. Matisse's almost sketchy style reflected his attempt to construct an image with a "wider meaning, a more comprehensively human image" (Goldwater and Treves 411).

His overall goal was to create an experience for the viewer that made a lasting impression at the same time that it expressed a universal understanding of humanity. Toward this goal, he traveled to Tangiers and Morocco, further influencing his style toward experimentation with *odalisques*. Matisse's interest in the exotic is clearly visible in *Odalisque sur la terrasse* (1922–23). He worked largely in both Paris and the French Rivera during this odalisque period. The setting for this work consists of an exotic looking room with a terrace view of the beach. The costuming of the nudes also appears to have eastern influence. *Odalisques*, or the painting of nudes read as concubines, became a common subject for Matisse because it provided a means by which he could present nude women to the public in an acceptable manner (Gilot 170).

The imagery in this piece typifies Matisse's work. His figures are central to the interior space and dominate the work. In *Odalisque sur la terrasse*, Matisse's figures appear flattened and although they maintain their central importance, they seem almost to become a part of the overall decorative interior (Elderfield 90). In fact, Matisse himself held that "A picture should...always be decorative..." (Elderfield 51). Because Matisse believed that "the chief aim of color should be to serve expression as well as possible" (Goldwater and Treves 412), the choices in this piece appear striking, making the piece aesthetically pleasing to the viewer. Matisse's intentions were clear: "What I dream of is an art of balance, of purity and serenity devoid of troubling or depressing subject-matter...." (Goldwater and Treves 413). Matisse indeed searched for this ideal through a combination of color, subject and feeling.

[Mikeda Cannon, *Class of 2007*]

167

Sun over Rock Outcrop, 1924
Thomas Moran (American, b. England 1837–1926)
Oil on canvas, 35.5 x 63.7 cm., 14-1/16 x 25-1/16"
Gift in Memory of Drs. Fritiof and Regina Fryxell, Augustana College Art Collection, with Conservation Services Donated by Mr. Barry Bauman, 2007.44.13

First-time travelers headed north toward Grand Canyon find breath-taking views. Almost without warning they find themselves gazing down into the mile-deep and seemingly endless Canyon, one of Thomas Moran's favorite subjects. Here easily and unbelievably seen are the mountain panoramas like his colorful *Sun over Rock Outcrop*. Throughout the world very few locations allow one to easily look toward such colorful mountain peaks, clouds, and even an occasional rainbow.

Like many nineteenth-century American artists, Thomas Moran began landscape painting as a member of the Hudson River School, the first formal *school* of landscape painting in the United States. With the growth of Romanticism, America's unspoiled landscape was hailed as a virtual *Garden of Eden* in comparison to well-known European scenes. These views appealed to a growing middle class market and typically depicted the gentle summer and fall views along the Hudson River. Following the Civil War, however, such idealistic regard for the East, both North and South, was challenged, and many artists sought new vistas, free of war associations.

Manifest Destiny became a driving force and in 1871, Moran travelled westward as a member of a team, led by Major John Wesley Powell, charged with capturing images of the beautiful and exotic American West. In 1872, Congress, inspired by the photographs of William Henry Jackson and Moran's colorful paintings, established Yellowstone National Park, ultimately leading to the further environmentalist step in 1916 of establishing the National Park System. Until his death in 1926, Moran continued to explore scenic areas of the West, especially Grand Canyon. Undoubtedly the colorful paintings of Moran led to the inclusion of Grand Canyon to the list of our National Parks.

During the latter years of his life, Thomas Moran spent most of his time at the South Rim of Grand Canyon with his daughter Ruth. Much of his work at this time, of course, featured the colorful and ever changing Canyon. However this painting certainly is not of the Canyon. It seems most likely to be of Green River country, an area he explored in the late 1800s with the Powell party and his friend, Jackson. Though Moran's work in general was not photographic in detail, this painting has more of a mystical character than most of his paintings. In this manner, it seems to relate more to the luminous qualities of the Luminist movement of the second half of the nineteenth century, fueled perhaps by a more transcendental than pictorial aim. The beauty and regard for the wonders of the West are breathtakingly captured in this late, visionary landscape created two years before Moran's death.

[Melbert E. Peterson, *Professor Emeritus of Chemistry and Director Emeritus, John Deere Planetarium*]

1667. Teton Range from the East, 1882
William Henry Jackson (American 1843–1942)
Albumen print photograph 1667, 55.6 x 152.2 cm., 21-7/8 x 59-7/8" image
Gift of Mrs. C.L. Horberg, 1955, to Augustana College, 1990.56

In today's world of instant point and shoot imagery snapped by pocket-sized digital cameras, we tend to forget just what an effort it took to create a photograph like William Henry Jackson's 1878 image, *1667. Teton Range from the East.* Mules and wagons were needed to carry the glass bottles of chemicals and glass plates (ranging in size from 5 x 8" up to 20 x 24"). A supply of water and a complex series of chemical procedures were necessary to fix the negative image. Careful packing, sure-footed mules and luck were needed to get those delicate glass plates safely back the thousand miles to home. This particular large (22 x 60") photograph, printed in 1882, was seamlessly stitched together from three separate negative plates.

Above all other media, William Henry Jackson's photographs of the west brought those distant mountains back to the eastern populations and spurred westward expansion by sparking the imagination of masses of city dwellers. At least in those days the camera did not lie. In contrast to the Hudson River School painters' romantic depictions of the Appalachian, Adirondack, Rocky, and Sierra Nevada Mountains, Jackson's wet plate images portrayed the true West. What you saw was what you were going to get when you got there, and those sights truly were inspirational; even today, in this era in which any image from anywhere on Earth (and beyond—catalogue 210) can be accessed instantly via the web, people still make pilgrimages of thousands of miles around the world to special, sacred mountains. Jackson's photographs promoted a sense of national pride and helped spur Congress to establish the world's first national park in order to preserve the region's beauty for future generations.

Many people believe that knowing more about the natural world will lessen its spiritual value. I believe the opposite. As long as we don't confuse knowledge with wisdom, I strongly affirm that the more we understand about the natural world, be it physically, chemically, biologically, or geologically, the more wondrous it becomes. As Dr. Fritiof Fryxell, renowned, long-time Augustana geology professor and Teton ranger, wrote in his book, *The Tetons: An Interpretation of a Mountain Landscape*, "True appreciation of landscape comes only when one is alive to both its beauty and its meaning."

Beyond the beauty portrayed, a wealth of scientific data still can be gleaned from these old images. In order to assess the effects of global warming, modern climate researchers have used this photograph to study the retreat of alpine glaciers prior to the advent of modern measuring studies. Jackson would have been proud that his photographic contributions as part of the F. V. Hayden United States Geological Survey of the Territories in the 1870s are still valued for their artistic and scientific qualities even today.

[Michael B. Wolf, *Professor of Geology*]

169

Golden Aspen (Rocky Mountain National Park, Colorado), 1928
Sven Birger Sandzén (Swedish American 1871–1954)
Oil on board, 30.4 x 35.3 cm., 11-15/16 x 13-7/8"
Gift of Dr. Eugene C. and Mrs. Barbara B. Wittenstrom and Mr. Clarence F. and Mrs. Barbara B. Wittenstrom, Jr., In Memory of Their Parents, Rev. Clarence F. and Mrs. Edna A. Wittenstrom, Sr., Class of 1928, and In Memory of Their Grandparents, Rev. Carl J. and Mrs. Anna A. Johnson, Treasurer of Augustana College under President Andreen, Augustana College Art Collection, with Conservation Services Donated by Mr. Barry Bauman, 1986.12.8

In 1894, Birger Sandzén (1871-1954) left his native Sweden to begin a teaching position at Bethany College in Lindsborg, Kansas. The plains quickly became an inspiration for his landscape paintings, scenes which would have been quite different than those he was familiar with in Sweden, especially in terms of light (Lindquist 18, 67). Although this part of the country is not well-known for majestic beauty, "[w]hat may have seemed commonplace to some viewers was exciting for Sandzén" (Lindquist 65), and the thrill of his new homeland only increased after seeing the Rocky Mountains for the first time. He wrote to his wife expressing his wish that he might "be able some day to evolve the means by which he could put on canvas the intense excitement he felt in their presence" (Lindquist 69). His very personal reaction to the contrast of the old world with the new would indeed lead him to develop a painting style that captured this excitement.

In *Golden Aspen*, we observe signature elements that have come to define a typical Sandzén landscape. The use of a brilliant gold in the trees highlights the subject of the painting, but what is perhaps most striking is the seemingly unnatural shades of purple and pink that appear in the sky, the rocky banks, and their reflection in the water. His use of vibrant color emphasizes his unique interpretation of the effect of light on this scene. Sandzén's wide brushstrokes and thick application of paint is another representative characteristic of his paintings, a technique that captures his perception of the lines and shapes of the rocks and trees. It is a style that is well-suited to the rugged, untamed country he reproduces in his paintings.

In contrast to many Swedish immigrants of the time, Sandzén was quite cosmopolitan; before coming to the United States, he studied with Anders Zorn in Stockholm and even had an opportunity to study for a short time in Paris. During his years in the United States, he also traveled to the East and West Coasts, Mexico, and back to Europe (Lindquist 39-42). His greatest inspiration, however, came from the Rocky Mountains and a relatively isolated life in Lindsborg, which "became more than a destination—it became his artistic destiny." (Kirn and Maurer 57). Sandzén portrayed his landscapes as "an ideal world, tinged sometimes with the pink glory of dawn, gilded sometimes with the burnished rose of dusk...[h]is idealism [was] directly related to the great adventure of his life, his coming to the New Land" (Kaplan 29). Sandzén's experience as a Swedish immigrant in America afforded him a unique lens through which he viewed his surroundings, and ultimately contributed to the development of a remarkable painting style.

[Jennifer Horrell, *Assistant Professor of Scandinavian Studies*]

170

Two Boats on Water with Cloudscape, n.d.
William Wendt (American 1865–1946)
Oil on canvas, 50.7 x 61.2 cm., 20 x 24-1/16" image
Gift of Alex Adelman and Robert Ubillus, Augustana College Art Collection, 2006.44

William Wendt's style is likened to that of the Impressionists and is emblematic of the character of most West Coast artists. But why was Impressionism so admired and utilized by these Californian artists when the movement had essentially ended in France, its birthplace, decades earlier? Impressionism was still considered new and exciting to Americans at the turn of the century and the style seemed particularly compatible to the California atmosphere—as if the two were made for each other. Pure Impressionists advocated the use of bright, naturally vibrant colors which captured the effects of sunlight on objects and employed "sketchy" painterly brushstrokes in order to focus on the aesthetic elements, simply "suggesting" shape and line. "The lay public seemed receptive, and California artists saw the style as bright, colorful, and upbeat in feeling, appropriate for interpreting the state's attitude, color, and sunlight" (Moure 161).

Like his French role models, Wendt preferred composing his images *en plein air*, or out in front of nature, rather than compiling many drawings from nature within a studio toward a finished painting, as was typical of conservative academic artwork of the past. Wendt actively pursued nature and felt a strong kinship with God through landscape. He would often hike into the wilderness and find natural compositions rather than taking elements from the landscape and manipulating compositions.

Wendt's *Two Boats on Water with Cloudscape* is characteristic of his subject matter and style. Unfortunately, the original title of this painting by Wendt remains unknown. Yet the vibrant colors and expressive brushstrokes are typical of his mature style and luminous optimism.

In Augustana's painting, Wendt employed mostly vibrant and stunning shades of blue combined with subtle tans and large areas of white to contrast the brilliant colors against each other. Viewers gaze out onto the water, past two sailboats, towards magnificent blue and beige valleys. Huge billowing clouds roll in as if the heavens were speaking through the artist. Most likely painted *en plein air*, as Wendt's other images, this piece brilliantly represents the artist's characteristic style and passionate reverence toward nature.

[Randi Higel, *Class of 2008*]

171

The Potter – Plate 426 [Nampeyo], 1922 from 1906 photograph
Edward Sheriff Curtis (American 1868–1952)
Photogravure, 39.4 x 29.0 cm.,15-1/2 x 11-3/8" image
The Olson-Brandelle North American Indian Art Collection, Augustana College, 2005.1.264aa

In this photograph by Edward S. Curtis simply called *The Potter*, we see a woman at work painting traditional designs on a clay pot. While the image itself seems straightforward, the story behind it is complex. The subject is the famous American Indian potter named Nampeyo. Although she passed away in 1942, she remains one of the best-known Native American potters.

Nampeyo bridged distinct eras in Native American history, from independence to the reservation system. Because she is often credited with introducing Pueblo pottery to tourists and collectors, she also acted as a different kind of bridge, from the Pueblo peoples to the dominant culture. Nampeyo is most often associated with the Hopi, an American Indian tribe that is one of a number of related Pueblo cultures whose homelands are found in what is today Arizona and New Mexico. On the surface of this photograph, we simply see Nampeyo sitting and painting a pot, but in that act she also bears the weight of a whole cultural tradition. She embodies the pottery-making of the generations of women who came before her. And her small act creates a gift to the future generations of women who in turn bear the tradition for their daughters.

Given her fame and influence in reviving this art-form, it was no wonder that in 1906 Edward S. Curtis decided to photograph Nampeyo doing something that seems so simple on the surface and yet was in reality so powerful—sitting on a sheepskin spread out across the floor painting a pot. In front of her are several other pots, some finished and others perhaps waiting to be painted. With deft brushstrokes she applies handmade paints to the clay pot in her hand, using a piece of yucca as a brush.

Although part of Curtis' aim was to document what he assumed were vanishing American Indian cultures, there is no doubt that much of his work was purposefully romantic and sentimental, and that he consciously controlled the subject matter of each photograph (Coleman VI). Images like *The Potter* do not represent candid moments in the lives of American Indians; instead, like a studio artist—or more to the point, like the portrait photographer he was—Curtis posed the subjects, carefully chose which objects to include in each image, and actively "directed the scene."

[Adam Kaul, *Associate Professor of Anthropology*]

172

Large Polychrome Olla, ca. 1920–25
Nampeyo of Hano (ca. 1857–1942) painted by Fannie Lesou Polacca Nampeyo (ca. 1900–1987), Hopi-Tewa, Arizona
Ceramic, hand coiled and outdoor fired, 47.2 x 42.2 x 43.1 cm., 18-1/4 x 16-1/2 x 16-7/8"
The Olson-Brandelle North American Indian Art Collection, Augustana College, (34-56 HOP) 2005.1.35

What made Nampeyo stand out from other potters was her new *modern* style, which was rooted in ancient pottery. Even as a young girl, her designs were distinctive, and she was later influenced by the *Sikyatki* style, one of the most famous prehistoric Hopi wares (from the 14th-century C.E. village of Sikyatki at the base of First Mesa). Her fascination with this style is reflected not only in her designs but also in the quality of her pots. She and her mother discovered clay that was similar to the ancient Sikyatki type.

Sikyatki pottery generally had many painted geometric and life designs, applied to flat-sided jars without necks, or to the center of the bottom of shallow, wide bowls with incurved rims. Nampeyo's pottery, on the other hand, produced jars with prominent necks, and her designs covered most of the entire surface of the pot. Bowls retained their low, wide shape, but the interior design varied greatly. Furthermore, Nampeyo's pottery included much iconography which related to Sikyatki style. It may be questionable whether or not all of the signs had a particular meaning; however, considering the importance of religious feasts and living in harmony with nature, many of the symbols were related to Hopi culture.

The pot was made between 1920–1925 and was likely painted by Nampeyo's daughter Fannie. By 1920, because Nampeyo became legally blind, her daughters often helped her in painting designs on the vessels. According to scholar Susan Peterson, "[Nampeyo's] lack of sight did not seem to diminish her art….She began to add tactile decoration, such as corrugated coils that she textured with a pointed stick, in place of some of her painting" (Peterson 57). The globular shape of the jar, called *globose* by Barbara Kramer, was a type usually used for storage (Kramer 180).

As far as icongraphy is concerned, it is hard to relate all the designs on this jar to particular symbols, because some are unique. There are many U-shaped cloud emblems, feather symbols, an arrow, and the *gnwela* (drawn as a curved stick, suggestive of germination and the spreading of life). The painting on this particular piece is clearly more abstract than that on earlier pieces by Nampeyo, a reflection of Fannie's style.

[Ewa Wojewoda, *Class of 2006* and
Kent R. Olson, *Class of 1961*]

173

General Logan and Party at Pueblo Zuni, 14 September 1882
(George Benjamin) Ben Wittick (American 1845–1903)
Wet-plate albumen print photograph, 10.9 x 18.0 cm., 4-1/4 x 7-1/8" image
Purchase with Gifts of Dr. Kurt Christoffel and the Reynold Emanuel and Johnnie Gause Leak Holmén Endowment Fund for the Visual Arts, Augustana College Art Collection, 2011.8

For a quarter century (1878-1903), Ben Wittick (1845-1903) who learned and practiced photography in Moline, Illinois, documented the lives of Native tribes in the American Southwest. There these years saw the final U.S. military victories over the Native peoples and their confinement to reservations, the expansion of the railroads, a boom in white settlement and the beginning of tourism. The tribes of the Southwest were subjected to enforced assimilation into the dominant white culture. This period brought radical change and cultural upheaval to these peoples and Wittick's photographs documented his subjects' confusion over their cultural identity. During his years in the Southwest, Wittick supported himself through his photography because he was able to produce images that appealed to prospective buyers seeking (what they imagined to be) authentic images of the life of the Native inhabitants. Thus Wittick's photos often blended real and imaginary aspects of that life to maximize their commercial potential.

General Logan and Party at Pueblo Zuni, September 14th, 1882 was shot while Wittick was accompanying a party that included Major General (U.S. Army, retired) John A. Logan (1826-1886) to the Zuni Pueblo. Largely forgotten today, Logan then held a position of national prominence. After distinguishing himself during the Civil War, Logan, a radical Republican, represented Illinois in the House of Representatives (1867-1871) and in the Senate (1871-1877; 1879-1886). Logan was a prime mover in the founding of the Grand Army of the Republic and the creation of Memorial Day. In 1884 he ran unsuccessfully as the Republican Vice-Presidential candidate. In September 1882 Logan and his wife were enjoying an extended visit with their daughter and son-in-law in Santa Fe (Jones 158).

This image was produced using the cumbersome wet-plate process in which the entire photographic process from negative plate preparation through to its development required completion before the plate dried (about 10 minutes)—all *in situ* under potentially challenging environmental conditions. This photograph is one of Wittick's late wet-plate images. Soon afterward he adopted the dry-plate process in which plates were prepared in advance and developed later in the studio. Here a wide view of the traditional Zuni multilevel stone pueblo dwellings shows the Logan party in the foreground. (Logan is the stout man wearing a topcoat and a light colored hat in the middle foreground.) The focus of Wittick's composition is the extensive network of stone dwellings. The humans appear largely oblivious to the photographer and are insignificant compared to the dwellings. Wittick documents a type of traditional dwelling that soon disappeared from the Zuni Pueblo to be replaced by the one-story concrete block dwellings commonplace there today. The spatial relationship of the humans (whites and Native Americans) in the photo is telling. This seems a testimonial to the reality of two cultures in close proximity yet worlds apart. The general's party does not appear to be attempting any meaningful interaction with the Zuni. The Zuni appear to be scrutinizing the unusual strangers. Thus the photo reflects a gulf between these cultures that persists to this day.

[Kurt Christoffel, *Professor of Chemistry*]

Whirligig of Native American Indian in Canoe, early 20th century
Artist unknown
Wood and paint, 49.1 x 40.0 x 16.5 cm., 19-3/16 x 15-3/4 x 6-1/2"
Paul A. Anderson Chair in the Arts Collection Purchase, Augustana College Art Collection, 2001.39

Growing up in a relatively rural area, the pivotal event of the year was always the town fair. Vendors from all over the country would make the pilgrimage to our small town, hauling thousands of pounds of steel that would magically unfold into rides and food stands. Colorful tents would spring into shape overnight, only to be populated in the morning by every imaginable craft item—custom carved wooden toilet seats with matching carved Kleenex boxes, air-brushed t-shirts, candles formed in the shape of every breed of dog imaginable, and of course, whirligigs.

Unable to be confined to a tent, these whimsical creations whirled close to the walkways, inviting fair-goers to indulge their child-like wonder. Miniature kinetic sculptures, these usually hand-crafted pieces react to every whim of the wind. Despite their kitschy connotation in contemporary culture, whirligigs have appeared for centuries in many works of art. Though few if any whirligigs survive from the time of Hieronymus Bosch, a Dutch painter during the Early Netherlandish Renaissance, this artist depicted many *whirligigs* (Gibson 9-15).

Said to have originated as miniature versions of the windmills that punctuate the Dutch landscape, whirligigs survived as an art form through the time of Bosch into the 19th century. As evidenced by a letter written by Caroline Elizabeth Wilde Cushing (daughter of Massachusetts Justice Samuel S. Wilde) in 1829, where she comments on the whirligigs she had seen in Bordeaux, France (Wilde 256-269). Had Ms. Cushing traveled the countryside in her native land, she might have encountered some whirligigs there as well, as the tradition was brought to America from Europe.

This particular whirligig depicts a generic Native American, replete with brightly painted headdress and paddles, seated in a canoe. Probably whittled, this whirligig was most likely made by hand for a private residence sometime in the early 20th century, and enjoyed a long life exposed to the elements, judging by the wear on the paint job. So persistent is this art form that it still enjoys a certain folk popularity, attested to by the prominent presence of whirligigs for sale at my hometown's annual fair.

[Veronica Smith, *Class of 2012*]

175

Caught in the Circle, n.d.
Frederic Remington (American 1861–1909)
Offset Lithograph originally published in 7 December, 1901 as double-page spread, *Collier's Weekly*, 30.2 x 39.7 cm., 11-7/8 x 15-5/8" sheet
Paul A. Anderson Chair in the Arts Collection Purchase, Augustana College Art Collection, SDC2010.42

Frederick Remington rose to prominence as a painter and illustrator between 1890 and 1915. His scenes of the ruthless environments and fearless fighters of the American West seemed to contrast mightily with the industrialized East and Midwest, where work was becoming ever more rule-bound and a flood of immigrants seemed to threaten the jobs and cultural supremacy of Euro-Americans. For viewers at the time, Remington's raw West suggested a return to a more *natural* time, when men were invigorated rather than depleted by their responsibilities. As working-class men felt increasingly *unmanned* by their dependence on owners' wages and middle-class men bowed to the repetition and femininity associated with desk jobs now often held by women as well, psychologists like G. Stanley Hall argued that boys needed to cultivate their inner "savage self" in order to recover the vigor intrinsic to manhood. Remington's good friend Theodore Roosevelt lauded the healthful effects of the "outdoor life" and rejoiced in the fact that the Spanish-American War of 1898, in addition to catapulting the U.S. onto the world stage as a colonial power, would literally turn boys into men. In his famous 1899 speech, "The Strenuous Life," Roosevelt exhorted Americans that "the timid man, the lazy man, the man who distrusts his country, the over-civilized man, who has lost the great fighting, masterful virtues, the ignorant man, and the man of dull mind... all these, of course, shrink from seeing the nation undertake its new duties." Sternly, he reminded his public that "We do not admire the man of timid peace."

Roosevelt anticipated a new era for America as colonial power, and artists like Remington looked to the American West, a region of earlier conquest by European and later American powers, for inspiration. While, like Roosevelt, Remington was an Easterner—he painted from his New York studio—he regarded the West as a place where men had defined themselves by assuming responsibility in life-and-death situations: fighting Native Americans, fending off a raging bull moose, guarding a precious source of water from competing cattlemen. As an illustrator who created more than 2,500 paintings, drawings, and sculptures, Remington helped to create the "myth of the West"—where the stoic, tragic, gallant cowboy resisted the forces that would confine him—even as it was rapidly disappearing. By the time he painted *Caught in the Circle* (catalogue 175) in 1914, the so-called "Indian Wars" of the West were over, and the violent confrontations between white and native that had captured the American imagination for well over a century were being replaced by the reality of the cultural conquest of the West. Many Native Americans were confined to reservations, barbed wire criss-crossed the formerly open range, and white and indigenous men alike were more likely to be working-class cogs than heroes of the open range. Remington's paintings, while realistic in their style and detail (Remington began his career as a journalist), are decidedly works of the imagination.

176

The Cowpuncher, or **No More He Rides,** n.d.
Frederic Remington (American 1861–1909)
Offset Lithograph, originally published as *Collier's Weekly* cover, 1901, 40.2 x 30.2 cm., 15-7/8 x 11-7/8"
Paul A. Anderson Chair in the Arts Collection Purchase, Augustana College Art Collection, SDC2010.41

Art historians have noted the gendered and racialized imagery of Remington's paintings: in this case, men with their guns pointed outward protecting themselves against a faceless, encircling enemy, even as one of their own assumes a fallen and "feminized" position. In this standoff between white men and native, it's unclear who will triumph; one man's gun even seems to be lowered, a sign that he was losing power. While a reading of Freudian imagery seems to be a stretch, when we consider that Remington's contemporaries believed that men's sedentary, indoor lives might lead to a loss of virility—a depletion of their "vital sources"—and that Roosevelt himself was deeply concerned with the possibility of "race suicide"—a declining birthrate among westernized nations as couples delayed marriage and limited numbers of offspring—this interpretation gains credence. The image of the encircling racial *Other* who would confine white men to a narrow sphere of influence impressed upon American men the necessity of proving themselves against such limiting and suffocating others—or die trying. The image of the cowboy such as *The Cowpuncher* (catalogue 176) that Remington and his contemporaries (illustrators like Charley Russell and writers like Owen Wister, author of the 1902 novel *The Virginian*) helped to create survived well into the 1960s, as screen heroes like John Wayne, James Stewart, and Henry Fonda re-enacted the conflict of men beset by civilization on the one side and savagery on the other. In such films, Native Americans represent the wild, untamed self that men both fought against and longed to be, while women often represented the alluring yet confining call of safety, domesticity, and familial duty.

Certainly viewers today recognize the messages about masculinity implicit in this image, for many are still present in our popular culture. As war drags on in the Middle East, work is outsourced to other countries, and young men find themselves outnumbered by women at colleges, we still look to images like this one to find meanings for manhood. Films like *The Hurt Locker* (2008) and *127 Hours* (2010) suggest that dusty, foreign soils and harsh landscapes are still fertile grounds for forging a sense of self in the face of the ruthlessness of nature and the folly of boyish choices—but at enormous cost. We also confront the ironic masculinity of the *Old Spice Guy*, in which we're invited to mock definitions of manliness that are impossible to uphold. Men and women who viewed *Caught in the Circle* (catalogue 175) in 1914—when the U.S. was witnessing a devastating war abroad—may have wondered whether war in the trenches of Europe would bring about power or destruction. Likewise, young men today may wonder how to confront the pressures that surround them, and whether the traditional tools of masculinity can still work in a postmodern world. What does it mean to *man up* in the early 21st century? What are the rituals and experiences that confirm masculinity? Does becoming a man involve facing up to the responsibilities of work, school, and family, or is it only forged through a flight from such responsibilities, to face dangers where you either win or die trying?

[Jane Simonsen, *Associate Professor of History and Women's and Gender Studies*]

177

An Evening on a Canadian Lake, n.d.
Frederic Remington (American 1861–1909)
Offset Lithograph originally published as double-page spread, *Collier's Weekly* , 18 March, 1905, 30.0 x 40.2 cm., 11-7/8 x 15-7/8" sheet
Paul A. Anderson Chair in the Arts Collection Purchase, Augustana College Art Collection, SDC2010.40

A calm, placid lake underscores a weathered canoe as it glides through the water, two rugged men and their dog aboard. The dark green diagonal of the tree line is smoothly contrasted by the silver of the lake. There is a hopefulness inherent in the bright early morning light, and the men pause mid-stroke to look towards the sun.

This piece's subject matter is a stark departure from the action-packed Western scenes Frederic Remington is best known for—cowboys, Indians, stampeding horses, and soldiers—but in sentiment, this image is remarkably similar to the rest of Remington's work. Remington was for the majority of his artistic career a painter, and illustrator, and his images of life on the plains graced the pages of *Collier's Weekly* (in which this particular image was published) as well as in *Harper's Weekly, The Century Illustrated*, and *Scribner's Magazine*. Heralded as an accurate recorder of life on the American frontier, Remington helped foster a new American identity through showcasing the cultural diversity and the natural bounty of the young nation. While this particular work concentrates on a Canadian lake, this composition still engenders the thrill of exploration (not to mention the adventure of *Manifest Destiny*) that gripped the nation during the latter part of the 19th century.

Remington's paintings and illustrations, while primarily focused on the dynamic movements of his subjects, also share a sense of vast space. In almost all of Remington's two-dimensional compositions, the landscape plays a prominent role in the overall composition. While the details of the action in the image often take precedent, perhaps in the incredibly realistic rendering of a dusty cowboy's spurs or in the glistening sweat on a horse's flanks, the setting of these dramatic scenes serves the vital purpose of foil to the action. More importantly, Remington's background landscapes embodied the hopes of a nation bent on expansion—just as Remington's skies and rolling plains (in the case of this particular work, the virgin forest and pristine waters) seem to extend forever in every direction, as did the dreams of the American people whose horizons at the turn of the 20th century seemed limitless.

[Veronica Smith, *Class of 2012*]

Still Life of Fruits and Flowers in Blue and Yellow Vase, n.d.
Artist unknown (American)
Reverse glass painting, 35.8 x 25.5 cm., 14-1/8 x 10"
Paul A. Anderson Chair in the Arts Collection
Purchase, Augustana College Art Collection, 2001.36

Reverse glass painting is a medium that dates as far back as the early sixteenth century in Europe and was first documented in China during the middle of the eighteenth century (Beggerow). The technique, however, did not make its way to the United States until the 1830s. Shortly after this time, there was enough interest in this skill that it was taught at women's boarding schools, much like samplers, and instructions appeared in magazines with stencils available by mail. Designs were mostly wreaths, flowers or floral baskets (Ketchum), similar to Augustana's piece. The genre of still life painting gained popularity with the growing middle class and also with the rise of Impressionism in the nineteenth century. Traditional academic subject matter trailed behind the goal of aesthetic color harmony. The harmony seen in this piece, with its bold primary colors of blue and yellow, along with complementary colors of blue and orange, draws the viewer's eye to the center of the painting. The subject matter is what classifies it as still life.

The technique behind a reverse glass painting is done in *reverse* from traditional paintings. The finest details are painted first, such as the pupil of an eye or the center of a flower. Larger portions of the painting are done after this, and finally the background is filled in. This leaves little room for error while building and completing the piece. The finished painting is thus a mirror image of the original painting as the glass is ultimately turned over and displayed with the paint behind it. In this manner, the original details are effectively reversed to the front of the composition and through frugal Yankee ingenuity, the glass serves a dual purpose as *canvas* for the painting as well as protection for the framed work of art. The challenge lies in ensuring the glass does not break over the years, as that would effectively *break* the painting as well.

Although this reverse glass painting is anonymous, we can assume that it was made by a Victorian period woman as females were taught crafts like these in order to prepare them to be wives and to decorate their homes. Their construction also served as a form of hobby much like crafts today. Because it was produced by an untrained artist, we may classify this work as *folk* art. Contrary to *fine* art produced by trained artists, folk art serves a more decorative purpose rather than an elevated didactic one. Yet it has become more prized and valuable over the past several decades for its ability to capture an original and fresh view, directly from eye to hand, without the benefit of a filter through formal academic training. Reverse glass paintings were also sometimes incorporated into mirrors, clocks, lamps and other furniture further emphasizing their decorative purpose and bringing the craft closer to the women who generally painted them and the domestic setting in which they were placed.

[Emma Burns, *Class of 2012*]

179

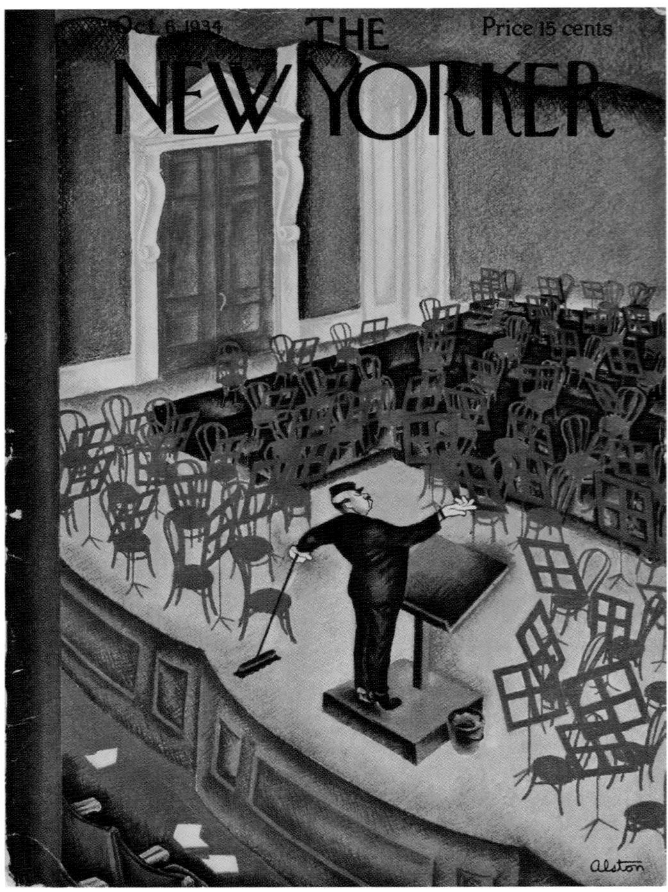

Cover of *The New Yorker* magazine, 6 October 1934
Charles Henry Alston (American 1907–1977)
Offset Lithograph, 30.2 x 22.3 x .5 cm., 11-7/8 x 8-3/4 x 3/16"
Paul A. Anderson Chair in the Arts Collection Purchase, Augustana College Art Collection, SDC2010.17

The New Yorker magazine cover from the October 6th, 1934 issue by Harlem Renaissance artist, Charles Alston, resonates today with a similar power it must have originally held. That power is based upon different circumstances but it makes a strong impact on the eye, mind, heart and soul. There are still many in the United States today who face very real barriers to seeing their true potential recognized.

The United States was a very different place in 1934. This was well before the many triumphs in domestic struggles for civil rights which would come in upcoming decades. Despite ambition, talent or even education, many Black people were limited to menial jobs due to racist laws and practices of the time. In Alston's painting the Black janitor has to wait, until the wealthy patrons as well as musicians have cleared out of the symphony hall at the end of the night, to have his moment of imagination. In that society, pretending to conduct the empty chairs would be the closest he would get to doing it. Surely this was a fleeting moment. This dignified man would have to step down and attend to the trash and seats that needed to be put back in place.

Now in the modern-day United States, eight decades later, there have been many strides in areas of race relations. But, the bitter reality is that there are still many people who can only imagine their dreams coming close to being true. In almost all cases, the laws limiting achievement have been struck down. But now, almost more than ever, there are serious struggles for the "have-nots." There are ever widening gaps in wealth. There are fewer and fewer people at the top holding more and more of the nation's wealth. On top of that, families of color find themselves holding less and less wealth when compared to their white counterparts. As much as we laud the progress that has been made, the scene in Alston's painting could easily fall into place in our modern times. The janitor could still be a Black man or he could be a Latino immigrant. He could even be a displaced White worker. America has changed while staying the same.

[Christopher M. Whitt, *Assistant Professor of Political Science*]

180

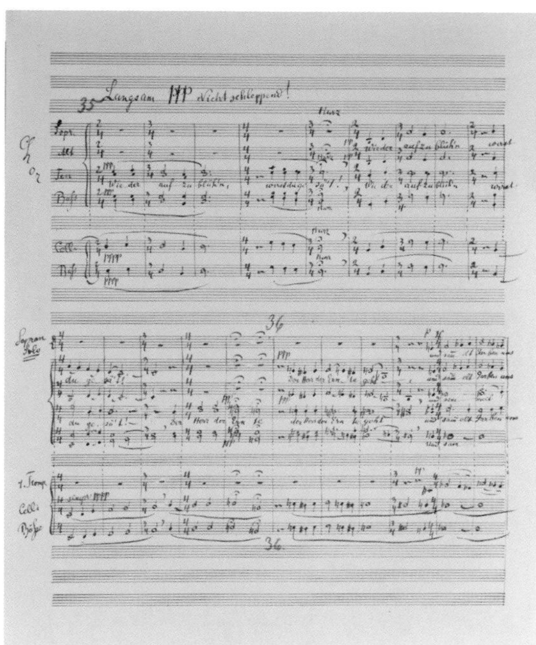

The initial statement of the Klopstock Ode Movement V in **Gustav Mahler Symphony No. 2 in C Minor "Resurrection,"** 1888-94
Gustav Mahler (1860–1911)
Page in printed book, facsimile, published by the Kaplan Foundation: N.Y., 1986, 21.1 x 26.2 cm., 8-1/4 x 10-1/4"
Lent Courtesy of Dr. Daniel Culver

Theodore Adorno said (famously) about the music of Gustav Mahler: "Pedestrian the musical material, sublime the execution" (Adorno 61). I would like to take a moment to comment on what all of the fuss was about Mahler. As one gazes intently on the full score of the *Second Symphony*, the musical images that informed Mahler become clear. Now, I should remind the reader and listener that it was precisely the pedestrian musical material that Mahler employed which caused such consternation among his critics. In turn-of-the-century Vienna, there was an accepted, customary understanding of what was appropriate music for the formal concert hall. The graceful and elegant themes of Mozart, Beethoven, and Brahms were considered the *sine qua non* of musical utterance. Enter Gustav Mahler with his extraordinarily fertile imagination, along with a penchant for irony and paradox. His audacious inclusion of folk song, *Heuriger Musik* (music of the wine tavern), military marches, natural sounds (cowbells and bird calls), and the use of *Klezmer* music from the *Shtetl* all served as the musical idea for his thematic material.

This all goes to the question of originality—that final arbiter of worth and force in the late 19th century. The severest judges of Mahler assessed his music as nothing more than a haphazard agglomeration of sound. The seeming heterogeneity of style for which Mahler was accused was something of which he was aware. Perhaps the criticism had to do with a kind of schizophrenic character shift in the symphonies; one only has to contrast theme groups in any of his first movements to understand an almost apocalyptic change of mood within movements. The contrasts of moods and mode, banal and serious, lyric and aggressive were considered by some as a profanation of the symphonic ideal. Maybe a dose of regrettably ugly and vulgar anti-Semitism was also at play. Whatever the criticism, it was precisely these observations regarding his music which, for many, were the touchstone of his genius. Some have tried to categorize all of his material—a peculiar central European fixation. For example, the consummate Mahler biographer, Henry-Louis de La Grange, has identified the following categories descriptive of Mahler's output: quotation, quotation from memory, self-quotation, borrowing, allusion, echo or reminiscence, similarity, and homage (de La Grange 127). Obviously, scholars of Mahler seldom agree on much of anything. However, it is safe to say that the idea of "Music about music in Mahler" (Ibid.) is central to a deeper understanding of the score and its musical intentions—intentions, which if we are to believe Mahler himself, are devoid of program and simply an expression of Mahler's world.

The use of the banal in a high art, as music was considered to be, was for some an inexcusable intrusion on artistic sensibilities. For others, like Theodore Adorno, Arnold Schoenberg, and Luciano Berio, transformation of the ordinary into the magisterial was the true genius of Gustav Mahler. The score shown here of the opening statement of the *Klopstock Ode* appears on the surface to be a harmless enough setting of a highly regarded text proclaimed by a chorus of many. But, closer examination reveals that Mahler does not merely state the obvious. Rather, he continually and subtly recasts the original material so that a wonderful transmogrification of the gesture is illuminated. Mahler, it becomes abundantly clear, is incapable and unwilling to simply quote himself directly. The spinning out of the musical material, yes, sometimes mundane musical material, achieves an artistic transformation that still moves us in a sensuous way, impossible to describe adequately. Ludwig Wittgenstein, no advocate for the music of Gustav Mahler, at least got it right when he said at the end of the *Tractatus Logico-Philosophicus*, "What we cannot speak about we must pass over in silence" (Wittgenstein 89).

[Daniel Culver, *Henry Veld Professor of Music*]

181

Sunday Morning, 1939
Thomas Hart Benton (American 1889–1975)
Lithograph, published by Associated American Artists, New York , edition of 250, 24.4 x 32.3 cm., 9-1/8 x 12-3/4" image
Purchase with Gift of Jeff Abernathy and Rebecca Wee, Augustana College Art Collection, 2005.9

Widely known by others as one of the premiere "Regionalists" by portraying the true America of the Midwest, Thomas Hart Benton depicted a country that was at odds with the modern technologies of the early twentieth century. While the majority of the art world embraced abstract representations, Benton depicted representational art, based on what he knew best: scenes of rural America drawn mostly from his upbringing in Missouri and the surrounding area.

As an art student, he studied abstraction early in his career, but decided to make a conscientious effort against this movement as his art matured. *Sunday Morning* was originally sold either by mail order or through a department store. By distributing the lithographic print in this manner, Benton's art found a democratic means toward patronage in order to reach the masses for a relatively inexpensive price tag. Wedged between the Great Depression and World War II, Benton and other Regionalists reflected a tenacious inward turning *Americanism* in response to the profound uncertainties of the day. In this manner, they illustrated a traditional, *realistic* view, reminiscent of the *Good Old Days*, in sharp contrast to the edgy styles imported from Europe at the time. As Benton famously stated following his European study, "…a windmill, a junk heap and a Rotarian have more meaning for me than Notre Dame or the Parthenon" (Dizard 2).

Sunday Morning illustrates an Arkansas sharecropping community, and thus, Benton portrays a bygone era that was becoming less and less common in America. Although the church is prominent in *Sunday Morning*, its scale in relation to the figures is skewed, as the figures would not be able to fit comfortably inside the structure. The group of four about to enter the church appears to have a sense of duty, judging by their stance and posture. Under the large tree, a young couple appears oblivious to the social traditions and constraints found inside. Instead, their freedom, both figuratively and theoretically, mimics the contradiction between the world of modernism and the nostalgic world of the America of yesteryear.

[Michelle Richmond, *Class of 1995*]

182

Seed Time and Harvest, 1937
Grant Wood (American 1891–1942)
Lithograph, published by Associated American Artists, New York, edition of 250, 18.9 x 30.7 cm., 7-7/16 x 12-1/8" image
Paul A. Anderson Chair in the Arts Collection Purchase, Augustana College Art Collection, 2000.30 Art © Estate of Grant Wood/Licensed by VAGA, New York, NY

During the 1930s, a popular artistic genre emerged out of America's heartland. Grant Wood, along with other notable Midwestern artists, such as Thomas Hart Benton (catalogue 181) and John Steuart Curry, developed the idea of Regionalism for a country that was weak and torn apart by the *Great Depression*. Wood, as illustrated in *Seed Time and Harvest*, felt the need to portray an Agrarian myth—the need to work by hand. He refused to recognize the age of industry that was sweeping the nation. The *Pointillist* (Post-Impressionist dot application of paint) technique is evident in *Seed Time and Harvest* in his use of tiny dots to represent highlights and shadows that ultimately consume the entire work.

Wood's most famous painting, *American Gothic*, presents a sort of zoom-lens view of stereotypical Iowa farmers. In *Seed Time and Harvest*, however, we see his more typical genre scene framed within a Regionalist landscape. Wood created numerous works depicting the fertile rolling hills of the heartland and the labor needed to tend to those farms. As seen in this piece, he used simplified figures in order to achieve a sense of realism. On the whole, the composition seems rather plain, yet upon closer examination, the minute details in the grass, haystacks and corn become evident.

There is a deep sense of iconography rooted in this lithograph. Wood wanted the American people to understand the dignity of hard work that still survived in the rural communities of this country. At a time when many were moving to industrialized cities, he reminded Americans that there were still farmers who remained in the country and made their living through traditional manual labor.

Wood engaged his audience through his use of *chiaroscuro* (shading with light and shadow.) The presence of the haystacks is emphasized through the long shadows, indicating early morning or late afternoon, depending on the vantage point. The dark interior of the shed leaves the viewer pondering what might be inside. The shadows also perhaps allude to the idea of a long summer's day coming to an end, as if he is working from dawn until dusk, and must complete his tasks before the cold winds of winter blow.

[Mary Feeney, *Class of 2007*]

183

Winter, ca. 1989
Robert Daughters (American b. 1929)
Oil on canvas, 22.7 x 30.5 cm., 9 x 12"
Gift of George J. Schlenker, Augustana College Art Collection, 2003.1

The American Southwest, its beauty and wonderment, has been the inspiration for many artists throughout the ages. Such breathtaking scenery bewitched Robert Daughters and became one of his favorite subjects to paint. While attending the Kansas City Art Institute and School of Design, he met his wife, and upon their marriage in 1953, they spent their honeymoon in Taos, New Mexico where he was moved by the scenery and culture. Seventeen years later, after success and recognition in commercial art, the Daughters relocated, first to Santa Fe in 1970, then two years later to Taos ("Striking").

Redefining himself in his new surroundings, Daughters developed an aesthetic influenced by Post-Impressionists, Paul Gauguin (catalogue 132) and Émile Bernard, characterized by intensity and expressionism concentrated in jewel like colors, often delineated in black. This technique, referred to as *Cloisonnism* as it imitates the jewel-like effect of traditional enamel and gold cloisonné work, lent Daughters' paintings a simplicity and luminosity equal to his vision of the Southwest ("Striking"). Like a musical composer, Daughters strove to create harmony through balancing elements of color, light, and composition.

In *Winter*, viewers glimpse the magnificent and vivacious mountains that encompass half the composition. Our attention is immediately drawn to the Southwestern snowcapped mountains in the background. Daughters highlighted the mountain's ridges through dark blue shadows, like wrinkles on a face, reflecting the passing of time. Thick brushstrokes of pinks and purples further detail the mountainous facade. The middle ground is characterized by the warm and rich colors of the plateaus and desert plains, vividly contrasting against the dark mountain behind. The plateaus are outlined by *cloisonnist* black lines, inspired by the Post-Impressionist technique favored by Daughters. In the foreground, Daughters painted the rustic brush in black with blue outlines. The manner in which Daughters paints this composition, places viewers within the brush, like an audience gazing intently and eagerly awaiting an orchestra to begin playing. His composer's approach is also evident as the composition is arranged with complementary harmonies of light and shadows. Robert Daughters' depiction of the American Southwest is executed perfectly through his illustration of the vivid colors and light which captures the timelessness of the region with which he fell in love.

[Griselda Mata, *Class of 2012*]

184

Seining Minnows, 1938
John Bloom (American 1906–2002)
Oil on canvas, 70.8 x 71.0 cm., 27-7/8 x 28"
Partial Gift of David '72 and Cyndy Losasso, with Additional Funding through Gift of the Reynold Emanuel and Johnnie Gause Leak Holmén Endowment Fund for the Visual Arts, and Mr. and Mrs. Victor and Isabel Bartolome, and Mr. Daryl Empen '91 and Dr. Cynthia Wiedemann Empen '92, with Conservation Services Donated by Mr. Barry Bauman, Augustana College Art Collection, 2007.9

What we experience when we view a painting or read a novel or poem is the result of a negotiation between the work itself and our own interests and history we bring to that work. My first look at *Seining Minnows* sent me back to Mark Twain, one of the Midwest writers I spent much of my career teaching. They seemed similar in both choice of subject and technique.

Take *Tom Sawyer*, for instance. When that novel was first published in 1876, readers must have been shocked. They were used to novels with high literary style. Boy heroes like Little Lord Fauntleroy talked like miniature adults, dressed in black velvet and lace, and embarked on fantastic adventures. Now here, in Tom Sawyer was a boy who spoke and acted like a real boy, catching bugs, curing warts with dead cats, and running small con games. The language in which Twain told his story was equally plain.

The Midwest writers who followed Twain used similarly common subjects and plain language, from Carl Sandburg's poems about women breaking eggs to bake a cake as the sun rises on the Illinois prairie to Edgar Lee Masters' townsfolk who maintained their petty quarrels from the grave. There are very few searched for Holy Grails or Annunciations in Midwest literature.

The same thing is true of Bloom's painting. Seining minnows would have been a familiar subject for anyone living along a river in the 1930s. It was especially familiar to Bloom himself. He and his father often fished for bass in the Wapsipinicon River or on Crystal Lake near DeWitt, Iowa. Getting minnows for bait was the first step.

At first glance, such familiar subjects and simplicity of technique may seem artless, as they did to Twain's early literary critics who refused to admit him to literary circles. But of course they were wrong. Ernest Hemingway was later to claim that "all American literature begins with Mark Twain." Twain's language may be plain and simple, but he chose each word carefully and accurately. He knew what he was doing, and as a result, Tom Sawyer and Huck Finn have become universal folk heroes around the world. As one of the Massachussetts Bay Puritans said in defending their plain style of writing, "It is also an art to conceal art." Imagine how far Carl Sandburg would have gotten if he had tried to be "literary" and had written "the vapors arrive shoreward on miniature feline digits" instead of "the fog comes in on little cat feet." Twain rightly believed that much of what passes for high literature was, in fact, pretense.

John Bloom was just as careful an artist as Twain. Among Augustana's art collection are several preliminary sketches for *Seining Minnows*. They show Bloom moving his characters slightly to get just the right perspective, and moving from detailed drawings of creases in the pants and rolled-up sleeves to a version so simplified that the men might as well be from Ireland, Greece, or Spain as the Wapsipinicon. As for the poses, drawing our attention to the hands in the net, that pose, too, seems universal. It could be Huck and Tom catching a frog, or it could be the Holy Family.

I have found that some works that dazzle me when I first approach them soon lose their luster. Some that appear to be simple grow on me. John Bloom's *Seining Minnows* grows on me.

[Roald Tweet, *Professor Emeritus of English and Conrad Bergendoff Professor Emeritus of Humanities*]

185

Autumn Afternoon on the Mississippi River, 1915
Jonas Olof Grafström (Swedish American 1855–1933)
Oil on canvas, 91.5 x 137.2 cm., 36 x 54"
Gift of Augustana College Art Association, 1983.171

Olof Grafström arrived in the United States in 1886 at the age of thirty-one. Trained at the Swedish Academy of Fine Arts in Stockholm, Grafström studied landscape painting under Per Daniel Holm (1835-1903) who was sympathetic to Romanticism and schooled in the Barbizon and Düsseldorf traditions (Kirn and Maurer 22). It is therefore not surprising that once Grafström settled in the Midwest, he would link his Swedish landscape training with the robust Romantic landscape tradition already established in the United States.

Grafström taught at Augustana College from 1897-1926. As Professor of Painting and Drawing, he educated in a large classroom on the third floor of Old Main. The windows offered a commanding view of the Mississippi River. *Autumn Afternoon on the Mississippi* presents a sweeping panoramic view of the river and the warm, autumnal landscape surrounding it. This painting relates to the season and coloring of the American Hudson River School. The composition is nearly half water and half sky, looking toward the bend in the river that defines the Quad Cities. A paddleboat in the distance helps delineate the scale and perspective and serves as a reminder of technological progress in the heartland. The figure establishes scale and seemingly invites viewers to search beyond to the distant vista, reminiscent of American Luminist compositions with their calm, mirror-like water surfaces fading, via atmospheric perspective, into the distant horizon.

This painting, nearing its own centenary, seems appropriate following the 2010 sesquicentennial commemoration of the founding of Augustana College along the Mississippi River. Landscape painting has a long and distinguished history both in the United States and at Augustana College in particular. From the nineteenth through the twentieth centuries, it served as an emblem of the unspoiled paradise offered in America in comparison to the more developed and *historical* landscape of Europe. The area along the Mississippi was rapidly transitioning and the figure amidst this natural beauty might also serve to remind us of the profound Romantic belief in *man's* spiritual relationship with nature.

[Catherine Carter Goebel, *Editor*]

186

Southern Iowa View, 1986
James Konrad (American 1943–2011)
Oil on canvas, 91.2 x 151.8 cm., 36 x 59-3/4"
Augustana College Art Collection Purchase, 1986.8

This pairing of paintings represents an intentional break in chronology for an otherwise art historical book. Such thematic license seems appropriate to link two historically revered Augustana art professors, each enriching the college for over twenty years. James Konrad was born in Iowa and served as a U.S. Navy medic during the Vietnam War. He earned his B.F.A. and M.F.A. in printmaking and painting from Drake University and came to the Quad Cities as the first Artist-in-Residence at the Davenport Municipal Art Gallery (now the Figge Art Museum). His expertise in the color and chemistry of paint was furthered through his work as a color specialist and paint formulator. Jim was hired in 1989 as an assistant professor of art in Augustana's Department of Art and Art History. His expertise enabled him to teach a number of courses and media, including drawing, painting, two-dimensional design, printmaking and art education.

Konrad was a recognized artist for his strong, realist still life painting as well as his beautiful Midwest landscapes, particularly centered as with this work, on the Iowa vistas of his youth. Jim was a master in utilizing artistic materials, not only in creating artwork but also in his sensitive conservation of the works of others. This Iowa landscape reflects a complementary love of nature and artistic breadth akin to his predecessor, Olof Grafström. Jim's artistic eye and skillful touch lovingly captured the sweeping beauty of the Midwest.

Konrad was also pivotal in building the pedagogical art history collection featured in this book. He and I spent numerous hours of lively, collegial conversation over the past twenty years, examining works of art from our respective perspectives, in order to determine suitability for the teaching collection. Jim had an impeccable eye for the connoisseurship of fine art which he lent to his superb conservation of paintings. He brought to life numerous works which enabled the college to build an outstanding teaching collection. He often commented on the thrill and artistic engagement of "tracing the brushstrokes of the masters" as he preserved their works. He also graciously taught art history students conservation and printmaking techniques. Konrad modeled genuine collegial art and art history collaboration within a liberal arts framework.

It is important to note in this publication, not only his talent as an artist and teacher, but also his steady contribution to *Liberal Arts through the AGES*. At the time of his death, he was finalizing his research on Josef Albers' *Homage to the Square*. Following his death, the Josef and Anni Albers Foundation kindly gifted a print from this famous series in Jim's memory (catalogue 196). The high regard of the two Augustana presidents during Jim's tenure is evidenced by the fact that this particular painting has hung in the President's Office through the administrations of both President Thomas Tredway and President Steven Bahls. Furthermore, upon his retirement, President Tredway commissioned Jim to paint his presidential portrait, now hanging in the college boardroom alongside portraits of other past presidents. Jim Konrad was a gifted artist, generous teacher and cherished colleague—he will be remembered and missed.

[Catherine Carter Goebel, *Editor*]

187A&B

187A

Save Freedom of Speech/ Buy War Bonds, 1943
Norman Rockwell (American 1894–1978)
Offset lithograph poster, image published in *The Saturday Evening Post*, 20 February 1943, 71.0 x 50.9 cm., 28 x 20" sheet
Paul A. Anderson Chair in the Arts Collection Purchase, Augustana College Art Collection, SDC2006.32d Printed by permission of the Norman Rockwell Family Agency Book Rights Copyright © 2011 The Norman Family Entitles

187B

Save Freedom of Worship/ Each According to the Dictates/ Of His Own Conscience/ Buy War Bonds, 1943
Norman Rockwell (American 1894–1978)
Offset lithograph poster, image published in *The Saturday Evening Post*, 27 February 1943, 71.1 x 50.9 cm., 28 x 20" sheet
Paul A. Anderson Chair in the Arts Collection Purchase, Augustana College Art Collection, SDC2006.32a Printed by permission of the Norman Rockwell Family Agency Book Rights Copyright © 2011 The Norman Family Entitles

One of the early magazines, the *Saturday Evening Post*, began publication on August 4, 1821. The *Post* focused on current events and featured prominent writers of fiction and nonfiction. In 1916, *Post* editor George Horace Lorimer purchased two cover illustrations by 22-year-old artist, Norman Rockwell. Rockwell's illustrations are noted for the stories that they suggest. His "stories" connote All-American values and celebrate everyday experience. To create these depictions of life, Rockwell would meticulously stage each image. He hired models, preferring his friends, family and neighbors over professionals. He then costumed them, and surrounded them with the necessary props. Initially, he would sketch these scenes, but later turned to photography to preserve the images that he would eventually draw (Rockwell).

These four images, the *Four Freedoms*, are among Rockwell's best-known illustrations. On January 6, 1941, in his State of the Union speech to Congress, with the intent of garnering support for the Lend-Lease plan that would provide needed resources for Great Britain, Franklin Delano Roosevelt (FDR) articulated four essential freedoms that the United States should seek to defend. These were freedom of worship, freedom of speech, freedom from fear and freedom from want (Crowell 265). Later that year after U.S. entry into World War II, Rockwell, wanting to assist in the war effort, created four sketches for posters that would illustrate each of the freedoms. The four finished oil paintings were reproduced in the *Post* in early 1943.

The first to appear was *Freedom of Speech* on February 20, 1943, accompanied by an essay from Booth Tarkington. It features a working man standing to speak at a town meeting. His plaid shirt and casual, stained-jacket contrasts with the more formal white-collar attire of other attendees. On February 27, 1943, *Freedom of Worship* was printed along with an article by Will Durant. The only image with text ("EACH ACCORDING TO THE DICTATES OF HIS OWN CONSCIENCE") "portrays representatives from different faiths, different racial backgrounds, different ages, and both genders, providing a spectrum of people with whom most Americans can identify" (Olson).

187C&D

187C

Ours...to Fight For—Freedom From Want, 1943
Norman Rockwell (American 1894–1978)
Offset lithograph poster, image published in *The Saturday Evening Post*, 6 March 1943, 71.2 x 50.9 cm., 28-1/16 x 20-1/16" sheet
Paul A. Anderson Chair in the Arts Collection Purchase, Augustana College Art Collection, SDC2006.32c Printed by permission of the Norman Rockwell Family Agency Book Rights Copyright © 2011 The Norman Family Entitles

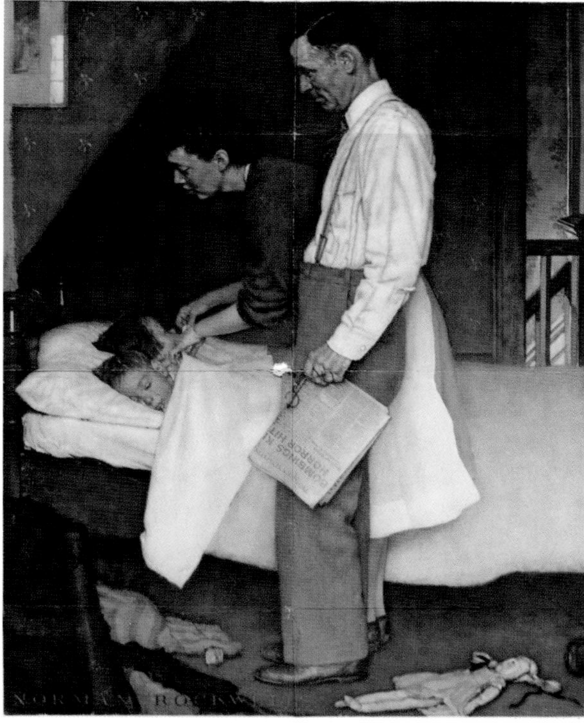

187D

Ours...to Fight For—Freedom from Fear, 1943
Norman Rockwell (American 1894–1978)
Offset lithograph poster, image published in *The Saturday Evening Post*, 13 March 1943 , 71.0 x 50.9 cm., 28 x 20" sheet
Paul A. Anderson Chair in the Arts Collection Purchase, Augustana College Art Collection, SDC2006.32b Printed by permission of the Norman Rockwell Family Agency Book Rights Copyright © 2011 The Norman Family Entitles

Along with an essay by Carlos Bulosan, *Freedom from Want* was featured on March 6, 1943. In it a multi-generational family gathers at the table to partake in the annual holiday meal. Rockwell noted, "I painted the turkey in 'Freedom from Want' on Thanksgiving Day. Mrs. Wheaton, our cook (and the lady holding the turkey in the picture), cooked it, I painted it, and we ate it. That was one of the few times I've ever eaten the model" (Rockwell 196). While seemingly glib about the creation of this illustration, Rockwell later expressed disappointment in this image and one other, *Freedom from Fear*. "He felt they came off as smug, especially to Europeans lacking in comfort of distance from the battlegrounds that Americans at home enjoyed" (Claridge 311)

The final image, *Freedom from Fear* appeared on March 13, 1943 with one of the last writings of Stephen Vincent Benet. (Benet died on the day of publication) (Murray and McCabe 62). While toys lay lifeless on the floor, young parents tuck their children into bed. The father grasps a newspaper depicting the carnage of war. For Rockwell, *Freedom from Fear* erred "by allowing American viewers to sigh in relief that they tuck their children into bed safely each night, in sharp contrast to the victims of the bombings alluded to in the newspaper the father holds" (Claridge 311).

The *Four Freedoms* were immediately popular with the American public. Over 25,000 sets of prints sold. The U.S. Treasury, realizing their propaganda value, organized the Four Freedoms War Bond Show. The four paintings were displayed in 16 cities, ultimately raising over $130 million (Rockwell). Frequently Rockwell autographed copies of the illustrations. Although Rockwell's meticulous attention to exact detail was well-known, not so well-known was his ability to omit detail so as to promote varied identifications (Olson 16).

[Ellen Hay, *Professor of Communication Studies*]

188

Untitled, 1980
Willem De Kooning (American 1904–1997)
Offset color lithograph, 79.4 x 71.2 cm., 31-1/4 x 28-1/16" image
Paul A. Anderson Chair in the Arts Collection Purchase, Augustana College Art Collection, 2002.14 © 2011 Artists Rights Society (ARS), New York

Willem de Kooning was one of the most influential Abstract Expressionist artists of the twentieth century. Abstract Expressionism, and particularly *action* painting, was a movement in which the artist painted rapidly and forcefully on large canvases in an effort to intuitively express feelings and emotions. To an Abstract Expressionist, spontaneity was thought to draw out the creativity from the artist's subconscious. In the 1930s, de Kooning's art began to develop a distinct appearance. He started out painting letters on canvases, recreating and shifting them into gestured statements as his final product (Hess 23).

De Kooning extended his process-oriented approach in his most famous works representing the abstract figurative paintings of women. Through his *Woman* series, he explored the abstract figure in space while experimenting with shapes and colors. His many depictions of women were controversial because the figures were distorted and looked grotesque.

Untitled is a 1980 color lithograph that might be an abstract depiction of a woman's figure in a landscape scene. The woman looks to be in profile with an American flag behind her and landscape beside her. De Kooning defined his own concept of space by the way he arranged the landscape and the figure. Although this is a lithograph, the bright colors and thick, expressive *brushstrokes* make the piece look three-dimensional and reveal a sense of movement similar to his action paintings. At the top of the image, the flowing blue lines and the yellow might represent the sky and the sun, while the brown and green near the bottom suggest land. The curving red brushstrokes near the face hint at a flag. Although the loose swabs of paint look as if they were done in a hurry and suggest spontaneity, the artist actually placed his gestured strokes with care.

Another technique that de Kooning explored was closing his eyes while painting so he could concentrate inwardly to intensify his feelings and "to disconnect perception from preconception" (Butler 169). This distanced him from imposing proper proportions and conventional form, which made his figures more keenly felt and accurately expressionistic.

[Sneha Konda, *Class of 2007*]

189

Constellation von 5 Formen (Constellation of 5 Forms), 1956
Jean (Hans) Arp (French 1886–1966)
Color lithograph, 54.5 x 38.5 cm., 21-1/2 x 15-3/16" image
Gift of Polly Fehlman '46, Augustana College Art Collection, 2001.21 © 2011 Artists Rights Society (ARS), New York / VG Bild-Kunst, Bonn

It could be an egg, sunny side up. Or maybe it's a summer sea, white sails billowing, hot sun spilling into endless blue. Or (and this is the most likely) it is symbolic of nothing. Well, not exactly nothing, but more of *nothing* than something. This kind of quixotic, paradoxical statement is typical of the Dada movement, which was a reactionary form of artistic expression that responded to the extreme violence and subsequent disorder of World War I (Frey 12). The Dadaists weren't really a united force. Rather, they were a magmata coalition of artists who were connected only in their vehement opposition to just about everything. Dada, according to the *Dada Manifesto* of 1918 (which is pointedly ironic), is a testament to almost universal numbness after the atrocity of widespread warfare. "How can anyone hope to order the chaos that constitutes that infinite, formless variation: man," the manifesto beseeches, and more optimistically: "After the carnage we are left with the hope of a purified humanity" (Tzara 5). Dada is active simplicity, a rejection of everything that had been termed "art" in past generations (Frey 12).

Described by the Metropolitan Museum of Art as "fragile and poetic," (Geldzahler 22) the work of Hans Jean Arp is associated with the Zurich Dadaists. The poetic attribution to Arp's work was not hyperbole—the artist was also a wordsmith, winning literary acclaim from critics and scholars alike (Hancock 122). During his Dada period (ca. 1916-1920s), Arp primarily worked in the medium of collage on paper or wood relief. This particular piece is an example of prototypical Dada serendipity— the lighter yellow, white, and gray figures on the pictorial plane seem to be placed (or dropped) precariously and lend a sense of impermanence to the viewer, as if they could begin to float aimlessly to a new position the moment the viewer looses interest.

Just as his contemporary Vasily Kandinsky (catalogue 153) utilized color and form to allow art to create itself (Robbins 145), Arp also had a sense of the organic, almost biological tendency for a work to grow into meaning. This philosophy of creation is in keeping with the Dada mantra of hope: that as a species, perhaps we too will grow into a meaning beyond violence and destruction.

[Veronica Smith, *Class of 2012*]

190

Les Mille et une nuits **(The Thousand and One Nights)**, 1950
Henri Matisse (French 1869–1954)
Color lithograph, 30.6 x 81.0 cm., 12-1/16 x 31-7/8" image
Gift in Honor of Dr. and Mrs. Thomas William Carter through Drs. Gary and Catherine Goebel, Augustana College Art Collection, 2008.21 © 2011 Succession H. Matisse/Artists Rights Society (ARS), New York

As the leader of the *Fauves*, French Expressionists, Matisse always demonstrated a remarkable feel for color and pattern, often tinged with sensitivity toward exoticism. This piece is a brilliant mix of vibrant colors, abstract shapes and brash lines. During his recuperation from serious surgery, Matisse fashioned brilliance of necessity and invented a new art form, the *cut-out*, rooted in a pair of scissors and painted paper.

In June of 1950, Matisse commenced work on a large, twelve-foot panel inspired by the *Arabian Nights*. This series of stories, originally told in Arabic, began to be collected around 1000 CE and was traditionally said to have been brought together by protagonist *Scheherazade*. Scheherazade's life was threatened by her new husband, the once cuckolded King Shahryar, who planned to kill all his future wives in the night while they slept. To avoid death, Scheherazade entertained the king for 1001 nights by telling him a different story each night.

Suffering from insomnia following his illness, Matisse perhaps felt a bond with Scheherazade as they both feared the uncertainty of the night. Through strategic placement of subjects, the composition tells an interesting story within its narrative. From left to right, we read a burning Persian lamp, reminiscent of Aladdin's magic lamp, releasing smoke from its spout which leads us to a dancing blue figure, perhaps a genie, as well as to the central panel which indicates the various phases from night to day.

This image is followed by the silhouette of a once burning Persian lamp, now dark and extinguished, while the oval lines and shapes of the final image evoke the morning sunrise. These separate elements within the narrative, placed in consecutive order, tell a new story: a story about the passage of night to day and the queen's relief that she has survived yet another night. The readings might also be interpreted as revealing bits and pieces derived from various Arabian tales. The center of the composition suggests a storm at sea, as in the tales of Sinbad, culminating in the entrance to a cave, like that of Ali Baba, terminating with the dawn, when Scheherazade "falls discreetly silent" (Cowart et al 169). Less is indeed more, perhaps, as one grasps intuitively for greater meaning, fragile and fugitive like the magic from Aladdin's lamp.

[Randi Higel, *Class of 2008* and
Catherine Carter Goebel, *Editor*]

191A-D

Blue Nude I-IV or ***Nu bleu I-IV***, 1952
Henri Matisse (French 1869–1954)
Series of 4 lithographs printed by Fernand Mourlot Printers and published 1958 in *Verve* magazine, 35.6 x 26.4 cm., 14 x 10-3/8" sheet; 35.7 x 26.1 cm., 14-1/16 x 10-1/4" sheet; 35.5 x 26.3 cm., 14 x 10-3/8" sheet; 35.5 x 26.4 cm., 14 x 10-3/8" sheet
Paul A. Anderson Chair in the Arts Collection Purchase, Augustana College Art Collection, 2007.6a, b; 2007.7, 2007.8.1a, b; 2007.5a, b

Although Henri Matisse never enjoyed especially good health, he was left chronically bed-ridden later in life, having survived an operation that neither he nor anyone else really expected him to survive. It was then that Matisse began working extensively in colored paper, forgoing the relatively more arduous work of producing paintings on canvas. Matisse himself failed to see any real disconnect between his previous artistic output and this new work in cut paper: he simply referred to this new activity as "painting with scissors." This unique experiment produced a series of remarkable cutouts, including these strikingly sensual, and yet oddly spiritual, *Blue Nudes*.

The severe abstraction of the *Blue Nudes* certainly shows a strong continuity with some of Matisse's earlier artistic concerns. Some of his previous work in paint aimed not to depict some particular thing: a specific woman, plant, or fruit, located in a specific time and place. The paintings seem rather to communicate the essence—or the *idea*—of the things being depicted.

The *Blue Nudes* certainly manifest that same concern. The images clearly don't depict any specific woman. They aim rather to depict femininity, and especially feminine sensuality, itself. In the original cutouts, and in these lithographs, Matisse offers a purified glimpse of female sensuality, one communicated through his own vision of it.

Those reflections obviously echo two great philosophers in the Western tradition: Plato, from ancient Athens, and Arthur Schopenhauer, from 19th-century Germany.

Plato famously argued that bodily desires provide a stumbling block to any genuine understanding of reality. He thought that appreciating the timeless essence of reality required a distancing of the intellect from the spatiotemporal cares of the body.

Schopenhauer simply extended that line of thought to the realm of art. He claimed that people could never attain genuine understanding—or lasting happiness—as long as they were obsessed by their everyday concerns, by their day-to-day desires. Thus the value of art, as Schopenhauer saw it, lies precisely in its ability to release us from the tyranny of our desires. When we properly confront great art, he thought, our desires evaporate in an appreciation of a true, timeless reality. That possibility explains how the *Blue Nudes* manage to be *both* gorgeously sensual *and* utterly anti-pornographic.

One final reference addresses the obviously spiritual nature of the *Blue Nudes*. It reports Matisse's own answer—at exactly the time he produced these cutouts—to the question whether he believed in God. "Yes," Matisse wrote, "when I am working."

[Noell Birondo, *Visiting Assistant Professor of Philosophy*]

192

Adam and Eve and the Forbidden Fruit, 1960
Marc Chagall (Russian/French 1887–1985)
Color lithograph, 35.3 x 25.6 cm., 13-15/16 x 10-1/8" sight
Lent Courtesy of Private Collection in Memory of Dr. Thomas William Carter © 2011 Artists Rights Society (ARS), New York/ADAGP, Paris

This lithograph produced by Marc Chagall is one of a series titled *Drawings for the Bible*, published in 1960 by *Verve*. Fifty signed copies of this piece were produced in addition to 6,500 unsigned copies. The importance of biblical themes for Chagall is evident in this lithograph series and from another also illustrating the Bible that was published in 1956. He often used themes associated with the Bible in his work in other media, including tapestry, mosaics, sculpture, oils and stained glass. Not without controversy, the theme of crucifixion was central in a number of his works. "Since my earliest childhood I have been captivated by the Bible. It has always seemed to me the greatest source of poetry of all time. Ever since then I have sought its reflection in life and art. The Bible is like an echo of nature, and this is the secret I have tried to convey" (Baal-Teshuva 222-223).

The depiction of *Adam and Eve and the Forbidden Fruit* illustrates this echo of nature—and of the biblical story. Unlike many readers who wish to interpret the stories of Adam and Eve as literal historical events, Chagall captures the "echo" of the story in this illustration. The intensity of the event is heightened by the bold colors typical of Chagall's work. The commonly expected motifs of the serpent and the apple (Is there really a mention of an apple in a close reading of the biblical texts?) are juxtaposed with other elements that are enigmatic—another characteristic of Chagall's style. In Chagall's story, while Eve has the central role, Adam, holding the fruit in his hand, looks out at the viewer (with a slight smile on his face?). This Adam and Eve are the stuff of dream and imagination. The world they inhabit lives in the depths of all who tell this story as their story of "origins." This story of origins, especially as the account of the loss of innocence and the wellhead of pride and disobedience of humankind, has become a central story in Western culture. The tension between this darker part of the story (told in Genesis 2–3) and the judgment by God that he "saw all that he made, and look!—it was exceedingly good" (Genesis 1:31) has informed much of the struggle in defining humanity down into the modern and post-modern period.

[Robert D. Haak, *Professor of Religion, Associate Dean and Director, Center for Community Engagement*]

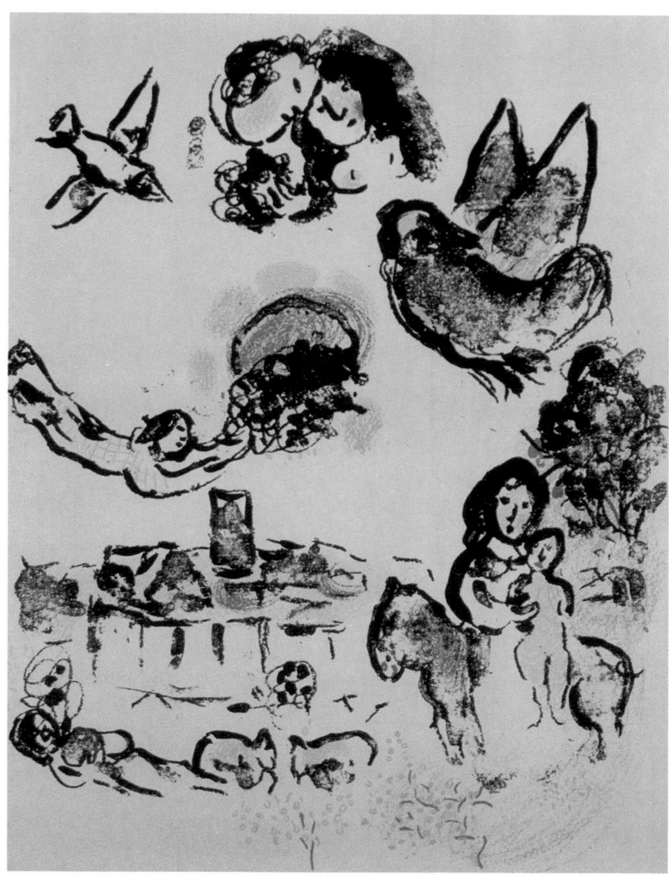

Nocturne à Vence, 1963
Marc Chagall (Russian/French 1887–1985)
Color lithograph, from *The Lithographs of Marc Chagall*, volume 2, 31.8 x 24.1 cm., 12-1/2 x 9-1/2" sight
Lent Courtesy of Private Collection in Memory of Dr. Thomas William Carter © 2011 Artists Rights Society (ARS), New York/ADAGP, Paris

Marc Chagall is widely recognized as both a pioneer of the Modernist movement and as the preeminent Jewish artist of the world. Within his long and widely respected career, we see influences of Cubism, Symbolism, Fauvism and Jewish folk culture. What is truly emblematic in his works is the use of color with its solid, bold backgrounds and painterly, poetic figures. In fact, Picasso remarked in the 1950s, "When Matisse dies, Chagall will be the only painter left who understands what colour really is" (qtd. in Wullschläger). This statement is wholly applicable to Chagall's *Nocturne à Vence* of 1963, in which we see images of a dream-like narrative translated through the juxtaposition of colors. Creations such as this with their combination of bold, primary hues and religious sentiment relate nicely to another medium Chagall was well known for—stained glass. In fact, Chagall was revered for his work on the cathedrals of Reims and Metz, the windows at the United Nations headquarters and the Jerusalem windows in Israel.

This particular image is of great interest in that it combines traditional *Chagallesque* elements (religious cues emblazoned by striking colors) with some unique insertions as well. His depiction here of a night at Vence, a town in the French Riviera, is a subjective purposeful demonstration of how he viewed the nightlife in that area. He has adopted a sense of mysticism in his translation, combining references to technology (the airplane in the top left corner), theology (an angel in flight along with a depiction of Mary and Jesus), and romance (the devoted lovers in the top center). All of these elements hint at points of direct significance or popularity in the Riviera culture through the eyes of Chagall.

In 1963, when this lithograph was produced, Chagall was residing in Côte d'Azur, a Mecca for artistic genius. Other greats such as Henri Matisse and Pablo Picasso had used the South of France as both a home and a source of inspiration. The dream-like waves of color and motion that sweep across Chagall's work produced during this period reflect the vibrancy of the region. The combination of his elegant, minimalist brushstrokes and his unprompted use of disparate imagery evokes a sense of intrigue in the viewer. One is left wondering if an actual visit to Vence could generate such a trancelike, imaginative response as Chagall has depicted in his lithograph.

[Katherine E. Goebel, *Assistant Editor*]

194

Yan Face, 1963
Pablo Ruiz y Picasso (Spanish 1881–1973)
Painted red earthenware pitcher, numbered 99/300, 25.8 x 11.3 x 15.6 cm, 10-1/8 x 4-3/4 x 6-5/8"
Paul A. Anderson Chair in the Arts Collection Purchase, Augustana College Art Collection 2001.10 © 2011 Estate of Pablo Picasso/Artists Rights Society (ARS), New York

Pablo Picasso's ceramic vase straddles Modernist and Post-Modernist modes of connoisseurship. In his seminal essay, *Art in the Age of Mechanical Reproduction* (1936), Walter Benjamin heralded that the age of reproducible images would liberate objects from their aura. *Aura* is the superstition that invests some objects as sacred. In this, Benjamin assumes that markets have the power to create appetites. Markets create the demand for the sacred. The shift isn't from presence to absence, but rather when the object gets invested. All objects bought or sold have two distinct periods: production and distribution.

One of the inventions of modernism—in the epoch sense, defined as the point Proto-Renaissance artist Giotto (Giotto di Bondone 1266/7-1337) painted perspective in a fresco, was the invention of the myth of the author. The object mimics the sense of the sacred by being the plastic manifestation of the maker's genius. An example would be when James Turner first started out doing forgeries, now these are worth more than the originals. Since Turner's intent was to make the work indistinguishable from the original, it is only the myth of his genius that creates the higher sense of value.

Once an artwork is made, it gets distributed. Manufacturing an object obliterates any sense of authorship. But manufactured objects get invested with aura through their distribution. Consider that in 2006 Rawlings manufactured over 2,000,000 baseballs annually. On September 23rd, Chris Capuano threw a ball which Barry Bonds hit out of the park, breaking Henry Aaron's record. Being innately superstitious, humans invest—this ball, which is identical to every other ball manufactured, gets invested with aura. The absurdity of this ball not being the chew toy for a collie, much less fouled off the previous inning, creates its sense of aura.

Picasso's *Yan Face* resonates with elements of both modes of connoisseurship. In the modernist sense, Picasso tantalizes the viewer with slight references to his genius. The deceptively simple images obscure two hallmarks of Picasso painting. First, Picasso flicks lines and brushstrokes with supreme confidence. The quick gestures are gracefully exact. Picasso welds his brush like a fencer. By using black slip on red earthenware, Picasso references Greek red vessel ceramics. Again, many of the artist's works contain erudite references. The face even has a few cubist elements, where profile and straight on depictions merge. On the other hand, the form itself is almost *kitsch*. There are, or at least were, thousands of exact duplications of this form. Only by coincident does this work get culled from the pile.

Yan Face appeals to both the Modernist and Post-Modernist sense of connoisseurship. Benjamin asserted that the Market created the appetite among humans to distinguish some objects as sacred. Picasso proved this appetite is far more innate than construction.

[Anthony Merino, *Class of 1988*]

Helmet Head, 1963
Henry Moore (British 1898–1986)
Bronze with green patina, gold-surface bronze, edition of 6, 47.6 x 28.7 x 36.2 cm., 18-3/4 x 11-5/16 x 14-1/4" without base
Gift of Alex Adelman and Robert Ubillus, Augustana College Art Collection, 2006.42
Reproduced by permission of The Henry Moore Foundation

Henry Moore helped usher in modernist sculpture. He was born in 1898, allowing him to fully witness twentieth-century effects of globalization and war on western art before his death in 1986. After discovering non-western sculpture in the late 1920s, the famous British sculptor veered away from traditional sculpting practices. *Helmet Head* (1963) elegantly illustrates why Moore was at the forefront of modernism. It is one of six editions in a series that explores concepts of layers of exposure and protection.

Moore created abstracted human forms, often focusing on women with their children. *Helmet Head* is made of bronze with green patina and gold surface bronze. Moore described his inspiration for the series: "I think it may be the interest I had early on in armour, in places like the Victoria and Albert Museum where one used to wander round as a student in the lunch hours. And it may be that I remembered reading stories that impressed me and Wyndham Lewis talking about the shell of lobster covering the soft flesh inside. This became an established idea with me—that of an outer protection to an inner form, and it may have something to do with the mother and child idea; that is where there is the relation of the big thing to the little thing, and the protection idea. The helmet is a kind of protection thing, too, and it became a recording of things inside other things. The mystery of *semi-obscurity* where one can only half distinguish something. In the helmet you do not quite know what is inside" (Moore *Christian Science Monitor,* quoted on the Henry Moore Foundation Website).

These were not the first works in which Moore explored the idea of an inner and outer form. When examining his sculptures and drawings, this concept can be traced to 1940, but not explored again until 1948-50. In 1950, he created his first series of *Helmet Heads* which resemble armor-like shapes, "evoking memories of the Second World War, in which soldiers and civilians alike used protective helmets and masks...as the outbreak of hostilities in Korea threatened to escalate into a wider international conflict and may reflect Moore's anxieties over the threat of nuclear war" (Tate Modern Website). The issue of protection in times of war complements his earlier theme of mothers protecting their children. In the 1960s, Moore returned to the *Helmet Head* series with rounder, more organic forms such as Augustana's example, which reward the curious viewer, upon closer examination, with a glimpse of the object within.

[Julianne Medel, *Class of 2009*]

196

Homage to the Square: Full, from **Ten Works** portfolio, 1962
Josef Albers (German-American 1888–1976)
Screenprint, 28.0 x 28.0 cm., 11 x 11" image
Gift of Josef and Anni Albers Foundation in Memory of James Konrad, Augustana College Art Collection, 2011.10

In teaching students about color theory, two lessons are indispensible: the nineteenth-century color wheel of chemist Michel-Eugène Chevreul and the *Homage to the Square* series by artist Josef Albers. In the former, the physics of light is delineated as a tool to teach component colors created through the breakdown of light. Chevreul's theories were essential to nineteenth-century art, particularly evident in the colorful works of French Impressionism and Post-Impressionism. Albers continued such experimentation in color theory through his *Homage* series. Inspired by Post-Impressionist, Paul Cézanne and further allied with the theories of contemporary, Piet Mondrian, Albers began this series in 1950 and continued exploring such "interaction of color" for twenty-six years. He aimed for "visual experience rather than psychological revelation or historical reference: the aspects of color and line and form, as well as of nature and man-made objects, that are universal and valid in any place and at any time" (Weber, Albers Prints).

Albers' design was based in the fundamental order of architecture and design, rooted in his early teaching in the Bauhaus school in Germany. His *Homage to the Square* series was the "ultimate achievement of his life" (Weber 7). Albers described these works in painting and prints, as "'platters to serve color.' They are hymns to the infinite possibilities, both physical and spiritual, of hue and light" (Weber 7). The series is based on a format of nesting squares, as illustrated in *Homage to the Square: Full.* These are weighted toward the bottom while centered left and right. There is order yet complexity as "the incremental distances underneath the central squares are doubled to left and right of them and trebled above" (Weber 8).

The conception upon first glance may appear deceptively simple. Yet there is a sort of *magic* that occurs that denies a singular interpretation. Albers stated: "In action, we see the colors as being in front of or behind one another, over or under one another, as covering one or more colors entirely or in part. They give the illusion of being transparent or translucent and tend to move up or down" (Weber 8). Take time to focus only on the center square in order to visually absorb the color. You will be rewarded with a transformative experience. "The interaction of colors is multifarious; perfectly flat areas appear shaded; the squares grow darker near one boundary and lighter near another. Nothing is as it seems" (Weber 8). Albers humbly concluded: "How far this has been successful is for others to decide" (Weber 9). As art and art history professors, and their students, have acknowledged for over half a century, and as viewers may discern, Albers' success is timeless.

[James Konrad, *Adjunct Professor of Art*
and Catherine Carter Goebel, *Editor*]

Composition with Semicircular Shapes, ca. 1970
Sonia Delaunay (French 1885–1979)
Color aquatint, artist's proof, 49.1 x 39.6 cm., 19-1/4 x 15-1/2" image
Paul A. Anderson Chair in the Arts Collection Purchase, Augustana College Art Collection, 2001.11

Sonia Delaunay, along with her esteemed husband Robert Delaunay, helped to found the movement of *Orphism*. This faction of artists largely focused on the depiction and relation of bold colors and shapes within a composition. Orphism simultaneously moved away from a noticeable aim of perspective and naturalism, seeking instead compositions that speak through a language of prismatic hue and delineated swerves of paint. The subject matter is devoid of real figures, opting instead for anthropomorphic, and sometimes even geometric, shapes that allow viewers to approach the overall image any way their eye is compelled.

The artists strove for an optical appeal from a dialect of color that is universal. In fact, Delaunay's line of work extended to textile and stage set designs due to its ability to captivate the eye. There is no objective truth in the work and there is no regional focus within the composition. While speaking at the Sorbonne in 1927, Delaunay stated, "If there are geometric forms, it is because these simple and manageable elements have appeared suitable for the distribution of colors whose relations constitute the real object of our search, but these geometric forms do not characterize our art" (Cohen 207). More broadly, there is no single intention—rather, the viewer is to interpret the arrangement of form and function as he or she sees best, particularly in regards to the way the colors interact with each other.

The juxtaposition of prisms within her works recalls Michel Eugène Chevreul's study of the color wheel along with the *Pointillist* movement, made famous by such artists as Georges Seurat and Paul Signac. In *Composition with Semicircular Shapes* (1970), we see a composition that has seemingly been split into four quadrants by intersecting curvilinear lines. Delaunay employed a wide range of color, from light grays to harsh blacks, expressing her interest in color range. The consecutive, randomized strokes of color are both optically enticing and meaningfully subjective. One becomes lost traveling from luminescent swerve to swerve, the result of which is an absorbing, self-activating animation of the print. Delaunay enjoyed a great deal of success during her lifetime, in the latter portion even being commissioned to complete designs for costumes, furniture, automobile exteriors and murals. In fact, Italian modern painter Alberto Magnelli told her in the early 1960s "she and Braque were the only living painters to have been shown at the Louvre," (qtd. in Baron and Damase 170) an honor typically reserved for those artists within the traditional art historical canon.

[Katherine E. Goebel, *Assistant Editor*]

198A&B

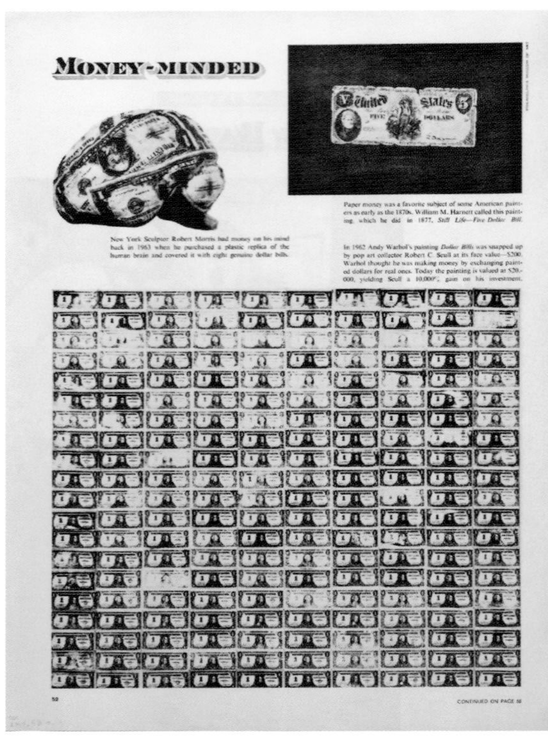

MONEY-MINDED

New York Sculptor Robert Morris had money on his mind back in 1963 when he purchased a plastic replica of the human brain and covered it with eight genuine dollar bills.

Paper money was a favorite subject of some American painters as early as the 1870s. William M. Harnett called this painting, which he did in 1877, *Still Life—Five Dollar Bill.*

In 1962 Andy Warhol's painting *Dollar Bills* was snapped up by pop art collector Robert C. Scull at its face value—$200. Warhol thought he was making money by exchanging painted dollars for real ones. Today the painting is valued at $20,000, yielding Scull a 10,000% gain on his investment.

Money-Minded and **Art You Can Bank On**, 1969
Related to Andy Warhol (American 1928–1987)
Printed magazine page, published in *Life* magazine, 19 September 1969, p. 52, 34.6 x 26.0 cm., 13-5/8 x 10-5/16" sheet
Purchase through Gift of Paul and Marty Pearson, Augustana College Art Collection, SDC2010.48.a, b © 2011 Artists Rights Society (ARS), New York

Sotheby's Contemporary Art Evening Auction New York 11 November 2009, 2009
Related to Andy Warhol (American 1928–1987)
Printed auction catalogue, 27.0 x 21.0 x 1.0 cm., 10-5/8 x 8-1/4 x 1/2"
Purchase through Gift of Paul and Marty Pearson, Augustana College Art Collection, SDC SDC2010.47.a, b

When Andy Warhol's *200 One Dollar Bills* came up for auction at Sotheby's in November 2009, the painting sold for $43.8 million. If you wonder what is going on here, you are asking the signature question of art criticism.

The story goes that when an art dealer advised Warhol to paint what he liked best, the answer was, "Money." Warhol wasn't crass, just honest. The average person expends $2.2 million in a lifetime. That's a lot of bills. But you can look at something every day and never see it. Case in point: can you name the creature peeking out from the "1" in the upper-right corner of a dollar bill? (Hint: look closely.) In art as in life, seeing is the first step to understanding.

200 One Dollar Bills was one in a series of "Dollar Bill" paintings Warhol created in March/April 1962. Some featured single bills; others displayed group formats like the *Campbell's Soup Can* paintings completed earlier that year. New with this series was Warhol's use of a silkscreening process which made the serial images more exactly the same, thereby suggesting the fabulous plenitude of American consumer society but also themes of uniformity, monotony, and impersonality.

When *200 One Dollar Bills* was first exhibited, people wondered, "Is this art?" A more difficult question follows: what is money?

Try this: take a dollar bill and tear it in half. If you are like most people you'll have trouble bringing yourself to do this. A dollar is just rag paper, yet somehow it resists annihilation. Knowing what money is made of does not get at what money *is.*

Deeply religious, Warhol attended Catholic mass nearly every day. In church he heard Jesus warn that Mammon is a jealous god demanding complete allegiance. That money has a demonic power makes sense to people, on Sundays. Other days of the week, Americans have favored the more pragmatic view that money is a swell friend indeed.

Mostly, people take money for granted. Warhol's *200 One Dollar Bills* reminds us that the existential questions surrounding money are ever with us, if we will but look at money to see it for what it is.

[Lendol Calder, *Professor of History*]

199A&B

Diane von Furstenberg, 1984
Andy Warhol (American 1928–1987, né Andrew Warhola)
Polacolor ER, 9.5 x 7.3 cm., 3-3/4 x 2-7/8" image
Gift of the Andy Warhol Foundation, Augustana College Art Collection, 2008.12.12 © 2011 Artists Rights Society (ARS), New York

Diana Ross: Silk Electric, 1982
Andy Warhol (American 1928–1987, né Andrew Warhola)
Album cover, transfer lithograph (RCA release), 31.3 x 31.5 cm., 12-5-16 x 12-3/8"
Paul A. Anderson Chair in the Arts Collection Purchase, Augustana College Art Collection, SDC2010.28 © 2011 Artists Rights Society (ARS), New York

Pop icon Andy Warhol worked in various media throughout his career, but by the early 1960s, photography became a major impetus for his creative energy. In 1970, Warhol purchased a Polaroid *Big Shot* camera. What other technology was better suited to the tastes of Warhol than the Polaroid camera? Warhol reveled in mass-produced art and was fascinated by the instant, as well as instantly disposable, notion of celebrity. As he moved through the New York art and club scenes, Warhol always had his camera in hand in order to document the world of glamour and celebrity, and the ever-changing cast of characters with whom he mingled. The Polaroid camera allowed him to capture, with his characteristic voracity, everyone from the famous, such as Muhammed Ali, Georgia O'Keefe and, as seen here, *Diane von Furstenberg* (199A), to the completely anonymous everyday pedestrian. Such snapshots also enabled him to circumvent copyright infringement challenges inherent in his commercial images. Most of Warhol's Polaroids were used as studies for eventual silk-screen portraits and were never formally exhibited during his lifetime.

In 1982, Warhol designed the cover for Diana Ross' music album, *Silk Electric* (199B). The design was based on a previous Polaroid print taken by Warhol of Ross at his *Factory* studio. The look as a whole should elicit *déjà vu* for the viewer in relation to the adjacent Warhol Polaroid piece. The hair, make-up, and over the shoulder pose closely resemble Warhol's Polaroid portrait of *Diane von Furstenberg* (199A). Warhol would often cover his subjects' faces in white *kubuki* makeup and finish the look with intense red lips and dark eyes. By doing this his celebrities are stripped of their individuality. They become commercialized and easily reproduced along the lines of Warhol's famous *200 Campbell's Soup Cans* and other familiar *popular* consumption goods. By comparing the elements of his Polaroid portrait with this stylized translation into lithography, one can discern the duality of commercial realism and abstraction in the transformation of a person into a commodity. This is possibly a comment from Warhol on the nature and idea of celebrity.

[Emily Cox, *Class of 2011*]

200 

Crak!, 1963–64
Roy Lichtenstein (American b. 1923)
Offset color lithograph on white wove paper, 62/300, published by Leo Castelli Gallery, New York, 47.2 x 68.7 cm., 18-9/16 x 27-1/16" image
Paul A. Anderson Chair in the Arts Collection Purchase, Augustana College Art Collection, 2000.59 © Estate of Roy Lichtenstein, 2011

In *CRAK!*, Roy Lichtenstein illustrated the commercial themes of Pop Art and culture while exploring his graphic themes of war, violence and women. At the same time, he demonstrated a distinctive style and visual appeal. Lichtenstein, perhaps most associated with the comic strip style, took the low-art of the comic and elevated it to a form of *high-art* that was and remains in great demand, hanging in museums and galleries world-wide.

An initial viewing of *CRAK!*—with its red flare bursting forth from the rifle, disconcertingly piercing our picture plane with obvious violence—begs the question: "At whom is this French woman firing her gun?" Is she a Resistance fighter shooting at the enemy? Is this meant to be an anti-war statement or an argument for the "Good War" conception of World War II, stemming from Lichtenstein's own experience serving in the army in Europe during World War II? At a yet deeper level, could the violence be aimed directly at the state of art itself? While stylistically this French woman may be seen as merely an object with her stylish beret, arched brow and long lashes, it is interesting to note that she does not assume the role of victim as we find with many of Lichtenstein's other cartoon women (Waldman 113-127). Rather, she is in a position of dominance and assertion and takes on a heroine-like role, though admittedly in cartoon form.

With Lichtenstein, it is critical to understand not only *what* is printed and painted but how it was executed. The simplicity of color and line is so smooth, un-painterly and commercial in appearance, that the final result gives no hint of the skill required to produce it, almost appearing to be a reproduction even when original. Here in *CRAK!* we see the prominence of white and black punctuated with an acidic yellow and a deep red. The contours imitating printed ink are bold and deep, emphasizing the compositional flatness existing on a single plane. The cropped frame focuses and intensifies the drama and immediacy unfolding before us, giving the composition a snapshot-like effect.

[Beth Repay Swanson, *Class of 1987*]

201

Skid Row, 1969
Robert Indiana (American b. 1928, né Robert Clark)
Color lithograph, 21.1 x 21.2 cm., 8-5/16 x 8-3/8" image
Paul A. Anderson Chair in the Arts Collection Purchase and Gift of Geoff Heeney, Apollo Fine Art, Augustana College Art Collection, 2008.10.1 © 2011 Artists Rights Society (ARS), New York

The spectacle of Robert Indiana's work lies within its ability to be simplistic and optically dazzling at the same time. As a member of the Pop art movement in New York in the 1950s, Indiana worked to construct images that were bold and iconic, often employing short words or symbols to convey great meaning to the masses. His most famous piece, *LOVE* of 1964, made a great presence in the United States, and continues to stand as a timeless image.

This lithograph is particularly interesting because it portrays the artist himself in a very modern way. He has captured his character by juxtaposing color, words and symbols in a sort of abstracted, geometric pattern that persuades viewers to piece together the character puzzle before them. We see the first three letters of his last name placed diagonally in the center of the composition, declaring the space as his own. Below that we find the year it was produced and the title of the piece, *Skid Row.* The work reflects a sort of urban motif, perhaps one inspired by street signs, subway stops or taxi cab stencils.

At first glance, we feel as though the overall image is carefully sliced into sections, creating a sense of symmetry. However, upon closer inspection, a great deal of incongruity and odd placement lies amidst a sea of haltingly brazen hues. Our first instinct, perhaps, is to feel cautioned or stopped due to the color combination. But, ironically, it's a piece that is instead supposed to draw us in further, calling on our intuition to interpret the intricacies. We are left wondering how the clues fit together. How may the yellow, black and white relate to a certain aspect of Robert Indiana's persona? What is the significance of "tiger" and the number "71?"

Like the other artists involved with the Pop movement, there is an obvious commentary on commercialism present in the piece—perhaps in this particular instance one of the over-produced signs throughout a city in which no one takes an individual interest. However, this sign is of interest, for no detail goes without significance. Swirls of three simple colors arranged in a rigid, yet randomized fashion thus represent a man, a mentality and a larger artistic movement.

[Katherine E. Goebel, *Assistant Editor*]

202

Sorcerer's Village, 1972
Romare Bearden (American 1914–1988)
Color screenprint, 41.5 x 49.8 cm., 16-3/8 x 19-5/8" image
Paul A. Anderson Chair in the Arts Collection Purchase, Augustana College Art Collection, 2001.26 © Romare Bearden Foundation/Licensed by VAGA, New York, NY

Romare Bearden is notable as one of the most successful modern African-American artists of all time. Although he is best known for his bold collages, Bearden spent his artistic career in constant progress, attempting to create distinctive and purposeful art along the way. Bearden believed that artists should visually order the chaos of the world (Schwartzman 197). His main concern for his art was that its space, aesthetics and color all worked together. *Sorcerer's Village* is a prime example of Bearden's *signature* style. In the fashion of collage, he created this serigraph by means of bold color and forms reminiscent of Piet Mondrian's works with their "interlocking rectangular relationships" (Greene 4). Color was an important theme within his work, with gray employed in order to "move from one thing to another, to hold the bright colors in a certain balance" (Schwartzman 196).

Although most of the bold colors within the piece are primary, Bearden also employed secondary colors for effect, making them appear more important. For example, the face of the figure that may be the sorcerer has yellow tinges but is predominantly purple. Faces lacking purple are no less important, yet effectively contrast with those that do. At the same time, the figure in the lower left corner has no face at all, perhaps causing some discomfort for the viewer. Another in the upper right corner has a red face, suggestive of aggression (the color red is usually a dominant color), yet this figure appears non-threatening. Heavily cropped, it appears fearful or wanting, seemingly reaching for another. Finally, the person in the window looks completely self-involved. And perhaps this is a good element, since like the sorcerer, if he did look directly at the audience, the result could be frightening. Every figure in this piece is individually intriguing as well as challenging in its relation to the others. *Sorcerer's Village* is a wonderful example of the careful and intelligent work of Romare Bearden, and while he left it up to each observer to decide what his work depicted, he also furnished clues as to how to relate to each piece.

[Mikeda Cannon, *Class of 2007*]

203A&B

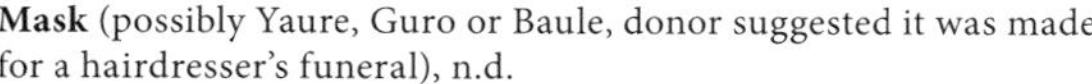

Mask (possibly Yaure, Guro or Baule, donor suggested it was made for a hairdresser's funeral), n.d.
Artist unknown, Ivory Coast, Africa
Carved, painted wood, 48.5 x 16.5 x 9.2 cm., 19-1/4 x 6-5/8 x 3-1/2"
Gift of Betty L. Beer Franklin, Augustana College Art Collection, 2004.18.2

Figural Mask, (possibly Yaure, Guro or Baule) n.d.
Artist unknown, Ivory Coast, Africa
Carved wood, 45.0 x 16.5 x 12.0 cm., 17-3/4 x 6-1/2 x 4-3/4"
Paul A. Anderson Chair in the Arts Collection Purchase, Augustana College Art Collection, 2004.22

Little is known about these two masks in terms of their makers and dates of origin. The *hairdresser's* mask (203A) has been identified as a creation of the Yaure from central Ivory Coast, but the ethnic group that created the figural mask (203B) is uncertain. Stylistic features suggest that it too stems from the Ivory Coast; it may also be Yaure, but could derive from the Guro to the west or the Baule, the Yaure's eastern neighbors. While the three cultures possess their own languages and local traditions, they have never been isolated groups; due to their geographic proximity, over time they adapted features of each other's politics, religion, and art (Bacquart 40-41; Visona 194; Vogel 35 and 288). The two masks bear the refined formal features common to the region. While the Yaure mask is much more geometric than the figural one, both faces are pensive and idealized, with small, closed mouths and semicircular, downcast eyes to signify the importance of maintaining secrets. The oval-shaped faces each have a broad forehead, perhaps a sign of intellectual strength. The smooth and lustrous surfaces intimate clean and healthy skin. Also typical are the triangulated decoration along the cheeks and the elaborate coiffures parted on both sides, topped by some kind of ornament—on these two masks, a comb-like structure and a female figure (Bacquart 41; Visona 189; Vogel 141). Kneeling females signify fertility in many African cultures, and thus could mean something similar in this context. The Yaure mask was purportedly created for the funeral of a hairdresser, which might explain the comb-like projection at the top; however, these "horns" appear on a number of masks, and their exact significance, if any, remains unknown (Bacquart 42; Vogel 162).

For most Africans, the value of art lies not in its status as a completed "thing," but in what it does: communicating with the spirits, marking life's transitions, and defining cultural principles (Cole 34-41; 88). A mask is part of a larger spectacle that involves costume, music, dancing, and audience involvement. Although rooted in longstanding local traditions, African art must act. Meaning is thus rarely fixed or static, a fact that is further impacted by ever increasing cross-cultural exchanges, which these two masks aptly demonstrate.

[Margaret Morse, *Assistant Professor of Art History*]

204

Haitian Market, ca. 1986
Alexis Patrick (Haitian active 1986)
Oil or acrylic on canvas, 31.6 x 40.8 cm., 12-1/2 x 16"
Lent Courtesy of Private Collection in Memory of Dr. Thomas William Carter

Alexis Patrick painted a traditional aspect of life in Haiti—a Haitian market, which is the main venue of commerce. According to many Haitians, the market place is Haiti's answer to *one stop shopping*. The origins of Haitian markets may have been either French or West Africa and existed as early as 1803. These markets may be located in a short distance or could be as far as 20 miles away from the village. The center of a town acts as a major *entrepôt* which is linked through bus routes depending on seasons.

The market is the heart of the economic life of the peasants. While agriculture is a primarily male occupation, the marketing of the produces remains in the hands of the women. Most peasant women have experience of going to the market to sell or buy vegetables and other necessities and so they nearly always can say that they are daughters of traders (Underwood 5). James G. Leyburn, in his book *The Haitian People*, writes "One of the characteristic sights of Haiti is the seemingly endless procession of women coming down from the hills trudging, or rather swinging majestically along, with a great load on the head, or riding on the haunches of a tiny donkey loaded with bulging panniers" (196).

The women spend all day in the market and often they spend the night too in order to finish selling or buying things. Most often they are accompanied by small children. The market also acts as the social gathering for the women where they frequently get "their fill of companionable gossip" (Leyburn 197). Amid the bustle, the gossip and "the endless buzz of tongues" this becomes "distinctly ladies' day" (Underwood 12). Many think that since the family structure of the peasants is matriarchal in some ways, it is natural that the women should attend to the business dealings of the market place. However, Haitian women "keep the proceeds of their own economic activities" (Bellegarde-Smith 28) and often use it to open small businesses after taking care of the household financial needs. This shows their entrepreneurial spirit.

The autonomy and economic importance of the Haitian peasant women contrast sharply with the lives of élite women. Although the Haitian economy is in a shambles, people have been impressed with the vigor, the color and the socio-economic importance of the local markets as the painting communicates. Though this is a painting of 1986, one can envision the powerful Haitian spirit by imagining women going to the market after the 2010 earthquake with this approach: *Sélavi* (That is life).

[Umme Al-Wazedi, *Assistant Professor of English*]

205

Machu Picchu Farmers, ca. 2009
María Uyauri (Peruvian 1955-),
NOVICA in Association with National Geographic
Cotton, acrylic and other fibers; wooden toothpicks; wall hanging, 84.6 x 98.0 x 4.0 cm., 33-1/4 x 38-5/8 x 1-1/2"
Paul A. Anderson Chair in the Arts Collection Purchase, Augustana College Art Collection, 2010.8

Artist María Uyauri consciously blends past and present in this tapestry. She celebrates key aspects of indigenous life in the Andes: harvesting the staples of maize and potatoes from terraced fields, the use of llamas and alpacas as pack animals as well as sources of wool and meat, and the weaving of colorful fabrics. The terraces where these men and women work have been farmed since the time of the Inca civilization (1200s-1500s). Doña Uyauri celebrates that civilization and its continued heritage by placing her farmers in the shadow of Machu Picchu, a city built at the behest of Inca imperial authorities. The focal point of the background is a mountain soaring more than 2700 meters high; historians believe that Huayna Picchu once housed Incan high priests. Although forever known to locals, Machu Picchu received international attention only in the first decades of the 1900s, when U.S. historian Hiram Bingham "discovered" it. To this day, conflicts continue between the Peruvian government and Yale University, where Dr. Bingham worked, regarding artifacts that Dr. Bingham and his researchers removed from the site. Machu Picchu has been designated a Peruvian Historical Sanctuary and a UNESCO World Heritage Site.

A harder to see, yet absolutely crucial part of this piece is the context of genre. *Machu Picchu Farmers* is part of the *arpillera* tradition, which first gained international recognition during the 1970s. At that time, women in Chile began gathering in small groups and, using rags and old clothing, created fabric appliqué scenes that depicted the hardships of life under the military dictatorship headed by General Augusto Pinochet Ugarte (1973-1990). They called these pieces *arpilleras*, or burlaps, for the castoff fabric sacks used as the backing. Their creators became known as *arpilleristas*; they comprised a social movement that defied the dictatorship in many ways: by simply gathering together in groups (which the military had criminalized); by selling their artwork to help provide for their families during difficult economic times (which directly countered the gendered norms of the regime); and by sending messages to international observers about the disappearances, torture, and assassinations occurring in Chile. (See Augustana's collection of Chilean *arpilleras* for a sampling of such messages.)

Women in other countries of Latin America soon adopted the *arpillera* as both a method of protest against violence and repression, and as a means of income. Although the creator of this tapestry no doubt lived through the violence associated with Peru's Sendero Luminoso (Shining Path) insurgency (1980s-early 1990s) and Alberto Fujimori's repressive rule (1990-2000), this particular piece was not necessarily a response to those experiences or a call for international solidarity. Instead, the rather romantic scene of *Machu Picchu Farmers*, created circa 2009, was probably intended as a means to earn some money. Doña Uyauri was born in Lima in 1955, likely to a family of limited economic means. As a member of a women's support group, she learned the craft and business of *arpilleras*. Today, she is an independent artisan; with help from her husband and son, she creates pieces with happy themes including festivals, harvests, weddings, and markets.

[Molly Todd, *Assistant Professor of History*]

206

Confrontations, 1986
Victoria Mamnguqsualuk (b. 1930) and Magdalene (1931-1999) Ukpatiku (Inuit, Baker Lake, Canada)
Stonecut and stencil, ed. 7/45, 60.2 x 85.6 cm., 23-3/4 x 33-3/4" image
Gift of Kathy Bulucos Memorial Collection to Augustana College, 2010.61.29

Confrontations was created in 1986 by two Inuit artists, Victoria Mamnguqsualuk and Magdalene Ukpatiku. The composition depicts two Inuits being attacked, while on a hunting expedition, by bears, snake-lizards, and a spirit form that combines human, snake/lizard, and wolf characteristics. Inuit culture, very much like the cultures of indigenous peoples across the planet, is immersed directly within Nature, not apart from it. Hunting scenes, as depicted in *Confrontations*, are rendered through a myriad of artistic media by the Inuit people because they strike at the heart of Inuit culture: the inexplicable, yet absolutely essential, confrontations of humans and animals in the wild.

Within Inuit culture, it is well known that sometimes the hunters can become the hunted (as evidenced by *Confrontations*). Whether for sustenance, clothing, tools, or trading purposes, the Inuit culture is dependent for its survival upon the wild fauna of Northwestern Canada and the Arctic region. Either out of respect for Nature, or fear of it, renditions of the hunt and animals are frequently seen in Inuit art.

This collaborative piece originates from the Inuit community of Baker Lake, which is located near Canada's geographic center in the Northwest Territories. To best appreciate Inuit works such as *Confrontations*, it is essential to have an understanding of the environments from which these works originate. According to the Government of the Northwest Territories website: "[The Northwest Territories] is 1.17 million square kilometers of mountains, forests and tundra threaded by wild, clean rivers feeding thousands of pristine lakes...Nature is in balance here. You can view rare wildlife species, from white wolves to white whales...herds of bison, prowling bears, moose and caribou by the thousands" ("Explore").

Confrontations is an ideal piece to illustrate the artistic techniques employed by Inuit printmakers from the Baker Lake community. Vigorous activity, multiple characters, and flattened two-dimensional perspectives are used to depict Inuit myths and lore, rather than actual events. The Inuit artist uses the mundane (the hunt) to express the sacred (the duality of life and death).

Mamnguqsualuk and Ukpatiku worked on many other prints together in various co-operative studios in Baker Lake, such as *Catching The Fish Mother*, which depicts two Inuits catching anthropomorphized fish. These studios offered local artists the opportunity to share ideas, teach techniques, procure supplies, and ultimately market and sell their wares all across the world. The importance of printmaking for the Inuit people of Baker Lake cannot be overstated. Kyra Vladykov Fisher summarizes this point: "The history of printmaking in Baker Lake is also the history of a people going towards self-sufficiency and nationhood: 'a culture employing art unconsciously for identity while moving inevitably into the unknown'" (Fisher 192).

[Joshua Schipp, *Class of 2009*]

Symbolic Imanpa Abstract, ca. 1995
Jackie Peaqcc (Imanpa Community of Mt. Ebenezer, N.T., Australia)
Oil on canvas. 24.7 x 38.3 cm., 9-3/4 x 15-1/16" image
Paul A. Anderson Chair in the Arts Collection Purchase, Augustana College Art Collection, 2010.15

The Aboriginal peoples of Australia have been subjected to dramatic transformations and hardship over the last century, and yet they have tried tenaciously to preserve their indigenous cultures. This painting is by Jackie Pearce, an Aboriginal woman from the community of Imanpa in the Northern Territory of Australia, who is descended from a long line of well-known Aboriginal artists. Sue Verlander, who runs the Imanpa Arts organization, tells us that Jackie Pearce and her two sisters were taught to paint at an early age by their mother, Emma Inkamala.

Many aspects of the piece are very traditional, and yet it was created using Western materials—acrylic paints on canvas, placing the piece firmly in the current era following the changes brought by Western society. The use of tiny dots to create patterns and figures, reminiscent of French Post-Impressionist *Pointillism*, is probably the most recognizable feature of traditional Aboriginal aesthetics. Verlander informs us that the images and symbolism tell a very traditional story, too. "The painting," she wrote, "is a bush-tucker dreaming story where a man and woman are out in the desert in search for food. Instead of looking for plants this couple wants to hunt the *goanna* [lizard], and search for eggs of the *kuniya* (python snake) as well as the goanna's eggs. We see [them] protecting their eggs from the hunters."

Bush-tucker is a descriptive term for wild foods taken directly from the environment. In the past, it was vitally important to teach children how to survive by hunting and gathering, and in an oral culture without writing, education came in the form of storytelling and visual art. Originally, these educational drawings would have been made in the sand, but today they are painted with more permanent materials and are sold to outside art collectors. Imagery in Aboriginal art is either abstract or figurative, and this piece includes both. The python and the goanna lizard are clearly figurative, while the man and the woman are represented in abstract by the U-shapes inside the circles. The U-shapes represent people in Aboriginal art because it is the shape that remains in the sand after a person has been sitting. We can also see that the man and the woman have brought their hunting and gathering tools with them—spears, digging sticks, and boomerangs among other things.

As this painting vividly illustrates, traditional Aboriginal culture has, thankfully, not been swept away by the tide of Westernization.

[Adam Kaul, *Associate Professor of Anthropology*]

208

Spring Rain, ca. 1992
Toshiko Takaezu (American b. 1922)
Ceramic sphere, 50.8 x 56.2 x 55.7 cm., 20-1/8 x 22-1/8 x 21-7/8"
Gift of Mrs. Jean F.P.W. Walgren, Augustana College Art Collection, 1993.37

Toshiko Takaezu was born of Japanese immigrants on the Hawaiian Islands in 1922. She studied ceramics, design and weaving at the University of Hawaii, after which she enrolled in Cranbrook Academy of Art in Michigan. Takaezu later remarked of her artistic education, "Hawaii was where I learned technique; Cranbrook was where I found myself" (Sewell). At Cranbrook, Takaezu was introduced to one of her most influential mentors, the Flemish ceramicist Maja Grotell. Grotell was known for her large, sturdy forms created on the wheel. After graduating, Takaezu adopted many similarities to Grotell. She began her career making modest functional vessels, and gradually evolved into closed forms of the 1960s, which led to the development of Moon pots (large spheres) and increasingly bigger closed forms, sometimes as large as standing 6ft tall. While her forms change in shape and size they carry her signature of painterliness in the poured and brushed glazes.

Takaezu's major formal development of the late 1950s involved closing form, creating an uninterrupted surface to develop her glazing and color palette (Koplos). Her color does not appear as a solid, but as an atmosphere. It suggests landscape and evokes space. She uses both layering and a dispersal of misty color to create illusionary dimension. The glazing technique is a full body experience and evokes the action painters of her childhood. She combines movements of controlled dripping, splashing, pouring, dipping, and brushwork to create representational form (Strickland). In the 1960s, she also began inserting into the closed forms a paper-wrapped wad of clay that after firing would make a subtle sound when the pot was moved. This noise incorporates the sense of hearing, while the visual display involves the sense of sight.

Takaezu's *Spring Rain* (ca. 1992) is one of her *moon* forms. She developed this form in the late 1960s. These are constructed pieces made of joined hemispheres. The lower hemisphere evokes water, while the upper hemisphere appears to depict land and air. Takaezu encompasses the elegiac qualities of nature in her forms. Her color range is subdued and includes splotches and drips. This specific moon form suggests a calm landscape seemingly disturbed by the arching drops of spring rain. Takaezu stated her goal for such work, "To me an artist is someone quite special. You are not an artist simply because you paint or sculpt or make pots that cannot be used. An artist is a poet in his or her own medium. And when an artist produces a good piece, that work has mystery, an unsaid quality; it is alive" (Sewell).

[Victoria Richmond, *Class of 2011*]

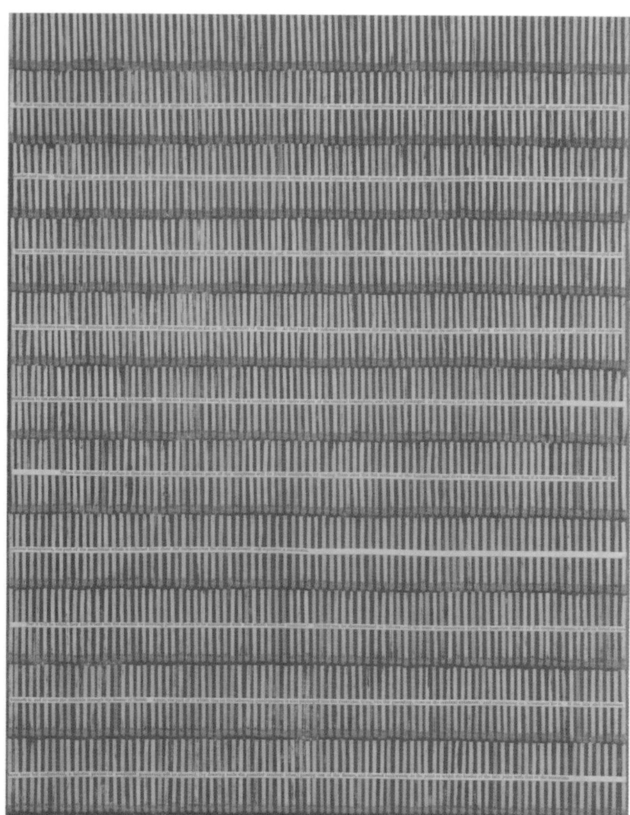

Untitled, 1991
David Moreno (American b. 1957)
Matchsticks, silk cloth, commercially-printed text, tempera, collage on canvas, 61.2 x 45.7 cm., 24 x 18"
Gift of Paul A. Anderson Estate, Augustana College Art Collection, 2005.11 © The Artist, courtesy of the artist and Feature Inc., New York

Paul Andrew Anderson graduated from Augustana College in 1971 with a double major in Business Administration and Economics, earning an MS degree in Agricultural Economics from Purdue University in 1973. He was highly successful at commodity trading, becoming a full member of the Chicago Board of Trade at the young age of twenty-seven. He was elected President of Ferguson Grain in 1977 and by 1987, began to reduce his trading activity in order to devote more time to other interests. In 1980 when Paul was thirty years old, he met Allen Schuh and they enjoyed a committed gay partnership until Paul's death from AIDS in 1992.

According to Allen Schuh, Paul established the Paul A. Anderson Chair in the Arts so that the beauty and intellectual stimulation of the visual arts would have a strong and lasting presence at Augustana. He wanted students to see original works of art in person and become knowledgeable about the aesthetics, meaning and history of that art within a supportive academic environment. Augustana's art collection reflects this alumnus' profound vision, ranging historically from ancient through contemporary and representing diverse cultures. These resources enhance Augustana's teaching mission through projects such as *Liberal Arts through the AGES*, supported through the Paul A. Anderson Chair.

Paul Anderson was an astute art collector who built an impressive personal collection, particularly focused on the artistic response to the AIDS epidemic. Many of these works, such as *Untitled* by David Moreno, deal with the sobering tragedy left in the wake of this deadly disease. Allen Schuh donated the two ancient Roman glass pieces in this book (catalogue 5A and 5B)—originally gifted from Allen to Paul—as well as this contemporary work by Moreno from Paul's own collection of contemporary art related to AIDS topics. Moreno, like many modern artists, creates conceptual works with multiple associations. He also demonstrates twentieth-century experimentation with multi-media, including *found* objects and collage. In this context, the very real wooden matchsticks are carefully aligned in eleven horizontal rows, recalling such multiplied images as Andy Warhol's Pop art *Campbell's Soup Cans.*

Yet there is more to Moreno's work than the sleek finish of commercial art. The matchsticks are distinct and individual while their assemblage is linked and softened by a gossamer *skin* of silk. Furthermore, upon closer analysis, the matchstick rows are *dissected* by scientific, anatomical texts, perhaps related to autopsy, that commence with: "We shall suppose in the first place, a vertical section of the skull and the spine to be made, so as to lay open their cavities." From a distance, the work's immediate impression suggests Color Field and Minimalist paintings. But further examination implies that Moreno was also commenting on the current state of the AIDS epidemic when medical and political progress appeared stalled. Each individual connects as a bridge to a larger community, whether local or global, while the virility of the spread of disease seemed to go unchecked. Both the artist, Moreno, and the collector, Paul Anderson, called for greater compassion and research to spare humanity from such an inferno.

[Catherine Carter Goebel, *Editor*]

210

Horsehead Nebula, 5 October, 2000
Adam Block, Betty Peterson and Mel Peterson (1930–2011)
Digital photograph taken at Kitt Peak, National Optical Astronomy Observatory (NOAO)
Full size image is 1522 x 1006 pixels
Image Provided Courtesy of the Augustana College Department of Physics

To a casual observer, the universe seems static and unchanging. The stars we see in the sky appear to be immortal, always showing the same color and brightness night after night. This however is an illusion, the universe is dynamic and constantly changing, but the dynamic nature of the universe can only be detected by careful observation. *Horsehead Nebula*, an astrophotograph by Mel Peterson and his wife Betty Peterson, helps us to see the complexities of the universe. Discovered in 1888 by Williamina Fleming at Harvard Observatory, the *Horsehead nebula* is located fifteen hundred light years away in the constellation of Orion. For most of astronomical history, the nature of these diffuse objects was not clear, but using the new tools of photography and spectroscopy available in the late 19th century, scientists were able to determine that nebulae are clouds of dust particles and hydrogen gas. The galaxy is composed not just of stars, but enormous amounts of diffuse material between the stars. Inside the *Horsehead nebula* (and other interstellar clouds) new stars are constantly being formed. These stars will slowly evolve over billions of years and eventual die, returning their material back to the interstellar medium from which new clouds and eventually new stars will be made. The *Horsehead nebula* gives us a glimpse into the great cycle of stellar birth, life and death in our galaxy.

Dr. Mel Peterson (who graduated from Augustana in 1953 and was a member of the chemistry department from 1958 to 1995) was deeply involved in the work of Augustana's John Deere Planetarium from the day it was dedicated in 1969. He served as its second director from 1988 to 1999 and remained highly active in its operations until his death in July 2011. In that time, he gave planetarium shows, observing sessions and open houses to the thousands of school children and members of the general public that visit the facility every year. Mel had a passion for teaching astronomy, for sharing beautiful images of the heavens and for helping people to understand the beauty and complexity of the physical properties that govern the universe. Thanks to Mel Peterson, thousands of people got a chance to see the universe in a whole new way.

[Lee Carkner, *Associate Professor of Physics and Astronomy, Director, John Deere Planetarium*]

Bibliography

Adorno, Theodore W. *Mahler: A Musical Phsiognomy.* Trans. Edmund Jephcott. Chicago: University of Chicago Press, 1992. Print.

Agosín, Marjorie. *Tapestries of Hope, Threads of Love: The Arpillera Movement in Chile.* Rowman and Littlefield, 2007. Print

"Albert Charles Lebourg." *AskART.* AskART, 2011. Web. 31 July 2011.

"Albert-Charles Lebourg." *FADA.* FADA, 2011. Web. 31 July 2011.

"Albumen Print." *Wikipedia.* Wikimedia Foundation, 14 April 2011. Web. June 2011.

Alford, Roberta M. "Fransisco Goya and the Intentions of the Artist." *Journal of Aesthetics and Art Criticism* 18.4 (1960): 483. *JSTOR.* Web. 2011.

Anderson, Dan. "Toshiko Takaezu 1922-2011." *Ceramics: Art & Perception* June 2011: 105. *Academic Search Premier.* EBSCO. Web. 25 July 2011.

Anderson, Ronald. "Théodore Roussel." *Tate.* Tate, n.d. Web. 7 June 2011.

Antal, Frederick. *Classicism and Romanticism.* New York: Harper and Row, 1973. Print.

Antiques. (June 1962): 582. Print.

Appiah, Kwame Anthony. "Why Art? Why Africa?" *Africa: The Art of a Continent.* Ed. Tom Phillips. London: Royal academy of Arts, 1995. Print.

"Art Institute of Chicago Museum Studies." *Ancient Art at the Art Institute of Chicago.* 20.1 (1994): 78-91. Print.

"Artwork of the Month." *Walker Art Gallery.* National Museums Liverpool, May 2008. Web.

Asleson, Robyn. *Albert Moore.* London: Phaidon, 2000. Print.

Augustine. *City of God.* Print.

Baal-Teshuva, Jacob. *Marc Chagall 1887-1985.* Taschen: New York, 1998. Print.

Bachert, Hildegard. "Collecting the Art of Käthe Kollwitz: A Survey of Collections, Collectors, and Public Response in Germany and the United States." *Käthe Kollwitz.* Ed. Elizabeth Prelinger. New Haven: Yale UP, 1992. 117-132. Print.

Bacquart, Jean-Baptiste. *The Tribal Arts of Africa.* New York: Thames and Hudson, 1998. Print.

Bailey, Anthony. *John Constable: A Kingdom of His Own.* London: Vintage, 2007. Print.

Bailey, Colin B., and Joseph J. Rishel. *The Annenberg Collection: Masterpieces of Impressionism & Post-Impressionism.* Philadelphia: Philadelphia Museum of Art, 1989. Print.

Banks, Thomas R. "Pavo." *Liberal Arts through the Ages.* Ed. Catherine C. Goebel. Rock Island, IL: Augustana College, 2005. 266. Print.

Barker, Godfrey. Foreword. *Albert Goodwin,* R. W. S. 1845-1932. By Chris Beetles. London: Chris Beetles, 1996. Print.

Barners, Susan, et al. *Van Dyck: A Complete Catalogue of the Paintings.* New Haven: Yale UP. Print.

Baron, Stanley, and Jacques Damase. *Sonia Delaunay: the Life of an Artist.* New York: Abrams, 1995. Print.

Barratt, Carrie Rebora, and Ellen G. Miles. *Gilbert Stuart* New Havew and London: Yale University Press, 2004. Print.

Barron, Stephanie. *Degenerate Art: The Fate of the Avant-Garde in Nazi Germany.* Los Angeles: Los Angeles County Museum of Art, 1991. Print.

Baudelaire, Charles. "The Painter of Modern Life." *Selected Writings on Art and Literature.* Trans. P.E. Charvet. Hammondsworth: Penguin, 1972. Print.

Beach, Milo Cleveland. *Mughal and Rajput Painting.* New York: Cambridge University Press, 1992. Print.

Beetles, Chris. *Albert Goodwin, R. W. S. 1845-1932.* London: Chris Beetles, 1996. Print.

Beggerow, Alan. "Reverse Glass Painting – Centuries Old Art Form." *eArtfair.com.* eArtfair.com, 30 January 2008. Web. 7 July 2011.

Bell, Daniel Orth. "New Identifications in Raphael's School of Athens." *The Art Bulletin* 77.4 (Dec. 1995): 638-646. Print.

Bellegarde-Smith, Patrick. *Haiti, The Breached Citadel.* London: Westview, 1990. Print.

Bénézit, E. *Dictionaire des Peintres, Sculpteurs, Dessinateur et Graveur.* Vol 3. Paris: Editions Gründ, 1999. Print.

---. *Dictionaire Critique et documentaire des peintres, sculpteurs, dessinateur et graveurs de tous les temps et de tousles pays par un groupe d'ecrivains specialistes francais et étrangers.* Vol. 8. Paris: Gründ Paris, 1999. Print.

Berlioz, Hector. *Memoirs of Hector Berlioz.* Ed. David Cairns. New York: Alfred A. Knopf, 1969. Print.

Bierley, Paul E. *John Philip Sousa, American Phenomenon.* Columbus: Integrity, 1973. Print.

Bingham, Hiram. *Lost City of the Incas.* Phoenix Press, 2003. Print.

Binski, Paul. *Medieval Death: Ritual and Representation.* Ithaca: Cornell UP, 1996. Print.

Blackwood's Edinburgh Magazine (1839): 43-47. Print.

Blair, John, and Nigel Ramsay, eds. *English Medieval Industries: Craftsmen, Techniques, Products.* London: Hambledon, 1991. Print.

Boaden, Ann, and Sherry C. Maurer. *Dr. Fritiof Fryxell: Explorer in Search of Beauty.* Rock Island: Augustana College, 1991. Print.

Boardman, John. *Athenian Black Figure Vases: A Handbook.* New York: Thames & Hudson Ltd., 2000. Print.

---. "Greek Art and Architecture." *The Oxford Illustrated History of Greece and the Hellenistic World.* Eds. John Boardman et al. Oxford: Oxford UP, 1988. Print.

Bohstedt, John. "The Myth of the Feminine Food Riot: Women as Proto-Citizens in English Community Politics, 1790-1810." *Women and Politics in the Age of the Democratic Revolution.* Eds. Harriet Applewhite and Darline Levy. Ann Arbor, MI: The U of Michigan, 1993. 21-60. Print.

Bolton, Ethel Stanwood and Eva Johnston Coe. *American Samplers.* Boston: The Massachusetts Society of the Colonial Dames of America, 1921. Print.

Boon, K. G. *Rembrandt: The Complete Etchings.* Trans. Elizabeth Willems-Treeman. Secaucus: The Wellfleet Press, 1962. Print.

Boorsch, Suzanne. *The Engravings of Giorgio Ghisi.* New York: The Metropolitan Museum of Art, 1985. Print.

Borelli, Jane. "Red-figure Dish with Running Female Figure with Wreath and Ivy-garnished Phiale." *The Paul A. Anderson Art History Collection.* Ed. Catherine Goebel. Rock Island: Augustana College, 2001. 18. Print.

Bowler, Peter J. Evolution: *The History of an Idea.* Berkeley: University of California Press, 1989. Print.

Brake, Laurel. Rev. of *Landseer: The Victorian Paragon by Campbell Lennie. Victorian Studies.* Apr. 1978: 412-413. Print.

Brant, Sandra, and Elissa Cunningham. *Small Folk: A Celebration of Childhood in America.* New York: Dutton, 1980. Print.

British Museum. Trustees of the British Museum, 2011. Web. 4 August 2011.

Bradley, William S. *Emil Nolde and German Expressionism: A Prophet in His Own Land.* Ann Arbor, MI: UMI Research, 1986. Print.

Breen, T.H. "The Meaning of 'Likeness': Portrait Painting in an Eighteenth-Century Consumer Society." *The Portrait in Eighteenth Century America.* Ed. Ellen G. Miles. Newark: U of Delaware, 1993. 44-49. Print.

Broude, Norma, and Mary D. Garrard. *Reclaiming Female Agency: Feminist Art History after Postmodernism.* Berkeley: U of California, 2005. Print.

Broude, Norma. "Mary Cassatt: Modern Woman or the Cult of True Womanhood?" *Woman's Art Journal* 21. 2 (2000-01). JSTOR. Web. 3 July 2011.

Brown, Christopher. *The Drawings of Anthony van Dyck.* New York: Pierpont Morgan Library, 1991. Print.

Brown, Michelle. *Understanding Illuminated Manuscripts: A Guide to Technical Terms.* Malibu: The J. Paul Getty Museum, 1994. Print.

Brumbaugh, Thomas B. Personal Interview.

Buckley, Peter J. "Francisco José de Goya y Lucientes, 1746-1828." *American Journal of Psychiatry* 166.3 (2009): 292. *Academic Search Premier.* Web. 2011.

Burns, Sarah. *Inventing the Modern Artist: Art and Culture in Gilded Age American.* Danbury, CT: Yale UP, 1996. Print.

Bussagli, Marco, ed. *Rome: Art & Architecture.* Slovenia: Könemann, 1999. Print.

Bussière, Emile. *La Vie et l'oeuvre de Gaston Bussière: Peintre, illustrateur, graveur.* Paris: Librarie des Amateurs, 1932. Print.

Bye, Arthur Edwin. *Pots and Pans or Studies in Still Life Painting.* Princeton: Princeton UP, 1921. Print.

C., L. Rev. of *Lely and the Stuart Portrait Painters: A Study of English Portraiture Before and After Vandyck,* by C. H. Collins Baker. *The Burlington Review* (Nov. 1913): 110-113. Print.

Calvert, Karin. *Children in the House.* Boston: Northeastern UP, 1992. Print.

Caccioli, David. "Bowl." *The Paul A. Anderson Art History Collection.* Ed. Catherine Goebel. Rock Island: Augustana College, 2001. 22. Print.

---. "Red-figure Dish with Running Female Figure with Wreath and Ivy-garnished Phiale." *The Paul A. Anderson Art History Collection.* Ed. Catherine Goebel. Rock Island: Augustana College, 2001. 18. Print.

---. "Double Cosmetics Tube." *The Paul A. Anderson Art History Collection.* Ed. Catherine Goebel. Rock Island: Augustana College, 2001. Print. 20.

Calder, Alexander. *Calder: An Autobiography with Pictures.* New York: Pantheon, 1977. Print.

Calkins, Robert. *Monuments of Medieval Art.* Ithaca: Cornell UP, 1979. Print.

Cardinal, Roger. *The Burlington Magazine.* 145.1202 (1998): 385-387. Print.

Casteras, Susan P. Rev. of *Sir Edwin Landseer,* by Richard Ormond, et al. *The Art Bulletin* 66.2 (1984): 344-346. Print.

Chadwick, Whitney. *Women, Art, and Society*. London: Thames and Hudson, 1990. Print.

Chateaubriand, François-René. *Atala/René*. Trans. Irving Putter. Berkeley: University of California Press, 1980. Print.

Chevalier, Denys. *Maillol*. Trans. Eileen B. Hennessy. New York: Crown, 1970. Print.

Chiego, William J. *Sir David Wilkie of Scotland*, 1785-1841. Raleigh: North Carolina Museum of Art, 1987. Print.

Cifelli, Peter. Letter to the author. Feb. 2000. TS.

Cink, Calvin R. "Whip-poor-will (Caprimulgus Vociferus)." *The Birds of North America Online. Birds of North America*, n.d. Web. 29 Sept. 2008.

Cikovsky, Nicolai, Jr., et al. *Winslow Homer: An Exhibit Catalog.* Washington D.C.: National Gallery of Art, 1995. Print.

Clament, Russell T., and Annick Houze. *Neo-Impressionist Painters*. London: greenwood, 1999. Print.

Clark, James M. *The Dance of Death in the Middle Ages and the Renaissance*. Glasgow: Jackson, Son & Company, 1950. Print.

Cleaveland, Mary. Personal Interview. Feb. 2001.

Cohen, Arthur A. *The New Color of Art*. New York:Viking Press, 1998. Print.

Cole, Herbert. "Art as a Verb in Iboland." *African Arts* 3.1 (1969): 34-88. Print.

Cole, Thomas R. *The Journey of Life: A Cultural History of Aging in America*. Cambridge: Cambridge UP, 1992. Print.

Cole, Thomas. *Thomas Cole's Poetry: The Collected Poems of America's Formeost Painter of the Hudson River School*. York, PA: Liberty Cap, 1972. *University of Virginia Library*. Web. 30 July 2011.

Collins, Marsha. *The Dance of Death in Book Illustration*. Columbia: University of Missouri, 1978. Print.

The Columbia Electronic Encyclopedia. 6th ed. New York: Columbia UP, 2005. *Infoplease*. Web. 2005.

Cowley, Robert L. S. *Hogarth's Marriage a-la-Mode*. Ithaca: Cornell UP, 1983. Print.

Craven, Wayne. "Colonial American Portraiture: Iconography and Methodology. *The Portrait in Eighteenth Century America*. Ed. Ellen G. Miles. Newark: U of Delaware, 1993. Print.

Cuppleditch, David. Phil May: *The Artist & His Wit*. London: Fortune, 1981. Print.

Cushing, Caroline Elizabeth Wilde. "Letter from Caroline Elizabeth Cushing, 1829." *Letters: Descriptive of Public Monuments, Scenery, and Manners in France and Spain*. Vol. 1. Newburyport, MA: Allen, 1832. pp. 256-269. Print.

"David Laing." *Edinburgh University Library*. The U of Edinburgh, n.d. Web. 17 February 2005.

Dayagi-Mendels, M. *Perfumes and Cosmetics in the Ancient World*. Jerusalem: The Israel Museum, 1989. Print.

Dearth, Dan. "Civil War's Carnage Led to Medical Advances." *Antietam.com*. Herald-Mail, n.d. Web. June 2011.

Delahunt, Michael. "Woodcut." *ArtLex Art Dictionary*. Michael Delahunt, 2005. Web. 20 April 2005.

Delaunay, Robert, and Sonia Delaunay. *The New Art of Color*. Ed. Arthur A. Cohen. New York: Viking, 1978. Print.

Delevoy, Robert, Catherine De Croes, and Gisell Ollinger-Zinque. *Fernand Khnopff*. Brussels: Lebeer-Hossman, 1987. Print.

Delouche, Denise. "Painters in Britanny." *Tourisme Bretagne*. Comité Régional du Tourisme de Bretagne, n.d. Web. 2005.

Department of Islamic Art. "The Art of the Mughals before 1600". *Heilbrunn Timeline of Art History*. The Metropolitan Museum of Art, 2000. Web. October 2002.

De Sanna, Jole. *De Chirico and the Mediterranean*. New York: Rizzoli International Publications, Inc., 1998), 278.

Diethe, Carol. *Nietzsche's Women: Beyond the Whip*. Berlin: Walter de Gruyter & Co, 1996. Print.

Dillon, Sheila. *The Female Portrait Statue in the Greek World*. Cambridge: Cambridge UP, 2010. Print.

Dizard, Wilson P. *Inventing Public Diplomacy: the Story of the U.S. Information Agency*. Lynne Rienner, 2004. Print.

Dowling, John. "The Crisis of the Spanish Enlightenment: Capricho 43 and Goya's Second Portrait of Jovellanos." *Eighteenth-Century Studies* 18.3 (1985): 331-332. JSTOR. Web. 2011.

Druick, Douglas, and Michael Hoog. *Fantin-Latour*. Ottawa: National Gallery of Canada, 1983. Print.

Du Maurier, Daphne. *The Young George Du Maurier*. New York: Doubleday, 1952.

Easton, Elizabeth Wynne. *The Intimate Interiors of Edouard Vuillard*. Washington: Smithsonian Institution, 1989. Print.

"Edith Cavell." *Royal Norfolk Regimental Museum*. Royal Norfolk Regiment, n.d. Web. 14 July 2011.

Ekserdjian, David. *Parmigianino*. New Haven: Yale UP, 2006. Print.

"Eliot Clark." R. H. *Love Galleries*. R. H. Love Galleries, n.d. Web. 7 June 2011.

"Eliot Candee Clark (1883-1980)." *Bodega Bay Heritage Gallery*. N.p., n.d. Web. 7 June 2011.

"Eliot Clark (1883-1980)." *Gallery C*. Gallery C, n.d. Web. 20 May 2011.

Ellridge, Arthur. *The Triumph of Art Nouveau: Mucha*. Italy: Terrail, 1994. Print.

"*Encyclopédie ou Dictionnaire raisonné des sciences, des arts et des métiers, par une société de gens de letters: Sculpture en tous genres, Elevation du marbre: Planche, Iere*." *The ARTFL Project*. U of Chicago, n.d. Web. 2005.

Empen, Cynthia Wiedemann. "Symbolism and Psychological Modernism in Fernand Khnopff's *Un Masque á la Tenture Mauve*." 1995. MS.

"Erich Heckel (1883-1970)." *Brücke Museum*. Brücke Museum, 9 Mar. 2005. Web. 20 April 2005.

Errington, Lindsay. *Tribute to Wilkie*. Edinburgh: The National Galleries of Scotland, 1985. Print.

"Explore Canada's Northwest Territories." *Government of the Northwest Territories*. Gov. of the Northwest Territories, n.d. Web. 9 July 2011.

Favro, Diane, et al. "Rome, Ancient." *Grove Art Online*. Oxford Art Online, 22 Jan. 2010. Web. 2010.

Feld, Stuart P. "'Nature in Her Most Seductive Aspects': Louis Comfort Tiffany's Favrile Glass." *The Metropolitan Museum of Art Bulletin*. 21.3 (1962): 101-112. Print.

Ferguson, George. *Signs and Symbols in Christian Art*. New York: Oxford UP, 1958. Print.

Ferguson-Wigstaffe, Sarah. "'Points of Contact': Blake and Whitman." *Romantic Circles Praxis Series*. Nov. 2006. Web. 25 May 2011.

Fisher, Kyra Vladykov. "The Baker Lake Printmaking Revival." *Arctic* 50.2 (1997): 192. Print.

"The 5th New York Volunteer Infantry." *Duryee's Zouaves*. Company A, 5th Regiment, New York State Volunteers Duryee Zouaves. 1996. Web. June 2011.

Fleming, John, and Hugh Honour. *The Penguin Dictionary of Decorative Arts*. New York: Penguin Books, 1989. Print.

Fleming, Stuart J. *Roman Glass*. Philadelphia: U of Pennsylvania Museum of Archaeology and Anthropology, 1997. Print.

Flothuis, Marius. "Kapellmeistermusik." *Mahler-Interpretation: Aspekte zum Werk und Wirken von Gustav Mahler*. Ed. Rudolf Stephan. Mainz: 1985. 9-16. Print.

Fox, C. Rev. *Phil May, His Life and His Work*, by Simon Houfe. Print Quarterly 20 (2003): 166. Print.

Foy, Jessica H. and Thomas J. Schlereth, eds. *American Home Life, 1880-1930: A Social History of Spaces and Services*. Knoxville: U of Tennessee, 1992. Print.

Franseco, Poli. "Giorgio de Chirico: From Avant-gardist to Maverick: Seventy Years of Metaphysical Research." *De Chirico and the Mediterranean*. Ed. Jole de Sanna. New York: Rizzoli, 1998. Print.

Freitas, Leo John. "Phil(ip William) May." *The Dictionary of Art*. Ed. Jane Turner. Vol. 20. London: Macmillan, 1996. Print.

Freud, Sigmund. "Consciousness and the Unconscious." *The Ego and the Id*. Trans. J. Riviere. London: Hogarth, 1927. 8-18. Print.

---. *The Interpretation of Dreams*. Trans. A. A. Brill. New York: Random House, 1950. Print.

---. "The Origin and Development of Psychoanalysis." *American Journal of Psychology* 21.2 (1910): 214. *JSTOR*. 2011.

Frey, John G. "From Dada to Surrealism." *Parnassus* 8.7 (1936): 12. Print.

Frey, Julia. *Toulouse-Lautrec: A Life*. London: Viking, 1994. Print.

Friedman, Barry, et al. *Fernand Khnopff and the Belgian Avant-Garde*. New York: Friedman, 1983. Print.

Fryxell, Fritiof. *American Annual of Photography*. (1939). Print.

---. *The Tetons: Interpretation of a Mountain Landscape*. 7th ed. Grand Teton Natural History Association, 1995. Print.

Gauss, Ulrike. *Marc Chagall: The Lithographs: La Collection Sorlier*. New York: Distributed Art, 1998. Print.

Gay, Peter. *Freud: A Life for Our Time*. New York: Norton, 1998. Print.

Geldzahler, Henry. "Jean Arp." *The Metropolitan Museum of Art Bulletin* 30.5 (1972): 225. Print.

"George Du Maurier, Illustrator and Novelist (1834-1896): An Overview." *The Victorian Web*. Brown University, n.d. Web. 18 Sept. 2004.

George, Waldemar. *Aristide Maillol*. Greenwich, CT: New York Graphic Society, 1965. Print.

Gerdts, William H. *Art Across America: Regional Painting in America, 1710-1920*. New York: Abbeville, 1990. Print.

---. *Art Across America: Two Centuries of Regional Painting, 1710-1920*. Vol. 3. New

York: Abbeville, 1990. Print.

Getlein, Frank. *Mary Cassatt Paintings and Prints*. New York: Abbeville, 1980. Print.

Getscher, Robert H. *The Stamp of Whistler*. Oberlin: Oberlin College, 1977. Print.

Gibson, Walter S. "Bosch's Boy with a Whirligig: Some Iconographical Speculations." *Netherlands Quarterly for the History of Art* 8.1 (1975-1976): 9-15. Print.

Gilbert, Creighton. "The Prophetic Women." *Michelangelo on and off the Sistine Ceiling*. New York: Braziller, 1994. Print.

Giorgi, Rosa. *European Art of the Seventeenth Century*. Los Angeles: Getty Publications, 2008. Print.

"The Girls' Book of Poetry. A Selection of Short Pieces Lyrical, Descriptive, Pathetic, and Narrative. From British and American Poets." *UC Santa Barbara*. The Regents of the University of California, n.d. Web.

Gleeson, William. "Waving the Black-and-White Bloody Shirt: Civil War Remembrance and the Fluctuating Functions of Images in the Gilded Age." *E-rea* 8.3 (2011): n. pag. Web. June 2011.

Goebel, Catherine. Augustana College. Rock Island, 2004. Lecture.

Goebel, Catherine, ed. *Liberal Arts through the AGES*. Rock Island: Augustana College, 2006. Print.

---. *Liberal Arts through the AGES: A Sesquicentennial Celebration*. Rock Island: Augustana College, 2007. Print.

---. *Origins of Modernity*. Rock Island: Augustana College, 2005. Print.

---. *The Paul A. Anderson Art History Collection*. Rock Island: Augustana College, 2001. Print.

---. *Tracing Line Through Time: A Whistler Centenary Exhibition*. Rock Island: Augustana College: 2002. Print.

Gordenker, Emilie. *Anthony van Dyck and the Representation of Dress in Seventeenth-Century Portraiture*. Turnhout: Brepols, 2001. Print.

Great Britain. Oakland: Lonely Planet, 2005. Print.

Green, C. M. C. *Roman Religion and the Cult of Diana at Aricia*. Cambridge: Cambridge UP, 2010. Print.

Groom, Gloria. *Edouard Vuillard, Painter-Decorator: Patrons and Projects*, 1892-1912. New Haven: Yale UP, 1993. Print.

Grossman, Janet Burnett. *Looking at Greek and Roman Sculpture in Stone: A Guide to Terms, Styles, and Techniques*. Los Angeles: Getty Publications, 2003. Print.

Gunderson, Jessica. *Impressionism*. Mankato, MN: Creative, 2008. Print

Gunter, Liz. "Dürer's Narrative Style." *Realism and Invention in the Prints of Albrecht Dürer*. Durham: The Art Gallery, University of New Hampshire, 1995. Print.

Hall, James. *Dictionary of Subjects and Symbols in Art*. New York: Harper & Row, 1979. Print.

Hammond, Smith. *Albert Goodwin, R. W. S. 1845-1932*. Leigh-on-Sea: F. Lewis, 1977. Print.

Hancock, Jane H. "Jean Arp's The Eggboard Interpreted: The Artist as a Poet in the 1920s." *The Art Bulletin* 65.1 (1983): 122. Print.

Hansen, Richard K. *The American Wind Band: A Cultural History*. Chicago: GIA Publications, 2005. Print.

Harris, Jean C. *Édouard Manet: The Graphic Work*. San Fransisco: Wofsy Fine arts, 1990. Print.

Harwood, Barry. Introduction. *Reflections: Arts & Crafts Metalwork in England and the United States*. New York: Kurland-Zabar, 1990. Print.

Harthan, John. *The History of the Illustrated Book: The Western Tradition*. London: Thames and Hudson, 1981. Print.

Hess, Earl J. *The Rifle Musket in Civil War Combat: Reality and Myth*. Lawrence: Kansas UP, 2008. Print.

Homer, Winslow. "Letter to George G. Briggs, 19 February 1896." *Archives of American Art*. Smithsonian Institution, 2011. Web. 12 April 2011.

Houfe, Simon. *Phil May: His Life and Work*. Aldershot: Ashgate, 2002. Print.

Houston, R. A. *Literacy in Early Modern Europe*. New York: Longmans, 1988. Print.

Hopkins, Eric. *Childhood Transformed: Working-Class Children in Nineteenth-Century England*. New York: Manchester UP, 1994. Print.

Huisman, Phillippe, and M.G. Dortu. *Lautrec by Lautrec*. Secaucus: Chartwell Books, 1964.

Hunter, Sam, John Jacobus, and Daniel Wheeler. *Modern Art*. New York: Prentice-Hall, 2004. Print.

Hutchinson, Jane C. *Albrecht Dürer: A Biography*. Princeton: Princeton UP, 1990. Print.

Hyslop, Lois Boe. *Baudelaire: Man of His Time*. New Haven: Yale UP, 1980. Print.

Illick, Joseph E. *American Childhood*. Philadelphia: Pennsylvania UP, 2002. Print.

Irwin, David. *Neoclassicism*. London: Phaidon, 1997. Print.

Isings, C. *Roman Glass from Dated Finds*. Groningen: J.B. Wolters, 1957. Print.

Ives, Colta. "An Art for Everyday." *Pierre Bonnard: The Graphic Art*. New York: Abrams, 1989. Print.

Johnstone, Pauline. *The Byzantine Textile in Church Embroidery*. Chicago: Argonaut, 1967. Print.

Jones, Colin. *The Cambridge Illustrated History of France*. New York: Cambridge UP, 2001. Print.

Jones, James P. *John A. Logan: Stalwart Republican from Illinois*. Tallahassee, FL: UP of Florida, 1982. Print.

Kadinsky, Wassily. *Concerning the Spiritual in Art*. Trans. Michael Sadlier, et al. New York: Wittenborn. 1947. Print

Kaplan, James M. "My Search for Birger Sandzén." *Swedish-American Historical Quarterly* 56 (2005): 29. Print.

Kapp, Reinhard. "Schumann Reminiszenzen bei Mahler." *Musik-Konzepte: Sonderband Gustav Mahler*. Eds. Heinz-Klaus Metzger and Rainer Riehn. Munich: 1989. 325-361. Print.

Kasson, Joy S. "The Voyage of Life: Thomas Cole and the Romantic Disillusionment." *American Quarterly*. 27.1 (1975): 42-56. JSTOR. Web. 20 July 2011.

Kearns, Martha. *Käthe Kollwitz: Woman and Artist*. Old Westbury, NY: Feminist Press, 1976. Print.

Keene, Charles Samuel. "Chronic!" *Punch*, Or *The London Charivari* 1 Nov. 1884: 224. Print.

Kellogg, Louise Phelps. "The Paul Revere Print of the Boston Massacre." *The Wisconsin Magazine of History* 1.4 (1918): 377-387. Print.

Kelly, Richard. *The Art of George du Maurier*. Aldershot: Scolar, 1996. Print.

Ketchum, William C. "Reverse-Glass Painting." BookRags. *BookRags*, 2011. Web. 7 July 2011.

Keynes, Milo. "The Portland Vase: Sir William Hamilton, Josiah Wedgwood and the Darwins." *Notes and Records of the Royal Society of London*. 52.2 (1998): 241. Print.

Kirn, Mary Em, and Sherry Case Maurer, eds. *Härute—Out Here: Swedish Immigrant Artists in Midwest America*. Rock Island: Augustana College, 1984. Print.

Knoppers, Laura Lunger. "The Politics of Portraiture: Oliver Cromwell and the Plain Style." *Renaissance Quarterly* 51.4 (1998): 1282-1319. Print.

Koenigsaecker, Patty. Personal Interview.

Koch, Robert. *Louis C. Tiffany's Art Glass*. New York: Crown, 1977. Print.

Kollwitz, Hans, ed. *The Diary and Letters of Kaethe Kollwitz*. Trans. Richard Winston and Clara Winston. Evanston, IL: Northwestern UP, 1988. Print.

Koplos, Janet. "An Unsaid Quality." *Ceramics Monthly* 59.3 (2011): 38-43. *Academic Search Premier*. EBSCO. Web. 25 July 2011.

Kramer, Emil. "Double Cosmetic Tube." *Liberal Arts through the AGES: A Sesquicentennial Celebration*. Ed. Catherine Goebel. Rock Island: Augustana College, 2007. 6. Print.

Kuhn, Charles. *German and Netherlandish Sculpture 1200-1800*. Cambridge: Harvard UP, 1965. Print.

Kunczik, Michael. "British and German Propaganda in the United States from 1914 to 1917." *Propaganda in the 20th Century: Contributions to its History*. Ed. Jürgen Wilke. Cresskill, NJ: Hampton Press, 1998. Print.

La Grange, Henry-Louis. "Music about Music in Mahler: Reminiscences, Allusions, or Quotations?" *Mahler Studies*. Ed. Stephen E. Hefling. Cambridge: Cambridge UP, 1997. Print.

Laillet, Helene. "The Home of an Artist: M. Fernand Khnopff's Villa at Brussels." *The Studio* 67 (1912): 202. Print.

Landau, David and Peter Parshall. *The Renaissance Print*, 1470-1550. New Haven: Yale UP, 1994. Print.

Larsen, Erik. *L'opera complete di Van Dyck*. Vol. 2. Milan: Rizzoli, 1980. Print.

Laurencin, Marie, and Charlotte Gere. *Marie Laurencin*. New York: Rizzoli, 1977. Print.

Layard, George Somes. *The Life and Letters of Charles Keene*. London: Sampson Lowe, 1892. Print.

Levitine, George. "Some Emblematic Sources of Goya." *Journal of the Warburg and Courtauld Institutes* 22.1-2 (1959): 126-127. *JSTOR*. Web. 2011

Levy, Darline and Harriet Applewhite. "Women and Militant Citizenship in Revolutionary Paris." *Rebel Daughters: Women and the French Revolution*. Eds. Sara Melzer and Leslie Rabine. New York: Oxford UP, 1992. 79-101. Print.

---. "Women of the Popular Classes in Revolutionary Paris, 1789-1795." *Women, War, and Revolution*. Eds. Carol Berkin and Clara Lovett. New York: Holmes and Meier, 1980. 9-35. Print.

Leyburn, James G. *The Haitian People*. Connecticut: Greenwood, 1980. Print.

Lindquist, Emory. *Birger Sandzén: An Illustrated Biography*. UP of Kansas, 1993.

Print.

Lohrey, Derek van. Personal Interview. 9 June 2005.

Lopez, Robert. "Minerva." *The Paul A. Anderson Art History Collection*. Ed. Catherine Goebel. Rock Island: Augustana College, 2001. 58. Print.

Loring, John. *Louis Comfort Tiffany at Tiffany & Co.* New York: Abrams, 2002. Print.

Lucie-Smith, Edward. *Henri Fantin-Latour.* New York: Rizzoli, 1977. Print.

---. *Symbolist Art*. London: Thames and Hudson, 1985. Print.

MacDonald, F. Margaret, Patricia de Montfort and Nigel Thorp, eds. *The Correspondence of James McNeill Whistler, 1855-1903.* University of Glasgow. University of Glasgow, 2003. Web. 2011.

Mack, Maynard, ed. *The Poems of Alexander Pope, Volume VII: Translations of Homer.* London: Methuen, 1967. Print.

MacLeod, Anne S. *American Childhood: Essays on Children's Literature of the Nineteenth and Twentieth Centuries*. Athens: U of Georgia, 1994. Print.

Mamnguqsualuk, Victoria, and Magdalene Ukpatiqu. *Catching the Fish Mother.* 1979. Museum of Inuit Art, Toronto. *MIA Gallery.* Web. 9 July 2011.

Marter, Joan M. *Alexander Calder.* New York: Cambridge UP, 1991. Print.

Mathews, Nancy Mowll. *Mary Cassatt: A Life*. New Haven: Yale UP, 1998. Print.

McConkey, Kenneth. *British Impressionism*. New York: Abrams, 1989. Print.

McMillan, James. *France and Women 1789-1914: Gender, Society and Politics*. New York: Routledge, 2000. Print.

Miesel, Victor H., ed. *Voices of Expressionism*. Englewood Cliffs: Prentice-Hall, 1970. Print.

Mikalson, Jon D. *Ancient Greek Religion*. Malden, MA: John Wiley and Sons, 2009. *Google Books*. Web. 9 Aug. 2011.

Miles, Ellen G. *George and Martha Washington: Portraits from the Presidential Years.* Washington D.C.: National Portrait Gallery, Smithsonian Institution, 1999. Print.

Mitchell, Sally. *Daily Life in Victorian England.* Westport: Greenwood, 1996. Print.

Moorjani, Angela. "Käthe Kollwitz on Sacrifice, Mourning, and Reparation: An Essay in Psychoaesthetics." *MLN* 101.5. (1986): 1110-1134. Print.

Mundy, Jennifer. "Brussels. Magritte" *The Burlington Magazine*. 140.1143 (2003): 411-412. Print.

Nichols, Arlene Katz. "Biography as History: Making and Shaping American Art in the Eighteenth Century." *Likeness & Landskips: A Portrait of the Eighteenth Century.* New York: Hirschl & Adler Galleries, 2002. Print.

Nickell, Joe. *Pen, Ink, and Evidence*. New Castle, DE: Oak Knoll, 2003. Print.

Nietzsche, Friedrich. *Human, All Too Human*. Trans. R.J. Hollingdale. New York: Cambridge UP, 1986. Print.

---. *Thus Spoke Zarathustra*. Trans. Walter Kaufmann. New York: Penguin Books, 1981. Print.

Nehamas, Alexander. "The Sleep of Reason Produces Monsters." *Representations*. 74 (2004): 37. Print.

Norwich, J.J. *England & Wales*. New York: Knopf, 2000. Print.

O'Donohue, John. *Wisdom of the Celtic World*. Sounds True, 2005. CD.

Opfell, Olga S. *Special Visions: Profiles for Fifteen Women Artists from the Renaissance to the Present Day.* North Carolina: McFarland & Company, 1991. Print.

Ostergard, Derek E. *Bent Wood and Metal Furniture: 1850-1946*. New York: American Federation of Arts, 1987. Print.

Oxford Art Online. Oxford UP, n.d. Web. 2011.

Papanikolaou, Father Basil. Personal Interview.

Parker, Robert. "Greek Religion." *The Oxford Illustrated History of Greece and the Hellenistic World*. Eds. John Boardman et al. Oxford: Oxford UP, 1988. Print.

Partridge, Loren. *Michelangelo: The Sistine Chapel Ceiling, Rome*. New York: Braziller, 1996. Print.

Pausanias. *Description of Greece*. Print.

Peck, Amelia. "American Needlework in the Eighteenth Century." *Heilbrunn Timeline of Art History*. The Metropolitan Museum of Art, 2000. Web. Oct. 2003.

Pécrus, Jean, and Serge Pécrus. "Charles Pécrus." Trans. Colleen Jaycox. Lisieux, Fr. 1979. Lecture.

Pennell, Joseph. *The Work of Charles Keene*. New York: R. H. Russell, 1897. Print.

Perucchi-Petri, Ursula. "*Japonisme* in Bonnard's Work." *Pierre Bonnard: The Graphic Art*. New York: Abrams, 1989. Print.

Petronius. *Satyricon*. Print.

Pietrangeli, Carlo et al. *The Sistine Chapel: a Glorious Restoreation*. Ed. Pierluigi de Vecchi. New York: Abrams, 1994. Print.

Pisano, Ronald G. *William Merritt Chase*. N.Y.: Watson-Guptill, 1979. Print.

---. Pisano, Ronald G. *William Merritt Chase: Still Lifes, Interiors, Figures, Copies of Old Masters, and Drawings*. Vol. 4. New Haven: Yale UP, 2010.

Plato. *Plato's the Republic*. Ed. G Ferrari. Trans. T. Griffith. Cambridge: Cambridge UP, 2000.

Pliny the Elder. *Natural History*. Print.

Popovich, Ljubica. "Observations on the Russian Icon in the Paul A. Anderson Art History Collection." Rock Island: Augustana College, 2001. Print.

Poulet, Anne L., and Alexandra R. Murphy. *Corot to Braque: French Paintings from the Museum of Fine Arts, Boston*. Boston: Museum of Fine Arts, 1979. Print.

Powell, Earl A. *Thomas Cole*. New York: Abrams, 1990. Print.

Prelinger, Elizabeth. *Käthe Kollwitz: Woman and Artist*. New York: The Feminist, 1976. Print.

---. "Kollwitz Reconsidered." *Käthe Kollwitz*. Ed. Elizabeth Prelinger. New Haven: Yale UP, 1992. 13-86. Print.

Prettejohn, Elizabeth, ed. *After the Pre-Raphaelites: Art and Aestheticism in Victorian England*. New Brunswick: Rutgers UP, 1999. Print.

Price, David Hotchkiss. *Albrecht Dürer's Renaissance: Humanism, Renaissance, and the Art of Faith*. Ann Arbor: U of Michigan Press, 2003. Print.

Price, Simon. *Religions of the Ancient Greeks*. Cambridge: Cambridge UP, 1999. Print.

Rabinow, Rebecca. "Édouard Manet (1832-1883)." *Heilbrunn Timeline of Art History*. The Metropolitan Museum of Art, Oct. 2004. Web. July 2011.

Rago, David. "Regionalism in American Coppersmithing." *Reflections: Arts & Crafts Metalwork in England and the United States*. New York: Kurland-Zabar, 1990. Print.

Read, Herbert, ed. *The Thames and Hudson Dictionary of Art and Artists*. London: Thames and Hudson, 1984. Print.

Reid, Herbert. *The Thames and Hudson Dictionary of Art and Artists*. London: Thames and Hudson, 1985. Print.

Reid, Jane Davidson. "Hebe." *The Oxford Guide to Classical Mythology in the Arts, 1300-1990s*. Vol. 1. New York: Oxford UP, 1993. 490. Print.

Reitsma, Ella. *Maria Sibylla Merian & Daughters: Women of Art and Science*. Amsterdam: Rembrandt House Museum, 2008. Print.

Rewald, John. *Seurat*. New York: Abrams, 1990. Print.

Reynolds, Graham. *Turner*. Oxford: Oxford UP, 1969. Print.

Rice, Patty C. "Powers and Symbolism of Amber." *Amber: Golden Gem of the Ages*. Bloomington: AuthorHouse, 2006. *Google Books*. Web. 8 July 2011.

Rich, Daniel Catton, and Degas Edgar. *Edgar-Hillaire-Germain Degas*. New York: Abrams, 1985. Print.

Rilke, Rainer Maria. *The Selected Poetry of Rainer Maria Rilke*. Trans. Stephen Mitchell. New York: Vintage Books, 1989. Print.

Ring, Betty. Appendix. *Girlhood Embroidery Volume I*. New York: Knopf, 1993.

Rives, James B. *Religion in the Roman Empire*. Oxford: Blackwell, 2007. Print.

"Robert Daughters." *Meyer Gallery*. Meyer Gallery, 2011. Web. 07 Aug. 2011.

Robbins, Daniel. "Vasily Kandinsky: Abstracton and Image." *Art Journal* 22.3 (1963): 145. Print.

Robinson, Fred Miller. *The Man in the Bowler Hat: His History and Iconography*. Chapel Hill: U of North Carolina, 1993. Print.

Rodgers, Davis. "Sir Peter Lely." *The Oxford Companion to Western Art*. Ed. Hugh Brigstocke. Oxford: Oxford UP, 2001. *Oxford Art Online*. Web. 22 June 2011.

---. "Talismanic, Amuletic, and Folk Medicine." *Amber: Golden Gem of the Ages*. Bloomington: AuthorHouse, 2006. *Google Books*. Web. 8 July 2011.

Roseblum, Robert, and H. W. Janson. *19th Century Art*. 2nd ed. Upper Saddle River, NJ: Prentice Hall, 2004. Print.

Rosenbaum, Robert. *On Modern Art: Selected Essays*. New York: Abrams, 1999. Print.

Rosenthal, Angela. "Exhibition Review." *Eighteenth-Century Studies*. 121.1 (2002): 602. Print.

Rossi, Angelina. "Le sibille nelle arti figurative italiane." *L'Arte*. 18 (1915): 209-221, 272-285. Print.

Rubin, James H. *Impressionism*. London: Phaidon, 1999. Print.

Rubinstein, Charlotte Streifer. *American Women Sculptors: A History of Women Working in Three Dimensions*. Coston: Hall, 1990. Print.

Sandell, Renee. "Marie Laurencin: Cubist Muse or More?" *Women's Art Journal* 1.1 (1980): 23-27. JSTOR. Web. 18 July 2011.

Sardar, Marika. "The Art of the Mughals after 1600". *Heilbrunn Timeline of Art History*. The Metropolitan Museum of Art, 2000. Web. October 2003.

Saward, Susan. *The Golden Age of Marie de' Medici*. Ann Arbor, MI: UMI Research, 1982. Print.

Saunders, Richard H. and Ellen G. Miles. *American Colonial Portraits*, 1700-1776. Washington D.C.: The National Gallery of Art, 1987. Print.

"Schatzbehalter." *SMU.edu*. Southern Methodist University, 2011. Web. 4 Aug. 2011.

Schenk, Herras. *Frauen Kommen ohne Waffen: Feminismus und Pazifismus.* Munich: Beck, 1983. Print.

Scherer, Barrymore L. "Enigma Variations." *Art and Auction* (2000): 111. Print.

"Schools, Styles, & Artists: Market Place Paintings." *Haitian Art Company.* Haitian Art Company, n.d. Web. July 2011.

Scott, Casper. "The Boston Massacre." *American History* Aug. 2008: 22-23. Print.

Sear, Frank. *Roman Architecture.* Ithaca: Cornell UP, 1983. Print.

Seaton, Beverly. *The Language of Flowers: A History.* University of Virginia Press, 1995. *Google Books.* Web. 12 July 2011.

Sellin, David. *American Painters on the French Scene: 1874-1914.* New York: Beacon Hill Fine Art, 1996. Print.

Sellin, David, and James K. Ballinger. *Americans in Brittany and Normandy: 1860-1910.* Phoenix: Phoenix Art Museum, 1982. Print.

Sewell, Darrell. "The Poetry of Clay: The Art of Toshiko Takaezu." *Ceramics Monthly* 52.10 (2004): 42-44. *Academic Search Premier.* EBSCO. Web. 25 July 2011.

Shestack, Alan, ed. *The Complete Engravings of Martin Schongauer.* New York: Dover, 1969. Print.

Slatkin, Wendy. *Women Artists in History: From Antiquity to the Twentieth Century.* Englewood Cliffs: Prentice Hall, 1990. Print.

Southgate, Therese M. "The Cover." *Journal of the American Medical Association* (1999): 214. Print.

Spicer, Joaneath A. "Anthony van Dyck's Iconography: an Overview of its Preparation." *Van Dyck 350.* Ed. Susan J. Barnes and Arthur Wheelock, Jr. Washington, D.C.: National Gallery of Art, 1994. Print.

Stanwood, Ethel, and Eva Johnston Coe. *American Sampler.* Boston: The Massachusetts Society of the Colonial Dames of America, 1921. Print.

Stedman, Edmund Clarence, ed. *A Victorian Anthology*, 1837-1895. Boston, 1895. *Bartleby.* Web.

Stern, E. Marianne. "Roman Glassblowing in a Cultural Context." *American Journal of Archaeology* 103.3 (1999): 441-484. Print.

Stern, Steve J., ed. *Shining and Other Paths: War and Society in Peru, 1980-1995.* Durham: Duke UP, 1998. Print.

Steyaert, John. *Late Gothic Sculpture.* Ghent: Ludion Press, 1994. Print.

Stokstad, Marilyn. *Art History.* 2nd ed. Vol. 2. New York: Abrams, 2002. Print.

Stratis, Harriet and Martha Tedeschi, eds. *The Lithographs of James McNeill Whistler.* Chicago: Art Institute of Chicago, 1998. Print.

Stott, Annette. "Floral Femininity: A Pictorial Definition." *American Art.* 6.2 (1992): 60-77. JSTOR. Web. 20 June 2011.

Stratis, Harriet, and Martha Tedeschi, eds. *The Lithographs of James McNeill Whistler.* Chicago: Art Institute of Chicago, 1998. Print.

Strickland, Carol. "Master of Art and the Art of Living." *Christian Science Monitor* 06 Oct. 1997: 10. *Academic Search Premier.* EBSCO. Web. 25 July 2011.

"Striking the Right Note: The Well-Made Life of Robert Daughters." Ascribe. net. N.p., 2011. Web. 07 Aug. 2011.

Swanson, Robert N. *Religion and Devotion in Europe, c. 1215-c. 1515.* New York: Cambridge UP, 1997. Print.

Sweet, Frederick A. *Miss Mary Cassatt: Impressionist from Pennsylvania.* Norman, OK: U of Oklahoma, 1966. Print.

Taws, Richard. "Material Futures: Reproducing Revolution in P. L. Debucourt's Almanach National." *Art Bulletin* 92.3 (2010): 169-187. Print.

"Testimony of Pastor Le Seur." *The Edith Cavell Website.* The Rev. Phillip McFadyen and David Chamberlin, 2011. Web. 14 July 2011.

Thayer, Bill. "The Cities and Cemeteries of Etruria." *Bill Thayer's Website.* U of Chicago, 2011. Web. 9 Aug. 2011.

Thiem, Gunther. *Prints by Erich Heckel and Karl Schmidt-Rottluff: A Centenary Exhibition.* Los Angeles: Los Angeles County Museum of Art, 1965. Print.

Thomason, Richard, Phillip Dennis Cate and Mary Weaver Chapin. *Toulouse-Lautrec and Montmartre.* Princeton: Princeton UP, 2005. Print.

Tibbe, Monika. *Lieder und Liedelemente in instrumentalen Symphoniesätzen Gustav Mahlers.* Munich: 1971.

Tolstoy, Leo. *What is Art?* Trans. Aylmer Maude. New York: Funk & Wagnalls Company, 1904. Print.

Turner, Elizabeth Hutton. "Calder and Miró: A New Space for the Imagination." *Calder/Miró.* Ed. Elizabeth Hutton turner and Oliver Wick. Washington, D.C.: Philip Wilson, 2004. 34. Print.

Turner, Jane, ed. "Ramberg, Johann Heinrich." *The Dictionary of Art.* 34 vols. New York: Grove's Dictionaries, 1996. Print.

Tzara, Tristan. *Seven Manifestos and Lampisteries.* Print.

Underwood, Frances W. "The Marketing System in Peasan Haiti." *Anthropology* 60: 3-33. Print. "The United States, 1600-1800 A.D." *Heilbrunn Timeline of Art History.* The Metropolitan Museum of Art, 2000. Web. Oct. 2004.

United States Bureau of the Census. *Historical Statistics of the United States 1789-1945.* Washington D.C.: United States Dept. of Commerce, 1949. *U.S. Census Bureau.* Web. 20 July 2011.

Vasari, Giorgio. *The Lives of the Painters, Sculptors, and Architects.* Trans. Arthur B. Hinds. Vol. 3. London: J.M. Dent & Sons, 1927. Print.

Vedder, Lee A. *John James Audubon and the Birds of America: A Visionary Achievement in Ornithological Illustration.* San Marino: Huntington Lib., 2006. Print.

Visona, Monica, ed. *A History of Art in Africa.* New York: Harry N. Abrams, 2001. Print.

Vogel, Susan Mullin. *Baule: African Art, Western Eyes.* New Haven: Yale UP, 1997. Print.

Vogt, Paul. *Erich Heckel.* Recklinghausen: Aurel Bongers, 1965. Print.

Voragine, Jacobus. *The Golden Legend: Readings on the Saints.* Trans. William Granger Ryan. Vol. 2. Princeton: Princeton UP, 1993. Print.

Wagner, Margaret. *The American Civil War: 365 Days.* New York: Abrams: 2006. Print.

Waldman, Diane. *Roy Litchenstein.* London: Tate Gallery, 1968. Print.

Ward-Perkins, John B. *Roman Architecture.* New York: Abrams, 1977. Print.

Weber, Nicholas Fox. *Josef Albers: Homage to the Square.* Barcelona: Casa Luis Barragán, 2009. Print.

---. *Josef Albers: Prints 1916-76.* London: Alan Cristea Gallery, 1999. Print.

Wechsler, Herman J. *Great Prints and Printmakers.* New York: Abrams, 1967. Print.

Wellington, Hubert, ed. *The Journal of Eugène Delacroix.* Trans. Lucy Norton. Ithaca: Cornell UP, 1980. Print.

Wernick, Robert. "Declaring an Open Season on the Wisdom of the Ages." *Smithsonian* 28.2 (1997): 72-80. Print.

West, Shearer, ed. "Minerva (Greek: Athena)." *The Bulfinch Guide to Art History: A Comprehensive Survey and Dictionary of Western Art and Architecture.* New York: Bulfinch Press, 1996. Print.

Wheelock, Arthur K., Jr., et al. *Anthony van Dyck.* Washington, D.C.: National Gallery of Art, 1990. Print.

Whistler, James McNeill. "Mr. Whistler's 'Ten O'Clock.'" *The Gentle Art of Making Enemies.* London: Heinemann, 1892. Print.

White, Barbara Ehrlich. *Impressionism in Perspective.* New Jersey: Prentice-Hall, 1978. Print.

White, Christopher. *Rembrandt and His World.* New York: The Viking Press, 1964. Print.

White, Eric Walter. *The New Grove Dictionary of Music and Musicians.* Ed. Stanley Sadie. 6th ed. Vol. 18. London: Macmillan Publishers Limited, 1980. Print. 20 vols.

Whitley, Derek Pepys. *George Du Maurier.* New York: Pellegrini & Cudahy, 1948. Print.

Wichmann, Siegfried. *Japonisme: The Japanese Influence on Western Art Since 1858.* New York: Thames, 1999. Print.

Wieck, Roger. *Painted Prayers: The Book of Hours in Medieval and Renaissance Art.* New York: Braziller, 1997. Print.

---. *Time Sanctified: The Book of Hours in Medieval Art and Life.* New York: Braziller, 2001. Print.

Wilcox, Timothy. Rev. of *The Prints of Théodore Roussel: A Catalogue Raisonné*, by Margaret Danwoody Hausberg. *The Burlington Review* (May 1992): 317. Print.

Wilde, Oscar. *Salome.* Trans. Lord Alfred Douglas. London: 1894. Print.

Williams, Hermann W., Jr. *A Survey of American Genre Painting: 1750-1990.* Greenwich, CT: New York Graphic Society, 1973. Print.

Wilton-Ely, John. "'Classic Ground': Britain, Italy, and the Grand Tour." *Eighteenth-Century Life.* 28.1 (2004): 149. *EBSCOhost.* Web. 7 July 2005.

Witte, John. *Law and Protestantism: The Legal Teachings of the Lutheran Reformation.* New York: Cambridge UP, 2002. Print.

Wittgenstein, Ludwig. *Tractus Logico-Philosophicus.* Trans. D. F. Pears and B. F. McGuinness. London: Routledge Classics, 2001. Print.

Witzling, Mara R., ed. *Voicing Our Visions: Writings by Women Artists.* New York: Universe Publishing, 1991. Print.

Wölfflin, Heinrich. *Raphael's School of Athens.* Ed. Marcia Hall. Cambridge: Cambridge UP, 1997. Print.

Woodfin, Warren. "Liturgical Textiles." *Byzantium: Faith and Power (1261-1557).* Ed. Helen C. Evans. New York: Metropolitan Museum of Art, 2004. 18-19. Print.

Wullschläger, Jackie. *Chagall: A Biography.* New York: Knopf, 2008. Print.

Yeh, Susan F. "Mary Cassatt's Images of Women." *Art Journal* 35.4 (1976). *JSTOR.* Web. 3 July 2011.

Zellman, Michael D. *300 Years of American Art.* Secaucus: Wellfleet, 1987. Print.

Le Jardin du Luxembourg [The Luxembourg Gardens], Emma Ruff (n.d.) Catalogue 90, detail

"...I believe the study of art history helps us to deepen our understanding of ourselves and our world....Art enhances the life of the mind in a way that neither hardship nor illness can tear away. That is why Augustana has committed itself to giving generations of students the gift of understanding and appreciating art created throughout the world and throughout time."

Steven C. Bahls, *President of the College*
Liberal Arts through the AGES: Interdisciplinary Art Historical Inquiry